WITHDRAWN

Scientists and World Order

Scientists and World Order

The Uses of Technical Knowledge in International Organizations

Ernst B. Haas,
Mary Pat Williams,
and
Don Babai

University of California Press Berkeley · Los Angeles · London

University of California Press
Berkeley and Los Angeles, California

University of California Press, Ltd.
London, England

ISBN 0-520-03341-8
Library of Congress Catalog Card Number: 76-47981
Printed in the United States of America

 2 3 4 5 6 7 8 9

Contents

Figures and Tables

Acknowledgments

Work on this book began in the summer of 1973 with a series of exploratory interviews on the Berkeley campus of the University of California, using a sample of scientists and engineers who had worked in or for international organizations. The research design was worked out jointly by Haas and Williams. The bulk of the interviewing was done at the headquarters of various international organizations. It was split evenly between them and carried out during the first half of 1974. Don Babai joined us in the fall of 1975 and assumed major responsibility for chapter 9.

We wish to acknowledge that our work could not have gone forward without the intellectual help of a great many people. Over two hundred scientists and officials gave freely of their time and experience in talking with us in Washington, New York, Geneva, Paris, London, Brussels, Rome, Vienna, and London. The help we received in Berkeley requires special explanation. We enjoyed the advantage of discussions with many of the scientists for which Berkeley is known, though none is in any way responsible for the opinions we express in this book. Moreover, we profited from the stimulation received by participating in the Science Policy Colloquium—a discussion group composed in equal number of natural and social scientists headed by Reinhard Bendix—sponsored by the Institute of International Studies of the University of California, Berkeley.

This book is part of a program funded by the Rockefeller Foundation and housed in the Institute of International Studies of the University of California, Berkeley, known as "Studies on International Scientific and Technological Regimes." Our work could not have gone forward without the stimulation provided by the graduate students, visitors, and fellow faculty members associated with that project. We wish to single out Peter F. Cowhey, Branislav Gosovic, Gene Rochlin, and John G. Ruggie as indispensable contributors, though none of them is to be

blamed for any of our missteps. The Institute's support, through
its director Carl G. Rosberg and its chief administrator Cleo S.
Stoker, made it all possible. Research assistance was provided by
Benjamin Schiff and Michael Hatch. The manuscript was typed
by Nancy Roller, Bojana Ristich, and Susan Hartman. During a
portion of this period, Mary Pat Williams was supported by a
fellowship from the University Consortium for World Order
Studies, and Ernst Haas by a fellowship from the John Simon
Guggenheim Foundation.
    We are enormously grateful to all of them.

Berkeley and San Diego   Ernst B. Haas
Summer 1976   Mary Pat Williams

Scientists and World Order

PART 1

Knowledge, Action, and World Order

How Does International Science Relate to World Order?

In considering the order of the world at large, which will inevitably
continue to undergo historical change, what we need is a system of
homeorhesis rather than one of homeostasis. . . . The only type of
outlook which holds out any hope of being successful in this is one
which holds firmly that the central focus of interest, for mankind
in the next century or so, is in the improvement of the material
conditions of life.

C. H. WADDINGTON

I submit that it is the economist's task to guide politicians in the
elaboration of the proper international policies and their preparation,
that is, international economic planning.

JAN TINBERGEN

Over ten years ago, a group of internationally prominent natural and social scientists met to consider the elusive notion of "world order." Jan Tinbergen and C. H. Waddington
were among the participants, and the meeting was chaired by
Raymond Aron.[1] To some of the scientists the term meant the
need for planning a new order in a setting of ideological conflict.
Who would do the planning, since the ideological conflict was
identified with the character of existing societies and their leaders? The task of introducing a new order was considered to be
the duty of intellectuals in general and scientists of all kinds in
particular. How could such planning go forward if the substantive meaning of "world order" was itself a matter of conflict?
Aron proposed as a working definition, "Under what conditions
would men (divided in so many ways) be able not merely to avoid
destruction, but live together relatively well in one planet?"[2]

Since this is a book about the world order concerns of internationally active scientists and technologists, Aron's definition can
serve as our point of departure. But what does his formulation
have to do with scientists? The Czech microbiologist Ivan Malek
provided an answer:

The development of science, technology, and culture is proceeding at a rapid pace; the possibilities of a decent life for all men in the
world are growing from day to day; the period of colonial oppres-

sion is drawing to a close the world over, and the way to full development is being opened even for that part of mankind which
until recently was so humiliated; finally, man has come to understand some of the laws governing evolution not only in nature but in
human society as well and thus has an opportunity to try to build a
society which is in harmony with these laws.

In view of these possibilities, all those who have pondered these
goals and are trying to realize them in practice have a responsibility
to show how it is possible to advance a step further. In his efforts at
reforming the world, Comenius relied on the counsel of the "wise
men"; their counterparts at the present stage of mankind's development are *those men who base their reasoning and action on scientific
knowledge.* It is in this light that we, too, should view our responsibilities, and attack this problem with all the resourcefulness of
scientists who do not shrink from any new views of the problems
facing us and ways to solve them.[3]

Are scientists really responsible for a new world order? If so, is
this because they have laid claim to a special knowledge? Some
scientists think so.[4] And many nonscientists concur that the scientists' claim to special knowledge does empower them to prescribe major changes in a world so complex that the vibrations of
policy decisions shake the lives of all people. Consequently, we
wish to probe the attitudes of these scientists in international
organizations; we also wish to ascertain the specific role which
they play through these international organizations, and we wish
to know the extent to which their decision-making processes and
products reflect a consensual view of a scientific "mission." If we
are to live together relatively well on one planet, it behooves us to
discover whether the scientists working on this task speak with
one voice or with many.

One voice—a very strong one, indeed—urges that what is at
issue is the very survival of the species *homo sapiens:* Man must
adapt his sociopolitical institutions to biological imperatives. If
he fails to recognize a dynamic symbiosis between cultural and
biological evolution—and act on it with the wisdom of scientific
knowledge—then his species cannot survive. As authors of this
study we cannot accept this formulation. We doubt that the imperatives for survival are so simple or unilinear. We are not even
sure who or what is to survive, adapt, or evolve. We are not
convinced that scientific methods can or should be used uncritically for making political decisions. We are suspicious of using
mechanical, organismic, and cybernetic systemic formulations as
substitutes for political models and as definers of political
choice.[5] But we are sufficiently impressed by the pervasiveness of

these images to inquire into their presence in international programs; we recognize that the power of a world order model is not determined by our personal approval or disapproval.

The mathematician-philosopher Alfred North Whitehead once wrote, "Duty arises from the power to alter the course of events."[6] We agree with Whitehead. The power of scientists to alter the course of events is plain in the military realm of international relations. If it is not quite as obvious in the economic and social realms, the advent of such things as the Green Revolution, direct television broadcasting, remote sensing, and planning the transfer of technologies to poor countries serves to remind us that changing scientific knowledge has the capacity to change that course of the events we call the global politics of production and distribution.

When power and duty are systematically combined into a program of action, they result in institutionalized behavior—a kind of order. We are interested in the way scientific knowledge is likely to shape world order. This knowledge is currently produced by a technical elite, and there is frequently a tendency on the part of that elite to define its duty as being as objective as science itself is supposed to be. Objectivity is the hallmark of the world order which seeks to marshal knowledge for action. Do scientists really know best in the new world order? We very much doubt it. But if they think they know best, and if the institutions for remaking the world reflect this belief, then the world order of the future will indeed differ greatly from that familiar to us.

WHAT THIS BOOK IS NOT ABOUT

Painting with such a broad brush invites the expectation that we can settle the nagging questions about science, technology, truth, peace, plenty, and purity. The issue seems to call for an effort to make a portrait out of a puzzle. Our effort falls short of such an achievement.

At present, almost everyone suspects that science and technology are extremely important for the future of the world. Science spawns factual and theoretical knowledge, which, when translated into technology, promises not only to solve those problems which have plagued mankind, but also very possibly to trigger new ones. However, only more science and more technology are recommended as the probable cures for the new malady. Regardless of whether the problems are poverty, disease, illiteracy, or cultural deprivation, science and technology are believed capable of creating those conditions under which peace and equality can rule.

We do not know whether or not all of this is true. We know only that many important people think that this is true. We ought to have information on the extent to which international science and technology programs raise standards of living, incomes, health, education, self-confidence, but we have no systematic information on this subject. Hence we cannot tell to what extent these programs have been successful in creating conditions for peace and equality.

Many people believe that the scientific mode is capable of providing intellectual solutions to problems of peace and plenty even when it is not accompanied by technology. The professions of faith in the scientific method quoted here suggest that the human mind is able to provide rational answers to age-old questions simply by disciplining itself, by following the example of the scientific researcher.

We suspect that some of this may be true, but that the test of its efficacy is the impact of scientific programs on national and international policy. What does such a test suggest? The science of economics has certainly infected national monetary and fiscal policy, planning, and programing. It has also influenced the studies of international organizations—regional and global— even though no international policies and plans of great intellectual coherence have resulted from the effort. Systems engineering is undoubtedly responsible for the successful launching of space communications facilities and resource satellites. Have these efforts pacified or humanized international politics, or do they suggest a more benign world order? The answer is probably negative.

However, our book does not attempt to settle the issue. It provides no systematic information about the impact of scientific thinking on world politics. It offers no new insights into the way in which scientists and engineers influence the actions of politicians in order to change the quality of international life. We do not answer the question *"How* influential is science in ushering in a new world order?" But we believe that the evidence suggests that science *is* influential, if only because more and more decisions are reached solely through consultation with and through the participation of scientific experts.

We do not ask "What is the impact of science and technology on the international system?", nor do we ask "How important is science in changing our thinking about the future of world politics?" Both questions imply certain conceptions of the very notion of world order which we do not adopt in this book. Discussions of world order commonly address one of these themes: (1) the conditions of human progress, (2) the institutions for realizing them. Under what conditions *can* the world enjoy more peace, less military intervention, fewer revolutions, a closer approximation to equality, less hunger and disease, a more wholesome physical environment—this is one set of questions asked by students of world order. The answers range from utopian exhortations to technical formulas.[7] Questions about the impact of science and technology, in their physical or their intellectual formulation, are part of this universe of discourse.

Another set of formulations about world order stresses the institutional configurations which are likely to advance sought-after goals. Peace, plenty, and a wholesome environment are then studied in terms of power balances, alliances, blocs, federations, and international organizations. The question becomes which—if any—of these familiar institutions is most likely to bring about a given desired condition. Prescriptions about preferable world orders take the form of institutional arrangements designed either to downplay or to support one type of territorial unit or actor or another.[8]

The discussions over which Raymond Aron presided were brought to grief by the inability of the participants to agree on a single set of desired conditions and by their division of opinion regarding the optimal institutional formula. Contemporary international negotiations labeled as committed to the search for alternative world orders do not seem to fare much better. We suspect that this approach to world order questions cannot be fruitfully applied to an inquiry about the work of internationally active scientists. Their influence—if any—is likely to be more indirect, longer in coming, and less capable of being observed empirically.

It seems obvious that the world political system has not changed dramatically since 1960. Power is still distributed most unevenly. The gap between rich and poor countries is still widening. While nation-states confer, confront, and connive more than ever in multilateral fora, the power of multilateral institutions to force a change in policy on one of their members remains as weak as ever. In the realm of science and technology, the bulk of the world's physical and intellectual resources is controlled by the Soviet Union and the United States. Their decisions and dispositions are likely to have much more impact on the diffusion of technology and on the conditions of international life associated with the possible impact of science than do the programs of all international organizations taken together. To be

sure, there are few fields of science which are not now, in some
measure, within the programmatic purview of international organizations. But they do not include the most massive research
and development efforts, the most challenging fields of basic
research, or those portions of scientific and technological knowledge which have military relevance even when they can also be
applied to the improvement of life. In short, we grant that the
bulk of the world's scientific and technological effort is not under
international control. International science covers only a small
part of the iceberg, and probably not even the tip.

   Why, then, do we study it? Why devote a book to the relationship between science and world order, focusing on international
programs, if we cannot assess the impact of science on the international system, nor measure the role of science in changing the
pattern of international cooperation? The effort is worthwhile
because it addresses the cognitive dimension underlying, and
probably preceding, such impacts. It is of course likely that science and technology will influence the configurations of international life quite apart from the work of the United Nations and
the International Council of Scientific Unions. However, programs organized by these institutions illustrate and exemplify
those aspects of science which command enough *common interest*
among nations to become visible in terms of budgets, personnel,
and global discussion about ends and means. They *are* the extent
of the current international technical and political consensus.
Moreover, they are articulated through the *only* global institutions enjoying some political legitimacy, all possible alternatives
being for the present in the realm of utopia. Barring a major
moral or institutional breakthrough or a sudden and universal
raising of consciousness, whatever will happen in terms of collective efforts to make the globe safer, wealthier, and cleaner will
occur as a result of expectations and goals mobilized in and
through international organizations resembling the familiar
ones. By mapping the cognitive terrain on which current thinking and action is developing, we make possible the eventual assessments necessary for dealing with the aspects of world order
concerned with the good life and the institutions needed for
providing it.

WHAT THIS BOOK IS ABOUT

   This book is designed to shed light on two questions: (1) What
do scientists involved with international organizations believe
about the relationship between specialized knowledge and col-

lective action for the achievement of economic, social, and political goals?; (2) is there evidence that international science and technology programs have become more comprehensive and more ambitious in linking specialized knowledge to expanding economic, social, and political goals? In short, we ask whether or not the sophistication of thinking about international science and its effects, and the skill in building programs intended to serve changing goals, have evolved in some manner. The answers will suggest the contours of cognitive world orders now operative or easily conceivable.

It would be gratifying to know whether or not a change in the perceptions of scientists was the cause underlying the advent of more ambitious programs. If we could say that a given idea, a certain discovery, or an identifiable network of specialists triggered the development of a political consensus, which in turn legitimated a new international program, we would make a definite demonstration about the impact of science on collective problem-solving. While we can offer occasional evidence of such a link, our materials do not suffice for making a comprehensive case. We *cannot* insist on a causal model which stipulates changing specialized knowledge as the independent variable, a new world order as the dependent variable, and the programs of international organizations as the intervening set of factors.

Yet we proceed on the hypothesis that this chain of events is plausible even if we cannot prove its existence. Granted, the new world order implied here is confined to the *consensual* aspects of science, to those concerns which are in fact linked to changing specific material and cultural conditions high on the agenda of international discussion. The status of our model is heuristic. It is designed as a preliminary mapping of events and relationships. Our data neither confirm nor destroy it; the model simply gives some plausible order to our inquiry. Hence it is pretheoretical and heavily dependent on definitions and assumptions derived from what we think we already know about the behavior of scientists and the interaction between experts and politicians.

Consequently, it makes more sense to talk about components of the argument than it does to discuss independent and dependent variables. Two key components—the perceptions of scientists and the programs of international organizations—provide the data from which we wish to extract conclusions about the direction of movement of a world order defined in cognitive terms. The outcome which interests us is a continuum of syndromes which groups the various ways in which specialized knowledge and social goals can interact so as to produce a better life. The items on this continuum, the various syndromes, we label "world orders." They suggest consistent ways for making collective decisions about the features of life which science and technology are capable of influencing. The two components, perceptions and programs, are not linked to each other in a determinative fashion. Both exist and both are thought to tell us something about outcomes. It is certainly true that, in empirical terms, the perceptions of internationally active scientists are antecedent to, and of causative significance in, shaping the programs of international organizations. In a loose sense, therefore, the international programs do intervene between perceptions and outcomes. But we cannot specify, hypothetically or empirically, how much and what kind of perception is required for triggering a given organizational response. We can and do indicate the degree of concordance between the perceptions of scientists and the evolution of organizational programs. Further, we can and do specify the significance of the concordance with respect to alternative world orders.

Our data for the two components are derived from different sources and are subjected to different modes of interpretation. The perceptions of internationally active scientists were obtained by means of interviews and discussions. The results, though not the interpretations, are the work of the respondents themselves. They classified themselves with respect to their opinions and experiences regarding the relationship between specialized knowledge and social action. We then used their classifications to arrive at an assessment of their significance with respect to alternative world orders. The second set of data, however, was culled from the activities, documents, and claims of international organizations. The authors did the classifying and the sorting. We imposed our model of decision-making and institutionalization on the programmatic materials in an effort to relate these to concerns about cognitive world orders.

The purist will object that our demonstration is flawed because we include aspects of cognitive world orders in the very definition of the causal components, instead of using the customary method of defining independent and dependent variables in terms of mutually exclusive dimensions and concerns. And we did indeed subject the interpretation of our data to these prior definitions, though we did not arrive at them until after the data collection process was completed. Why did we do this?

Our enterprise is predicated on the belief that we should incorporate in the research what we take to be established and known, or at least what can be plausibly taken for granted. In Chapter 2 we present an argument drawn from the literature on science and society which incorporates a fully "rational" model of world order, a cognitive stance in which there is presumed to be a direct and powerful relationship between knowledge and appropriate social action. This model will serve as the most ambitious and the most powerful vision of a different world order throughout the book. But we know, even before engaging in empirical research, that such a model does not now characterize national and international decision-making on science and technology. Hence we would be attacking a straw man if we confined ourselves to using our data to knock down this model. Therefore, in Chapter 3, we present two additional cognitive models which might link knowledge to social action, based on what we already know about the behavior of scientists and politicians.

We claim to know too much already. And we legitimate our prior imposition of definitions of world orders on our data by virtue of this claim. What do we know? Three key assumptions are made: (1) Scientific knowledge is increasingly important in shaping political decisions regarding international collaboration in the fields of environmental protection, industrial development, and agricultural progress; (2) international organizations are very important instruments for observing the extent and scope of this cooperation; (3) scientists are influential as advisers to politicians, not as autonomous actors. The first two assumptions will now be examined; the third is developed in Chapter 3 because the thrust of its meaning undermines the reliance on a consistently rational model.

THE ASSUMPTIONS:
SCIENTIFIC KNOWLEDGE AND
THE ROLE OF INTERNATIONAL ORGANIZATIONS

We are concerned with identifying and projecting the world views of scientists working in international programs. We believe that such an exercise will help in imagining how world order might be transformed. One need not accept a particular vision of a new world order to be persuaded of the utility of such an effort. Some commentators identify a new world order with specific values: peace, prosperity, tolerance, openness. Others see it in terms of benign new institutions: world government, regional federations, international regimes for the commons of the planet. Still others define it negatively, as the transcendence of the nation-state substantively and institutionally. The train of thought most central to our concern identifies a new world order with the advent of a new rationality for making collective decisions, leading to comprehensive planning as the institutional outcome. Knowledge, therefore, is a crucial element in the conception. If René Dubos is right, science is a key component in such knowledge:

> ... Science is at present evolving from the description of concrete objects and events to the study of relationships as observed in complex systems. We may be about to recapture an experience of harmony, an intimation of the divine, from our scientific knowledge of the processes through which the earth became prepared for human life, and of the mechanisms through which man relates to the universe as a whole. A truly ecological view of the world has religious overtones.[9]

In short, the acceptability of the proposition that knowledge matters crucially is dependent on the persuasiveness of certain assumptions: that experts count, that knowledge is becoming more consensual, and that it can influence political action.

Processes of choice now underway in international politics *already* suggest that expert knowledge is affecting political action, and cognitive maps are undergoing significant change. Such changes may not be final or determinative, but they are sufficiently pervasive to justify the assumptions underlying our inquiry. Experts have not replaced politicians; but they are advising politicians on issues never before on the international agenda, and they are designing programs of research and action with a potential for altering the way in which we interpret the international system. Their views comprise one of the main symbolic constituents of man's collective interpretation of his place and evolution on this planet.[10]

Item: In 1974 the SALT II negotiations were temporarily suspended in order to give the "experts" time to work out force-level equivalents acceptable to the Soviet Union and the United States.

Item: Since 1972 U.N. efforts to work out globally acceptable policies of protecting the natural environment have been increasingly informed by the notion that all industrial and agricultural activity must be reevaluated in terms of the overall carrying capacity of the biosphere.

Item: In 1974 the world shortage of oil at low prices, the level of agricultural productivity in South Asia and Sahelian Africa, rainfall, and erosion patterns were discussed for the first time as interrelated phenomena.

The list could be expanded at will. Prescriptions derived from scientific knowledge—fragmentary or final—are no longer confined to programs of "international scientific cooperation," the sharing of technology, the holding of symposia, the launching of exploration "decades." Such prescriptions now make themselves felt in the way foreign ministers and ministers of finance discuss trade and investment policies. Scientific advisers are not philosopher-kings, but they seem to be standing ever closer to the throne. This fact alone justifies our inquiry into those beliefs which relate to international programs and organizations.

But why focus on international organizations in mapping this growing influence of scientists? To be sure, international organizations made up of sovereign states using the global media to dramatize their confrontations are not ideal illustrations of Platonic rationality at work, or even of Aristotelian rationality. However, they are all we have and are likely to have for some time.

In scientific, and even in some political circles, there is talk of transcending these confrontations with new principles. A prominent physician and cancer researcher made this observation:

> Maybe altruism is our most primitive attribute, out of reach, beyond our control. Or perhaps it is immediately at hand, disguised now, in our kind of civilization as affection or friendship or love, maybe as music. I don't see why it should be unreasonable for human beings to have strands of DNA, coiled up in chromosomes, coding out instincts for usefulness and helpfulness. I think it is likely true for all my friends, and I don't see why your family and friends should be any different.[11]

If love can be identified with the chemistry of genetic structures, it can presumably be bred deliberately in future generations. Hence the world is not the indefinite captive of selfishness institutionalized in international organizations and their members. But then, love may also result from such confrontations. Pierre-Elliot Trudeau is reported to have told the Habitat conference,

> It is clear that in order to survive, we will be forced to socialize ourselves more and more. What is actually meant by "socializing"? From a human viewpoint, it means loving one another. We will thus have not only to tolerate one another, but to love one another in a

way which will require of us an unprecedented desire to change ourselves. Such a change will be more drastic than a major mutation of our species. The only type of love which would be effective in the tightly packed world we already live in would be a passionate love.[12]

Such a love might, of course, result in an even more tightly packed world. Nevertheless, whether through genetics or through consciousness-raising, alternatives to the organized self-ishness of international politics are being discussed.

We believe that it is safer to assume, for the foreseeable future, that neither breakthrough will occur. If change comes, it will come as a result of the kinds of confrontations featured in the work of international organizations. They mirror the world of politics, its claims and dissensions as well as its compromises and agreements. And they are the only institutions which capture the crowning of a new consensus with an active program designed to meet some agreed-on social needs. Bilateral science programs merely incorporate the partial consensus implied by a momentary pairing of national objectives. Only multilateral institutions approximate a mirror of the more permanent and the most general trends. A few recent events illustrate why we make this assumption.

Item: When, after the oil embargo of 1973, the major oil-importing nations could not agree on a formula including the pricing of oil, the creation of a pooled reserve, the conditions of access to such a pool, and measures for conserving oil (including R & D on new energy sources), they created the International Energy Agency with a mandate to perfect the package.

Item: As the developed and the developing countries proved unable to achieve agreement on the best and most equitable way of transferring technology from the rich to the poor, without at the same time strengthening the power of multinational corporations, they created a committee of experts and instructed UNCTAD to work out a code of conduct on transfer of technology.[13]

Item: When, in 1971, it became evident that the developed and the developing countries had rather different approaches and conceptions regarding global pollution and environmental degradation, they set up the U.N. Environmental Program as the agency for working out a compromise and launching a program to reflect the compromise.

Item: When, in 1975, the United States became increasingly concerned about unregulated and competitive sales of nuclear reactors and reprocessing plants to developing nations, it began the search for a formula looking toward the creation of multinational nuclear reprocessing centers, institutionalized consultation among sellers of equipment, and stronger safeguarding powers for the International Atomic Energy Agency.

PLAN OF THE BOOK

We have explained what we seek to show, and what not to show. We have made a case as to why science and technology under international auspices ought to be considered an important constituent in talking about future cognitive world orders, even if some of the most puzzling issues cannot now be settled. How do we go about the demonstration?

We first present the strongest case for scientific determinism in the discussion of world orders. This case is heavily influenced by constructs drawn from cybernetics, systems engineering, and studies of biological evolution. Organismic and cybernetic metaphors abound. For reasons to be explained later, we are reluctant to take these seriously as determinants of political choice, but we accept their intellectual salience as definers of a rational approach to the construction of a cognitive world order. This we do in Chapter 2.

However, the rationalist case, though preeminent as a heuristic benchmark, does not exhaust the possibilities. What we know about international decision-making permits us to posit two additional models. In Chapter 3, we therefore present a case against thoroughgoing rationalism by first developing our assumptions, based on the existing literature, regarding the actual role scientists play in the policy-making process. This discussion enables us to develop other reasonable mixtures of how specialized knowledge and the choice of political goals may come together. These will then give us the heuristic world order models to be matched against the perceptions of internationally active scientists and the programs of international organizations.

In Part 2 we present our data on the perceptions of these scientists. What are their personal beliefs about the connections between their knowledge and its application to social goals? What are their experiences as to how international organizations use knowledge in fashioning their programs? This material is presented in Chapter 4. We then extract from these perceptions the properties which illustrate various ways of approaching world order by constructing typologies of world order ideologies. In Chapter 5 these are explained and matched to the earlier discussion of world order models.

In Part 3 we take up the evolution of the science and technology programs of international organizations. Since this material is based on our analysis rather than on the responses of participating scientists, we introduce it in Chapter 6 with our typologies of international decision-making and institutional development. These concepts will be used to sum up the descriptive materials on nine science programs spread over the major specialized agencies, the United Nations, the International Council of Scientific Unions, the European Communities, and the Organization for Economic Cooperation and Development. We will insert into this description the perceptions of the respondents who participate in these nine programs, even though these perceptions do not necessarily match our observations. Hence their assessment of their role and impact will often differ from ours. The actual descriptions of the nine programs provide the material in Chapters 7, 8, and 9.

We conclude our inquiry in Chapter 10 by seeking to match and contrast our assessment of the program with the perceptions of our respondents. Having done so, we inquire again as to how the distribution of program perceptions matches the requirements of the various world order models. We explain how and why the present distribution confirms certain cognitive trends and we speculate how a slight shift in perceptions, some slight increase in knowledge, might alter the distribution in favor of a different cognitive order.

Notes

1. The conference is summarized, and the papers presented there published, in *Daedalus*, spring 1966. A number of additional papers were printed in the summer 1966 issue. The passages quoted from the papers of Jan Tinbergen and C. H. Waddington appear on pp. 545, 667, and 668 of the spring 1966 issue.

2. As quoted by Stanley Hoffmann, in "Report of the Conference on Conditions of World Order," *Daedalus*, spring 1966, p. 456. Predominantly, this idea of a better world order means a restratification of *power* and *authority* in international politics so that those who lack power (small states, significant nonstate groups) improve their power position vis-à-vis the large states and multinational corporations, resulting in a situation in which the authority of international organizations grows at the expense of state authority, as mankind realizes that all problems are interrelated and can be solved only by more centralized action. For a full argument of this position, see Richard A. Falk, *A Study of Future Worlds* (New York: Free Press, 1975). This is emphatically not the position taken by the authors of this study.

3. *Daedalus*, spring 1966, pp. 647–8. Our emphasis. The same point was made forcefully from a Comtian social science perspective by Helio Jaguaribe under the label of an unfolding and universal "operational rationality." See his "World Order, Rationality and Socio-Economic Development," ibid., pp. 607–26.

4. Jan Tinbergen used these words in describing how the Club of Rome seeks to define the priority issues facing the world in the last quarter of the century: "It should be

emphasized that these issues have not been selected on the basis of any political criterion, but of technical criteria which, *because of their technicality,* ought to have priority over political principles. The importance of this argument is enormous because, in the end, it means that if some politicians insist on the priority of their political principles they may well walk into the trap of contributing to the world's, and therefore their own, destruction." "A New International Order," *NATO Review,* December 1975, p. 9. Tinbergen here refers to the RIO study of the Club of Rome. Emphasis is ours.

5. For a critique of these conceptualizations, see Ernst B. Haas, "On Systems and International Regimes," *World Politics,* January 1975, and "Is There a Hole in the Whole?$1$1 *International Organization,* summer 1975.

6. Philip Boffey, *The Brain Bank of America* (New York: McGraw-Hill, 1975), p. *xvii.*

7. This approach is illustrated by the publications of the World Order Models program and its journal *Alternatives.* See, for instance, Rajni Kothari, *Footsteps into the Future* (New York: Free Press, 1974), and Jagdish N. Bhagwati (ed.), *Economics and World Order* (New York: Free Press, 1972).

8. This approach is exemplified by the publications of the Trilateral Commission and, from a different perspective, the Dag Hammarskjöld Foundation and its affiliates in Geneva and Mexico City.

9. Rene Dubos, *A God Within* (New York: Scribner's, 1972), pp. 42–3.

10. The speculative literature on this point is as rich as the descriptive literature is deficient. For the only comprehensive description of international scientific activity available, see Jean Touscoz, *La Coopération scientifique internationale* (Paris: Editions Techniques et Economiques, 1973). This work is a handbook of activities relating to science and technology carried out by intergovernmental organizations, intergovernmental bilateral programs, multinational firms, and international nongovernmental organizations, and it has an excellent bibliography. The only comprehensive political analysis of these programs and their relationship to the evolving interaction among scientific research, technological complexity, and international action is Eugene B. Skolnikoff, *The International Imperatives of Technology* (Berkeley: Institute of International Studies, 1972). Much material on the role of scientific experts in such programs can be gleaned from the first major *tour d'horizon* undertaken under legal auspices in John L. Hargrove (ed.), *Law, Institutions, and the Global Environment* (Dobbs Ferry: Oceana Publications, 1972). For selected case studies on the role of experts, see John G. Ruggie and Ernst B. Haas (eds.), *International Responses to Technology,* special issue of *International Organization,* summer 1975.

11. Dr. Lewis Thomas, "Altruism," *New York Times Magazine,* July 4, 1976, p. l09.

12. As quoted in Friends of the Earth, *Not Man Apart,* vol. 6, no. 12, p. 1. It is reported that Barbara Ward and Mother Theresa made similar statements at Habitat. For a reasoned and elaborate argument advocating world order views combining science and humanism, see Victor Ferkiss, *The Future of Technological Civilization* (New York: Braziller, 1974).

13. See Miguel S. Wionczek, "Draft Outline of an International Code of Conduct on Transfer of Technology" and "Notes on Technology Transfer through Multinational Enterprises in Latin America," *Development and Change* 7 (1976), pp. 135–55, 175–93.

Chapter 2

Knowledge and Action: Rationalism and its Assumptions

In this chapter we offer a summary of views expressed by prominent scientists claiming a sweeping mandate for inserting their knowledge into the act of political choice. In the aggregate, the thrust of this view proclaims the duty of scientists to assure nothing less than the survival of man in the face of challenges brought about by the misuse of both science and technology.

Science is thought capable of suggesting what *ought* to be done in order to assure man's survival; it can tell us about the limits on political choice. Put less sweepingly, science as knowledge at least tells us what must *not* be done if we are to increase the chances of survival. Science and engineering as method limit choice by telling us what *can* be done. These methods attempt to specify ends and to enumerate the means; they also seek to mesh ends and means in such a way as to maximize efficiency, speed, and magnitude of impact. How *will* this be done? Experts will increasingly advise the politicians who make the crucial choices. In a global society in which access to knowledge is deemed crucial, the possessors of that knowledge will be in a position to insert their views into the processes of decision-making. In the aggregate, their beliefs constitute a model of world order geared entirely to the objective of *social* survival, as distinguished from the currently accepted model of nation-state survival. It is mankind—and not a subset of the species—which is to survive.

The increasing importance of scientific and technological experts might not suggest any particular world order model if it were not for the *style of thought* which tends to be typical of many such scientists. These scientists implicitly or explicitly stress the "connectedness" of processes and structures; this, in turn, leads to universal imperatives derived from the presumed uniformity of nature. Therefore, such scientists tend to argue, man's survival in the biosphere imposes new and different kinds of political choices. These choices must respect the substantive *knowledge* accumulated by science and, probably more important, the *methods* used in accumulating knowledge. A more "rational" world order is implied by this dual imperative: Instead of confrontations and negotiations among states informed by cultural symbols considered obsolete, the world ought to be governed by the new symbols, by people and institutions cognizant of the limits on choice demonstrated by science and informed by methods of choosing which are capable of seeing things as wholes.

THE DOMINANT METAPHOR: MANAGED EVOLUTION

Our interest is the identification of a "dominant metaphor" which links knowledge to action. Such a construct predicts comprehensive world order views. A single metaphor of great persuasive power may be identified with an equally appealing program for a new world order. A mixture of metaphors implies ideological competition. The absence of any metaphor would suggest that nothing very specific about a new world order can be culled from the beliefs and experiences of international scientists.

There is, of course, a multiplicity of dominant metaphors in contemporary science. The oldest—the mechanical metaphor of Newtonian lineage—is rarely used by scientists when they discuss world order, though it frequently crops up in the constructs employed by economists and political scientists. Biologists working in the Darwinian tradition favor the organic metaphor. They conceive of organisms in dynamic interaction with their physical environment. The parts of the organism were conceived as a whole; each part has a function which must be carried out in complement with all other functions so that the whole can adapt and survive in a changing environment. Malfunction implies death or decay. The contemporary application of the organic metaphor is evident in the writings of many ecologists. They argue, in effect, that our knowledge of natural processes of interaction enables us to predict which species will survive under given conditions. The physical and chemical properties of the biosphere—in its "natural" state and in its man-altered form—provide the independent variables for indicating the potential for survival. Political purpose is then imputed from the analysis: The organic metaphor suggests what ought to be done to protect the biosphere through the medium of regulation, legislation, and adjudication.

The third dominant metaphor is derived from computer science and cybernetics. It features the flow and use of information in large and complex "systems." The kind of information used by organisms determines whether they will adapt and survive; the manner in which they assimilate, screen out, interpret, and incorporate information becomes crucial. The language used to describe these processes comes to resemble the familiar vocabulary of ethics and political theory.[1] In discussions of world order the cybernetic metaphor takes the form of "whole systems" constructs so defined and engineered as to maximize mankind's capacity to survive.[2] Adherents of the organic and the cybernetic metaphors share similar concerns but differ in the sweep of their prescriptions: The biologists generally confine their recommendations to the wiser management of the *physical* environment; adherents of the cybernetic metaphor show more interest in the joint management of the *physical* and the *social* environments, thus committing themselves to a much more ambitious program of political action.

The metaphor which dominates current discussion of a rational world order is the "evolution" of biological-cultural wholes to a global situation promising the survival of the human species. This construct contains elements of the organic metaphor on nature and society. The metaphor stresses mankind as a whole, not societies and nations. Survival, while still conceptualized as the organic connection of separate parts all contributing to a common purpose, is seen to depend on appropriate feedback loops, information processing techniques, and search routines. Man- computer simulations have become the operational symbol of the dominant metaphor.

However, such a metaphor involves *planning* the evolution of man, for example, by prescriptions for zero growth and resource management. Man, as part of nature, has done for millenia what "comes naturally"; he has acted out his evolutionary potential by seeking to make himself master of the very environment into which adaptation is supposed to be taking place. In other words, unlike all other species known to us, his manner of adaptation has taken the form of manipulating the environment, *not* of accepting it as given. In acting naturally (presumably), he also has so altered his environment that his chances to survive in the future are thrown into doubt, unless he changes his ways. The scientist's approach to world order calls for such a change. A different world order is one in which the environment—now threatened by man's "natural" behavior—will be deliberately manipulated by a wiser man so as to remain hospitable to his continued evolution.[3]

Evolution toward what? Is the wiser man more or less "natural" than his now-flourishing but rapacious ancestor? To what extent is the deliberate (and therefore political) intervention in natural processes a part of nature, or is intervention something alien superimposed on it? At this point in our summary of views, we step back to comment on the meaning of the argument. Why do we combine the views of systems thinkers and exponents of ecological management into a single metaphor? Why do we call it a metaphor and not scientific knowledge?

We call the argument metaphoric because it imputes social meaning to a scientific theory which was originally devoid of it. A large number of prominent scientists, though by no means all, are comfortable with this imputation and use it for postulating what governments ought to do, and refrain from doing. They claim a scientific warrant for the definition of political purpose. Their argument amalgamates components drawn from the ecological management and systems management perspectives, even though these two need not and do not always cohere in a single claim. And since we are investigating the ideological power of the metaphor in international scientific programs, we find it important to focus these views even if, in so doing, we combine strands which do not command combination. A disaggregation of the metaphor is in fact encountered in the world order models which will be found to compete with the rational case.

A brief excursion into the meaning of the concept of "survival" will illustrate why we call the argument a metaphor. We demonstrate the epistemological difficulties involved in transposing a concept from a biological to a cultural and political setting. In Darwinian evolutionary theory, the notion of survival is verbal shorthand for biological processes involving genetic continuity and change vis-à-vis physical and organic conditions. It does not involve choice, action, deliberation, will, or learning. Survival in contemporary discourse on food, population, energy, nuclear weapons, aggressiveness, conflict over pure water, comes to mean the recognition and management of crisis. In other words, it implies all the characteristics *not* present in the intellectual context from which the term is borrowed and "adapted" to make a programmatic point. The contrast in meaning is starker than the word suggests: Survival in Darwin was associated with progress, with the faith in the comprehensive unfolding of rationality through history in which most nineteenth-century scientists believed, whether they had read Hegel or not; now, when no such faith in metarationality prevails, survival means only the marshaling of such energy as we have to stave off catastrophe.

The evolution of a wiser man as the "end" or "purpose" of biological and cybernetic processes is very different from the physical survival of a given species. A question such as this, most scientists argue, cannot be adequately dealt with on the basis of biology, ecology, and genetics.[4] They think that this conundrum evokes the need for a significantly different form of social organization than now exists. And to understand what this organization might look like, the direction of cultural—as opposed to biological—evolution becomes a matter of direct interest. Moreover, the relationships between cultural and natural systemic characteristics—or "systemic coupling"—become a central matter of concern. While this calls for an examination of historical patterns and future possibilities for social adaptation as studied by anthropologists, the attempted coupling of natural and social systems also raises the question of whether or not the metaphor is now being extended to another level, and whether or not science validates the coupling process. In either event, the argument now begins to address the social and political purposes implied by the need for survival.

Systemic coupling is described as follows in an ingenious analysis by Anatol Rapoport. Man is a "successful" species because, in terms of longevity, he has been around twice as long as the average for species; and because his doubling time is now thirty-five years! This may be because "cultural evolution," through the development of a collective intelligence, is superimposed on biological-physical development, which has remained unchanged since Cro-Magnon times. Cultural specialization, through language primarily, is the main mechanism of human evolution. But which cultures are "successful"? No taxonomy of cultures is very persuasive as a "survival indicator," and the analogy cannot be worked out by imputing a "struggle for existence" to cultures in the same sense as interspecies competition in a physical environment. The analogy can be established by examining the mechanism of reproduction. The criterion of "success" for a species is the numerical value of its reproductive processes; the criterion of "success" of a culture is the numerical value of the reproduction of its artifacts—language, institutions, cities, attitudes, values. However, since all these items are systemically interrelated, the net survival value of the cultural reproduction process is determined by the functionality of the linkage, just as in biological evolution the functionality of anatomical-biochemical interactions determines successful adaptation. In short, the simple numerical incidence of a single cultural item is *not* a valid indicator of the survival value of the culture in which it is embedded.

According to Rapoport, the functionality of the linkage is determined by the feedback process. Positive feedback ensues when, superimposed on a given biological pattern, various cultural items mutually reinforce one another to produce a new cultural syndrome; negative feedback ensues when they neutralize one another. Cultural evolution can be accelerated if, in positive-feedback processes, a critical threshold of causal interaction is passed, as in the bandwagon effect. Obviously, for purposes of survival calculations, such positive processes may be destructive or beneficial. Positive feedback operates in both cultural and biological evolution. It can be checked in biological evolution by the extent to which the "explosion" remains within environmentally determined bounds. When numbers exceed ecological carrying capacity, Malthusian principles take over. When numbers grow as the environment changes, the environmental change may make adaptation impossible. In cultural evolution there are no analogous checks. Cultural changes cannot be related unambiguously to cultural survival. Nevertheless, the sketching of positive-feedback patterns in culture facilitates prediction and analysis as to *which* cultural items are functional for survival of the species (even though there is disagreement on which human values are worth fostering or restraining).[5]

What difference does this make for a more rational world order? The case for a scientifically legitimated world order is strong to the extent that cultural imperatives are tightly linked with biological and ecological injunctions. Even such political artifacts as international decision-making mechanisms would then become subject to survival imperatives derived from superior knowledge thought to rest on universality, objectivity, and replicability. If it could be argued unambiguously that such and such a syndrome of cultural traits must be associated with a given level of evolutionary development, then prescriptive statements about desirable future cultural steps could be made—for example, that world government is necessary for man's survival. If, in contrast, the parallelism between cultural and biological systems is metaphorical rather than literal, the compellingness of such arguments is considerably reduced.

Glenn T. Seaborg, certainly an experienced statesman of science, expressed himself fairly literally on this point when he argued, "We now see the world evolving into an ecologic, economic, and ethical whole. Science and technology have created the conditions leading to this viewpoint, and they have created the instruments to observe it; and if they have fostered many of the problems related to it, they are also capable of giving us the knowledge and tools to solve these problems."[6] He called on his fellow scientists to "expand their action to the international scene," to work for a world of peace, fulfillment, and dignity "through the achievement of a worldwide unified economy." He described science and technology as "the leading forces in an evolutionary unification of man" simply because science itself is universal and the truths it discovers become a revelation for all mankind. Science is to close the gap between outmoded cultures and the rational promise of a better future by removing biases, misconceptions, and outmoded ideas. And scientists, as experts, are the agents of this transformation:

> It is up to the world's scientists and engineers to exercise great leadership, not only in focusing the attention of their communities and countries on these problems but in developing practical solutions that can be rapidly put into effect by industrial and political leaders. The problem of the industrialization of the developing countries in a humane and sensible way provides a great challenge to the world community of scientists and engineers.[7]

Whether as metaphor or analog, the most general argument usually holds that there is a serious lag between the pace of "adaptive" cultural evolution and the "needs" of biological survival. Having transformed his global environment by virtue of his scientific and technological prowess, man now endangers his survival because he has failed to fashion values and institutions and symbols of communication to warn himself of the damage he has done, and he has failed to foster behavior less likely to be self-destructive. Therefore, if survival is to be "planned," the two evolutionary patterns ought to be brought into phase. The remaking of political institutions then constitutes one step in the reform. Competitiveness, aggression, conflict enter the picture as the evolutionary villains.

Two current variants of the prescription can be discerned. Some scientists who seek to link cultural and biological patterns conceptualize survival on the basis of a positive-feedback mechanism. Such remedies as zero economic and population growth, collaborative resource management, and deliberate measures to diversify the gene pool will not restore the global ecosystem to the equilibrium point which it may have occupied in the past. Instead, new policies—which must be developed by new values and institutions—will lead to trends that will bring about equilibrium at a different point, thus restoring the world to a steady state in an aggregate and abstract sense. Survival strategies involving deliberate positive feedback thus imply cooperation, brotherhood, trust. The realization of such values and practices constitutes the appropriate cultural evolution for many who take this approach.[8]

This conceptualization contrasts sharply to the more familiar approach of scientists who think in terms of negative-feedback processes, of adjusting culture to nature so as to obtain self-corrective or homeostatic mechanisms which automatically restore the ensemble to a state of equilibrium. Waddington coined the term *homeorhesis* specifically to suggest the inadequacy of this formulation.[9] But since scientists cannot be certain what the "end" or final product of evolution might be, they differ on what survival implies in terms of more rational political purposes. To be sure, there is little disagreement that nuclear war is bad, that energy should be conserved, and that the biosphere should be kept below a certain level of pollution. But there is less agreement as to what kind of new cultural pattern may be required. Yet the imperatives of *some* pattern of cultural evolution must be evoked.

Put differently, the question is as follows: Assuming that cultural traits legitimating conflict were functional in the past and may remain so in the future, how much aggressiveness can the cultural system tolerate short of self-destruction (that is, nonsurvival)? Rapoport answers this question by saying that "man's destructive aggressiveness against nature may be a manifestation of a need to assert his autonomy in the immature stage of humanity." Autonomy, he says, is a desirable cultural trait, and the search for institutionalized power is undesirable in terms of survival. "When man's autonomy is fully established, that is, as his capacities have become more fully realized, only so much 'aggression' may be expected to remain as is needed to guarantee the maintenance of the human race as an autonomous entity. (In system-theoretic terminology, this would mean to maintain a steady state."[10]

Scientists who seek to *prescribe* cultural and political responses on the basis of this chain of reasoning act in the role of political theorists. For Rapoport, the principle of "autonomy" is the ethical imperative which should characterize man's relationship to nature (and to other men). "Therefore, if Man's uniqueness is embodied in his *awareness* of his autonomy as the most precious gift of evolution, men must address themselves to the task of dismantling the fortresses of entrenched power."[11] Dubos argues that science "can provide a more factual basis for options by giving the statistical probability that certain consequences will result from new technological and social practices. Since awareness of likely consequences plays a large role in decision-making, scientific knowledge can become an important criterion in the evaluation of old value systems and perhaps in fostering the development of new ones."[12] Harrison Brown feels reasonably certain that as man exhausts easily available mineral resources, he will perfect technologies to extract them from any kind of rock. This is likely to lead to the end of technological civilization either because the rich countries will exploit the poor even more than heretofore, or because the poor will make war on one another. Therefore, we must make a "series of rational decisions" to create, now, a worldwide civilization "which can perpetrate itself indefinitely and in which people can live comfortably and in peace with each other."[13]

Our summary of scientific views on world order has stressed *why*, in an evolutionary perspective, science is entitled to stipulate political purposes. It has sought to make the case as to *why* scientific knowledge ought to be considered as a guide to rational choice. The claim is based on the substance of that knowledge, on the demonstration of connectedness which permits the inference that all parts are combinable in a larger system of knowledge, a system that also contains the laws of what is possible to man in the future.

By no means all scientists accept this view of the world. Richard Crossman, minister for science and technology in the first Wilson cabinet, gave a different emphasis to the issue when he argued that his should be the "first science-based government in Britain. Science-based in two senses. First, that it recognizes the enormous importance of technological change. And second, that it bases its actions on a scientific assessment of the facts."[14] To Crossman this implied social democracy, public ownership, educational reform—in short, "that rational solutions can be achieved with the voluntary assent of an educated people."[15] However, to Crossman this did not mean that scientists should function as political theorists. Many prominent scientists put the emphasis on the quality of the information science can add to the policy-making process, how science can improve *methods* rather than political purposes.[16]

The view we have summarized so far, however, includes *both* claims: The substance of scientific knowledge as well as scientific methods of inquiry entitle science to specify political purpose. We now turn to the discussion of method in a rational approach to world order. Many scientists accept only the portion of our summary which deals with methods. Those scientists who are also political theorists, however, subscribe to both.

METHODS

There are few scientists who would argue that, in any direct sense, science is capable of "preempting" or "replacing" politics. In a world order model indebted to science and scientists the political decision-makers would still be politicians, elected or otherwise. Infusing political choice with scientific impulses involves less the replacement of the decision-making personnel than the introduction of new cognitive styles. The emphasis is therefore on *how* future decisions could and should be made.

Before discussing this further we wish to illustrate the point with one important set of recommendations for reforming "science for policy." The Brooks report of the OECD recommends that the technological applications of pure research be made part and parcel of a more systematic approach to economic control, industrial development, education, and the safeguarding of the quality of life. The scientific method—in the form of data banks, formal models of large systems, and the use of social indicators—is to be featured. Science is to be made "relevant" to social needs by these means. Social science is to become part of the ensemble, instead of remaining a stepchild. The aim is to advance the orderly development of societies too complex to rely on market mechanisms and incentives. International research and forecasting are the methods. Were the report implemented, it would effectively subordinate national investment in R & D, secondary and higher education, social welfare, foreign aid, and the setting of policy priorities to an international technocracy of experts whose work is unified by a common commitment to *a methodology*.[17]

The basis for such a commitment is the conviction on the part of scientists that "facts," especially the facts concerning nature, are less problematical and ambiguous than "values." Politicians and lay publics disagree and argue over values. Scientists discover facts. Such views are common even though it is agreed by scientists that it takes much debate and work to succeed in establishing the facticity of phenomena and processes. More important, once a consensus on the factual character of a set of phenomena has been established, this consensus will prevail even if the scientists involved hold clashing opinions on religion, politics, ethics, sex, and food. This is the meaning of the universality and objectivity of science.[18] That being so, established families of facts act as cognitive constraints, in much the same fashion as political ideologies, on possible courses of action. *But the special virtue of scientific knowledge is the universality of the meaning of the constraints over political ideologies.* In that sense, then, science can civilize politics.

When scientists speak of rationalizing politics, of imposing a more rational view on political actors, of changing the cultural system in the direction of more rationality, they are urging politicians to respect these constraints. It is facts which promote rationality, and rationality so defined ought to simplify political choice by eliminating from consideration many options which would be plausible candidates for action in the absence of good information. Since the social sciences are sometimes considered capable of generating good information, they also ought to figure in the improvement of rationality.

What is good information? Do facts speak for themselves? If not, how must they be manipulated or interpreted to qualify as good information? Is good information in biology equatable, for purposes of political choice, with good information in economics and social anthropology? Are fields of knowledge additive, multiplicable, combinable? These are the kinds of questions which preoccupy scientists in their capacity as technicians of political choice. Being master of a methodology implies a set of attitudes and predispositions with respect to such questions, though not agreement on all details. A variety of answers is given; they amount to a set of convictions that science *does* offer a rationality superior to choice informed only by values.

Good information is not a compendium of self-evident facts, though at the simplest level it would be agreed that just knowing that the level of pollutants in the air is above a certain threshold will be useful. Useful for what? For predicting illness or discomfort. The interface between health and pollution, however, requires an understanding of the connections between the organism and its physical environment, of two systems. Information almost always depends on the acceptance of a scheme of interpretation before it can be considered good. A methodological consensus among scientists thus presupposes the acceptance of schemes of interpretation. Various kinds of *systems* provide the most common schemes in contemporary discussion. By being accepted as a framework for interpretation they become cognitive simplifiers. They make possible the reduction of countless facts to summary statements of explanation and, perhaps, prediction.

"Natural systems" is a powerful cognitive simplifier increasingly employed in those branches of science most closely related to international and national policies. Ecological and resource management are obvious examples. But natural systems constructs also make their appearance in the design of policies relating to education and to the diffusion of technology in late developing countries, as, for example, through the notions of energy transfer and cybernetics.

The methodological difficulties faced by systems constructs are severe. And the ideological salience of the systems view as the main cognitive simplifier is far from unchallenged. Let us look again at the example of pollution used previously. Some scientists will treat facts pertaining to the organism as one system and the environmental aspect, the typical mode of interaction between an organism and its nonphysical setting, as another. The intellectual task then becomes the coupling of the two cognitive simplifiers. More commonly, however, both systems will be integrated into a single construct; they become "subsystems" (or subroutines in computer language) of one single system. It makes a great deal of difference which approach prevails. If a single system is used, the causal arrows will be drawn more heavily and determinatively than if the task is seen as a more tentative linking of discrete systems. The firmness and finality of the recommendation resulting from the cognitive scheme will differ in the two cases. Good information still depends on the intellectual assumptions one makes, and a reliance on the power of natural systems alone will not still controversy.

The controversy is exemplified by the ongoing discussion of the key concepts to be used in systems constructs. Older systems approaches rely heavily on the notion of "function." The activities, units, components, and processes being combined by the analyst are expected to serve some biological or cybernetic purpose. Function implies a built-in teleology. Purposiveness is imputed to the phenomenon by the human observer, not proclaimed by the phenomenon itself. Inferences about optimal quantities of aggressiveness in social systems, for example, depend on a teleological judgment of the utility of aggressive behavior in the "tasks" facing the society. Such judgments, in turn, are influenced by the prior choice as to whether social and biological systems are separate but subject to coupling, or whether they are subsystems of the same overarching construct.

It is therefore not surprising that, in the absence of general agreement on a teleology, there is some preference for abandoning the concept of "function." The notion of "structure" has come to the fore instead. It is meant to capture processes and syndromes of behavior which persist over time and thus demonstrate a capacity to survive. However, there seem to be almost as many candidates for the label of "structure" as there are structuralists, even though the specification of structures eliminates the need for imputing purposes to inanimate forces or inarticulate organisms, including primitive societies observed by articulate anthropologists. If the purpose of the cognitive simplifier is to link knowledge to political choice, not much clarity is gained by redefining systems approaches in structural terms.[19]

Hence, systems theorists increasingly advance the concept of "control" as the means for deciding how to couple discrete systems or combine them in single systems. Control is easily matched to management through better understanding, to deliberate manipulation of physical and social forces thought in need of better performance. Good information about control in natural systems might be considered an important clue on how to manage the cultural systems relating to world order.[20]

Social systems theories are not in short supply. They are also used as cognitive simplifiers, whether or not it is legitimate to use them as analogs to their natural systems cousins. Their impact on schemes for improving world order needs no emphasis. Notions of control abound in them. Their purpose is either to facilitate choice by mapping out the most efficient, rational, or optimal action path to a desired social outcome (as in systems analysis, cost/benefit studies, and operations research) or to enhance our understanding of complexity by showing the links between actors and/or processes in society, economics, and politics (as in structural-functional systems in sociology, anthropology, and political science). Systems analysis, of course, is already a social methodology in common use. Some scientists now also include structural-functional models in the conceptualization of national and international "control problems," as is implied in the social indicators movement.[21]

Our discussion of the links between biological and cultural evolution has shown that a scientific approach to world order seeks to link natural with manmade systems. A desire to bring about such an epistemological and cognitive marriage is common to a scientist's approach to world order issues. How to do this remains a much-debated issue. In the absence of an agreed-on formula, the method of multidisciplinary collaboration on scientific projects (especially projects relating to social needs) is now favored. Action programs, particularly in the field of ecology, while formerly handled almost exclusively by physical and biological scientists, now commonly include social scientists whose ideas and methods are to be "plugged into" the natural systems already used by the biologists.[22] The bulk of the effort remains eclectic. Lively debate among rival approaches continues. All that matters for us is that various multidisciplinary and systemic modes of working are currently accepted as the way of meshing the methods of natural and social scientists, and thus of influencing choice.

In the rational model, then, scientists believe they possess a methodology superior to political confrontation and debate as a means of making choices in fields dependent on information from the natural sciences. Their methodological commitments involve the marshaling of good information designed to constrain choice in the form of various systemic constructs, which increasingly include systems analysis and models of social systems. Thinking in terms of highly abstract models relying on the use of computers, therefore, is becoming relevant to the designing of a different world order.

SCIENCE AND A RATIONAL WORLD ORDER: SUMMARY

We have attempted to isolate some key themes scientists stress when they think about taking an active hand in shaping a new world order dedicated to welfare and survival—an objective commonly operationalized in terms of the survival of the species *homo sapiens* in the face of such dangers as nuclear war, famine, resource depletion, genetic deterioration, overcrowding, or the poisoning of the biosphere. This collection of catastrophes is conceptualized by some scientists as an irreversible process of entropy in the man-environment system; it is seen by other scientists as a reversible process resulting from faulty negative feedback. Both groups share a belief in the ability of science to sketch the cognitive links required to understand the interaction of systems of natural and man-caused behavior. Some, but not all, believe that knowledge of biological and cultural evolutionary dynamics can be connected within a context of physical determinism and stochastic processes. Almost all believe in the superiority of certain methods of investigation and demonstration which feature systematic thinking—usually in quantitative terms—and which therefore are able to perform "better" than the simple confrontation of rival political goals in the "technical sphere" of fashioning policy. Most believe in efforts to marshal

knowledge of systems and of methods in such a way as to
influence politicians without taking their place, by advising
politicians from within government and by being near government as "insiders," not simply as members of the plurality of
interested voices who normally clamor for attention.

It may be objected that this ideal type is rigged in favor of
science in that it ignores the challenges to scientific rationality
now common in the philosophical and polemical literature. Our
formulation seems to accept the special claim to knowledge as
profoundly salient just at the time when its legitimacy is being
widely questioned by scientists and the lay public alike. So it does.
Our reasons for proceeding in this fashion are due to the conviction that most of the complaints regarding scientism and the
overreliance on scientific modes of thinking are being dealt with
in such a fashion as to *confirm* the special position of theoretical
knowledge. Whatever is wrong with science, today's reformers
seem to be saying, can be fixed by methods and approaches
which will make decision-making *more* dependent on specialized
information processed in intricate ways. Consider systematic
technology assessment, development planning, environmental
impact studies, the modeling of complex processes and interactions, procedures of adversary science conducted within the
bounds of professional decorum, and even the deliberate linking
of science with humane values. All these involve experts more
intimately than before with policy choice. All call for more focused and systematic confrontation among disparate bodies of
knowledge, under the aegis of some profession other than politics as usually practiced. Nor is it seriously argued that crucial
goals in resource planning and environmental protection can
be chosen without the continuous input of specialized information which only scientists can provide.[23] We believe that our
portrait is safe because it does *not* overstate the potential role of
scientists. It simply seeks to present what is actually being said
so as to make it speak to the issue of world order. Whether it
applies to scientists working in international organizations remains to be seen.

What matters to us is the mixture of perceptions on the part of
internationally active scientists with respect to issues of world
order. We wish to explore whether and how their beliefs, actions,
and impressions conform to the themes of the overall portrait of
rationalism. Given that international choices regarding a future
world order are being made on the basis of confrontation and
bargaining among units (states) informed by goals derived from

ideologies of military, economic, and cultural security, do internationally active scientists and experts provide one or several alternative models transcending these ideologies?

Notes

1. See Karl W. Deutsch, *The Nerves of Government* (New York: Free Press, 1963); David E. Apter, *Choice and the Politics of Allocation* (New Haven: Yale University Press, 1971). For work exposing hidden normative biases implicit in cybernetic approaches to knowledge, and their social consequences, see C. West Churchman, *The Systems Approach* (New York: Dell, 1968), and Robert Boguslaw, *The New Utopians* (Englewood Cliffs, N.J.: Prentice-Hall, 1965).

2. Such concerns are illustrated by Harold and Margaret Sprout, *Toward a Politics of the Planet Earth* (New York: Van Nostrand Reinhold, 1971); Ervin Laszlo, *The Systems View of the World* (New York: Braziller, 1972); Erich Jantsch, *Technological Planning and Social Futures* (London, 1972).

3. This case was made eloquently and often by the late Eugene Rabinowitch. See "Responsibility of Scientists in Our Age," *Bulletin of the Atomic Scientists*, November 25, 1969, pp. 2–6, 26; "The Role of Scientists: Thoughts for 1971," ibid., January 27, 1971, pp. 2–4.

4. See Michel Batisse, "Environmental Problems and the Scientists," *Bulletin of the Atomic Scientists*, February 29, 1973, pp. 15–21. Batisse—while analyzing the human condition in terms similar to the argument being discussed here—doubts that scientists are able to deal with problems posed by value and preference priorities after the scientific demonstration has been made because such issues properly belong to the "sociosphere" and the "noosphere," which are only loosely coupled to the biosphere and the technosphere. A similar line of reasoning has led Peter Corning to suggest that one important task of political science in the "new era" should be the elaboration of a list of political values which enhance the human survival potential. See his "The Biological Bases of Behavior and Some Implications for Political Science," *World Politics*, April 1971.

5. Anatol Rapoport, *Conflict in Man-Made Environment* (Baltimore: Penguin, 1974), chap. 7.

6. For this and the succeeding quotations, see Glenn T. Seaborg, "Science, Technology and Development: A New World Outlook," *Science*, vol. 181, no. 4094 (July 6, 1973), p. 13. This article is the text of Seaborg's address as retiring president of the American Association for the Advancement of Science.

7. Ibid., p. 18.

8. Rapoport suggests that it is unnecessary to be informed in detail about the motivations, objectives, and purposes of human actors (individuals and collectivities) in sketching cultural systems of conflict. He argues that such system dynamics can be understood in describing their stochastic properties on the basis of the "logic of large numbers." He describes conflict as a structural-institutional characteristic of the cultural system, whose functionality with respect to the biological system is questionable. Hence institutional techniques of conflict management, as in the United Nations, are ineffective, because they address symptoms and not causes, and dysfunctional in an evolutionary sense because they do not recognize that sometimes conflict may be necessary for better adaptation. The causes of war lie in these stochastic processes, just as the causes of diseases can be described in such terms. Diseases can be treated basically, rather than symptomatically, only when these processes are understood. Hence, it is difficult to understand why he also argues that "as long as war continues to be institutionalized, the most valuable result of peace research would be a change in the conception of war, from that of a political instrument or a natural catastrophe or a disease to that of organized crime" (Rapoport, *Conflict*, p. 240; see chapter 15 for the argument on stochastic processes).

9. Norbert Wiener in 1962 questioned whether the achievements of technology were not creating negative-feedback conditions which "make one wonder whether we have not changed the environment beyond our capacity to adjust to it, and whether we may not be biologically on the way out." Quoted in René Dubos, *Reason Awake: Science For Man* (New York: Cambridge University Press, 1970), pp. 124–5. Dubos himself makes similar suggestions in ibid., pp. 245–6. The affinity of these formulations to Social Darwinism is quite obvious. Scientists leaning toward the negative-feedback formulations have something in common with those late nineteenth and early twentieth century Social Darwinists who projected evolutionary survival formulations into politics by means of advocating national self-assertion and the eugenics of racial purity. The later eugenic argument, stripped of its racial component, is equally consistent with this position, as are contemporary discussions of genetic engineering and cultural programs of compensating for genetic deficiencies. Scientists espousing the positive-feedback formulation (for example, Rapoport, Dubos, Rabinowitch, Dobzhansky) are no less Social Darwinist in their desire to make biological and cultural determinants cohere in a single evolutionary pattern tailored to their normative preferences. Both formulations involve an anthropomorphic bias in seeking to impute a direction and a desired "end state" to a process which is presumably given by nature.

10. Rapoport, *Conflict*, p. 249.

11. Ibid., p. 250. Emphasis in original.

12. Dubos, *Reason Awake*, p. 240.

13. Harrison Brown, "Resource Needs and Demands," International Council of Scientific Unions, *Bulletin* 19 (November 1969), p. 24. Brown later became president of ICSU. The vice-president of ICSU, Jean Coulomb, had other priorities, however, "The proper role of scientists is . . . to establish the truth and to announce it, rather than direct political arguments from it or put oneself in the service of technicians for studying the details." "Le Passé et l'avenir de la coopération scientifique internationale," ibid., p. 15. Leo Szilard and Albert Szent-Gyorgyi express views which make them political theorists in *International Science and Technology, The Way of the Scientist: Interviews from the World of Science and Technology* (New York: Simon and Schuster, 1962–1968).

14. *International Science and Technology*, p. 295.

15. Ibid., p. 300.

16. Three former science advisers to the president—George B. Kistiakowsky, Jerome Wiesner, and Donald F. Hornig—go out of their way to argue that they saw their job as keeping the necessity for making political choices out of their work by concentrating on technical issues and supporting science for its own sake. Ibid., pp. 202–5, 210–16, 220–5.

17. *Science, Growth and Society: A New Perspective,* Report on the Secretary-General's Ad Hoc Group on New Concepts of Science Policy (Paris: OECD, 1971).

18. We are summarizing views and attitudes, not expressing an opinion as to our agreement with them. The literature on this point is too well known to require citation here. Nor do we at this stage consider it necessary to enter into all the permutations of the fact-value controversy, or comment on the social science literature which disputes the accuracy of some scientific claims and insists on treating the scientific method as just another ideology. For a balanced view on philosophical commitment as opposed to practice, see especially Jerome R. Ravetz, *Scientific Knowledge and Its Social Problems* (New York: Oxford University Press, 1971). See Jürgen Habermas, *Technik und Wissenschaft als "Ideologie"* (Frankfurt: Edition Suhrkamp, 1968), for an argument that while—*pace* Marcuse—science and technology must not by their very nature be alienating, their being embedded in a social context of inequality and exploitation does tend to make them suspect and therefore a mere ideology. For empirical support that many scientists and engineers in fact see themselves as capable of offering special competence and knowledge as political actors, see A. A. Elliot, T. G. Hood, and J. E. Holmes, "The Working Scientist as Political Participant," *Journal of Politics,* May 1972, pp. 399–427.

19. See Jean Piaget, *Structuralism* (New York: Basic Books, 1970), for a discussion suggesting that structural theories do not decisively remove the difficulties inherent in systems theories.

20. For examples of this concept as used in a variety of natural systems theories, see Howard H. Pattee, *Hierarchy Theory* (New York: Braziller, 1973). The common thread of these theories, incidentally, is the notion of survival.

21. The most sophisticated discussions of the cognitive issues raised by the approach are Herbert Simon's. For critical discussions of the social costs of systems analysis, see Ida Hoos, *Systems Analysis in Public Policy* (Berkeley and Los Angeles: University of California Press, 1972), and for analyses of the political practice of systems analysis in the U.S. government, see Aaron Wildavsky, "The Political Economy of Efficiency: Cost-Benefit Analysis, Systems Analysis and Program Budgeting," *Public Administration Review,* December 1966. Large-scale application of both systems analysis and a type of social systems theory in international scientific programs is exemplified by the UNISIST data bank of UNESCO, which seeks to make available to all users everywhere appropriately coded scientific and technological information relating to the diffusion of technology, and by the similar system of UNEP relating to environmental protection.

22. The prominent example is the Man and the Biosphere program to be discussed further on. For an excellent survey of the multidisciplinary attempts to conceptualize linkages, see F. E. Emery (ed.), *Systems Thinking* (Penguin, 1969). General systems theory is used by Ervin Laszlo in an effort to conceptualize cognitive simplifiers for the natural and social sciences in dealing with world order. See his *The World System* (New York: Braziller, 1973) and *The Systems View of the World* (New York: Braziller, 1972).

23. Rapoport and Ferkiss, who show a marked ambivalence on the question of scientism and are acutely aware of science perceived as an alienating and dehumanizing force, argue forcefully that whatever is wrong with the science-society interface is going to be cured only by means of a more complete—if institutionally different—integration of science with society. For a more extended argument designed to show why and how the malaise concerning science is being attacked without downgrading the influence of scientists, see Haas, "Is There a Hole in the Whole?" *International Organization,* summer 1975.

Chapter 3

Rationalism, Pragmatism, Skepticism: World Order Models

If we suppose that all knowledge is ultimately inter-connected and reflective of the uniformity of nature, and if we suppose further that systems methods will help in elucidating the connections, many interesting political ramifications may become demonstrable. It may appear, for instance, that peace cannot be had without a different global system of education, and that education is useless until food and energy shortages are removed. If human pugnaciousness, in the form of competitive and mutually suspicious sovereign states, is due to the persistence of social and cultural habits which fly in the face of the "need" for cooperation, this need cannot be met until remedial measures are adopted in *all* the subsystems of the "war system."[1] Rationalism is the cognitive mode which commits itself to the identification of all these components in its search for comprehensive solutions based on a knowledge of nature.

But the rational stance is not the only possible one. Less sweeping claims by scientists are also encountered. Not all insist that political solutions are capable of being directly linked to a better understanding of the laws of nature. More complex links between expert knowledge and political action are conceivable and are recognized by internationally active scientists. These suggest cognitive models of world order in which scientific knowledge plays a different role than in the rationalist position. The purpose of this chapter is to chart these possibilities and to link them to world order models which assign a more modest position to the possessors of specialized knowledge.

A preliminary step must be taken first. In Chapter 1 we indicated that a key assumption of this enterprise is a conception of the scientific expert as *adviser* to politicians, not as an autonomous political actor. The explication of world order models is not possible without a prior statement as to why we cast specialists and experts in a subordinate political role. Who can say that the benign governance of philosopher-kings will never arrive? We believe, however, that we are safe in assuming that the day will not come very soon.

KNOWLEDGE, ADVICE, AND ACTION

We therefore dispense with the image of scientist-philosopher-king made familiar by Leo Szilard's dolphins: Scientists will not make a contribution to a different world order by earning recognition and authority as a ruling elite of knowledge-for-survival. However, if scientists are to function as the possessors of a politically relevant message and a special methodology in world affairs they must somehow influence policy-makers. How?

> Professors back from secret missions
> Resume their proper eruditions,
>   Though some regret it;
>
> They liked their dictaphones a lot,
> They met some big wheels, and do not
>   Let you forget it.

W. H. AUDEN

Scientists *do* believe, in principle, that their knowledge entitles them to give advice on many questions which they consider to be ill-understood by politicians. Whether that knowledge is indeed better, by standards other than those of the experts themselves, is not a relevant question for us. It is considered better by the experts, and their increasing presence in national and international administrations testifies that this self-judgment is accepted in some measure by nonexperts. The question that remains to be answered is how such advice is brought to bear on major decisions relating to international order.

The political roles of science and scientists are commonly described in the following ways. Some conceive of science as an "estate" linked to or coterminous with "the Internationale of science" or the "epistemic community" of scientists. We do not find this formulation helpful in our quest. Others describe the political activities of scientists in the language of interest group theory; we, however, do not define the role of international scientists as approximating that of interest groups. Still others define the issue of scientists in politics as a bureaucratic phenomenon and therefore treat international science programs as an instance of "supranational bureaucracy." For reasons to be developed, we do not consider this formulation appropriate for our purpose.

The conception of an estate, in Don Price's formulation, evokes the image of a community of like-minded people, united in terms of the ethos of their work and calling. An estate would exist if scientists of all nationalities, in their political advisory roles, were consistently committed to the Mertonian imperatives of universality, communality, disinterestedness, and organized skepticism. Even if we grant that the notion of the superior rationality of science presupposes the reality of these imperatives as attributes of the system of science, it does not follow that we must accept them as part of the daily catechism of the experts' behavior. The empirical and biographical literature which throws doubt on the reality of these canons as personal motivators seems quite persuasive to us.[2] That being so, the idea of a national or international scientific estate is simply an interesting figure of speech.

International science also has been described as an "epistemic community," a network of individuals and groups who are able to influence the future by virtue of their shared specialized knowledge of certain crucial phenomena. Since they sometimes make efforts to link this knowledge to programs and activities designed to create a future which differs appreciably from the past and present, individuals who belong to this epistemic community seek to use their knowledge as a way of organizing cognition collectively. The beliefs of this community, when translated into policies and programs, are sometimes seen as the institutionalized conscience of the community of knowledge devoting its energies to a combination of prophecy and problem-solving. The proof of the pudding is in the eating. The Pugwash Conference comes close to meeting the terms of an epistemic community in action, of the true Internationale of science. Its declining role speaks for itself.[3] No likely successor comes to mind.

Scientists, to be sure, do attempt to act as an interest group, both nationally and internationally. In doing so they make two claims: Their expertise entitles them to be heard in the discussion of public policy *in preference to* other interest groups because their knowledge is held to be less self-interested and more comprehensive; and their expertise gives them a special insight into the moral dangers posed by exclusive reliance on "official" scientific advice and is therefore an important corrective, especially with respect to military and environmental issues. This dual argument, however, throws doubt on the very disinterestedness of the advisory activity and has the effect of casting the scientists in the same role as any other interest group. They may simply represent *an* interest: consumers, the poor, backpackers, or a subgroup within science. Thus, their special claim to be heard is weakened.[4] The advocacy role, especially when it pits "government insiders" against "outsiders," may be extremely useful in opening up the decision-making process when it comes to the introduction of new technologies because it may show that knowledge is far less consensual than had been claimed by the "insiders." Nor is it necessary that scientists act only as spokesmen for "their" particular interests. If they resort to public debates, rather than panel discussions in the U.S. National Academy of Science, they would—as in the debate on the use of defoliants in Vietnam—be acting as political-moral guardians, as "the lower House of Science" to use Gerald Holton's phrase.

The point is that we can take no comfort either from the self-interested or the public-spirited variants of these activities. While they occur intermittently in the United States, these activities have not been routinized into a consistent pattern of interaction among organized scientists in and out of government. In fact, the form of the interaction remains an issue within the U.S. National Academy and the American Association for the Advancement of Science. In other countries, moreover, the issue hardly exists, and scientists do not act as a visible interest group. On the international scene there have been sporadic demonstrations of scientific interest group activity, as over NASA's Project West Ford and the issues of nuclear proliferation and arms control. However, they have been less than global in the interest they managed to arouse and have led to no permanent role. We see no evidence that these groups are growing in influence internationally. Hence we cannot rely on international interest groups of scientists for providing the link between knowledge and action which we seek.

Finally, the role of the scientist as bureaucrat is not fully germane to our concern. Most tellingly illustrated by the Manhattan Project, this role involves the comprehensive cooptation of scientific experts into the governmental apparatus in the context of an agreed-on mission. Government then takes over science for that mission, though in the process it may grant enormous and autonomous authority to scientists. The critical position of the possessor of special knowledge, however, is thereby eroded; the scientist becomes a bureaucrat, with all the attendant problems of dependence on the canons of bureaucracy, bureaucratic and financial survival—in short, the problems summed up under the label "Big Science."[5] Obviously, scientists have been enormously influential as bureaucrats at the national level. Their very prestige on some policy questions in the United States probably derives from their occupancy of bureaucratic roles in the period since World War II. However, since there is no international counterpart to the Manhattan Project and to the former U.S. Atomic Energy Commission, we cannot rely on this role as a link for tying international scientific thought to world order models. We are forced again to come back to the advisory role as the crucial one.

The role we have in mind is suggested by Bell's discussion of the characteristics of knowledge in post-industrial society. Theoretical knowledge and access to such knowledge are central to such societies:

> In the post-industrial society, what is crucial is not just a shift from property or political criteria to knowledge as the base of new power, but a change in the *character* of knowledge itself. What has now become decisive for society is the new centrality of *theoretical* knowledge, the primacy of theory over empiricism, and the codification of knowledge into abstract systems of symbols that can be translated into many different and varied circumstances. Every society now lives by innovation and growth, and it is theoretical knowledge that has become the matrix of innovation.[6]

Linked to this phenomenon, Bell continues, is the all but universal commitment to an orientation to the future. Almost all societies now seek to "plan," to allocate resources in the service of a future different from the present. This, in a sense, constitutes the raison d'être of the bulk of international programs. A new kind of knowledge is thus impressed immediately into the service of a political program designed to lead to a better life for all. This combination, Bell believes, creates the potential everywhere for the special political power of the possessors of this knowledge, the expert who is often also a scientist. Under conditions where knowledge is considered a precious resource, scientists and research people located in universities and research institutes are likely to become politically dominant. Their means of power is the ability to influence those charged formally with decision-making. Their claim to legitimacy is their specialized skill, and their exercise of authority depends on their position in political organizations. Neither patronage nor inheritance, but education alone, when employed in such a nexus, becomes the means of access for the individual (even if it leads to cooptation). Indeed, the individual possessor of education comes into his own *as an individual* rather than as a member of a party, group, or family.

Bell warns, and we agree, that this development need *not* imply the advent of technocracy as the predominant mode of governance. He argues, and we agree, that the very trend toward the meritocracy of education implies active resentment on the part of those left out or displaced. Moreover, since the level of education is rising everywhere and the ideal of social equality is being both pronounced and promoted, the concentration of decision-making in the hands of individuals suspected of playing sorcerer's apprentice with our lives is likely to lead to greater demands for "participation."

We make a point of this because there is inherent in the rationalist approach to world order issues a hostility to "politics" as uninformed and self-interested confrontation. The rationalist would prefer to see an "end to ideology" and casts himself in the role of hastening that demise by maximizing his influence as a knowledge specialist. If, as Bell and we think, political confrontation, both national and international, is likely to increase over issues heavily infused with specialized knowledge, the case for world order constructs less indebted to rationalist assumptions becomes a strong one.

This characterization of scientists as purveyors of a highly valued resource gives us the basic concept we seek: Internationally active scientists are a meritocracy who, in principle, if not always in practice, subscribe to the Mertonian imperatives. They believe that their craft is, on balance, "progressive" and that it can—some say it should—be linked to fashioning better policies to assure human survival. They also believe that their methods can make a unique contribution toward that end. While organized into voluntary associations which correspond to their professional specializations, a more important operational aspect of their organization is the fact that scientists tend to work in "invisible colleges." These informal groupings coexist with formal organizational links and often animate them in terms of programmatic and cognitive emphasis. Scientists are in principle dedicated to the achievement of human welfare; but in day-to-day practice they are also preoccupied with the bureaucratic imperatives of assuring the continuity of their work with mandates, projects, personnel, and budgets. They may have begun their scientific careers as pure researchers, but their involvement in socially relevant programs which are institutionalized and bureaucratized makes their work germane to world order considerations. The purposes underlying the application of science and technology remain inextricably linked to the exercise of political choice. But that choice persists in being embedded in rival hierarchies of goals, and it is subject to being interpreted in terms of clashing models. The advent of the scientific adviser and official has not displaced politics.[7]

Meritocracy is the end neither of politics nor of ideology. The basic claim of the scientist is that his knowledge is transideological, but much depends on how this claim is formulated. If the ideologically flawed knowledge of the politician can be displaced through good information, the scientist may be claiming that ideology is obsolete *because* scientific knowledge can *simultaneously* address the issue of consensual means *and* expanding agreement on ends. This claim is acceptable only if we presuppose that the ends of policy are given: peace, plenty, a purer physical environment. If there is no conflict on what these symbols mean, then the designing of a survival strategy becomes an exercise in methodology, the very methods at which scientists are recognized experts. If the symbols remain as ambiguous as we believe them to be, we cannot presuppose an agreement on ends which is meaningful for practical purposes. Not all scientists claim to be providing better information on both ends and means. Many prefer to confine the argument about a superior methodology to the realm of means alone. While their participation may infuse programs with additional information of an objective character, their role does *not* imply the end of ideology as long as the information cannot settle debate over ends and purposes.

If neither politics nor ideology is clearly banished from the world order models of scientific advisers, in what ways can their advice be justified? While scientific knowledge may appear to dictate some very specific choices regarding war and peace, poverty and plenty, consumption or conservation of energy, these choices are still justified as "technical" by most scientists. Hence we are face to face with the vexing issue of what is "political" and what is to be regarded as "technical"—a point never laid to rest in theory or in practice. And yet it matters for us. Scientists, whether they subscribe to the rational model or not, consider their advice to politicians to be something different from counsel given by lawyers, foreign area specialists, or military men. Scientists believe that they base their advice on good information, on what is known or knowable according to canons of objective investigation, not on ingenious arguments, imputed motives, or professional tradition. In short, they claim an epistemological foundation for their advice which differs, in principle, from the contributions to policy made by other professions. Hence, when advice is given on international programs which may have the effect of stimulating the acceptance of new models of world order, the character of that advice acquires a special status. If it is indeed more objective (that is, more "technical") than the lawyer's, it should have a greater impact on the future of the world.

Some have attempted to distinguish between the technical and political realms by claiming that different decision-making processes characterize each. Technical decisions are made by panels of experts; political decisions by legislatures, citizens, committees, or military juntas. Usually this effort at differentiation breaks down when it is discovered that presumably objective panels of experts engage in the same kind of negotiation and bargaining as their political counterparts when they cannot agree on the purposes informing their deliberations. Efforts have also been made to distinguish the technical from the political on the basis of the subject matter or the issue being discussed: waging war, writing tax laws, fixing agricultural support prices are political; assuring airport safety, preventing oil spillage at sea, and eradicating smallpox are technical. The distinction soon breaks down too, when it is shown that the previously technical issue suddenly becomes "politicized," that is, made controversial because a number of interests and actors have important stakes in how it is resolved. As actors reassess their interests, issues have a tendency not to remain in the class to which the analyst assigns them.

The difference between the technical and the political is to be found in the cognitive maps of the decision-makers, in the way questions are put. Let us define "political" as the realm of inquiry and deliberation which addresses the large issue of the future of mankind and of nations, and the choices that must be made in order to assure their welfare. "Technical" issues then refer to "good information" and its application to the processes of making such choices; the "technical" deals with the means and styles of knowledge that create the infrastructure for decision. Are scientists in governments, then, technicians? The boundary between technical and political roles *is* crossed if the scientist has the right to *initiate* discussion, to *link overtly* the matter of national and international welfare to the choice of techniques and information, and if *he* can *frame* the question to be addressed without being restricted by his bureaucratic or political superiors. Only if scientists merely *respond* to questions, *defined* by their superiors and *restricted* to rigid ends-means or cause-effect matters, can we

say that the distinction between a technical and a political competence is being observed. Therefore, scientists who are recruited
en bloc to "run" a public program which is considered vital are
active politically as well as technically. So are scientific advisers
who actually shape the ends of policy, even though in theory they
are simply supposed to answer specialized questions put to them
by their political superiors. The same would be true of scientists
organized into a fifth estate and of scientific interest groups.[8]

This contrast is well expressed in the judgments of two scientific advisers to chief executives. Sir Solly Zuckerman makes the
"technical" argument:

> A scientist is as yet no better equipped to predict the consequences of
> the applications of scientific advances than is the next cultivated
> man. On the other hand, because of their professional knowledge,
> scientists are in a better position than others to appreciate the nature
> of what is bringing about social transformations. . . . It is in that
> sense only that I see science having an active and effective social
> function.[9]

Donald Hornig, in contrast, urges a "political" role. Scientific
advisers ought to participate in the identification of overall national goals *and* assess priorities among scientific programs as to
their capacity to attain them.[10] We think that the position taken
by Hornig is exceptional. Most scientists involved in governmental programs profess a cognitive perspective which is closer to the
view expressed by Zuckerman. This view is "technical" also in the
sense of being nonideological. It asks no questions about ultimate goals, about the social values to be served by scientific participation in government. Hornig's view, however, obscures that
distinction. The scientist is to give advice on how specialized
knowledge relates to values, then even to participate in defining
values. This makes the enterprise distinctly ideological. It can be
considered scientific only if the methods used in selecting values
conform to the canons of objective research—a tall order.[11]

The continuum defined by a "purely technical" and a "purely
political" mode of giving advice should be considered a key ingredient in the study of science and politics. The rationalist,
because he claims to be specifying the information needed *for*
action as well as the purpose *of* action, acts in an ideological
capacity. The technician who confines his advice to listing the
properties of pollutants entering the atmosphere does not. Both
are present in international organizations, and both may have a
role in working for different world orders.

We now list the typical institutional expressions which scientific participation in international programs can take while remaining true to the restricted role of the scientist:

1. International *administrative and research* agencies. These are funded with public money and employ scientists, physicians, lawyers, and engineers to fashion programs with a social purpose, based on theoretical knowledge. The expert is a bureaucrat, though not in the exalted position of the managers of the Manhattan Project or Project Apollo. He is constrained by legislation and directives defining his work, imposed by nonexperts, even though the expert may successfully influence the content of his mandate. The World Meteorological Organization furnishes an example, as do several other U.N. specialized agencies. The experts do not govern; they carry out mandates provided by conferences and boards of national delegates.

2. International *advisory bodies* to political decision-makers or decision-making fora. These are asked to make restricted recommendations toward the implementation of socially sanctioned objectives when specialized knowledge seems required. The advice may or may not be taken. The U.N. Advisory Committee on the Application of Science and Technology to Development is such an organ.[12]

3. International groups of experts *collaborating* in the advancement of some scientific enterprise. Such work, by its nature, cannot be done by a single researcher or unit; it requires the consent and help of governments and/or international organizations. While such efforts seek to advance the interests of the participating scientists, they differ from classical interest group activities in that no attempt is made to shape fundamental national or international policy as it relates to matters of future collective welfare. Mission-oriented professional organizations and the specialized bodies of the International Council of Scientific Unions illustrate this type of activity.

4. *Consultants* and *advisers* to international governmental bodies, who are called on *occasionally* and intermittently to help in shaping a program, but whose advice is not directly related to the definition of the ultimate social or political objectives of such programs.

We have deliberately loaded the definitional dice in favor of the importance of the *knowledge* being dispensed—and against the exercise of direct political *power*. Our reason for doing this is to remain faithful to those characteristics of the contemporary political and scientific scene which we consider as given. We have also formulated advisory roles so as to obscure the legitimate distinctions that can be drawn between scientists as administrators, scientists as independent agents acting in their individual capacities, and scientists acting as instructed delegates or representatives in interbureaucratic and international negotiations. We do so because of the demonstrable interchangeability and overlap of actual behavior by experts irrespective of formal position; these classifying devices seem to predict very little about actual behavior among scientists.[13] We have cast the scientist in the difficult role of using his special knowledge as his major weapon in the effort to influence politicians, to adopt courses of action to improve human welfare, because this seems to be the predominant state of affairs.

ORGANIZATIONAL IDEOLOGIES: ENDS AND MEANS

Scientists who seek to fashion international programs of action depend on budgets, personnel, and bureaucratic links to national agencies, and they are subordinated to routinized patterns of making decisions on allocations and priorities. In short, international scientific advisers depend on *institutionalization*. It is through the medium of institutionalization that a relationship to world order can be imagined.

This is no different from what we normally refer to as "organizational ideologies." Adherents of an ideology seek to organize their views collectively, to identify its parts and their interrelationships. They seek to define and choose independent and dependent variables, as well as the mental techniques which allow the adherent to move from one variable to another. Scientists tend to differ from the members of other professions only insofar as the choice of variables and the manner of relating them is a function of substantive scientific commitments and past experiences. If the dependent variable is some version of a new world order, however, the scientist has entered the arena of debate over political goals and futures. He has embraced an ideology. If he also succeeds in getting the United Nations or the Food and Agriculture Organization to accept this ideology as *its* paradigm, model, or dominant metaphor guiding global action, the ideology has been institutionalized. Our empirical task is to determine whether this has, in fact, occurred. If so, is a single program dominated by a single ideology, or can we identify several competing ones?

The range of possibilities for world order implied by the acceptance, or partial acceptance, of an ideology can be illustrated schematically. Suppose we are considering the reorganization of the United Nations system so as to enable the organization to mount multilateral programs designed to advance economic de-velopment in the Third World *and also* improve methods for global environmental protection. Clearly, such an effort raises the questions of difficult trade-offs between economic welfare and "quality of life" considerations which have characterized the actual United Nations discussions since 1972. Suppose further we simplify the reorganization issue by distinguishing between (1) the *goals* underlying the program to be mounted and (2) the scientific *knowledge* considered applicable to mounting such a program (economics, biology, chemistry, meteorology, and so forth). The participants may agree or disagree with one another on either or both dimensions (see Figure 1).[14]

Goals may include, for example, any or all of the following: increasing national GNP by a certain amount; rapid indus-trialization through the unplanned application of all new technologies; planning of trade/investment between developed and underdeveloped countries; limiting pollution; controlling population growth; committing raw-material-importing coun-tries to fixed prices and supplies; guaranteeing employment levels and controlling inflation; seeking to prevent genetic dam-age due to industrial activity; planning the entire world economy instead of relying on market forces; subordinating national growth rates to economic *and* biological "limits to growth" con-siderations; working for world government.

All of these goals have been and are being advocated by prom-inent scientists as guides to a better world order. Many are also advocated by politicians. The most comprehensive of the goals —global planning for ecological and/or economic purposes

FIGURE 1
Goals versus Knowledge: Static

		Goals of Action	
		Participants agree	Participants disagree
Knowledge for action	Participants agree	Rational computation	Selective negotiation
	Participants disagree	Pragmatic assessment	No model specifiable

and world government—are usually justified in terms of an evolutionary-cybernetic metaphor. As goals become more modest and piecemeal, the elaborateness of the dominant metaphor used to justify them also declines. At the lowest level of complexity, the informing figure of speech remains that of the free market. Each desired end goal, with the exception of the unplanned intensification of economic growth, represents a complex hierarchy. Such end goals subsume a series of sequentially interdependent subgoals. The planning of some future state of affairs then depends crucially on whether or not the subgoals are considered combinative in terms of some overall satisfactory cost-benefit calculus. It is also common, however, that what we have labeled subgoals will be treated by some decision-makers as end goals in their own right. Such a choice then implies a mental construct in which one planner may consider the cause-and-effect chain thought to lead to the attainment of the end goal as a system in its own right, whereas another planner would consider the same chain as a subsystem within a larger model. What is considered an end goal by one appears as an instrumental goal to another. A particular planner may have a given hierarchy in mind, but another may not share his vision.[15]

Whichever hierarchy of goals prevails is a function of the particular model, or cognitive map, the advocate chooses to adopt. It is crucial to recognize that a particular cognitive map does *not* appear in nature. Any model depends centrally on the recognition that not all objectives can be attained simultaneously, that some may be (in the short run, at least) mutually contradictory, and that the model must therefore provide a method for calculating trade-offs between costs and benefits. Put differently, the attainment of any cluster of goals above the level of simply accelerating the diffusion of all new technologies is highly dependent on the kind and amount of technical knowledge available. An understanding of cause-and-effect chains is crucial for justifying models and hierarchies of goals. The marshaling of this knowledge is the province of the scientist associated with international program-making. Hence it matters crucially whether the knowledge which goes into this process is in fact consensual.

Knowledge for action, then, is the area preeminently occupied by experts, advisers, planners. They are the people on whom decision-makers rely for background information, assessments of feasibility, projections of supply and demand, and for models delineating chains of causation toward the attainment of political goals. Put differently, the expert dominates the *means* considered relevant in making policy. The politician, however, remains preeminent in defining the goals of action and therefore dominates the conceptualization of *ends*. Hence future world orders depend crucially on the extent to which experts succeed in convincing politicians to accept their dominant metaphors.

Each combination of knowledge/action alternatives on our matrix suggests a different world order model because each must incorporate different modes of reaching agreement, and because the character of the stipulated goals changes. Each implies a different set of institutions and procedures for linking knowledge to action. Let us assume a static situation: At this time, which institutions would various actors in world politics seek to alter or create in the effort to reorganize the United Nations?

If all the participants agree on goals *and* background knowledge, the reorganization scheme becomes an exercise in rationally "computing" the optimal design (see Figure 1). If they accept the goal of "evolution for the survival of the species on the basis of better information on feedback patterns," the evolutionary-cybernetic metaphor becomes the organizational ideology of a revitalized United Nations. The world order model implied is very close to a version of world government, or at least world government for the purpose of maximizing both economic welfare and a wholesome environment. If the participants do not agree on either dimension, no world order model can be specified at all. This situation precludes any thought of direction and deliberate management. For our purposes—which include the use of knowledge for management—this is not a relevant model.[16]

The two intermediate possibilities are the most interesting for the purpose of imagining world orders designed for some deliberate management. When the participants agree on a set of goals but are in dispute concerning the adequacy of the existing knowledge base, the remedy at hand is to cooperate for improving the knowledge. Reorganizing the United Nations according to the logic of "pragmatic assessment" would then imply the creation of new research centers and programs in which competing claims to knowledge could be stated and tested further. It would also call for intensive cooperation with nongovernmental scientific programs. Technology assessment would become a logical international activity when, for instance, there is debate as to whether double-bottomed tankers will continue to cause oil spills. Moreover, continued disagreement among scientists concerning the adequacy of existing knowledge could be subjected to international adversary procedures as a result of which the decision-makers could make a choice.[17] As long as there is a prevailing conviction that things are knowable and can be linked to objectives on which there is agreement, pragmatic assessment and cooperation techniques provide the parameters for world order constructs. These constructs may be decentralized and temporary. They do *not* have to be consonant with a single dominant metaphor or a specific ideology. They *do* have to share a commitment to the unique role of scientific knowledge in aiding mankind.

"Selective negotiation" prevails when the participants can agree on background knowledge but dismiss it as irrelevant or uninteresting to the attainment of the clashing objectives which divide them in the first place. In many domains, this is an accurate description of the reality facing the United Nations. Much of the ecological and economic knowledge which goes into the actual reorganization debate is consensual. But governments do not seem to be very impressed with this when the knowledge runs counter to what they have in mind or when they fear that the use of the knowledge will favor their antagonists. And this is the situation which the evolution-minded scientist finds so intolerable: Politics is seen as defeating science. What does he say to the delegate who insists that his country is willing to accept pollution as the price it has to pay for industrialization? Solutions can then be found only by disaggregating the problem, by decoupling issues and by seeking a formula for dealing with single goals which are less divisive than the package of goals we have stipulated.

ENDS, MEANS, AND FUTURE WORLD ORDERS

The immediately preceding analysis was confined to a static situation. Let us now alter the rules of demonstration to imagine a longer timespan in which "learning" is thought to take place. Learning may occur in the sense that knowledge about means becomes more consensual. It is possible, for example, that scientists will come to agree on a single cause-and-effect model which lays to rest arguments over how much marine pollution is consistent with economically and biologically sanctioned principles of fisheries management. Goals may also change if politicians become convinced that certain very specific objectives can be realized only if they are subordinated to an expanding, or more complex, set of goals. This is the possibility we sought to suggest when we distinguished between the separate pursuit of end goals which, in another perspective, could be combined as subgoals serving some other ultimate end goal. Movement toward "expanding and interconnected goals" implies the adoption of a more comprehensive systemic perspective. Evolving policy on energy illustrates this possibility, as does the attempt to link the economic development of Third World countries to stable commodity export prices.

The matrix on Figure 2 gives us three "possible" world order models—possible in that they differ from the currently prevailing pattern. We shall use them in the remainder of this book in order to determine the extent to which the perceptions and experiences of internationally prominent scientists are consistent with each. We wish to suggest that the interaction between knowledge and action captured in the cells may be a changing one, that the manner and the time period allowed for the interaction can be imagined to entail different consequences. In the first matrix, emphasis is placed on a single decision or choice; in the second, the emphasis is on sequential and protracted choice. Further, the second matrix differs from the first in that the kind of interaction which takes place in each cell is more complex; it involves constant choices as to whether goals should or should not be systemically linked.

Both matrices are constructed from the viewpoint of the observer who takes for granted that collective choice tends to be made under conditions other than optimality. This stance thus differs from that of the rationalist who would prefer an optimal scheme, and from the view of the pragmatic politician for whom his craft is a very slippery art of the possible. We take for granted that most choices do not satisfy criteria of optimality, but we also

FIGURE 2

Goals versus Knowledge: Dynamic

		Political goals are	
		Specific	Expanding and interconnected
Expert knowledge becomes	More consensual	Pragmatic world order	Rational world order
	Not more consensual	No new world order	Skeptic world order

believe that political choice is more structured than is suggested
by the reminiscences of genial statesmen.

We remind the reader that we are dealing with the role of
experts. Obviously, decisions are made and events are launched
with minimal expert participation, or with none. Political goals
may expand or contract without any scientific input, and they
often do. Such decision-making may or may not be effective. A
political leader who convinces himself that no scientific body of
knowledge is available to help him determine his goals is not
necessarily acting ineffectively. But a political leader who disre-
gards expert advice because he finds knowledge to be unpalatable and irrelevant to his passionately held beliefs is surely be-
having less than effectively if his neglect of the known leads to
his demise. However, important as these two modes of action
are, they are not our concern. The particular action programs
which we are analyzing are animated by people who consider
themselves experts, are guided by expert knowledge, and who
do participate in the selection of political goals.

We now take up each cell and illustrate its possibilities by referring to the international debate on the future law of the sea.[18] At
the moment, some governments wish to maximize national control over off-shore resources, others are more interested in protecting the traditional freedom of the seas, and still others want
to subject mineral exploitation on the deep ocean bottom to
international regulation. In short, their goals are fixed and substantively specific in such a way that they remain divergent at a
low level of generality. Scientific consensus is very specific in
pointing to sources of marine pollution, the principles of
fisheries management, and the manner of prospecting for minerals.

1. The *rational* world order is the technocrat's delight: It
postulates that the cognitive horizons of politicians expand as
scientific knowledge becomes more consensual and is effectively
communicated. Increasingly, better knowledge preempts political confrontation as the route to action. Such is not the actuality
today; how do we get there? Suppose that scientists arrive at an
interdisciplinary consensus on fisheries, minerals, and pollution
and advance ideas on how these activities could be linked so as to
maximize benefits and limit losses for all. If they persuade governments, politicians will be forced to reexamine their earlier
goals and arrive at a redefinition which includes all or some of
these goals. It is this sequence which is captured in "rational
world order" alternatives. In the rational world order a scien-

tifically legitimated ideology is dominant. Scientists in such a setting play the role of political theorists.

2. The *pragmatic* world order model assumes that experts will behave as in the first example, but that governments will remain passive and fail to assimilate fully the message propounded by the scientists. In the law of the sea illustration, politicians will not formally reexamine their goals but will persist in separately seeking to maximize whatever goal is most highly valued. However, this means that politicians continue to share a minimal—if static—consensus, for example, a cleaner body of off-shore waters and preferential access for coastal fishermen in heavily fished waters. However, as knowledge of the cause-and-effect chains and the means for achieving this dual objective increases and becomes more consensual among the experts, the choice of means available becomes less ambiguous and the constraints facing policy more obvious. If politicians then merely continue to adhere to their minimal consensus, they put themselves in a position of having to deal *jointly* with pollution and fisheries— thus foreclosing certain past practices—even if they do not arrive at an expanding and interconnected set of new objectives. This mode of action does not call for self-conscious political reassessment. Nor does it always predict that the solution to scientifically identified issues must take the form of expanded international regulation or management. It does, however, mean that either choice is heavily influenced by a scientific argument or demonstration. The role of the scientist in this choice may well be ideological if he persuades his political superiors of the compelling nature of a particular set of linked issues. But such a role cannot be predicted exclusively by the pattern we seek to capture. Certainly the pragmatic world order includes the situation in which the boundary between the political and the technical role of the scientist may be blurred. In short, the organizational ideology of the pragmatic world order remains biased in the direction of the superiority of scientific knowledge, though less than in the case of the rational world order.

3. In the *skeptic* world order the relationship between knowledge and action becomes indeterminate. Goals do change, but not necessarily as a result of an increasing consensus among experts. Yet we do not mean to suggest that there is no interaction at all; this is not the case of "pure" political decision-making on the part of a creative statesman who sees interconnections ignored by his predecessors and colleagues, the Bismarcks, Lenins, and Maos of history. Suppose that politicians come to

realize that they cannot simultaneously obtain joint benefits from deep-ocean mining, coastal fisheries protection, and anti-pollution measures simply because their negotiating positions are too divergent and the costs and benefits of alternatives too diffusely distributed. They come to this conclusion in the face of continuing disagreement among experts on how to link environmental protection, prospecting for resources, and fisheries management. But recall that while the experts may disagree on how to link these activities, they are in considerable accord on how to deal with each one singly. In other words, "not more consensus" does not mean "no consensus."

In the face of such a situation, it is quite conceivable that agreements will be reached among the politicians, though they will not be as comprehensive and interconnected in substantive content as in the case of the rational model. They will be piecemeal and regional rather than global, grouping some activities in some areas, and others in different parts of the oceans. Such a world order would differ from the present because it would trigger numbers of decentralized package deals involving goals which would be more expansive and interconnected than is now the case. However, such a trend would owe little to a new consensus among the experts. The scientist plays the role of the technician in this construct. He is "on tap" because he is asked for advice from time to time on factual matters relating to certain goals. He is not given the opportunity to insert his ideology, his value preferences, into the decision-making process. Hence, fora and programs which meet this model show little of an identifiable organizational ideology.

4. The final model represents the situation in which the world finds itself today with respect to ocean issues. Expert opinion is consensual on single issues but no rapid movement toward interissue consensus is presently discernible. As for politicians, little of the movement toward partially linked issues imagined in the skeptic model can be discerned either. Most governments are sitting tight with respect to the regime they wish to see in the law of the sea. Since there is *no movement* toward a recognition of joint benefits from the linking of issues, this model suggests that a variety of different national solutions will eventually be adopted, thus confirming the present nation-state-centered world order. There is no semblance of an organizational ideology, unless one wishes to label a generalized *sauve-qui-peut* into exclusive national sovereignties as "organizational." The input of expert advice into the negotiating process is barely discernible at the international level, though at the national level the expert is consulted in his capacity as a technician.

Three of these models permit the possibility of movement from one type of world order to another. If the processes imagined in any *single* cell go on for a sufficient period of time, it is conceivable that the world order projected in *other* cells will be called into being. The futures implicit in a single cell, then, do not preclude the futures implicit in others. This is an important consideration once we are in a position to specify empirically some of the attitudes and experiences of the experts. Suppose that the characteristics of the skeptic order are numerically predominant among experts and politicians now, if not on ocean issues, then on some others. It is still conceivable, given the character of research and political sensitivity to changing ways of meeting welfare demands, that movement either into the pragmatic or the rational future will take place.

Each of these world order models implies its own set of procedures for making decisions, its own pattern of institutionalization. After we have examined the experiences and views of our international scientists, we turn to these in Part 3.

Notes

1. This terminology is used commonly in works advocating disarmament, and especially unilaterally initiated disarmament. It takes its salience from the conviction that scientifically demonstrable connections exist among personal insecurity, domestic inequality, international tensions and distrust, and unfulfilled economic needs. The totality of the interactions makes up the "system," which can be changed only if remedial measures are taken in the crucial components. See Jerome D. Frank, *Sanity and Survival* (New York: Vintage, 1968); Walter Millis and James Real, *The Abolition of War* (New York: Macmillan, 1963); Seymour Melman, *The Peace Race* (New York: Braziller, 1962). Frank is a psychiatrist, Melman an industrial engineer, and Millis a historian.

2. The attitudinal and institutional characteristics of the "scientific estate" are analyzed, with reference to the president's Science Advisory Council, by Avery Leiserson, "Scientists and the Policy Process," *American Political Science Review,* June 1965, pp. 408–16. For evidence that scientists-as-advisers do not predictably live up to the Mertonian imperatives, see Ravetz, *Scientific Knowledge;* H. Rose and S. Rose, "Knowledge and Power," *The New Scientist,* April 1969, pp. 108–9. Jean-Jacques Salomon summed up the matter this way: "As a body of truths and procedures or rules, science is universal in its validity and is unaffected by nation or any other claim to loyalty . . . but as a resource for national security or aggrandizement, as an instrument of economic and social welfare and collective prestige, science is subject to claims which are at present irresistible" (*Minerva,* summer 1964, p. 411). One can accept this judgment without also arguing that science and scientists are *exclusively* to be seen as national resources and that the Internationale of science is a myth, as is argued by Jean Meynaud and Brigitte Schröder in *Les Savants dans la vie internationale* (Lausanne: Etudes de Science Politique, no. 5, 1962).

3. See Joseph Rotblat, *Pugwash: A History of the Conference on Science and World Affairs* (London, 1967). By the time of the twenty-first conference (1971), which dealt with world security, environment, and development, a consensus could no longer be discerned, as the membership became more diverse nationally, professionally, and in terms of programmatic emphasis.

4. At the national level the most prominent group is the Federation of American Scientists, possibly a less influential body than its predecessor Federation of Atomic Scientists. See Donald A. Strickland, *Scientists in Politics* (Lafayette: Purdue University Press, 1968), and David Nichols, "The Political Attitudes of a Scientific Elite" (Ph.D. dissertation, Massachusetts Institute of Technology, 1968). A prominent international group is the World Federation of Scientific Workers, whose attitude on its role can be gleaned from an article by its secretary-general, E. H. S. Burhop: "Science in Contemporary Society—Is There a Crisis?" *Science, Medicine & Man* 1 (1973), pp. 75–85. The Pugwash Movement remains the most visible international group. The establishment of the Center for Science in the Public Interest illustrates the "interest group" approach in action. See Constance Holden, "Public Interest: New Group Seeks Redefinition of Scientists' Role," *Science,* July 9, 1971, pp. 131–2. Sir Rudolph Peierls argues that neither the pure research nor the public advocacy role is appropriate for scientists as advisers. He prefers the role of a dispassionate judge weighing the merits of competing arguments. "The Scientist in Public Affairs: Between the Ivory Tower and the Arena," *Bulletin of the Atomic Scientists,* November 1969, pp. 28–30. The same approach is advocated by Arthur Kantrowitz, "Controlling Technology Democratically," *American Scientist,* September-October 1975, pp. 505–9.

5. Some of these are summarized in polemical form by Daniel S. Greenberg, *The Politics of Pure Science* (New York: New American Library, 1967), and extrapolated into economics and politics by John K. Galbraith in *The New Industrial State* (Boston: Houghton Mifflin, 1967). For a treatment of the U.S. National Academy of Science as self-interested Big Science, see Philip Boffey, *The Brain Bank of America* (New York: McGraw-Hill, 1975).

6. Daniel Bell, *The Coming of Post-Industrial Society* (New York: Basic Books, 1973), pp. 343–4, and the remainder of his chapter 6. Emphasis in original.

7. See Stephen Cotgrove, "The Sociology of Science and Technology," *British Journal of Sociology,* March 1970, pp. 1–15; Diana Crane, "Transnational Networks in Basic Science," *International Organization,* summer 1971, pp. 585–601.

8. The debate over the ABM and SST decisions in the United States illustrates the crossing of the boundary by scientists into the political realm, *even when* the points being debated were "technical" in the sense of dealing with the feasibility and potential physical effects of the programs. See Charles L. Ruttenberg, "Political Behavior of American Scientists: The Movement against Chemical and Biological Warfare" (Ph.D. dissertation, New York University, 1972); Anne Hessing Cahn, *Eggheads and Warheads: Scientists and the ABM* (Cambridge, Mass: M.I.T. Center for International Studies, 1971). The "political" character of the debate by scientists is established by the demonstration that "technical" arguments were used very selectively in order to support or attack major welfare objectives relating to arms control and environmental protection. The most interesting instance in the story is the complaint by a pro-ABM systems analyst that the opponents of ABM either misunderstood or deliberately misinterpreted *technical* information to suit their political objectives. See Paul Doty, "Can Investigations Improve Scientific Advice?" *Minerva,* April 1972.

9. Sir Solly Zuckerman, *Scientists and War* (London: Hamish Hamilton, 1966), p. 161.

10. Donald Hornig, "Science and Government," *Proceedings of the Academy of Political Science* 28 (April 1966), pp. 169–82.

11. For a fuller development of the same point, see Robert S. Friedman, *Professionalism: Expertise and Policy Making* (Morristown, N.J.: General Learning Press, 1971).

12. At the national level, an enormous range of more specialized mandates prevails within this type of activity. These are listed, analyzed, and evaluated in the case of the U.S. government in *The Role of Science Advisory Committees in Government* (Washington, D.C.: U.S. National Academy of Sciences, 1972, appendix B). It is hardly a secret that the advisory process is subject to many kinds of deflections and abuses and that, not infrequently, the process of consultation is not only perfunctory but actually an exercise through which the government agency seeks to coopt scientific opinion. For analyses of these trends, see R. L. King and P. H. Melanson, "Knowledge and Politics: Some Experiences from the 1960's," *Public Policy,* winter 1971, pp. 84–101; Martin L. Perl, "The Scientific Advisory System: Some Observations," *Science,* September 24, 1971, pp. 1211–

15. For a comparison of some Western and Japanese patterns, see Ehud Harari, "Japanese Politics of Advice in Comparative Perspective," *Public Policy,* fall 1974, pp. 537–77.

13. Ruggie and Haas, *International Organization,* summer 1975, especially the articles by Brenner, Johnson, and Pendley-Scheinman.

14. This matrix is adapted from the seminal argument first presented in J. D. Thompson and Arthur Tuden, "Strategies, Structures and Processes of Organizational Decision," in J. D. Thompson et al. (eds.), *Comparative Studies in Administration* (Pittsburgh: University of Pittsburgh Press, 1959).

15. Herbert Simon distinguishes between goals and values. Values are ultimate conditions to be attained, and goals are the targets the planner sets himself for approximating those conditions. What we have listed as goals Simon would probably consider to be values. Our goals include instrumental targets and steps thought by many planners to be necessary for attainment of some ultimate condition. Simon's definitions are logically more satisfactory than ours, but since ours are meant to reflect the imperfections of the decision-making process, we have preferred a less clear-cut definitional distinction among types of goals and ends and means. See Herbert A. Simon, *Administrative Behavior: A Study of Decision-Making Processes in Administrative Organizations,* 2nd ed. (New York: Free Press, 1965), especially pp. 61–78 and chap. 4.

16. Our characterization of this situation as "no model," of course, does not mean that the situation is not a common one. It is. Decisions are often made somehow, even though there is agreement neither on background knowledge nor on goals. One might argue that many, if not most, decisions made in the United Nations are of this nature if they result from a mechanical majority united on the basis of a single nonoperational value. In such a context comprehensive solutions are not conceivable, but issue-by-issue solutions among some of the participants are still possible and do occur.

Some theorists of world politics, taking this situation to be the normal one, describe world order as "decentralized," "anarchic," "competitive," or "inchoate." Often they use the model of the free market as their dominant metaphor to show how actors reenact certain patterns of behavior as a result of such constraints as imperfect knowledge, limited power, and the need to hedge against these by means of alliances. Exponents of this view treat international politics as a game in which the rules are known and rarely change. Survival then means the playing of the game within the rules of prudence and measured restraint. The only actors who matter are the governments of sovereign states. Examples are provided by writers who use some version of balance of power theory as the key construct for dealing with world order.

We reject this view as being an overgeneralization on empirical grounds. Moreover, it is logically without value if we wish to imagine alternative world orders based on better knowledge. For empirical material showing the inadequacy of this conceptualization, see Robert O. Keohane and Joseph S. Nye, *Power and Interdependence* (Boston: Little Brown, 1977).

17. This view is implicit in suggestions for incremental reform of international institutions, both regional and global. See OECD, *Science, Growth and Society* (Paris: 1971); the "Cocoyoc Declaration," adopted by the participants in the UNEP/UNCTAD symposium on resource use, environment, and development strategies presided over by Barbara Ward, in *International Organization,* summer 1975, pp. 893–901; Seyom Brown and Larry L. Fabian, "Toward Mutual Accountability in the Nonterrestrial Realms," ibid., pp. 877–892.

18. For factual information on the Law of the Sea negotiations as they have evolved since 1967, see the special issue of *International Organization,* spring 1977, edited by Edward Miles.

PART 2

Attitudes and Experiences of Internationally Active Scientists

Chapter 4

The Complexity of Cognitive Patterns

To speculate about possible links between knowledge and action is one thing; to demonstrate the existence of such links in the minds of the scientists involved in a program is another. In this chapter we present the basic evidence we obtained on the beliefs and expectations of internationally active scientists. We now describe our sample, present the rationale for the questions posed to our respondents, list the questions, and present the overall distribution of responses. We then go on to analyze whether or not the professional and role characteristics seem to explain some of the patterns uncovered.

SAMPLE AND PROGRAMS

The authors conducted interviews with 146 individuals who are, or until recently had been, active in scientific programs of international organizations.[1] The interviews took place between May 1973 and September 1974. In terms of professional affiliation, the group was composed as follows:

Physical scientists	35
Biological and medical scientists	39
Engineers, oceanographers	37
Social scientists, lawyers	22
Diplomats	13

The diplomats and social scientists all had responsibilities in programs involving the application of the natural sciences to some social objective. The diplomats, considered in terms of their professional training and education, were either lawyers or natural scientists, thus qualifying as experts for our purposes. In terms of organizational role, the group looked like this:

Advisers/consultants to intergovernmental organizations	31
Officials of intergovernmental organizations	75
Officials of nongovernmental organizations	14
Delegates to intergovernmental organizations	26

Nationality was not a salient discriminating variable since well over 90 percent of the respondents were nationals of Western industrialized countries. A composite of role and profession gives us Table 1.

TABLE 1
Composition of the Sample

	Adviser	IGO official	NGO official	Delegate
Physicist	9	14	8	5
Biologist	10	20	4	5
Engineer	9	22	1	5
Social scientist	3	18	1	0
Diplomat	0	1	0	11

These 146 individuals do *not* constitute a systematic sample in terms of roles, professions, nationality, age, reputation, or influence. But the sample is unusual in terms of the overall extent of "expertness" and proximity to national and international governmental policy. Among our respondents we found the career achievements listed in Table 2.

TABLE 2
Highest Career Achievements in the Sample

Nobel laureates. —	4
Initiators and heads of international research centers or programs.[a]	13
High administrators of national research centers or programs.	24
Assistant directors-general in charge of scientific programs.[b]	5
Department heads in charge of scientific programs.[c]	24

[a]This includes officials of nongovernmental scientific organizations, and of major programs operated by such organizations.

[b]We chose the "assistant director-general" category in adhering to the terminology of the U.N. system. Equivalent individuals in other organizations often carry different titles.

[c]The titles of department heads vary with the type of organization. We included "directors-general" and equivalents in the E.C. and OECD and the heads of major divisions within the "departments" of the U.N. specialized agencies, since "departments" are usually headed by assistant directors-general. We also included *chefs de cabinet* in the European Communities in this category.

Individuals of lesser rank were concentrated on the upper levels of their respective hierarchies. The average age of our respondents was between forty-five and fifty.

Which criteria did we use in selecting respondents? Our chief criterion of selection was the nature of the *program* in which the individual was active. Having chosen the programs, we then sought interviews with persons who had been prominent in creating them, either as officials or advisers, or who were now working with such programs as administrators and national delegates. In short, the main principle of selection was the reputational and bureaucratic importance of an individual with respect to a given program. We therefore believe that our sample is *more* suggestive as a profile of modal attitudes and experiences because it contains a disproportionate number of influentials. It remains true, however, that the sample is deficient in the number of delegates we managed to interview, even by programmatic criteria. These individuals were affiliated with the following international organizations:

United Nations	23
U.N. Specialized Agencies	75
European Communities	14
Organization for Economic Cooperation and Development	14
International Council of Scientific Unions	15
Nongovernmental groups, miscellaneous	5

We deliberately selected programs conducted either by one or jointly by several of these organizations which were, in principle, relevant to issues of economic development, industrialization, resource management, and environmental protection. We biased the sample of programs in the direction of activities now perceived by many people to be directly related to the future social, political, and economic welfare of the world. Hence we selected, for instance, only those activities of the International Council of Scientific Unions and of UNESCO which have an easily identifiable "applied" component in preference to programs of basic research, even though some of our respondents had been active much of the time in basic research programs with an international dimension. Whenever this occurred, we were interested in their attitudes and impressions with respect to applied research, and we conducted the interview accordingly. Some of these programs exist as such with their own identifying title; in other instances we contrived the label by considering jointly the activities of several organizations, irrespective of the

actual administrative arrangements. We thus settled on the following "programs":

Program	Organizations involved	Respondents
Western European eco-nomic and R & D planning	European Communities OECD	13
Science policy and envi-ronmental planning in industrialized countries	European Communities OECD, CERN, NATO, ICSU	17
Public health and radiation safety	WHO, IAEA	13
Global environmental pro-tection and Man and the Biosphere	U.N., WHO, FAO, UNESCO, ICSU	19
Oceanography and meteorology	WMO, IOC, IMCO, ICSU	11
Application of science and technology to economic development	U.N., UNIDO, IBRD, UNESCO, ICSU	30
Application of science and technology to agricul-ture and fisheries	FAO	19
Water resource development	UNESCO, ICSU	10
Outer space	U.N., ICSU	13

Since there are no meaningful quantitative yardsticks for ranking the salience of these programs, we cannot make a claim that
the distribution of respondents among programs is statistically
systematic. As always, access proved to be an important determinant of inclusion. We now present our questions and the overall pattern of responses.

IS KNOWLEDGE COMPREHENSIVE AND SOCIALLY USEFUL?

We asked three questions designed to tap the *personal* attitudes
of internationally active scientists with respect to the quality of
knowledge, the comprehensiveness of the knowledge, and the
applicability of that knowledge to social needs. Most did *not* claim
to have possession of a superior body of knowledge:

1. "Scientific knowledge is superior to the kinds of knowledge
   used by politicians. If so, how?"   (N= 124)

1. Yes. 25.8
2. Not superior; different . . . 25.8
3. No. 48.4

The thoughtfulness and depth of the answers which we received here forced an equally thoughtful system of coding upon us. Respondents who told us that all options facing policymakers are effectively dictated, or are completely circumscribed, by the demonstrations and discoveries of the sciences were coded as believing in the unqualified superiority of scientific knowledge over the cognitive processes of politicians. Other respondents argued that scientific knowledge is superior in its own realm, but that normative judgments not informed by science are more important in the realm of politics. A related but variant view held that, while political choices ought to be based on value priorities, such priorities must be determined in part by what science unequivocally demonstrates. Respondents holding both views were coded as believing that "scientific knowledge is not superior but different." Finally, some stated that scientific knowledge has no special epistemological properties which distinguish it from political knowledge. Many thought that even if scientific knowledge were superior, it had little relevancy since all policy choices were fatally constrained by nonscientific considerations and were, in fact, made by political bargaining. Both views were coded as giving a "no" answer to our question, even though the reasons differ in the two instances. The implications remain the same in that they deny science any special role in shaping knowledge so as to constrain action.

If scientific knowledge is not considered "superior" by most of our respondents, is it felt to be comprehensive? The following question incorporates a scale of comprehensiveness: It starts with perceptions that associate the growth of scientific interdisciplinary interdependence with a laissez-faire approach to research and its uses; it ends with beliefs that public policy choices can be deduced from comprehensive natural laws, which are themselves the result of ever more comprehensive interdisciplinary formulations. Most scientists *do* believe that knowledge is expanding and that better understanding of the natural world *can* influence government in making more rational choices. Laissez-faire science is dead among our respondents.

2. "As an expert, how do you personally think your organization's work on (the relevant aspect of appropriate science/technology program) can make science useful for people's needs?" (N= 135)

1. It can't or doesn't.   14.8
2. By permitting free and unguided scientific research, knowledge and understanding will increase automatically as experts from several fields come to see their separate disciplines as being connected.   18.5
3. By uncovering laws of nature, scientific advice can be used to apply physical and biological laws to human and social activities and thus scientists can help governments make more rational choices in politically important matters.   54.8
4. It can do so by suggesting the existence of comprehensive systems of knowledge uniting separate disciplines from which rational choices governing social and human welfare can be deduced and by translating these choices into political programs.   11.9

But does a belief in the growth of interdisciplinary knowledge and the possibility of its aiding governments to make more rational choices also imply a belief in the unity of knowledge as a method for solving social problems?

3. "As an expert, do you personally think your organization's work on (the relevant aspect of appropriate science/technology program) is helpful in enabling men to link expanding knowledge to programs designed to improve human welfare?" (N = 134)
1. No.   21.6
2. Yes, because a fuller knowledge of the natural world enables governments to make more rational choices.   51.5
3. Yes, because methods used in the natural sciences can be usefully applied in other fields as well.   11.2
4. Yes, because the expansion of scientific knowledge and the general use of scientific methods can be used in the solution of human problems through government action.   15.7

This question is a scale of perceptions on the comprehensiveness of the scientific method in its applicability to international policies to improve human welfare. At the outer extreme it taps a belief in the unity of knowledge and the full applicability of the scientific method to all problems (response 4). At the opposite extreme it denies such a status to the scientific method as used in the work of international organizations (response 1). A large majority of our respondents minimized the unity of knowledge in this context, and a clear majority opted for a modest role of science in simply enabling governments to make more rational choices.

Since our sample quite obviously does not fully share the commitments we associate with scientists-as-political-theorists, it should come as no surprise that no sharp clustering of respect for science or alienation from it could be uncovered.

4. "As an expert do you personally feel that heavy reliance on scientific and technological knowledge and methods in dealing with human problems can have undesirable effects?" (N = 78) (Multiple answers possible)
   1. No. 38.5
   2. Yes, leads to fragmentation of nations along professional lines and to technocratic leadership and planning. 11.5
   3. Yes, leads to fragmentation of the world along developed/undeveloped lines. 23.1
   4. Yes, substitutes technique and means over a concern for social values. 35.9
   5. Yes, leads to overly concentrated public, military, and industrial power. 10.3
   6. Yes, leads to overly rapid and undigestible social change. 35.9

A finding that scientific and technological knowledge can lead to rapid and undigestible social change is not a vote of no-confidence in science, though a feeling that technique dominates values could be so interpreted. We were impressed by the number of respondents who, in voting no, told us that while most of these undesirable effects are indeed triggered by scientific progress, this was the inevitable price that had to be paid. We were equally struck by those who stated that the problem is not a result of reliance on the technology or the technique, but rather that undesirable effects are solely a function of unsophisticated manipulation and control.

It might be supposed that scientists concerned with programs relating to global welfare would consider themselves as representatives of global interests. The number that does so is far from overwhelming, especially since officials who strongly identify with their own organizations also tend to equate such loyalty with a representation of world interest.

5. "As an expert, do you feel that you are representing a group or a distinct interest in using your knowledge for policy-making?"   (N = 120) (Multiple answers possible)

1. No. 8.3
2. World interest, mankind. 36.7
3. Organization itself. 30.0
4. Interests of society in developed countries, industrial society. 5.8
5. Interests of society in underdeveloped countries. 5.8
6. Producers of technology. 1.7
7. Consumers of technology. 16.7
8. Your home country. 26.7
9. Your professional discipline. 31.7

DO INTERNATIONAL ORGANIZATIONS STRIVE FOR MORE
COMPREHENSIVE PROGRAMS?

We now turn to the organizational aspect of the link between scientific knowledge and political action: Do scientists see their organizations as mechanisms for evolving a new cognitive style? Our approach to this issue goes beyond eliciting the personal attitudes of our respondents. They are now asked to evaluate whether and how *their organizations* seek to link international programs in science and technology to meeting new social needs. The assessment of organizational experiences may or may not coincide with the respondent's personal views; his personal attitude may be one of disappointment with the quality of his organization's program, or he may consider it hopelessly utopian.

Our questions were predicated on the hypothesis that there is a relationship between increasingly complex understanding of cause-and-effect relationships in the realms of science and technology and an awareness of growing social complexity. The hypothesis, drawn from the literature on technological innovation and its impact on society, suggests that a cognitive shift occurs as people cease to associate unplanned innovation and diffusion of technology with an automatic improvement in the conditions of life.[2] There arises a concern with the unintended, and presently unforeseen, consequences of innovation and therefore with a desire to channel or control the process of innovation. An increasing understanding of the scientific aspects of knowledge is thus linked to a more comprehensive awareness of the way in which the technological application of that knowledge is able to change patterns of living, earning, producing, and enjoying—so as to exacerbate social tensions or to ameliorate them.

Such a cognitive shift is likely to imply a search for new social policies designed to yoke the kind and pace of innovation to the achievement of certain social objectives, instead of relying on a random pattern of technology diffusion. This would mean that efforts are being made to link hitherto discrete policy issues into more comprehensive packages. International organizations and the scientists working in them may become the fora in which this expansion of vision and action takes place. Increasingly the scientific and technologically relevant programs of international organizations would seek to link issues into policy "packages," to deal with problems in increasingly holistic ways, as suggested by the comprehensive survival strategies associated with the rationalist view.

We first inquired whether internationally active scientists perceive their international organizations as being actively engaged in linking scientific work to ever more comprehensive social and political goals. Respondents were asked to check only the *most comprehensive* item in the following question which accurately describes the purpose underlying their organizational programs. It was understood that the question represents a scale running from "least" to "most" holistic in the way in which issues are linked.

6. "Why should your organization seek to spread the use of science and technology?" (N = 140)
   1. To advance research because it is good in itself.   4.3
   2. To increase the utilization and effectiveness of specific technologies.   8.6
   3. While improving technology, also diffuse knowledge concerning it and enlarge the number of potential beneficiaries.   12.9
   4. To anticipate and control unwanted side effects of the technology in the physical realm.   19.3
   5. To identify more remote consequences of the technology, such as impact on employment, trade, family life, migration.   28.6
   6. To identify the most remote consequences, such as attitude change, political stability, tensions.   9.3
   7. To apply progress in your field to social and economic and political progress generally, particu-

larly through comprehensive international planning for developed and underdeveloped countries.   8.6
8. To link the research to a more comprehensive consciousness which stresses ecological interdependence, respect for the ecosystem, the use of knowledge of nature for comprehensive controls leading
to peace and to world government (regional government in Europe).   8.6

Well over half of the respondents saw the purpose of their organizational programs as the identification—and, in some cases,
control—of undesired consequences of science and technology.
While relatively few opted for very holistic purposes, the
number which saw the diffusion of scientific and technological
capabilities as an end in itself is also very small.

Demonstrating a commitment to programmatic comprehensiveness, however, is not enough to validate the overall hypothesis. We also have to demonstrate that scientists see their own
programs in the international organizations as being related to
the interests of people in member nations quite apart from their
personal convictions. The question, as put, calls for an assessment of the respondent's unit or organization in terms of the
impact it might have, given the purpose and the unfolding of
knowledge.

7. "In the opinion of your group, can scientific knowledge be
made useful for the interests of people in general?"
(N = 128)
1. No.   16.4
2. By permitting free and unguided scientific research, knowledge and understanding will increase
automatically as experts from several fields come to
see their separate disciplines as being connected.   18.7
3. By uncovering laws of nature, scientific advice can
be used to apply physical and biological laws to
human and social activities and thus scientists can
help governments make more rational choices in
politically important matters.   56.2
4. It can do so by suggesting the existence of comprehensive systems of knowledge uniting separate
disciplines from which rational choices governing
social and human welfare can be deduced and
translating these choices into political programs.   8.6

Faith in the capability of science to induce governments to make more rational choices carries over into the actual work of international organizations. Some respondents even thought that comprehensive ecological survival strategies are capable of being incorporated into organizational programs through pure deduction from the laws of nature.

Moreover, our respondents, in general, feel that their work is having an impact on politicians.

8. "The spreading of scientific knowledge influences the activities of politicians. If so, how?"   (N = 120)

    1. No.   17.5
    2. By showing that old issues and controversies are not relevant.   2.5
    3. By showing the existence of entirely new issues and fields of action.   18.3
    4. By showing in an obvious manner how various fields of action are linked and must be considered jointly, without implying the recognition of underlying or basic causative links of a logical or scientific kind.   41.7
    5. By showing how various fields of action are linked in terms of an underlying comprehensive logic and therefore must be solved jointly.   20.0

The question, again, is in the form of a scale designed to elicit responses which highlight "more" or "less" comprehensiveness in the way new knowledge is thought to influence political choice. The criterion of comprehensiveness is the scope of the cause-and-effect linkages being perceived. Showing that old issues are no longer relevant does not require much understanding of the complexity of natural and social linkages (response 2). Realizing that new issues and choices call for attention requires only a bit more understanding (response 3). For instance, it is now understood that transportation issues are no longer readily manageable by building new highways. Many people also realize that such things as new transport technologies and cheap public transit facilities pose general new issues. Moreover, they realize intuitively or empirically that there are cause-and-effect links among the use of automobiles, urban density, employment patterns, and air pollution. However, most people have no theory, or systematic model, for relating these items to one another. Response 4 in our scale therefore seeks to capture this non-theoretical linking of items. We find it surprising that almost half of our sample feels that politicians *have been* successfully taught this much about natural and social complexity. We find it even more surprising that one-fifth of our respondents feels that politicians have been successfully taught something about underlying and comprehensive patterns of causation.

Who are these politicians? The following question identifies the constituencies, or targets, to be influenced in the implementation of international programs.

9. "What group of people or body of opinion is successfully (or not) influenced by the work of your group?"   (N = 122) (Multiple answers possible)

   1. International political body—e.g., General Conference.   11.5
   2. International secretariat.   40.2
   3. International scientific or professional association.   9.0
   4. National governments, cabinet, ministers.   21.3
   5. Specific agency of national governments, single ministry.   49.2
   6. National interest groups.   4.1
   7. National scientific or professional associations.   15.6

DOES ORGANIZATIONAL PERFORMANCE MEET COGNITIVE EXPECTATIONS?

One might suppose that rationalistic cognitive sets about programs and access to nationally and internationally influential groups of political decision-makers might add up to positive experiences with respect to scientific programs. This is not the case. We probed our respondents' experiences with respect to the impact of their programs by asking them the following question:

10. "When politicians espouse rival objectives at the same time, how can planning based on scientific assumptions help bring coherence to the objectives?"   (N = 88) (Multiple answers possible)

   1. By the use of formal models, computers, and scientific forecasting methods.   14.8
   2. By the use of careful analysis based on good data, but not formal models or complicated programming techniques showing where objectives can and cannot be attained together.   33.0

3. By showing that means appropriate for the realization of objectives are not available, that costs are too great, and how available means can be combined to serve several objectives at once.   20.5
4. By building appropriate political coalitions around compatible objectives.   27.3
5. Issue does not arise.   27.3

The scale ran from the "most" formal-rational procedure (response 1) to the "least," that is, the most political (response 4). Results are difficult to interpret because of the large number of respondents who felt that this issue never arose in their programs. In any case, less than half the respondents opted for the more formal modes of conflict resolution in the scientific programs with which they were associated as characterizing their experiences.

We also expected that the convictions about the positive relationship between expanding knowledge and the need for more comprehensive linkages among policies might be experienced in actual programmatic impact. Our answers show this not to be the case.

11. "Would you say that your group has, over time, succeeded in showing the national governments and their agencies the true complexity of how sectors of action are connected and how more comprehensive policies are necessary in the future, instead of piecemeal (or ad hoc) solutions?" (N = 119)
  1. Yes.   42.0
  2. No.   58.0

And when we approached the matter from a slightly different direction, we obtained the same results:

12. "Is it easier than previously to achieve agreement on the role of science in the program of your group?" (N = 74)
  1. Yes.   43.2
  2. No.   56.8

Only an examination of the differences in impact among the actual programs can tell us when and where the most ambitious notions about the role of science in world order prevail in fact. The overall distribution of attitudes, expectations, and summaries of experiences gives little support to the wide currency of the rationalist type.

COGNITIVE CHARACTERISTICS OF ROLES AND PROFESSIONS

Nor are things radically different when, instead of looking at the entire sample, we examine the results for differences in perceptions among our four kinds of role incumbents. Since about half of the sample was made up of officials of international organizations, this group statistically dominates the response patterns. We therefore ask to what extent advisers, delegates, and officials of scientific nongovernmental organizations *differ* in their perceptions from the IGO officials.[3]

Advisers tend to believe in the superior or "different" status of scientific over political knowledge to a considerably greater extent than do the others. Advisers also, disproportionately, deny that they represent any constituency or interest, or else claim to represent the interests of the consumers of technology. In other respects, no special characteristics appear. Since most advisers are academics engaged in basic or applied research, these perceptions are to be expected.[4] Officials of nongovernmental organizations, whose primary activities lie in coordinating and servicing cooperative international research efforts, show a distinct preference for the more laissez-faire aspects of science in bringing about knowledge. They are skeptical about influencing governments toward rational choice in meeting people's needs, though they tend to believe that scientific knowledge is different from political knowledge. These scientists also stress their professional societies as their major constituencies, rather than mankind, world organizations, or their home countries. They are not interested in using the programs of their organizations for anticipating and identifying anything more remote than the undesirable physical consequences of innovations, and they do not advocate attempts by international organizations to use expanded knowledge to rationalize public choice. Consistent with their role as research administrators, they do tend to feel that politicians can be influenced by scientific knowledge because this knowledge represents a comprehensive system from which policies are deducible.[5] In short, they say that while comprehensive impact is possible, they do not find it particularly desirable.

Delegates to international organizations differ appreciably from these patterns. They deny any major difference between scientific and political knowledge, and they doubt that organizational programs are very useful in compelling rational choice in meeting welfare needs. Delegates, far more than others, see few undesirable consequences connected with the diffusion of science and technology: They may not believe in the superiority of the scientific method, but they certainly believe in the desirability of using its results! Not surprisingly, delegates feel that they represent their home countries. They believe that international organizations are unlikely to meet people's needs. Finally, they feel that scientific knowledge does progressively influence political choice by showing, intuitively, the more obvious links between branches of knowledge and their application to policy-making. Put differently, delegates tend to be skeptical on precisely the points which distinguish our rationalist cognitive portrait from other world order schemes, but they are pragmatically optimistic on the utility of science in producing better decisions.[6]

In all, the roles of internationally active scientists seem to predict relatively little about attitudes and perceptions. They predict nothing about the experiences associated with organizational programs. Matters are somewhat more complex when we turn to professions.

In determining the special cognitive characteristics of certain professions, we followed the same rules which we applied in our discussion of roles. It appears that biological scientists and engineers most faithfully represent the main lines of the overall cognitive patterns we found; the deviants tend to be physicists, social scientists, and especially diplomats.[7]

Physicists, as compared with the overall pattern, and with biologists and engineers, are more inclined to consider scientific knowledge as different from, but not superior to, political knowledge. They worry more than others about undesirable consequences associated with science with respect to technique taking the place of values. They cite the consumers of technology more often than other professions as their main constituency, but they also cite their own profession disproportionately. Physicists tend to be dubious about applying science to people's needs in a planned fashion and tend to see the progressive expansion of knowledge as the result of unguided research. They believe that formal models have effectively influenced the making of difficult choices. Even though they are disproportionately satisfied with the application of science in arriving at more comprehensive solutions to problems, they are also pessimistic about its becoming easier to reach agreement on the role of science in public policy. In short, physicists do *not consistently* depart from the overall pattern. We cannot safely identify them with any single type in our set of ideal portraits, though they do differ on some items from the total sample.

If physicists come somewhat closer to the rationalist type than do biologists and engineers, diplomats consistently deviate from it. They definitely do not believe that scientific knowledge is different from political knowledge. They express pessimistic personal attitudes and organizational evaluations about the progressive use of expanding knowledge to plan for people's needs. They do not believe in any direct benefits accruing from the planned use of science; nor do they believe in the capacity of unplanned science to make such a contribution. Yet they disproportionately fail to identify *any* undesirable consequences attendant on the application of science and technology. They do feel that scientific knowledge influences political choice by identifying new issues demanding action; they also see as proper organizational objectives the wider use of technology and identification of its longer range economic and social consequences. They tend to see political coalitions as the prevalent means of resolving conflict over programs, even though some also see rational weighing of costs and benefits of programs as conflict-solving techniques. Diplomats, overall, are less satisfied with the application of science to the fashioning of comprehensive solutions than are other groups. It seems that they expect more from science than do others, while also denying to science the attributes which supposedly make it a cornucopia of promises. Diplomats thus come off as consistently *not* meeting the cognitive characteristics of scientists as artisans of a new world order.

INTERNATIONAL SCIENTISTS AS A HETEROGENEOUS ELITE

The profile of scientists committed to a world order dedicated to the imperative of survival was constructed by us on the basis of the writings of visible, articulate, and concerned scientists acting as critics of the social order and of the role of science within that order. The profile, it seems, fails to capture accurately the complexity of the prevalent cognitive maps of scientists with responsibility for linking knowledge to international programs for human betterment.

One reason for the hiatus lies in the differing public postures of the elite of articulate critics and the elite of "working" international science administrators which furnishes our sample. We have already argued that we do not consider scientists to be a cohesive collectivity, a "community" in any meaningful sense, a "class," or even a single interest group. The fact that most scientists share certain beliefs about their calling and work *as scientists* cannot predict much about their beliefs as citizens, administrators, or policy-makers. Scientists are, however, an "elite," a group of people who, *because of* their work and calling, have disproportionate influence in the fashioning of certain public programs of action. They are an elite because they are recognized as the possessors and dispensers of a body of knowledge which is in great demand outside the field of scientific research. They are an elite simply by virtue of the fact that they are so considered by nonscientists, including politicians.

But in addition, these scientists profess a publicly declared mission: to improve mankind's chances by the better marshaling of knowledge for action. That said, however, sharp differences in the sweep of this claim become evident. Our respondents, for the most part, do not claim a public forum for their ideas (though some of the most prominent do). Moreover, their attitudes were elicited by us in a context of their work *in* a bureaucratic forum; we deliberately constrained them. Hence it should come as no surprise that the expressions we obtained are far more complex than the idealized cognitive styles with which we began our discussion.

We therefore sum up our overall findings by contrasting this complexity to the most demanding and most sweeping of our cognitive profiles, the rationalist who feels that the unfolding of scientific knowledge contains the basis for deducing the imperatives of a better world order.

Our rationalist-scientist committed to a survival-oriented world order knows what *must* be done to assure survival. His scientific knowledge permits him to specify appropriate social, economic, and military policies. However, our sample shows a marked reluctance to claim a special epistemological role for science, and we *cannot* therefore claim that our scientists "know what must be done." But there is a general feeling that the linking of knowledge to policy permits governments to choose more rationally: There *is* considerable faith that increasing knowledge will contribute to a better world even if the faith is not validated by elaborate scientific claims.

Our rationalist-scientist also knows what *can* be done to bring about a better world order because of his faith that the scientific methodology can be applied to political and social choice, that scientific forecasting is possible, and that better programs can be devised to deal with presently unintended and unanticipated consequences of technological innovation. How does this faith compare with our findings? We find little belief in the straightforward applicability of the scientific method in matters of social and political choice and the solution of social problems. We find that scientists do tend to evaluate their organizational programs as being directed toward the identification and control of un-

wanted social and economic consequences, but stop short of seeing these as part of a comprehensive world order plan. But we
also find that our scientists see their work as closely related to the
interests of humanity. Moreover, there is much support among
them for the proposition that the scientific methodologies of
greatest effectiveness feature techniques that make bargaining
over objectives unnecessary. In short, there *is* a vague faith in the
relevance of scientific work to fashioning a better world order in
terms of methods, even though that faith is less clearly based on a
sweeping philosophical acceptance of "the" scientific method
than the pure rationalist would have it.

Our rationalist-scientist is able to influence what *will* be done
by virtue of his role as an influential adviser to political decision-
makers, by virtue of acting on the blurred border between the
"technical" and the "political" realm. Our respondents by and
large address their advice to national and international agencies most appropriate for translating knowledge into policy;
their targets *are* the proper ones. However, the scientific knowledge diffused as a result of international programs tends to
influence politicians only in showing the more obvious cause-
and-effect links among policy items, not the comprehensive, systemic, and value-infused linkages discerned by some scientists.[8]
And our respondents do not agree that, over time, national officials recognize the complexity of issues and linkages among
issues, and the majority do not think that it is becoming easier to
incorporate scientific knowledge into policy-making. Taken as a
group, they cannot be said to play the advisory role in such a way
as to fuse basic survival values with their command of good information.

These findings leave a number of important questions unanswered. Is there a tendency for scientific advisers to be especially authoritative and effective when the body of knowledge at
their disposal is widely accepted? Are some scientific programs
more effective than others in preempting political choices? Are
advisers more effective when the professions involved in the
programs are self-confident about the status of their knowledge?
Are advisers most effective when their roles are played by individuals who occupy bureaucratic positions of influence nationally and internationally? Does it matter whether a given program
has a regional or a global constituency? These questions can be
answered only after we examine in some detail each of the programs covered by our study, a task to be done in Part 3.

In addition, our findings do not dispose of the question of the
relevance of scientific programs to alternative world orders.

True, the most "rational" cognitive profile with which we introduced this discussion is not supported consistently by the actual attitudes and experiences we mapped. It is still possible, however, that the less demanding world order models are more consistent with the distribution of responses, and that projections about the impact of international scientific programs can be made on the basis of these more modest alternatives. We examine these in the next chapter.

Notes

1. We use the word *individuals* as shorthand. Actually the term *role incumbent* would be more accurate since about ten individuals were interviewed in their separate capacities of adviser, official of a nongovernmental or intergovernmental organization, or delegate to such an organization. The responses of a given individual were often quite different depending on the role he had played.

2. For a sampling of this literature and its implications for social planning, see Todd R. LaPorte (ed.), *Organized Social Complexity* (Princeton: Princeton University Press, 1975).

3. In analyzing the data, we selected the 15 percent point as the significant threshold. In other words, whenever a given set of respondents differed by 15 percent or more from the total response figure, we selected the set as worthy of special attention.

4. All but three of thirty-one advisers were scientists and engineers.

5. All but two of our fourteen NGO officials were physicists and biologists.

6. Of our twenty-six delegates, eleven were diplomats by profession and five each physicists, biologists, or engineers.

7. Social scientists tended to follow the same pattern of deviation from the overall findings as diplomats, though on fewer items. Social scientists expressed strong fears that the application of science and technology would lead to technocratic leadership and overly rapid social change. They also tended to identify society in developing countries or in industrialized nations as their main constituency, and cited their professional associations less often than did any other profession. As for the purposes underlying organizational programs, social scientists called attention to foreseeing political consequences of applying science and technology and engaging in comprehensive planning. At the same time, in larger numbers than did other professions they expressed disappointment that the planning of the scientific content of these programs was not becoming easier.

8. Additional support for this particular conclusion comes from a question not answered by a sufficiently large number of respondents to justify inclusion in the overall discussion. When asked to indicate whether the program for which the respondent was responsible was designed to improve living standards, improve social harmony, increase equality, or bring about a specific political objective, 75 percent opted for the improvement of living standards. We consider this significant because it is the least demanding objective in terms of calling for an understanding of complex cause-effect links involving competing social values.

Chapter 5

Science and Organizational Ideologies

Scientists' attitudes and experiences in aggregate terms tell us little about their manifestations in the work of international organizations. We wish to discover which trends toward future world orders may be implicit in the attitudes and experiences. Our point of departure is provided by our introductory discussion of the relationship between knowledge and action. Four hypothetical models were developed to orient the inquiry. If political goals remain unchanged and expert knowledge remains fragmented, the existing order will continue to prevail. If experts remain in agreement on a certain minimum of scientifically demonstrable cause-and-effect relationships but fail to agree on more, while politicians continue to adhere to goals which differ widely but show a certain minimum common denominator as well, the evolution will be toward what we call a "skeptical" world order. However, if we stipulate increasing consensus among the experts and passive acquiescence on the part of politicians willing to be persuaded, political goals will expand without a formal agreement; the resulting world order will be "pragmatic." Finally, a "rational" world order is conceivable if consensual knowledge expands along with broader and more comprehensive common political objectives.

Our job now becomes the establishment of an empirical relationship between these possibilities and the work of scientists active in specific international programs. We bestow the label *organizational ideology* on identifiable clusters of attitudes and experiences which seem to approximate the conditions described in our four models. We do not argue, by definition, that a given organization or a given program is characterized by a given ideology. While this may turn out to be true in fact, our objective is simply to map empirically demonstrated clusters of coherent attitudes and experiences. We wish to use these as a means for mapping the distribution of scientific ideas in any given organization or program. By doing so we can eventually project the character of a given program in terms of its relevance to conceivable future world orders. We repeat: It is the *mixture* of ideologies we encounter which will be used as the predictor. We are not in search of pure types.

Why then use the term *organizational ideology?* That term was originally invented by students of large-scale organizations for discussing the manner in which leadership is exercised, socialization of personnel developed, and programmatic unity maintained. It was never assumed that such a body of beliefs would have to have the characteristics of the belief system of totalitarian states or movements.[1] Nor do we make such an assumption here. In fact, our data do not permit the full sketching of beliefs in any given organization because our sample was not constructed with that purpose in mind. We do maintain, however, that the notion of an ideology is appropriate in this context since the persons we are discussing are active in a bureaucratic setting, articulate shared objectives, make assumptions about the consequences of their programs, and defend their work by asking for mandates, funds, and facilities from political decision-makers. In short, they seek to cast their work in the shape of coherence among separate parts. This is the essence of an ideology. Its "truth" as an empirical matter is irrelevant. What matters is that a given group *believes* that the separate parts which make up its work and mission constrain one another in certain describable ways. We see no reason to exempt scientists and technologists from this usage, even though they may claim to be working in a style which is "beyond ideology." The fact remains, however, that our data on specific programs and organizations provide only a hint of the incidence of such ideologies, not a complete profile. Our objective is to project and *imagine* future world orders consistent with such beliefs, not to predict them with finality.

Our first set of data is based on the respondents' personal attitudes toward the epistemological quality of scientific knowledge, its comprehensiveness, the relationships defined by it, and the applicability of the knowledge to social needs. The second set of data is based on the ways in which scientists see their organizations as mechanisms for applying their knowledge, for outlining and elucidating courses of action, and for evolving a cognitive style able to influence politicians. Personal attitudes, then, speak to the issue of consensual *knowledge for* action; organizational experiences address the question of goals and the role of knowledge in defining the *direction of* action. In combination, these two sets of data ought to allow us to sketch the range of organizational ideologies and the options for world order they imply. We ought not to expect perfect coherence between personal attitudes and actual experiences; scientists who profess great faith in exercising a political role may well experience disappointment, but individuals with more modest expectations may well encounter a consensual political environment, depending on the program in which they work. The extreme case of the scientist-statesman is captured by the successful practitioners of rational computation. We know that our findings discovered very few such persons. Hence, the purpose of the analysis is to sketch other modal types with less deterministic implications for definite world order models.

These are captured in our typology of organizational ideologies, the combination of the two typologies derived by sorting personal attitudes and organizational experiences. We anticipate the full explication of each of the three by first identifying the key components of all (see Table 3).

TABLE 3
Summary of Three Typologies

Personal attitudes (N = 136)		Organizational experiences (N = 128)		Organizational ideologies (N = 122)	
Type	(Percentage)	Type	(Percentage)	Type	(Percentage)
Determinists (15.4%)	+	Deterministic planners	(14.8%)	= Rationalists	(9.8%)
Instrumentalists	(26.5%) +	Social forecasters	(27.3%)		
		Physical controllers	(18.0%)	= Pragmatists	(23.8%)
Skeptics	(38.2%) +	Random appliers	(17.2%)	= Skeptics	(29.5%)
Eclectics	(19.9%) +	Eclectics	(22.7%)	= Eclectics	(36.9%)

TYPOLOGY OF PERSONAL ATTITUDES

Our typology of personal attitudes held by the respondents runs from "most" to "least" determinative about the role of scientific knowledge in the construction of international programs. The types were derived by sorting opinions expressed on these questions:[2]

1. Scientific knowledge is superior to the kinds of knowledge used by politicians. If so, how?

2. As an expert, how do you personally think your organization's work can make science useful for people's needs?
3. As an expert, do you personally think your organization's work is helpful in enabling men to link expanding knowledge to programs designed to improve human welfare?

Having defined the typology, we then proceeded to inquire whether striking associations between the type of belief on these matters and other beliefs and experiences could be established. We wondered whether each type tends to associate with a specific group of clients and which—if any—type expresses particular concern about various undesirable consequences of science and technology. We also wondered whether the four types differ from one another in terms of experiences in influencing the activities of political decision-makers and national governments, in their reliance on various planning techniques, and in their success with respect to facilitating problem-solving and conflict resolution. We then proceeded to look for associations between our types and the role and professional properties of the sample.

Determinists come closest to our model of the scientist-statesman. They resolutely believe that scientific knowledge is epistemologically superior to other kinds of knowledge. Consequently, it is able to provide both a wisdom and a methodology capable of being translated into government action, of providing a rational basis for political decision-making. Such knowledge may take the form of physical and biological laws applicable to human and social activities or, more elaborately, of comprehensive systems of knowledge from which rational choices in any field or discipline can be deduced. Implicit in this view is the recognition that goals are almost always complex, and highly interdependent. Sometimes this complexity is seen as justifying an excessive readiness at scientific and technological intervention, thus leading to undesirable and/or unforeseen consequences. But such excessive readiness is rarely a cause for alarm because the technique, the methodology, will conquer. If good knowledge is combined with good method, the result must also be good. Where error has occurred, it has been the consequence of faulty application of technology or science—and it can probably be corrected with more technology or science. Technocratic leadership and formal planning are values seldom to be questioned. And these are values for humanity taken as a whole, for a clientele which is loosely defined as "world interest." Determinists tend to be reasonably confident in successfully influencing politicians and, among our respondents, they are dispropor-

tionately confident in having demonstrated to policy-makers
within their own organizations high-level systemic links among
pieces of knowledge. They also express greater faith than other
types of respondents in the successful use of formal models and
careful analysis in mounting action programs. They tend to believe that it is easier now than earlier to achieve agreement on the
role of science in international programs.

The second group in the typology of personal attitudes is the
instrumentalists. The respondents in this group believe that, in
some cases, the methods of the natural sciences can be usefully
applied in politics. They all share the belief that, by increasing
knowledge of any natural and/or social phenomena, scientists
can provide decision-makers with a rational basis for choice. In
general, however, the role claimed for science here is more modest than was assumed by the determinists. For the instrumentalists, scientific knowledge is capable of suggesting the *means* for
achieving political or other goals. But scientific technique is not
so powerful as to serve as a source for value judgments to define
political goals. The instrumentalists recognize a clear need for
planning based on careful analysis and good data, without insist-
ing on formal modeling. They see themselves in the role of helping politicians to decide what the targets/goals should be in any
given planning scheme and of providing knowledge in such a
way as to facilitate goal achievement. This injection of a highly
knowledge-intensive strategy into the bargaining process is regarded as legitimate by the instrumentalists because they consider scientific knowledge to be epistemologically different from
political knowledge, without being superior to it; science cannot
usurp politics, but it can offer a unique and important complement to it. Instrumentalists in our sample appear satisfied that
they have demonstrated to policy-makers the more obvious links
among pieces of scientific knowledge without claiming that they
have also established the more abstract systemic connections.
Like the determinists they see themselves as having influenced
policy-making by successfully reducing conflict through the introduction of factual information. Unlike the determinists their
natural target has been specific national administrative agencies.
When there is uncertainty over the means to be used and a weak
but acknowledged consensus on goals, the input of expert information is considered crucial to resolve or preclude conflict
and to map out a strategy of action.

Goals themselves are seen by the instrumentalists to exist in a
state of complex interdependency. Neither all elements of this
goals complex nor the efficacy of strategies for attaining the
goals can ever be fully understood by scientists or politicians.

Still, the instrumentalists do believe that they are capable of demonstrating better than politicians the manner in which the goals are interrelated and the way in which various means must be considered jointly in solving problems. Like the determinists, many think that it is easier now to achieve agreement on the role of science in organizational programs than earlier.

Skeptics, the third category in this typology, deny the existence of any epistemological difference between scientific and political knowledge. They doubt the validity of tying or applying scientific knowledge directly to meeting people's needs. At *best,* science might prove relevant when research is undertaken in a laissez-faire manner; nonprogramed scientific research might automatically produce the knowledge and understanding which is capable of providing linkages among different areas of knowledge. The job of the scientist is to do basic research. Hence the ability of international organizations to function as intermediaries, as translators from scientific knowledge to problem-solving, is questioned. The most to be gained from international programs is some general broadening of knowledge, which might serve as a basis eventually for more rational decision-making in the political world. Half of the skeptics express indifference to the undesirable consequences of the use of science and technology in policy. They are divided in their assessment of the impact of scientific knowledge on policy-making; a quarter of our sample sees a minimal impact, but almost half believes they have demonstrated the emergence of new fields demanding action and have shown the more obvious links among those fields. Skeptics lack faith in formal models as a mode of demonstration and prefer, much more than our other types, the use of political bargaining and coalition formation as a way of initiating new programs. They remain dissatisfied with their impact on governments. Not surprisingly, they also find that it is just as difficult now as earlier to achieve agreement on the role of science in policy-making.

Eclectics are the respondents whose answers to our questions do not fit into our hypothesized patterns. They profess views "inconsistent" with what we take to be logically supportive positions on the relationship between knowledge and action. Does that mean that nothing pertaining to world order can be said about this group? It is true that no *specific* ideology can be imputed to these individuals: Some eclectics support world government and total planning; others are content with the decentralized status quo; still others favor incremental reform which is likely to upgrade the role of scientists, implying cautious steps toward piecemeal planning. These possibilities suggest that the

numerical importance of the eclectic strengthens the argument
against the dominance of *any* single ideology or dominant
metaphor in the further development of international scientific
programs. Thus, for example, eclectics show the same division of
opinion on the impact of scientific knowledge on policy-making
as do skeptics. Eclectic respondents divide almost equally among
those who see formal techniques as effective aids to decision-
making and those who prefer political bargaining, though, like
the skeptics, they do not find it easier now than earlier to achieve
agreement on the role of science in mounting international programs.

The examination of personal attitude types in terms of roles
reveals that delegates are disproportionately skeptics and eclectics (see Table 4). Advisers account for the plurality of determinists and instrumentalists. Almost half of the IGO officials are
skeptics. There seems to be almost a linear relationship between
skeptic and/or unstructured attitudes on the one hand and direct
representational and administrative experience on the other.
How do we account for the fact that eclectics are so very prominent among the NGO officials? These individuals, whatever
their views on the power of scientific knowledge may be, tend to
doubt that the work of their organizations can be translated into
social action in a very direct way, and therefore they express reservations about the use of their knowledge for meeting people's
needs.

TABLE 4
Personal Attitudes by Role

	Advisers	IGO Officials	NGO Officials	Delegates	Total
Determinists	24.1	15.7	16.7	4.1	15.4
Instrumentalists	41.4	25.7	16.7	16.0	26.5
Skeptics	17.2	45.7	25.0	48.0	38.2
Eclectics	17.2	12.9	41.7	32.0	19.9

NOTE: Percentaging vertical.

Analysis by profession shows that the most noteworthy distribution again occurs among the skeptics, who account for two-
thirds of the diplomats and almost half of the engineers (see
Table 5). Skeptics are the most common type among all professions except physical scientists, where they take second place to
the instrumentalists. Determinists are disproportionately strong
only among the biological scientists.

TABLE 5
Personal Attitudes by Profession

	Physical scientists	Biological scientists	Engineers	Social scientists	Diplomats	Total
Determinists	9.4	24.3	17.1	14.3	0.0	15.4
Instrumentalists	40.6	24.3	25.7	23.8	0.0	26.5
Skeptics	25.0	29.7	48.6	38.1	72.7	38.2
Eclectics	25.0	21.6	8.6	23.8	27.3	19.9

NOTE: Percentaging vertical.

The distribution of personal attitudes among our nine programs is remarkable for its sharp clustering of types (see Table 6). The skeptics are predominant in three out of nine programs; they are the single strongest group in two more. Eclectics account for about a third of the respondents in four programs. Instrumentalists are powerful only in the outer space and public health programs. The greatest strength reached by the determinists is 33 percent of public health and 22 percent of science/

TABLE 6
Personal Attitudes by Program

Program	Determinist	Instrumentalist	Skeptic	Eclectic	N
European R & D	16.7	8.3	66.7	8.3	12
Developed Country Science Policy	17.6	29.4	23.5	29.4	17
Public Health	33.3	50.0	16.7	0.0	12
Global Environmental Protection/Man and the Biosphere	15.8	15.8	36.8	31.6	19
Science/Technology for Agriculture and Fisheries	22.2	22.2	22.2	33.3	18
Oceanography/ Meteorology	0.0	36.4	63.6	0.0	11
Science/Technology for Industrial Development	14.8	25.9	44.4	14.8	27
Water Resources	10.0	10.0	60.0	20.0	10
Outer Space	0.0	50.0	20.0	30.0	10
Total	15.4	26.5	38.2	19.9	136

NOTE: Percentaging horizontal.

technology for agriculture; every other program contains less than one-fifth determinists, and there are no representatives in oceanography-meteorology or outer space.

TYPOLOGY OF ORGANIZATIONAL EXPERIENCES

The first typology was designed to elicit the *personal* opinions of our respondents. We now turn to their actual experiences in an organizational context: How do they put their opinions to work in an international program? Personal attitudes relate to the issue of what kind of knowledge is available for action and how useful it is intrinsically, or to the understanding of cause-and-effect and ends-means relationships as validated by scientific knowledge. Here we address the question of the extent to which scientific knowledge is related to the definition and implementation of goals. Respondents were sorted in accordance to their responses to these questions:[3]

1. Why should *your organization* seek to spread the use of science and technology?
2. In the opinion of *your group,* can scientific knowledge be made useful for the interests of people in general?

The five-fold typology which emerged from the sorting process runs from "most" to "least" determinative in terms of the ability of science to shape organizational goal definition. Each type was then analyzed in terms of possible association with the same attitudes and experiences examined when we discussed the typology of personal attitudes.

Deterministic planners believe that their organizations can best and most profitably conduct their scientific/technological functions by linking research to comprehensive international planning, or to a "comprehensive consciousness" which embodies concepts of a natural and systemic interdependence of all things biological or physical, political or social. Many accept the notion that these goals involve technocratic plans for a world government. Obviously, this favors highly aggregated activity for their organizations—activity which seeks to cope with the more remote consequences of action, such as attitude change, political stability, and tensions. Planning becomes necessary in order to cope with the undesirable consequences of technology and to link the remedial actions to social, economic, and political progress generally. These scientists/technologists believe that their organizations are capable of successfully translating scientific knowledge into comprehensive programs applicable to human and social needs and ultimately of providing a scientific basis for decision-making. Deterministic planners believe that science, when manifested through their organizational programs, is capable of providing certainty both about means and about goals because their organizations can demonstrate that separate fields of action are subject to an overarching logic.

Social forecasters are interested only in the anticipation and avoidance of problems wrought by technology in both the socioeconomic realm (for example, employment, trade, family life) and in the political realm (political stability, attitude change); they do not carry their interest to the point of believing that the means are at hand for effectively controlling and managing such problems and therefore stress an organizational ability to forecast. There is a strong belief in the efficacy of scientific knowledge to provide politicians with a rational basis for decision-making.

Social forecasters consider their targets for action to be national agencies with real power, predominantly administrations and ministries with a mandate specific to a given field of regulation. Their clientele, therefore, is made up of their counterparts on the national level. The majority of forecasters is satisfied with the effectiveness of their programs. A majority feels that they have shown their clients the complexity of the linkage among fields of action and have persuaded them of the need for comprehensive rather than piecemeal solutions. Unlike the planners, social forecasters limit their confidence to having demonstrated to politicians the more obvious links among items of knowledge and action, without having persuaded them of any holistic underlying logic or system. Moreover, a majority feels that it is easier now than earlier to achieve political agreement on the role of science and technology in policy-making. But the pragmatism of this group is manifest in its refusal to link its success to the use of the most formal and scientific means of persuasion. Most of the pragmatic social forecasters consider their success in planning due to the use of good data and careful analysis rather than to formal modeling, and to their ability to demonstrate to politicians that the means for achieving certain objectives are not available, or that means can be combined to attain several objectives simultaneously.

Physical controllers want to anticipate and to control unwanted side effects of technology, *but*—unlike social forecasters—they wish to confine control to immediate unwanted physical side effects, such as pollution. They do not carry their concern to economic and political effects. This can best be achieved through

pure research, which automatically provides increased knowledge and understanding useful to decision-makers. Some, like
the social forecasters, also maintain that scientific laws can be
applied to the solution of social problems. In either case, the
emphasis is on the provision of a rational basis for decision-
making and, in particular, on the formulation of techniques
capable of problem-solution. The physical controllers do not believe in the efficacy of a single mode of planning. While they believe that they are capable of elucidating the linkages among
aggregate, interrelated, complex goals, they neither view this
process as deterministic nor do they feel capable of dealing with
the decisional implications of any other than the purely physical consequences of technology.

Within this niche, the physical controllers perceive their clientele to be their organization and their professional discipline;
they concentrate on national targets with power, such as national
governments, cabinets, ministers, and mission-specific agencies
of national governments, and on international secretariats.
Their clientele is therefore somewhat more diffuse than that of
the social forecasters, a situation which may account for the
mixed expressions of satisfaction with their work which these
respondents exhibit. Well over half believes that politicians eventually come to appreciate at least the more obvious linkages between separate scientific discoveries and the sectors of social and
economic concern in which these manifest themselves, thus making possible increasingly comprehensive solutions. But over
one-half also expresses disappointment with its immediate impact on politicians and policy. It may well be, then, that those
who see themselves as professionals with a disciplinary identification see their successes in their impact on the international
secretariat, but those who identify with a world interest are frus-
trated with a slow impact on national decision-makers.

Randon appliers believe that the most useful application of scientific knowledge—if any exists at all—comes from free and
unguided scientific research. Organizations seek to spread the
use of science and technology simply because this is a good in
itself, or in order to increase the use and effectiveness of specific
technologies, or to diffuse knowledge concerning technology to
enlarge the number of potential beneficiaries. All of this is best
done, however, only in regard to very specific, technological
activities, which rarely anticipate problems (even though negative side effects are sometimes acknowledged).

These scientific and technological laissez-faire predilections are also encountered in other responses elicited from the random appliers. They exhibit no pattern at all with respect to their experiences with planning and bargaining over program formulation. They are almost evenly divided regarding satisfaction with influencing politicians and attaining greater agreement on the role of science in program and policy-making. Almost half of this group can see no ill effects at all as flowing from technology. While one-third feels that politicians have been taught to see the more obvious links between scientific fields and the associated social effects, two-thirds gives widely scattered replies to the question of impact on politicians. Random appliers are unusual in identifying their home countries and their professional disciplines as their major clients, and they see their main targets of organizational action in their *national* professional associations and specific national administrative agencies. Yet there is some sense of a trust in technique, in procedure, which is reflected in the belief that free and unguided research will automatically increase relevant knowledge and create knowledge links. However, it should be made clear that this is not the same kind of belief in technique which we found among planners, forecasters, and controllers. That faith was in a technique capable of anticipating problems, of linking complex goals, or superseding purely political choice. The appliers evince a concern with rules tied to efficiency criteria and always to simple, specific activities. The aim is to ensure that actors do the correct thing to get the "most" out of a given technology.

Slightly more than one-fifth of the sample is *eclectic,* individuals whose organizational experiences do not correspond to any systematic clustering. Expressions of experiences with respect to planning, influencing politicians, and relations with clients show no significant patterns at all. However, eclectics overwhelmingly express dissatisfaction with their ability to show politicians how fields of policy are linked as a result of scientific work, and they are equally unhappy over their lack of success in producing agreement on the role of science in program formulation.

How are these five types of organizational experiences distributed among the organizational roles the respondents occupied? The results are presented in Table 7.

None of the four roles is dominated by a single type of organizational experience; but some of the clustering is striking just the same. Officials of nongovernmental organizations interpret their experiences as being considerably less holistic and comprehensive than do others. This is understandable if we bear in

TABLE 7
Organizational Experiences and Roles

	Deterministic planners	Social forecasters	Physical controllers	Random appliers	Eclectics	N
Advisers	26.7	20.0	30.0	13.3	10.0	30
IGO officials	10.9	35.9	10.9	14.1	28.1	64
NGO officials	14.3	7.1	28.6	35.7	14.3	14
Delegates	10.0	25.0	15.0	20.0	30.0	20
Total	14.8	27.3	18.0	17.2	22.7	128

NOTE: Percentaging horizontal.

mind that many of these respondents are primarily concerned with pure research and—as the lower percentage of eclectics among them suggests—have highly structured views on proper programs for their organizations: Their organizational experiences engender modest expectations. On the other hand, social forecasters are very strong among the officials of intergovernmental organizations, indicating that many *do* see themselves as having a mission to sensitize the world to the dangers and the promise of science in a systematically *scientific* manner. Considering that delegates cannot be readily assumed to share such an orientation, it is surprising that so many in fact do, and that a few even see the organizations to which they are accredited as playing a global planning function.

Professionally, biologists and engineers turn out to be the most likely to opt for holistic international programs, as shown in Table 8.

TABLE 8
Organizational Experiences and Professions

	Deterministic planners	Social forecasters	Physical controllers	Random appliers	Eclectics	N
Physical scientists	8.8	20.6	20.6	38.2	11.8	34
Biological scientists	23.7	31.6	18.4	13.2	13.2	38
Engineers	17.2	27.6	24.1	6.9	24.1	29
Social scientists	10.5	31.6	5.3	10.5	42.1	19
Diplomats	0.0	25.0	12.5	0.0	62.5	8
Total	14.8	27.3	18.0	17.2	22.7	128

NOTE: Percentaging horizontal.

While social scientists also opt heavily for such programs, the number of eclectics among them is so high as to cast doubt on the significance of this finding. Physicists are far more likely to settle for a more modest organizational program and for piecemeal procedures. The number of diplomats in this sample is too small to attach much importance to their distribution.

A much firmer pattern appears, however, when the individual programs are examined in terms of the typology of organizational experience (Table 9). A word of caution is required before we discuss the findings: A different analysis is necessary to enable us to say that a given program *is* concerned with deterministic planning or random application; what is shown here tells us *how scientists in the program perceive their work.* Later chapters will provide descriptions of the programs in which the authors' judgment will be juxtaposed against the participants'.

Deterministic planners are prominent only in developed country science policy; the sum of random appliers and eclectics dominates European research and development, science and technology for industrial development, science and technology for agricultural development, and the outer space programs. The middle range of scientists concerned with social and economic forecasting and the control of the physical side effects of technology predominates in public health, global environmental protection, oceanography/meteorology, and the water resources program. Put differently, the programs most directly linked to recognized economic and social concerns exhibit a fragmented approach, while programs involving the physical environment tend to a more holistic view. For practical purposes this finding is clearly more important than the pattern of distribution uncovered for roles and professions; hence it will be examined in greater detail in subsequent chapters.

TYPOLOGY OF ORGANIZATIONAL IDEOLOGIES

Our interest is the identification of typical views among internationally active scientists which tell us something about emerging "world orders." These views are equated with organizational ideologies which span a continuum from rationalistic holism at one extreme to skeptical incrementalism at the other.

A scientifically informed "world order view" is an ideology professed by an elite which purports to specify the kinds of policies which ought to be formulated; the ideology, then, speaks to both ends and means. The elite will take a uniform view with respect to the adequacy of scientific knowledge to furnish the

TABLE 9
Organizational Experiences and Programs

Program	Deterministic planners	Social forecasters	Physical controllers	Random appliers	Eclectics	N
European R & D	0.0	18.2	0.0	0.0	81.8	11
Developed Country Science Policy	40.0	6.7	33.3	6.7	13.3	15
Public Health	8.3	16.7	58.3	8.3	8.3	12
Global Environmental Protection/Man and the Biosphere	31.6	42.1	5.3	15.8	5.3	19
Science/Technology for Agriculture	15.8	31.6	10.5	21.1	21.1	19
Oceanography/Meteorology	0.0	54.5	27.3	9.1	9.1	11
Science/Technology for Industrial Development	8.7	26.1	4.3	21.7	39.1	23
Water Resources	14.3	28.6	28.6	14.3	14.3	7
Outer Space	0.0	18.2	18.2	54.5	9.1	11
Total	14.8	27.3	18.0	17.2	22.7	128

NOTE: Percentaging horizontal.

basis for policy, or to the lack thereof: The less agreement on the adequacy of the knowledge base, the less deterministic the case for scientific participation in policy-making must be. Agreement on means, therefore, defines the extent of the legitimacy claimed for scientific leadership. We sought to capture the extent of this agreement with our typology of personal attitudes and discovered that the range of *disagreement* is considerable.

World order ideologies are also defined by the extent of confidence of the elite with respect to its ability to produce political consensus on the objectives of policy. We have conceptualized the range as running from full agreement that all knowledge is systemically linked to the totality of human welfare to a preference for ad hoc technological "fixes" which arrives at policy piecemeal and without systematic integration of goals. A preference for ad hoc approaches implies a decision-making style which remains true to disjointed incrementalism and expects little by way of "educating" politicians. Elities who opt for the holistic implementation of goals, of course, must profess a good deal of confidence in the capacity of international organizations to play an active role. Their view of a future world order includes a vision of stronger international organizations endowed with a global planning function. Incrementalist elites lack such confidence and are content to work with weak organizations in the hope of gradually making an impact. Holistic elites are thus concerned with the dramatic upgrading of international institutions, whereas incrementalist elites are more likely to accept the status quo. Our typology of organizational experiences captures elite perceptions with respect to consensus on the degree of holism-incrementalism implicit in organizational programs. Again, we found that the range of ideological *disagreement* is striking.

How can we combine our two typologies to obtain a comprehensive picture of the range of organizational ideologies? The four-cell matrix (Figure 2, Chapter 3), pitting static or expanding knowledge against static or expansive objectives, yielded four possible "world orders." We have combined the two typologies to approximate the logic implicit in the matrix. Thus, world order constructs and organizational ideologies correspond in this manner:

Matrix		*Typology of Organizational Ideologies*
Rational	=	Rationalist
Pragmatic	=	Pragmatist
Skeptic	=	Skeptic, eclectic
No new world order	=	Skeptic, eclectic

The coding rules governing the assignment of respondents to one of the four types will be explained further on. At this point we repeat that we are impressed by the range of perceptions with which we are confronted and therefore do not wish mechanically to assign each type exclusively to a single world order cell. Neither do we wish to proliferate categories and complicate the typology. The result is the lack of complete correspondence between the "skeptic" world order cell and the respondents whom we describe as skeptics. The appearance of eclectics in the "skeptic" and the "no new world order" cells is due to the same concern.

The typology of organizational ideologies is shown in Table 10. The numbers in each cell refer to the number of respondents meeting the characteristics.

The core characteristics of each type are now summarized.

Rationalists believe that:

1. Science provides a methodology and a body of knowledge which is superior to other kinds of knowledge; science promotes systematic, comprehensive models of knowledge uniting sepa-

TABLE 10
Constituents of the Typology of Organizational Ideologies

Organizational experiences	*Personal Attitudes*			
	Determinists	Instrumentalists	Skeptics	Eclectics
Deterministic planners	4	8	3	5
Social forecasters	5	11	12	5
Physical controllers	5	8	5	4
Random appliers	4	4	8	4
Eclectics	1	3	14	9

Key:

Rationalists (N = 12)   Skeptics (N = 36)

Pragmatists (N = 29)   Eclectics (N = 45)

rate disciplines; science produces data translatable into international programs of social, economic, and political significance.

2. Heavy reliance on technology sometimes generates undesirable consequences, but these are either better than the original condition from which they emanated, or easily solved through additional technology.

3. Goals are complex, interrelated, interdependent. In order to deal with them, highly aggregated organizational activity is necessary. In order to achieve them, complex planning procedures, from formal modeling to studied analysis based on good data, are required.

4. Organizations can be effective partly because of the existence of good knowledge and good technique, but also because of the influence of scientists on political decision-makers. These same circumstances also allow the use of scientific information to help to resolve political conflicts.

5. The proper clientele of this activity should be the world as a whole.

Rationalists thus see a world already unified professionally and technocratically by science, and they envision a potential world similarly unified ideologically and politically. Poor decisions are the result of human (that is, political!) error, not of inadequate knowledge; numerous international and domestic problems exist because of poor decisions made by shortsighted decision-makers, not because of the inability of scientific knowledge to indicate solutions. Furthermore, international organizations provide excellent fora for demonstrating the universality of scientific knowledge and equally excellent media for translating this knowledge into specific programs relevant to all humanity. In fact, these international organizations offer the only conceivable means of concentrating sufficient knowledge to deal with a complex, interdependent world.

This view is illustrated by a respondent from the Food and Agriculture Organization (FAO). He explained that there are absolute biophysical constraints on land use which must largely determine policy-making. There is an inherent inability to satisfy national food needs by exclusively national means, if the problem is considered in terms of the costs of technology plus the risks of environmental degradation. Hence, proper global planning must take place and within the framework of these domestic physical constraints. Scientific knowledge preempts "stupid" political choices which are inspired by autarkic aspirations. Planning is necessary on a global scale, and the biophysical characteristics of soils are the major input variable to be used in planning. All of this then requires adjustment of national *and* international plans, of trade and agricultural production patterns.

Pragmatists believe that:

1. Scientific knowledge is not superior to political knowledge, but it is epistemologically different from it, thereby providing a unique and necessary companion to political decision-making. This is best accomplished either by the unplanned accumulation of more knowledge and understanding, or through the deliberate transference of physical and biological laws to human and social activities.

2. Scientific knowledge alone cannot fully determine political decisions, or goals. However, through mixed planning it can successfully suggest the means required to achieve these goals and thus provide an essential input into the goal-setting exercise.

3. Goals are recognized as being multifaceted, complex, and interdependent, and it is believed that scientific knowledge can demonstrate the linkages in knowledge which relate to these goals. However, it is acknowledged that not all problems are or can be known, and thus that anticipated and unanticipated problems will eventually have to be dealt with.

4. Organizations can best use their scientific and technological expertise to anticipate the more remote social and political consequences of technology. They can also be effective in dealing with the direct physical consequences of technology. In either case, the organization is concerned with more than just the immediate application and use of a new technology.

5. The clientele of the programs is either an organization or national societies; decision-makers to be influenced are national entities with power, such as cabinet members, ministers, and specific agencies of the national government.

Pragmatists believe that better decisions can be made and that some issues can be combined in packages. They assume that they have the expert knowledge to aid in the construction of such packages. However, this knowledge is an additional tool—not the entire machinery—in a decisional process which is characterized by bargaining over both goals and strategies. It is an inherently political process which is fed, shaped, refined—but not determined—by the inclusion of scientific knowledge. Policies and plans can always be improved by, and frequently require, expert information but, due to the complexity of the world, the inclusion of this expertise does not guarantee an absence of unanticipated and undesired consequences. At their best, international organizations can provide the optimal mixture of political and scientific decision-making: If the scientists are lacking, the resulting policies will most likely fail to be effective; if the politicians are lacking, the policies will most likely fail to be implemented. Again, we provide some illustrations.

A member of the United Nations Outer Space Committee views the satellite for India as part of a comprehensive plan which links remote sensing, direct broadcasting technology, and meteorology with development plans. For example, the satellite, as a technology, is seen as an opportunity to create a single national language, hasten birth control, and—even more removed—lessen the dependence of developing on developed countries by enhancing internal political stability. He sees scientists as important, though not indispensable, agents in this application of technology because the knowledge at their disposal can order and clarify choices facing politicians.

An adviser to the Pan American Health Organization expresses very deterministic views on the role of science in policy-making, but declines to apply these to the program of his organization. He feels that scientific advisers in the field of public health can indeed help governments in making more rational choices by, for example, applying the laws of genetics so as to eliminate the transferral of malfunctioning genes, thus producing "better" populations. He is sure that scientific knowledge is superior to political knowledge because it is "factual," "provable," and not subject to the semantic confusion and obfuscation considered typical of the language of politics. However, he is unwilling to see the program of his organization as anything more than the anticipation and control of the unwanted side effects of the technology of gene manipulation. His program is confined to controlling first-order physical side effects.

An official of the European Communities charged with designing a cooperative program for industrial research and development sees his task as facilitating the progressive linking into a single policy of work in such diverse sectors as metallurgy, information technology, medical technology, fusion power, and new technologies to reduce pollution. He is concerned with shaping the future of Western European technology and industry to improve the quality of life by, in effect, forecasting unwanted conditions and controlling the evolution of technology to avert them. He is confident that this can be achieved if the cooperative program is worked out by national officials charged

with similar tasks at home working closely with scientific experts
and engineers capable of doing the forecasting and funneling
appropriate information to policy-makers. Science, and especially information technology, is seen as a crucial ingredient in
fashioning better policies for highly industrialized society *as a
whole*.

We now turn to the *skeptics*. This type is heterogeneous because
it includes all respondents who consistently dispute that scientific
knowledge is sufficiently consensual to furnish unambiguous
means for international action; but it also includes determinists
and instrumentalists, in terms of personal attitudes, who identify
organizational goals which do *not* converge toward a comprehensive understanding of complexity and which, therefore,
confirm a policy of incremental tinkering. Those who are skeptical on grounds of personal beliefs in science account for 78 percent of the type, giving us a minority of 22 percent who do
believe that science is superior to, or at least different from,
political knowledge. Even though skeptical in this sense, however, 56 percent of the type identify with organizational goals
involving a commitment to planning or forecasting, though only
8 percent identify with deterministic planning.[4] In other words,
skeptics illustrate the phenomenon of cognitive dissonance.

Skeptics share the following mixtures of beliefs:

1. A strong majority sees no epistemological difference between scientific knowledge and political knowledge. This implies
that there is nothing about scientific knowledge which makes it
any more relevant to political, social, or economic decision-
making than any other kind of knowledge. A minority accepts
the views of pragmatists and determinists on this point.

2. If and when science does have anything to offer to
decision-makers, the relevant knowledge can best be obtained
through scientific research which is essentially unfettered by restrictions from outside of its own discipline. Freedom to conduct
research for its intrinsic rewards is a key value. Social relevance is
an incidental reward; it is produced automatically, not planned.
A minority, however, accepts the views of the pragmatists and
determinists.

3. The job of international organizations is to facilitate the
diffusion and application of new technologies, preferably in
such a way as to increase the number of people who will benefit
from the innovation. This is the belief of 44 percent of the skeptics. However, the other skeptics hold that the job of international organizations is to control unwanted physical consequences of technological innovation, and a few are committed

programmatically to forecasting social and political consequences of change, and even to comprehensive planning. However, respondents who incline toward the holistic program *lack* faith in the special quality of scientific knowledge in informing the planning process.

4. Skeptics at the higher end of the goal continuum acknowledge a high degree of interdependence between ends and means. Those at the lower end do not; in denying the existence of complex linkages, they prefer to deal with issues one by one rather than construct issue packages.

5. Skeptics tend to identify with their home countries and their professional disciplines rather than with wider clienteles. They see as the targets of their programs national interest groups, agencies, and professional associations.

These views sharply curtail the special role scientists are assigned in the other organizational ideologies. A scientist who attempts to enter the realm of politics has nothing unique to offer; he may even have less to offer than a politician due to his lack of experience in and acquaintance with the political. Scientists should be able to use international organizations to conduct research; technologists should be able to use international organizations to apply technologies; both should be able to use these organizations to disseminate information regarding their respective research and technologies, but neither is uniquely qualified to judge or determine how these activities relate to policy.

The composite nature of this type makes it necessary to illustrate the way in which divergent personal attitudes and organizational experiences can be combined. We therefore offer the following examples: (1) a deterministic planner who lacks faith in the deterministic quality of science; (2) a social forecaster similarly devoid of faith; (3) a physical controller who disputes the superiority of science; (4) a random applier who strongly believes in the superiority of science; (5) a random applier who lacks faith in science.

An adviser to the Pan American Health Organization (PAHO) defines public health as public welfare and thus subsumes under this rubric areas of employment, communication, transportation, power facilities, productivity, and equity of distribution, in addition to policies commonly related directly to the curbing of sickness. Public health, by being viewed as public welfare, is defined positively and made to include almost everything. Systems of knowledge determine the goals, the interrelationships among goals, and eventually the ways in which goals are attacked. However, this adviser does *not* derive this definition of

goals from any special body of knowledge. He does not invoke
science as the source of the goals, though he believes that a fuller
knowledge of nature will enable governments to make more
rational choices. But his view of policy formulation owes more to
a humanistic stance than to science.

An official of the Intergovernmental Maritime Consultative
Organization (IMCO) has a very relaxed attitude about the nature of science; it is seen as helpful in identifying the source of
social problems and needs and indicating some solutions, without being "special" in other ways. Yet he sees the work of IMCO
as influencing the methods of naval architecture, the prevention
of collisions, and the control of marine pollution in terms which
go beyond the engineering techniques involved. He sees IMCO
as linking its engineering and legal methods with the identification of quite remote consequences of these technological innovations, their impact on employment and trade. While it is too
much to claim a planning function for IMCO, this official certainly identifies a forecasting function.

An official of the Scientific Committee on Problems of the
Environment (scope) of the International Council of Scientific
Unions, though a biologist by profession, also makes no claims
for the special nature of scientific knowledge. While science, in
principle, *could* provide a factual and conceptual basis for a cohe-
siveness of expert views on environmental problems, and thus
influence politicians to make somewhat more rational choices, it
has had no such impact. There is no agreement on the "dependent variable" in environmental matters since the industrialized
and underdeveloped nations differ on the purpose of environmental protection policies. As more scientific information becomes available, the stronger the disagreement seems to become.
He sees the work of scope as the anticipation and control of
unwanted *physical* side effects of technological innovation, and
no more; but he does believe that scope is able to influence
government policy in simply making available the discoveries of
scientists in this field.

An official of the Food and Agriculture Organization (FAO),
with a special competence in the field of resource surveys
through remote sensing, strongly believes in the conceptual and
factual superiority of scientific knowledge. He has great faith in
phytogeomorphic theory and techniques for interpreting data
collected by satellite, and he feels that land use policy can and
ought to be decisively shaped through this approach. But in
terms of the work of FAO he is simply concerned with interpreting and diffusing the technique and the data, in the hope of
expanding the number of people who can benefit from more

rational land use. He is not concerned with possibly unwanted side effects, more remote consequences outside the field of land use, or the inclusion of the technique in large-scale planning apart from agriculture.

An official of the United Nations Industrial Development Organization (UNIDO) feels that *strategy* is a pompous word if used in an organization with a budget as limited as UNIDO's. Consequently, he feels that UNIDO is better off without even the pretense of a strategy, so as to allow the organization to fill the gaps left by the big bilateral aid programs. UNIDO is viewed as basically in the business of uncovering "recipes," establishing procedures for gathering and analyzing, via computers, data for each specific industrial sector. UNIDO should apply such computer recipes to the introduction of appropriate technology. This means working incrementally on highly specific, disaggregated targets. This official has no special faith in science or technology as such.

There is little point in specifying the mixture of beliefs and experiences of the *eclectics.* However, we should note that only four respondents of forty-five in this type could be characterized as either determinists or instrumentalists in their personal attitudes toward scientific knowledge, though the number of skeptics among them is much larger. In short, there is no question that as a "group" eclectics do *not* have a high regard for science as a source of factual or methodological structure in devising internationally useful programs. On the other hand, this lack of faith on the personal level does not prevent a third of them from characterizing their organizational programs as aiming at holistic planning, social forecasting, or at least controlling for physical side effects.

Cognitive dissonance is in evidence here too. "Pure eclectics," those who profess nothing systematic in terms either of personal attitudes or organizational experiences, account for only 20 percent of the type. The remainder profess enough of a set of beliefs to be available as allies of rationalists, pragmatists, and skeptics in particular organizational settings. Moreover, eclectics, while displaying no ideological uniformity, predict something important about a scientific world order: Their presence casts considerable doubt on the clear victory of *any* single view.

Mr. X, by our criteria, is an eclectic. But he has major responsibility for science policy in one of the most significant regional organizations. What does he believe? He denies that knowledge as marshaled by scientists is methodologically superior to nonscientific knowledge, but retorts that *any* comprehensive and systematic way of thinking about the continuities between technological innovation and social change is superior to the accepted way of making science policy decisions. He feels that heavy reliance on scientific knowledge *has* led to social fragmentation, stress on technique over values, overly concentrated military and industrial power, and undigestible social change. Planning science policy will not correct these evils; planning society, however, will. This requires a lofty view of man and his intellectual capability quite apart from any faith in *the* scientific method. X thinks that his organization is dedicated to the encouragement of comprehensive international social planning, though it has to rely on major crises before it can make a significant impact on politicians; it cannot rely on an automatic or gradual unfolding of scientific knowledge. In his experience, good data and careful analysis made available by his organization can bring coherence into national planning and has done so in several instances. But one cannot conclude from this that, over time, it becomes simpler to achieve agreement on the role of science in international programs. The opposite is more likely to be true.

The four types are distributed among the programs of interest to us as shown in Table 11. The breakdown speaks for itself. Rationalists dominate no program and are altogether absent from half of the programs. Pragmatists dominate only in public health, though they are a significant minority in agricultural development, and oceanography and meteorology. Skeptics dominate two programs relating to environmental questions and resource assessment; they are a significant minority in three more. Eclectics are strongest in the programs most closely tied to industrial, economic, and social planning; they dominate one such program and comprise the single largest group in three more. In the aggregate, these findings certainly do not support the arguments of those who see the future world order as heavily influenced by consensual knowledge of cause and effect and who expect an expanding circle of programmatic agreement on issues informed by the growth of knowledge.

CODING, COGNITIVE DISSONANCE, AND THE FUTURE

Eclectics, then, are far from irrelevant. If we were to consider their organizational experience as a more important predictor of conduct than their personal attitudes, the alliance of the minority of eclectics with planners, forecasters, and controllers would swell the ranks of these groups. If the same assumption were made about those who are skeptics in terms of their attitude

TABLE 11

Organizational Ideologies by Program

Program	Rationalist	Pragmatist	Skeptic	Eclectic	N
European R & D	0.0	18.2	0.0	81.8	11
Developed country science policy	33.3	13.3	13.3	40.0	15
Public health	9.1	72.7	18.2	0.0	11
Global environmental protection/Man and the biosphere	21.0	15.8	31.6	31.6	19
Science/technology for agriculture and fisheries	0.0	33.3	22.2	44.4	18
Oceanography/meteorology	0.0	27.3	63.6	9.1	11
Science/technology for industrial development	9.5	9.5	33.3	47.6	21
Water resources	0.0	14.3	57.1	28.6	7
Outer space	0.0	22.2	44.4	33.3	9
Total	9.8	23.8	29.5	36.9	122

NOTE: Percentaging horizontal.

toward the role of science but who nevertheless identify with ambitious organizational programs (for example, the first three examples presented in the preceding section on eclectics), the "alliances" would give us a different distribution of organizational ideologies than the one we prefer to adopt. Why, then, do we adopt it?

Our coding strategy is "to play it safe." We could have observed the basic rule of dissonance reduction: When personal attitudes are pitted against organizational experiences, it is the organizational experiences—and therefore the official goals of the organization—which are going to win out and thus force the personal doubts of role incumbents into the background of social causation. These doubts deal with the role of knowledge, with the use and availability of means. If we stress only ends and goals, it would be simpler to predict future world orders. However, we did not choose this strategy and therefore have our heterogeneous skeptic and eclectic types.

The coding strategy we have adopted consists of two rules: (1) When we have no reason to interpret the personal attitudes of respondents as precluding the eventual acceptance of organizational goals at variance with these attitudes, the principle of dissonance reduction is made to prevail; (2) when we do have reason to doubt the malleability of the respondents, their personal attitudes are coded as determining the type to which they are assigned. Our reasoning is as follows. Agreement on goals is the result of participation in a collective process of program-making, itself a socializing experience. Personal attitudes may or may not have undergone such a process, depending on the length and the intensity of involvement of a given respondent in the program. Hence, the mechanistic application of the principle of dissonance reduction would lead to absurd results: It would give us influential individuals who would be expected systematically to subordinate their personal doubts to the declared program of their organization. Subordination would make sense only if we could be sure that the organizational program were firm and consensual; we know that this is often not the case. It might make sense if we could be sure that the individual concerned would have a major impact on programs for a long time; in fact, we cannot be sure of this at all. Hence, we follow the conservative strategy of not coding such individuals as tending toward the direction of rationalistic holism.

But what would happen if we were to apply the principle of dissonance reduction? What if we stipulate that skeptics and eclectics whom we refused to classify otherwise in order not to guess at the way in which they might deal with their doubts *will* subordinate their personal views to the goals of their organizations. Such an exercise gives us the breakdown seen in Table 12. Visualized in the form of Table 10, it means extending to the right the areas now indicated for rationalists and pragmatists in order to include the skeptics and eclectics, as well as to include among the skeptics the eclectics who are presently located at the right of the "random appliers" row.

TABLE 12
Organizational Ideologies Redefined
(N = 128)

Rationalists	14.8%	(as opposed to 9.8)
Pragmatists	46.1	(as opposed to 23.8)
Skeptics	17.2	(as opposed to 29.5)
Eclectics	21.9	(as opposed to 36.9)

It is clear that any projection of world orders related to scientific thinking and experience must take into account a possible shift in ideological clustering which tends to feature the more holistic approaches to global welfare, even though such a projection is less conservative than the one we prefer. We return to this theme in the concluding chapter.

In the meantime, our original construction of organizational ideologies remains the most salient predictor of future world orders. What matters is how the ideologies cluster in the various programs selected for detailed study, and how they match our evaluation of these programs.

Notes

1. Our use of the term *ideology* is consistent with the definition offered by Philip E. Converse, "The Nature of Belief Systems in Mass Publics," in David E. Apter (ed.), *Ideology and Discontent* (New York: Free Press, 1964), pp. 207–8. For the application of the notion of organizational ideologies to international organizations, see Robert W. Cox and Harold K. Jacobson, *The Anatomy of Influence* (New Haven: Yale University Press, 1973), and Ernst B. Haas, *Beyond the Nation-State* (Stanford: Stanford University Press, 1964).

2. The typology is constructed as follows. We assign respondents to one of the four types according to their response patterns as summarized below. The numbers of items and options refer to the questions as presented in Chapter 4.

Determinists		Instrumentalists		Skeptics		Eclectics	
Item	*Options*	*Item*	*Options*	*Item*	*Options*	*Item*	*Options*
1	1	1	1,2	1	3	any other com-	
2	3,4	2	2,3	2	1,2,3	bination if two of	
3	3,4	3	2,3,4	3	1,2	the questions were	
						answered	

3. The following combinations of responses resulted in the derivation of the types. Numbers of items and options are the same as in Chapter 4.

Deterministic planners		Social forecasters		Physical controllers		Random appliers		Eclectics	
Item	*Option*	*Item*	*Option*	*Item*	*Option*	*Item*	*Option*	*Item*	*Option*
6	8, 7	6	5, 6	6	4	6	1,2,3	all other	
7	3, 4	7	3	7	2, 3	7	2, 3	combina-	
								tions if both	
								questions	
								were an-	
								swered	

4. This situation explains why it was not possible to identify skeptics mechanically with the "skeptic" world order cell, and eclectics with the "no world order" cell. Skeptics do not clearly correspond to the logic of the four cells because, in terms of their views on means, most fall into the "no agreement" cell whereas, in terms of their views on ends, they straddle the line between the cells since some believe in the possibility of attaining agreement on piecemeal policies while others identify with the evolution of a more comprehensive consensus on goals. Eclectics, on the other hand, should *not* be equated with the inhabitants of the lower left-hand cell, because the logic of that cell suggests that neither a broad consensus on goals (even by way of negotiation and bargaining) nor general agreement on means (through better knowledge) can ever be attained. Eclectics do not necessarily fit this picture; at best, only nine profess such views, while the remainder display more structured perceptions on one or the other of the dimensions, but not on both.

PART 3

The Evolution of International Science Programs

Chapter 6

Decision-Making and Institutional Attributes of World Order Models

---

The coal dust which the smokestacks of the Ruhr belch into the atmosphere settles in Sweden in the form of black snow. The hurricanes diverted from Florida by seeding them with silver iodine may ravage Cuba and destroy its sugar crop. Meteorologists are able to tell us why and how this happens and they can also suggest, once they can model large-scale atmospheric phenomena, how such events can be avoided. Work along these lines goes on in the World Meteorological Organization (WMO) and in its affiliated groups of scientists working in their individual capacities. How does this work enter the calculations of governments? How, if at all, does it change their perceptions of what is desirable and permissible? What institutions might be created as a result of changed perceptions?

We now take up the second major issue of our study: What is the relationship between the perceptions of internationally active scientists and the evolution of international cooperative programs for harnessing science to social objectives. Our concern with world order as implied by science cannot be limited to specifying the attitudes and experiences of key scientists. We must now ask whether and how these beliefs are linked to policy-making in international fora.

In Part 1 we defined the idea of "world order" as a way of linking knowledge to the making of collective decisions. These decisions, in turn, were imagined to call for comprehensive planning and thus for the creation of new institutions capable of formulating and implementing plans. The "perfect" rationalist world order would resemble a conclave of statesmen devoted to mastering the future by assuring everyone of a minimum standard of living and a wholesome physical environment. This conclave would be advised by a panel of scientists reasonably certain that they possessed the knowledge of nature—or were able to obtain it—which must be respected in order to meet these goals.

The facilities for obtaining, interpreting, and diffusing this knowledge would be created under international auspices. National activities would be mounted within the universally applicable constraints and opportunities thus demonstrated.

The material in Part 2 has shown that, while such views do indeed exist, and while the influential scientists advocating them are active in international scientific programs, their number is small and their impact hardly discernible. We now know that *there is no single view of a desirable future world order which is held by scientists as a group.* Scientists, despite their calling and despite their professional ethos with respect to the role of knowledge, *do not as a group subscribe to a model of international politics which transcends the practices now prevalent in collective international decision-making.*

At best, the attitudes and experiences of internationally active scientists suggest the prevalence of three different ideologies which imply future world orders. Each of these organizational ideologies incorporates a set of dimensions and properties which could serve as a model of the future. But they cannot be used to forecast three different and simultaneous world orders in any simple projection. We shall show in the following three chapters that the distribution of these ideologies among programs and among international organizations is such as to preclude a straightforward projection. We cannot say that UNESCO is tending toward rationalism and WMO toward pragmatism. Nor can we say that the program in public health suggests the advent of one model and the program in water resources that of another. The three organizational ideologies cannot be identified with single organizations and single programs. Most are represented in all organizations and all programs.

A more cautious projection is possible, however. Though all ideologies are represented, they are not present in equal measure. Consequently, after the reader has had an opportunity to acquaint himself with the substance of the programs, we will hazard an interpretation of each in terms of its relevance to one or the other of the models implicit in the ideologies. We do so by ascertaining which views predominate, and whether they are likely to prevail or undergo change. These judgments will involve us in an analysis of the degree of comprehensiveness achieved by each program. Then, in the final chapter, our judgments of comprehensiveness, juxtaposed against the expectations of decision-makers, will be used as a means for imagining the future of each program.

We stress that the focus of analysis now shifts. In Part 2 we established, on the basis of assessments furnished by the sample of internationally active scientists, the distribution of views pertaining to world orders implied by the substance and methods of science. We now superimpose our own judgments on these views. We also seek to integrate the perceptions of our respondents into the judgments we offer even when the two diverge. Our judgments are derived from the second set of data, substantive information on the origin and evolution of nine science programs managed by international organizations. This set of data is arranged so as to show whether and how the perceptions of scientists influence collective political decisions regarding the use of science in the attainment of social objectives. We are now dealing with the decision-making and institutional characteristics of international organizations which *mediate between* the perceptions of scientists and the evolution of policies which may suggest various outcomes approximating this or that world order. So far we have merely specified the *cognitive* characteristics, in principle and in terms of data, of world orders. What further steps now need to be taken?

First, each of the three organizational ideologies must be reexamined in terms of its relationship to speculation about future world orders. This undertaking requires a respecification of the world orders so as to pinpoint the *decision-making properties* of each and to explore *global institutions* appropriate for each style of making decisions. We will then be able to match our scientific programs to the world order typology in order to show which, on balance, comes closest to meeting the requisites of one or the other model.

ORGANIZATIONAL IDEOLOGIES AND WORLD ORDER MODELS: DECISION-MAKING

The task is the specification of how and why certain personal attitudes and organizational experiences suggest fixed modes of making decisions. Our task also compels us to show which institutions most logically go with modal decision-making styles. The amalgam of the cognitive properties guiding a given decision-making style and the institutional properties describing the fora in which the decisions are made is a world order model. We thus remain loyal to the proposition which has inspired this study: The types of knowledge available for making decisions are considered the crucial determinant of the *means* of action chosen; but the *ends* of action are defined by the political goals in the minds of the actors. And we reiterate that we envision the division of labor among actors to favor scientists as the definers of means and politicians as the fashioners of ends, at least in the kinds of international programs considered here.

In Chapter 1 we summarized this division of labor in a simplified form; in Figure 3 we add the percentage of our sample fitting each type.[1]

FIGURE 3
Knowledge and Goals in World Order Models

| | | Political Goals Are | |
		Specific	Expanding and Interconnected
Expert Knowledge Becomes	More Consensual	Pragmatic world order 23.8	Rational world order 9.8
	Not More Consensual	No new world order 22.1	Skeptical world order 44.3

Knowledge, as the definer of the ways of attaining goals, can be considered as becoming more unified and comprehensive as more powerful overarching concepts or metaphors come to connect diverse fields of inquiry, in various branches of the natural sciences as well as between the natural and social sciences. Cybernetically legitimated systems constructs are among the more familiar conceptual roofs. The possibility that knowledge is not becoming more consensual, however, does not imply a lessening of already existing understandings of links and connections; it simply means that no *new* conceptual bridges, no additional interdisciplinary breakthroughs are expected. The entry reflects our judgment of where the sciences are at the moment with respect to their relevance to policy-making in the international arena: The claim for the connectedness of knowledge is already very extensive, but it shows few signs of a quantum jump into a new master concept.

The opposite of a "specific" goal is an "expanding and interconnected" set of goals. The objective of limiting air pollution to a fixed threshold is specific; linking it to a design for automobile engines which are energy-conserving makes it expanding. A "specific" goal is one which addresses itself to a single dimension of government policy-making, such as establishing a floor price for certain agricultural commodities; that goal becomes "interconnected" with others when the floor price is determined on the basis of calculating future world food needs or nutritional levels. The shift is of enormous significance bureaucratically because it calls for the expansion of the number and types of individuals, expert and lay, who participate in decision-making. It also implies a different cognitive stance. Shifts on either of the dimensions are common. A professed desire to launch shifts on both dimensions is often encountered; its translation into actual policy is much less common.

In the international arena the Law of the Sea Conference of the 1970s illustrates the distinctions. A fisheries policy based on the maximum sustainable yield is specific; calculating the maximum sustainable yield in conjunction with the demand for fish would make it expanding, because it would call for deliberate policies for managing the size of the biological stock in conformity with commercial demand. Dealing with fish alone makes the goal of management specific; but if fisheries management were to be linked with a more general policy of improving nutritional levels in poor countries while also taking into account other commercial uses, the management policy would become both expanding and interconnected with other political goals. The original Maltese plan for an ocean regime was consistent with a rational world order. The actual solution adopted by the conference, in essence, implies no new world order at all, with some slight suggestion of movement toward the skeptical as far as the mining of the ocean bottom is concerned.

In the following chapters, then, our concern is with the cognitive path which leads from changing knowledge to political goals that are more comprehensive *and* more complexly linked than the goals sought earlier. Here we specify the nature of this path in terms of the typical ways in which decisions are made in international fora. We call attention now, not to the cognitive attributes of rationalists, skeptics, and pragmatists, but to the manner in which each typically interacts with others in actually deciding to mount international programs involving science and technology. We focus on the dynamics of issue-linkage. These decisions, of course, involve experts in interaction with politicians. Some of the politicians are themselves knowledgeable about science; others are not. The emphasis in what follows is on the interaction rather than the separate characteristics of each type of actor.[2] The character of the interaction is what distinguishes one world order from another.

How can we describe these distinctions more clearly? We are

dealing with three decision-making syndromes which differ from one another on these dimensions: (1) the knowledge used by the decision-makers; (2) collective learning of decision-makers; (3) the collective tactics adopted by the decision-makers to attain their objectives; (4) the shared objectives to which the decision-makers are committed; (5) the collective bargaining style used by the decision-makers. Even though experts and politicians interact on each of these dimensions, it is, nevertheless true that politicians are the more prominent and powerful actors with respect to defining shared objectives and engaging in bargaining. The mobilization of knowledge and the stimulation of learning provide prominent fields of activity for the experts, and the determination of tactics is shared by both sets of actors.

Knowledge

How does one decide that economics is no longer an adequate basis for making policy on questions of growth and national income? Such a decision must follow from a recognition that income alone is not good enough to define an appropriate "quality of life" because pollution, crowding, noise, and resource depletion involve social costs which cannot be conceptualized if we rely only on established economic methods. Knowledge of ecosystems and of urbanism, for example, now becomes relevant to policy-making on questions of national economic growth or nongrowth. New knowledge, then, refers to the addition of *substantive* fields of science to the armory of "good information" which policy-makers ought to have at their disposal. Furthermore, new knowledge also refers to *methodologies* which go with the marshaling of that information, with the interpretation of the information and its insertion in the political process of choosing. The issue is this: Do the actors *deliberately* search for new knowledge appropriate to the emerging issues? Do they believe that sufficient knowledge is already at hand to permit choice? Or, do they conduct a reluctant and ambivalent search for new knowledge, even though the existing knowledge base is considered generally adequate? In other words, we are not concerned here so much with the content of this knowledge as we are with the question of whether knowledge is marked by deliberate search, whether it is fixed, or whether it is reluctantly expansive.

A world order based on the *skeptics'* attitudes and experiences essentially follows the mode of decision-making known as disjointed incrementalism. Although a condition of uncertainty is acknowledged to exist, new knowledge is not deliberately sought. On the contrary, skeptics believe that past experience provides an adequate guide for the decision-making process; a routine is thus established in which new decisions emerge piecemeal from inadequately made prior decisions, only to be supplemented later with another set of piecemeal decisions.

The *rationalists'* ideology, however, chooses a comprehensive and deliberate search for new substantive and methodological lore. It seeks to capture all pieces of scientific knowledge within a formal, systematic framework. It opts for a search pattern in which almost everything can become relevant to choosing. Complex simulation models, cost-benefit analysis, and game theory, therefore, become important weapons in the informational armory. In the organizational literature, this type of decision-making is called "rational-analytic."

The *pragmatists'* ideology differs from both of the preceding in its treatment of new knowledge, but it does resemble the rationalists' more than the skeptics'. Pragmatists also seek new knowledge and attempt to establish connections among established islands of understanding; they are therefore consumers of intellectual constructs capable of providing cognitive bridges among disciplines. However, this search generally does not occur until there is sharp dissatisfaction with incrementalist procedures, until older objectives are questioned, new objectives are demanded, or until the rationality accepted as adequate in the past ceases to be a legitimate guide to future action. Furthermore, the pragmatists' ideology puts far less emphasis on the deterministic aspects of formal models and quantitative analysis than does the rationalists' ideology.

Learning

Presumably there is a connection between the mobilization of new knowledge and the lessons which decision-makers derive from that mobilization. How do actors learn? Learning processes can be thought of as resulting from the availability of new types of knowledge, or the uninformed recognition of new objectives may trigger "learning" which deliberately seeks new knowledge. There is no unidirectional path of causation. This dimension simply seeks to capture some fundamental differences in attitudes toward institutional learning—from the unselfconscious muddling-through of disjointed incrementalism to the emphasis on the need for learning which is channeled by fixed routines and institutional practices of a formal nature. The middle ground between these extremes is perhaps occupied by what Michel Crozier has called *apprentissage institutionnel*—"the process whereby members of a complex collectivity succeed in passing from a worn-out system of regulatory rules to a more elaborate system of rules which permits a larger scope for co-operation."[3]

In the *skeptics'* world order, actors do not agree on a clearly defined "single problem," and thus they eschew any desire to arrive at a comprehensive "solution." They engage in successive serial analysis to pinpoint where they went wrong; they correct failures of earlier decisions by seeking to make small changes. Put differently, the unintended and undesired results of earlier decisions cause small adjustments in later decisions.

In the *rationalists'* world order, however, efforts are made to identify systematically superordinate social values. After these are identified, the rationalist will seek to integrate these values into a single strategy by calculating the trade-offs among them. This results in an increasing number of interdependent utilities to be satisfied, and thus it leads to an ever-expanding scope of attempted solutions. Learning is the assimilation of the lessons derived from systematic synoptic analysis.

The situation is different in a *pragmatist's* world order. The pragmatist is a disappointed incrementalist who is not quite at ease with the holistic commitment of the rationalist. He subscribes to the necessity of seeking more comprehensive solutions and therefore to the utility of more complex and abstract cognitive models. But he comes to this conviction after having attempted incremental solutions to problems and with a belief that problem-solving can be improved "simply" by making incremental methods more sophisticated. The pragmatist "learns" by engaging in a partial "scanning" of the system of interdependencies which seems to underlie the unsolved problem, then attempts to link issues into packages which are more comprehensive than the skeptics'. But eventually he admits that the implementation of a given strategy may call for unlinking of the package, provided that the solution to smaller problems within the "whole" remains tied to the overall vision.[4]

Tactics

Here we are concerned with the kinds of tactical choices actors make in seeking their objectives, and the ways in which these might be affected by changing knowledge, changing rates, and changing kinds of learning. Specifically we need to ask what assumptions are made about the cause-and-effect links between means and ends, between tactics and strategy. It may be supposed that increasingly complex modes of choosing will be adopted if an understanding of more complicated patterns of causation develops. Means accepted uncritically at a point when objectives are fixed may come to be questioned when new objectives are added.

Within the *skeptics'* world order, decisions remain heavily tied to the *initial* set of goals shared by the actors. Departures from established tactics are a function of the degree of disappointment with the attainment of these initial goals. Policy choices may range from minimal new commitments, to the addition of major new tasks, or to the abandonment of a task.[5]

In the *rationalists'* world order, however, the emphasis in choosing tactics is quite different. There is an overriding goal and a cognitive model telling the decision-maker how separate modes of action in various sectors of policy interact toward the attainment of the goal. Hence, in terms of organization theory, program activities are "scheduled" according to a computation of optimality. As objectives change, due to feedback mechanisms included in the overall model, tactics for implementing subgoals are changed in proportion to the reassessment of priorities and optimal modes of action. In short, the choice of tactics is *not* constrained by the sum of the subgoals entertained by the actors (as it is in the case of the skeptic), but remains a dynamic function of the shared superordinate goal.

In the *pragmatists'* world order there is no reliance on either the initially shared sum of subgoals or any overriding single goal. Older goals are not dropped as new demands or issues come to the fore; they are incorporated and subordinated to these new goals. Since the initial goals may have included a schedule of performance, the rearrangement of goals then calls for an exercise in rescheduling which must include the attempt to satisfy the new demands that have arisen since the original consensus on goals was worked out. New issues, moreover, tend to arise suddenly in response to a sentiment of "crisis" and the pragmatic decision-maker is forced to undertake his rescheduling while *simultaneously* satisfying the new and the old demands. And yet he cannot take comfort from a massive concept of overall interdependence!

Objectives

We are not concerned here with the substance of objectives: These may include rapid economic development, increased public participation in opting for new technologies, clean air, or the planning of water resources in arid areas. What matters is the speed and suddenness involved in the articulation of *new* objectives and their relationship to the consensus on goals which existed prior to their advent. In OECD and the European Communities, for instance, the accretion of objectives relating to the freeing of trade and managing monetary stability was gradual and consistent with the initially shared goals of the members; but the evolution of demands relating to the environment, technological innovation, and rates of growth was not. These objectives were quite suddenly added to the older ones after 1968. The U.N. agencies had given practically no attention to the potential interplay between environmental and developmental objectives until the environmental nexus of concerns surfaced in 1971. On the other hand, the diffusion of new technologies appropriate to accelerating development had been on the international agenda since 1962; accretions were incremental rather than sudden and simultaneous.

How can these possibilities be associated with our three world orders? *Skeptics* fashion a consensus on goals by adding the subgoals dear to single actors into an agreed program. The implementation of the program, following the definition of the consensus, then features the attainment of these subgoals. In other words, *sectorally specific* goals are combined and added incrementally and slowly but are not meaningfully constrained by an overriding objective.[6] Skeptics react to the advent of new goals with uncertainty and hesitation. They are reluctant to change the prior goals, but if they cannot simply reject the new demands they seek to add them to the older set without raising questions about coherence and compatibility.

Rationalists, of course, proceed quite differently. The initial commitment in their world order is to a method of planning, a vision of interdependence of social goals and available knowledge. Sectorally specific subgoals, when they come to the fore, can always be accommodated by calculating their impact on the overall objective and by revising the master schedule. Rational planning calls for the continual reevaluation of the plan and the appropriate shifting of the constituent parts.

In a *pragmatic* world order, emphasis will be put on the *selective* linking of new and old goals. The pragmatist admits that the indefinite pursuit of disaggregated and sectorally specific policies will lead to mutually incompatible outcomes. Therefore, new goals cannot be simply added to the older ones. A periodic refocusing of shared objectives is thus necessary to obtain a more appropriate sense of priorities. These priorities, in turn, are partly defined by new understanding of cause-and-effect relationships among the previously distinct sectors. Refocusing thus implies the attempt to define a *new* consensus at appropriate intervals, a process illustrated by the ongoing debate over the proper mixture of environmental and economic growth objectives. However, these efforts are always a bit tentative because the older consensus never disappears completely. The goals implicit in it are still valued by important actors. Hence, unlike the case of the rationalist world order, the pragmatist stance eschews a firm cognitive commitment to a final new world order. The pragmatist leaves himself open to the dissipation of the new consensus.

Bargaining

How do the three world order models differ with respect to the bargaining behavior that produces the choice of new goals and tactics? The style of bargaining can range from the uncooperative extreme of a unit-veto system based on nonnegotiable demands and threats of withdrawal to the harmonious extreme of a variable-sum game in which the actors consciously seek to spread the benefits so as to reward the disadvantaged among them.[7]

Things are simplest in the *skeptics'* world order. The purpose of bargaining is making decisions to facilitate the attainment of the many subgoals, the sum of which constitutes the shared objective. Because that sum is a heterogeneous package, bargaining alternates among modes defined by a competitive zero-sum situation in which the minimum winning coalition carries the day (as opposed to a cooperative constant-sum game based on log-rolling and the offer of side payments). Package dealing occurs frequently, but the deals are confined to subgoals which are closely connected on substantive grounds, so that the amount of complex issue-linkage which occurs is quite limited.

In the *rationalists'* world order, bargaining is not of crucial importance because decisions tend to be computational. Since the evolving world model reflects changes in objectives, and since the cause-and-effect links among sectors and objectives are thought to be well understood, there is no need to resort to various kinds of coalitions and rewards in order to obtain a consensus. If such a need does arise, however, there is nothing in the cognitive model of the rationalist which clearly predicts one mode of bargaining or another.

In the *pragmatists'* world order, bargaining follows a pattern of cooperative variable-sum games based on a complex pattern of log-rolling. The log-rolling, however, tends to be more and more systematic in linking substantively disparate fields of policy to one another as changing knowledge demonstrates new cause-

and-effect links. Put differently, the bargaining pattern reflects the fact that actors learn to relate sectors of action which had been considered unconnected earlier in the process. Log-rolling can thus develop into a cognitively unified pattern of package-dealing which is based on the progressive understanding of causal links. Yet it will not develop to the point of cognitive unity represented by the rationalist world order because successive package deals do not necessarily add up to a realization of the "whole system."

Reconsider for a moment the distinction between specific and interconnected goals. Our description of decision-making attributes then presents us with a paradox: The skeptic world order actually looks more holistic than the pragmatic. The decision-makers following the skeptic mode are *more* likely to arrive at an expanding and interconnected set of goals than the pragmatic, *even though* they do not rely on an expansion of the knowledge available to them. How can that be? The answer is that goals and programs can and do expand without reliance on new knowledge. New knowledge is rarely so consensual as to approach certainty. New knowledge that does not tell political decision-makers unambiguously which goals can be easily met, and at what cost to other goals, will *not* automatically lead to a rationally unified collective program. It will lead to a temporary aggregation of goals and coordination of programs, to be followed by subsequent disaggregation into sector-specific activities.[8] The issue-linkage featured in this style remains fragmented. Adherence to the pragmatic mode therefore is far from leading us to a cognitively more unified world order by easy and regular steps. The skeptic, however, may stumble into expanding and interconnected programs because he follows the incremental mode; but he will do so without understanding, in terms of knowledge, *why* he arrives at such an outcome. Hence the finality of the program coordination and integration may well be doubted. New fragmentary knowledge which fails to become consensual will then trigger an "unlearning" sequence which will result in decoupling and separating programs previously unified. There is no systematic issue-linkage based on an increasing understanding of cause-and-effect links. Ecological and evolutionary ways of thinking will have no effect on the fashioning of political programs.

How does the cell containing *eclectics* fit into this scheme? Logically, its occupants cannot be identified with any evolution of issue-linkage because they do not make use of expanding knowledge and continue to adhere to separate and specific international program goals. However, this is not due to any overt commitment on the part of the policy-makers so classified. Their position results from their failure to be committed to a *consistent* view or a *cumulative* pattern of organizational learning. We encountered many instances in which eclectics professed partial views supporting the thrust of one or the other of the models. We also encountered some who identified with cumulative organizational program expansion, even though they lacked the attitudinal motivation to support such expansion in terms of their beliefs about science. The point is that international programs conceived and implemented by groups of individuals not markedly unified by a pattern of views and experiences regarding issue-linkage cannot readily make policy in a way which consistently supports one evolutionary direction or another.

We summarize the decision-making attributes of world order models in Figure 4.

FIGURE 4
Decision-Making Characteristics of World Order Models

Political Goals Are

	Specific	Expanding and Interconnected
Expert knowledge becomes more consensual	*Pragmatic* deliberate search for knowledge; learning via partial scanning; new issues superimposed suddenly; periodic refocusing of goals; package-dealing over wide range of issues.	*Rational* deliberate search for knowledge; learning via formal models; holistic "computation" of all issues; systemic arrangement of goals; no need for bargaining.
Expert knowledge does not become more consensual	*Eclectic* inconsistent mixture.	*Skeptic* no interdisciplinary search for knowledge; learning via incrementalism; slow expansion of issues; resistance to reconsidering goals; package-dealing over small range of issues.

ORGANIZATIONAL IDEOLOGIES AND WORLD ORDER MODELS:
INSTITUTIONS

Decisions are made by people working in institutions. Descriptions of world order models call for consideration of the kinds of institutions which appear appropriate for our three ways of making decisions. We will consider institutions in terms of a number of themes here expressed as questions. (1) What purpose is to be served by their activity? What capability for action on the part of member states is to be created or improved? (2) Since the management of knowledge is at the core of our concern, what instruments for managing knowledge are to be set up? (3) What division of labor between national and international agencies and activities is there to be? (4) Who is to make decisions in what kinds of institutions?[9]

Purpose and Capability

Actor purposes can be classified as follows. (1) The *acquiring* of a capability to act in a specific domain, either nationally or collectively: This may include creating the ability to make decisions, to analyze a situation, to set up new relationships, or to fashion physical goods. (2) *Making effective use* of an existing capability: This implies actions designed to perfect, adjust, or change decision-making norms or manufacturing facilities or habits of action so as to better exploit something already in place. (3) *Coping with the consequences* of a capability: This implies adjustment or change in an effort to undo previously unwanted and/or unanticipated results associated with the use of a capability. The more ambitious purposes subsume the less demanding, but the reverse is not the case. Any given organ, forum, or set of persons will usually seek to acquire and/or make effective use of some capability while also seeking to cope with the unwanted consequences of some other aspect of the same capability.

In general, *skeptics* limit themselves to the least complex of these purposes—the establishment of institutions which create a capability to act in the future. Examples of these institutions include data banks and monitoring systems, but do not include any built-in capabilities to deal with unforeseen consequences arising from their operation.

Pragmatists are more concerned with an established capability to act, although their belief in the expanding nature of knowledge does sometimes involve them with "coping." Essentially, however, they worry about how to make use of an existing capability in order to meet new issues, while simultaneously doing justice to the older issues.

The *rationalists* clearly possess the most complex purpose. It is only here, in their world order, that there is a manifest commitment to link the maintenance and acquisition of the capability to act with an overriding concern for the undesirable consequences of earlier decisions, and hence with a dedication to comprehensive "coping."

Instrumentalities and the Division of Labor

Instrumentalities run from the least to the most centralized. (1) *A common framework* seeks to affect national behavior through exchanges of information and common rules of reporting and record-keeping and commitment to certain agreed targets. In the language of organization theory, the division of labor sought here is confined to "pooling" separate capabilities without rearranging them in the search for a common product. (2) *A joint facility* is a more ambitious and demanding way of pooling capabilities by seeking to harmonize and standardize the behavior of the participants through the imposition of common routines and norms. The actors agree to a loose division of labor not merely by keeping one another informed but by changing routinized ways of doing things so as to meet an agreed standard. (3) *A common policy* is more demanding still. It calls for the ordering and scheduling of national behavior in such a way that the participants adjust their action to the planned needs of the collectivity by rearranging prior norms and patterns—a type of division of labor called "sequencing" in organization theory. (4) *A single policy* substitutes a centralized set of norms, plans, and objectives for the national ones. Since, in doing so, it absorbs the pre-existing commitments of the national actors, the resulting pattern of interaction (and the division of labor among the parts) is far more complex than in the other instrumentalities: The interaction is "reciprocal."

Common frameworks, joint facilities, single and common policies, moreover, can be identified with institutional mandates as to the use to be made of knowledge. Pooling, sequencing, and reciprocal interaction are all ways of managing knowledge in an increasingly complex fashion. Pooling requires only the collection and exchange of information without calling for changes in routinized behavior among the participants. It is appropriate for recognizing and describing a problem, but not necessarily for doing anything about it. Thus, it is an institutional choice particularly appropriate in a *skeptic's* world order model.

In the *pragmatists'* model, however, the actors feel committed not simply to understand a problem better, but also to do something about it: They must make collective decisions. Moreover, the decisions involve changes in prior routines, because the mixture of old and new issue areas calls for abandoning some past practices in favor of more highly coordinated alternative steps. The institutions to be set up, then, are joint facilities for common decisions, making use of knowledge in such a way as to create new sequences of action.

In a *rationalist's* world order, much more ambitious and complex collaboration is being sought. While in the pragmatic order joint decisions would still be implemented by the actors in their separate capacities, a rationalist stance calls for common and perhaps simultaneous implementation. Since the number of issues and problems to be dealt with simultaneously is much larger, the interactions among issues are more complicated, thus requiring the kinds of reciprocities illustrated by an industrial empire which is fully integrated both vertically and horizontally. This kind of goal requires a common or even a single policy for all the participants.

Types of Participants and Their Institutions.

The pooling of instrumentalities of action calls for very simple coordinating bodies when a common framework is at issue. Interbureaucratic committees of high civil servants suffice. When a joint facility is to be operated, however, a research staff may be necessary to devise the appropriate standards and norms; the staff need be no more than a working party of independent experts, convened when necessary. But it often develops into an international secretariat, which then comes to service the interbureaucratic committee. These institutions are sufficient for setting out common ground rules for national action. They will naturally tend toward issue-by-issue disaggregation of tasks in the effort to devise effective joint means of action appropriate for doing whatever their mandate demands—but no more. Sequencing is more ambitious, since priorities for action must be established. Some parts of the whole must act before others; some kinds of previously legitimate actions will become illicit. Creation of a common policy thus demands a capacity to make joint commitments; this is the task of councils of ministers and summit conferences, aided by lower level committees of national civil servants and rudimentary international staffs. It must be understood, however, that these lower level bodies are incapable of making commitments without the agreement of their superiors. A single policy, and the relationships of reciprocity which this implies, call for a full-fledged "government," whether in the classical federal tradition or in some other approximation.

We summarize these institutional attributes of the world order models in Figure 5.

FIGURE 5
Institutional Characteristics of World Order Models

| | Political Goals Are | |
	Specific	Expanding and Interconnected
Expert knowledge becomes more consensual	*Pragmatic* Purpose: to maintain and cope with capabilities. Instrumentality: joint facility for decisions. Division of labor: sequential. Institutions: decentralized, intergovernmental committees with varying mandates; tendency toward centralization through information provided by international agency.	*Rational* Purpose: to cope with consequences of capabilities. Instrumentality: common or single policy for implementation. Division of labor: reciprocal. Institutions: acceptance of a central plan will trigger international administration with executive power.
Expert knowledge does not become more consensual	*Eclectic* Inconsistent mixture.	*Skeptic* Purpose: to acquire a capability. Instrumentality: common framework for problem recognition. Division of labor: pooled. Institutions: problem recognition is increasingly centralized as new issues are added and international technical agencies expand; decisions are made by intergovernmental conferences, influenced by international agencies.

Despite other marked differences among the world order models, the conferences, committees, working parties, and groups of experts appropriate to our conceptualization do not differ greatly from type to type. It is idle to seek institutional specification in the international arena of joint policy-making in domains dominated by science and technology if we seek to apply the vocabulary of international and constitutional law. Such concepts as federation, confederation, regulatory commissions, and administrative procedure help very little in a setting in which there is no fixed territorial space whose institutional evolution can be judged. The application of terminal conditions used in regional integration theory, for instance, would be as misplaced as are projections based on the changing size of state units, the rise of nonstate actors, empires, condominia, and regional blocs.[10] We are not envisioning massive transfers of sovereignty to new territorial actors. We are concerned with specifying the implications of efforts at collective problem-solving for a wide variety of separate issues and tasks. Interest in these is not evenly or symmetrically distributed in the world now and may not be so distributed in the future. Participation and membership in the institutions may differ from issue to issue, and the commitment of single members to any one issue may wax and wane. The growth of functional interdependencies, then, is far from suggesting the structured and symmetrical ties which are implied in the effort to unite states in a new overarching legal framework. It could be said that a fully rational world order cannot be imagined without world government, but even that would be an overstatement. Pardo's plan for an ocean regime would have created a world government for the oceans; the Baruch plan might have resulted in one for nuclear energy. The most that can be said for the rational world order model is that it would imply "government" for the package of issues selected for rational management.

The same cannot be said of the other models. They call for various disaggregations of normal governmental functions. But they both rely on elaborate committees of instructed delegates of governments to negotiate appropriate rules of conduct, though they differ in the extent to which such committees are likely to be influenced by panels of experts and the research facilities of international agencies. Yet both ultimately depend for their authority on mandates issued by governments united in conference. Clearly, the customary distinctions among executive, legislative, and judicial powers have little relevance in such a setting, though the rational model contains something approximating an executive.

We can, however, rank the three models on a scale of "ultimate authority." Imagine a scale of authority which runs from highly centralized to completely decentralized among a large number of governing bodies seeking to make collective policy. At the more centralized extreme, the governing body has the power to issue binding norms limiting the behavior options open to the members; it is capable of directly implementing its decisions; it has the capacity to resolve conflicts among the members by handing down authoritative awards; and it has a monopoly on marshaling the knowledge which is to inform action. At the opposite extreme, decentralization implies that the member governments have consented to no such procedures. Uniformity of conduct is sought by means of nonbinding guidelines; decisions are implemented only through the administrative services of the members; conflicts are subjects of negotiation, not settled by awards; knowledge is the result of pooling the resources of the members, not the property of a technocratic elite at the center. Thus, in the *skeptics'* world order, ultimate authority rests indefinitely in the hands of the member states. In the *rationalists'* world order, it is the property of whatever central machinery is established. And in the *pragmatists'* world order, it is likely to be diffuse, shifting back and forth as issues are programmatically coupled and decoupled.[11]

IN SUMMARY: SOME CAVEATS

Armed with these distinctions among decision-making syndromes and institutional arrangements, we are now prepared to examine our international scientific programs in order to fit them into one or the other of our models. However, before proceeding to this task some caveats are necessary.

The following case studies will each contain two summary analyses—one based on the perceptions of our respondents, and one based on the perceptions of the authors. The self-perceptions of the respondents result from their roles as officials, advisers, or delegates. They have interpreted *their* experiences in terms of the jobs which *they* were asked to do, of *their* initiatives, *their* negotiations, *their* votes. The respondents were not asked to sum up their experiences by offering judgments of the collective and cumulative process of interaction. The authors, however, base their judgments on the interaction among advisers, delegates, and officials. They rate decisions and institutional behavior over a range of issues. To put matters differently, if the respondents err on the side of missing the forest because they are understandably preoccupied with trees, then the authors are more likely to be overimpressed with the forest at the expense of single trees. In any case, it is the task of the final chapter, supported by the strength of our data, to account for the discrepancies and to bring the two views together.

We stress that in the three chapters which follow we emphasize the extent to which nine international scientific programs have changed since their inception. We cannot speak directly to the issue of how successful these programs have been in shaping the lives and expectations of the national societies to which they are addressed. Nor can we offer evidence that these programs have visibly changed the distribution of power and influence in international politics. Our measure of success, then, is the extent to which these programs show an evolution from one mode of making decisions to another, from reliance on one set of institutions to another institutional syndrome. The measure of success is the degree of comprehensiveness in linking goals and the extent of reliance on increasingly consensual knowledge to inform political choice.

Hence the discussions of the programs will be couched in the vocabulary of the concepts introduced in this chapter. We are interested in whether and how more comprehensiveness in goals and knowledge was attained, not in recapitulating all aspects of all scientific programs mounted by international organizations. Nor are we able to explain in most cases the *precise* interaction of expert knowledge and political demands which accounts for whatever evolution we discovered. Hence the discussion cannot satisfy those interested in a descriptive catalog of international activities or students of international decision-making processes. Our materials seek to map the terrain that such a study should eventually fill in more completely and more satisfactorily. They advance concepts and suggest partial evidence useful for such an enterprise. Our immediate concern is confined to demonstrating the cognitive characteristics of program evolution and to linking them to alternative cognitive models of world order.

We group the nine programs as follows. Chapter 7 will take up activities of interest only to the industrialized countries in their mutual interactions. We discuss the efforts of the European Communities to arrive at a regionally collaborative R & D policy and the work of the Organization for Economic Cooperation and Development to fashion coordinated science and environmental policies for its member states. In Chapter 8 we examine global efforts to map and improve environmental conditions by examining global environmental research programs mounted by ICSU, UNESCO, and the United Nations (including the Man and the Biosphere program), collaboration in meteorology and oceanography under the auspices of ICSU, WMO, and IOC, work on water resources done by ICSU and UNESCO, and environmentally related public health programs under the jurisdiction of WHO. In Chapter 9 we examine international science and technology programs relating directly to the economic and social development of the Third World, including the marshaling of science and technology for industrial development as sponsored by UNESCO, the United Nations, and UNIDO, the application of science to agricultural development and fisheries under the purview of FAO, and the planning of outer space activities by ICSU and the United Nations.

Notes

---

1. See Table 11, Chapter 5, and the discussion preceding it for the rationale underlying the numbers. The number of skeptics does not correspond to the number given on that table because of the necessity of deciding how many eclectics professed views close enough to those of the skeptics to qualify them for inclusion in that category. We decided that the eighteen eclectics on the scale of personal attitudes who also identified with organizational goals which were not eclectic could safely be identified with a skeptical approach to world order issues. The residue of twenty-six eclectics constitutes the population in the "no new world order" cell.

2. Our discussion of decision-making syndromes and of institutional patterns is an adaptation of material presented in a discussion of regional integration under the stimulus of "post-industrial" experiences. See Ernst B. Haas, *The Obsolescence of Regional Integration Theory* (Berkeley: Institute of International Studies, 1975). The decision-making syndromes identified in that essay are more elaborate than the distinctions we use here and were made specific to the experience of the European Communities. The syndromes were labeled "incremental," "fragmented issue-linkage," and "rational-analytic," respectively. They correspond to skeptic, pragmatic, and rational in the present context. Some passages are carried over verbatim from this essay.

3. Quoted from an unpublished paper presented at the European Center of the Carnegie Endowment for International Peace, 1966. Our translation.

4. For the notion of "mixed scanning" as a planning strategy which seeks to combine the virtues of disjointed incrementalism and synoptic analysis, see Amitai Etzioni, *The Active Society* (New York: Free Press, 1968), pp. 282–8.

5. The dynamics of this process in a setting of incrementalism are captured by the notions of "spill-back," "spill-over," and "encapsulation." See Philippe C. Schmitter, "A Revised Theory of Regional Integration," in L. Lindberg and S. Scheingold (eds.), *Regional Integration: Theory and Research* (Cambridge, Mass.: Harvard University Press, 1970).

6. In the case of certain regional collaborative arrangements, however, the commitment to sectorally specific programs is conceived by the actors as consistent with the achievement of an overriding purpose to which the sectors are considered subordinate. The consensus underly-

ing the creation of the European common market illustrates this situation, since the founding governments thought of the separate sectors as adding up to an irresistable impulse toward European political unity. Our discussion of science and industrial policy in the E.C., however, shows that sectorally specific objectives are not easily reconciled despite the prior existence of a basic political consensus.

7. The discussion of bargaining modalities is adapted from Leon Lindberg, "Political Integration as a Multidimensional Phenomenon Requiring Multivariate Measurement," in Lindberg and Scheingold, *Regional Integration,* pp. 101–2.

8. For empirical evidence illustrating this sequence of events in international program-making, see Haas, *Obsolescence,* part 3.

9. Purposes and instrumentalities are based on the scheme elaborated by John Gerard Ruggie in "International Responses to Technology: Concepts and Trends," *International Organization,* summer 1975. Ways of classifying divisions of labor are derived from the work of J. D. Thompson and Peter Cowhey's studies of global energy management.

10. Hence the classification of possible outcomes of the regional integration process elaborated in Haas, *Obsolescence,* and in Haas, "The Study of Regional Integration," in Lindberg and Scheingold, *Regional Integration,* are not appropriate here. Nor are the world order models elaborated by Richard A. Falk in *A Study of Future World Orders* (New York: Free Press, 1975), because they are inspired by various possible regroupings of territorial actors.

11. The untidy mixture of institutions associated with the pragmatic world order model is essentially the same as that described as an "asymmetrical overlap" in Haas's discussion of regional integration. See Haas, "Study of Regional Integration," in Lindberg and Scheingold, *Regional Integration,* p. 31, and Haas, *Obsolescence,* pp. 83–5.

Chapter 7

Science and Technology
for Highly Industrialized Societies

Modern science and its offspring, industrial technology, originated in Western Europe and rapidly spread to the United States. By the beginning of this century, the industrial world included Canada, Japan, and Australia. While the same diffusion also occurred in Eastern Europe, the character of the political and economic institutions which came to prevail there has resulted in a different pattern of cognition and policy choice. For our purposes, highly industrialized societies are the countries of the West, the "first world," in the language of contemporary international confrontations, with the addition of Japan. The grouping is subjective in the sense that it relies on the self-definitions of these nations rather than on quantitative indicators of industrialization; it is objective in that the grouping corresponds to two major international organizations, two key attempts at collective management of certain problems associated with industrialization—the European Communities (E.C.) and the Organization for Economic Cooperation and Development (OECD).

What are these problems? Since science and technology originated in the West, it is hardly surprising that the effects should also be first experienced to the fullest by the West. Some problems are purely economic: how to combine free trade with national monetary management, how to enjoy both price stability and uninterrupted economic growth, how to implement national fiscal autonomy while also seeking to maintain competitive prices for one's exports. Other problems are both financial and intertwined with the mobilization of specialized knowledge: Can each country's industry finance the R & D needed for industrial innovation, or must the burden be shared through consortia and other modes of pooling resources? Should there be a planned industrial division of labor among countries professing free trade as the principle of mutual economic interaction? To what extent should proprietary knowledge be shared internationally? More and more commonly, the answers to these questions are linked to concerns over environmental degradation and re-source depletion. Should measures of energy conservation, the search for new energy sources, control of air and water purity, elimination of toxic substances, and sharing the specialized information necessary for all of these be done by each nation alone or by all jointly? Either choice affects the pattern of trade and investment in the group. Is science, and the universities and laboratories in which it is conducted, oblivious of social needs? Is research too expensive? Are there too many, or too few, scien-tists and engineers? Should science be subordinated to defined social needs, or should it be free to follow its own inclination? Is there too much science, or too little? Should science be used for determining social needs?

The two programs examined in this chapter have sought to deal with all of these problems by means of international col-laborative action. We look first at efforts mounted by the Euro-pean Communities, the program we label "European R & D." We then examine "Developed Country Science Policy," an amalgam of the separate programs maintained by three different organi-zations.

EUROPEAN RESEARCH AND DEVELOPMENT: THE EXPERIENCE OF THE EUROPEAN COMMUNITIES

We make the argument here that the *pragmatic* model accu-rately describes the institutional and decision-making patterns of the European Communities in its efforts to cope with the problems of industrialized societies. Our respondents, to be sure, see matters differently, a disagreement in perceptions which we take up in Chapter 10. We maintain that expert knowl-edge is gradually becoming more consensual, even though the main governmental actors continue to follow decision-making strategies of the task-oriented, specific kind. Decision-making is characterized by the deliberate search for new knowledge, re-liance on partial scanning, the need to deal simultaneously with old *and* new issues, periodic collective efforts at refocusing goals so as to do justice to both the old and the new, and the conse-quent need to engage in package-dealing over a wide range of issues which are not necessarily connected in substantive terms. The institutions used also conform to the pragmatic model. Actor purposes are concentrated on maintaining an existing capability and coping with the consequences of that capability. Joint facilities are most commonly used for accomplishing this, though there is evidence that common policies are emerging based on an increasingly sequential division of labor. Action is taken as a result of discussion in intergovernmental councils and committees with widely varying mandates, increasingly dependent on a centralized body of experts for the information on which decisions are based.

The Communities Program

Until quite recently, the efforts of the European Communities were, of course, concentrated on the implementation and further development of the Treaty of Rome. This implied an overwhelming concern with designing a common policy for trade, including the removal of all internal barriers to free trade, the free movement of capital and of persons, and the elaboration of a common commercial and tariff policy vis-à-vis third countries. Work was directed toward the perfection of the customs union and its evolution into a full economic union, which called for increasing attention to monetary, fiscal, and countercyclical policy issues.

The focus began to shift dramatically at the Paris Summit Conference of heads of state and government of October 19–20, 1972. At that time, a commitment was made to make further use of the Communities' capability by including in its program new items which directly related to the unresolved questions usually lumped together under the label "post-industrialism." Specifically, a commitment was made to the progressive implementation of a common policy with respect to scientific research and technological development by such new tactical arrangements as

> jointly selecting and drawing up a coherent set of long-, medium- and short-term objectives and the priorities to be complied with in achieving them;
> ensuring the coordination of national policies;
> determining those projects of Community interest on which work should go ahead;
> setting up permanent consultative machinery, through which the Member States can, whenever the need arises, decide on the common attitudes to be adopted vis-à-vis third countries or within international organizations;
> determining the resources required in order to achieve the objectives decided upon and choosing the administrative or technical structures best suited to this purpose.[1]

In the context of these new objectives, the Commission drew
up a plan which was quite unprecedented in the experience of
international collective efforts because it involved rigid sequencing by creating timetables, methods, and institutions for (1) the
coordination of national policies; (2) the promotion of basic research in member countries and in the E.C.; (3) specific E.C.
measures in the fields of medical research, energy policy, industrial development, and environmental protection.[2] We now describe each of these projects in somewhat greater detail. We
stress that the decision to enter these areas marks a sharp departure: Industrial and market growth was no longer being taken
for granted either as an automatic or as a necessarily desirable
process; efforts were to be made to forecast, assess, and channel
processes, that is, to subordinate them to a predecided set of
collective priorities.

Coordination of national R & D policies. Vague concern about duplication of effort among national R & D and the fears of some
that dependence on American technology was increasing had
triggered two prior efforts at coordination since the late 1960s. A
working group on coordination (PREST) had been set up, together with sectoral subcommittees, and a large number of "joint
projects" had been drawn up, only to result in inaction because
the members of PREST lacked the national bureaucratic authority
to see the projects through to completion. Moreover, the work
was confused by the simultaneous activity of a second coordinating body (COST), which also drew up projects for joint action
but grouped the E.C. countries with several important non-
members, notably Britain. The 1972 plan called for the abolition
of PREST and the creation of the Committee on Scientific and
Technology Research (CREST), to be made up of national representatives having primary responsibility for national R & D
planning, with the power to commit their governments.[3]

CREST was duly created in 1974, and it proceeded to examine
various programs, particularly in the field of energy R & D.
Specifically, this involved CREST in the Commission's action program, "Energy for Europe: R & D," which proposed coordinating national programs for energy R & D, carrying out research
of E.C. interest whenever necessary, encouraging certain research projects of more direct interest to industry, and exchang-
ing information on results of research, especially on techniques
suitable for industrial application. More importantly, the Commission recommended that CREST be responsible for the program's sequencing, that is, for coordinating national energy

R & D policies in accordance with a strict timetable, especially in regard to projects which could not be exclusively carried out at a national level (for example, thermonuclear fusion), projects which satisfied collective needs (reactor safety), projects which required a long-term effort (solar and geothermal energy), and projects for which market forces did not provide the necessary incentive (energy economy).

The Commission made additional proposals to the Council in 1975, which also required the overseer services of CREST. All were concerned primarily with structuring a deliberate search for knowledge about the unintended or unforeseen consequences of energy production and use (such as improving health protection against ionizing radiation) and for assessment of biological and ecological consequences of using nuclear energy and ionizing radiation. The Council approved programs on radiation protection, the environment, and the creation of a systematized reference data base.

The most significant proposal of the Commission for centralizing R & D in the energy field, however, has not yet been implemented by the governments. The Commission had also proposed the construction of a large-scale experimental device, the Joint European Torus (JET), for accelerating thermonuclear and plasma physics research. The Council initially failed to accede, in part because some governments favored the plasma physics component and others were more interested in thermonuclear fusion. CREST retains supervisory powers over the jointly arranged portions of plasma and fusion research previously agreed to pending full implementation.[4]

CREST was also requested to create a subcommittee which could concentrate on Communities R & D policies and programs for cooperation with the developing countries, including an initial program to define priority activities.[5] Eventually, CREST is to compare systematically all national and collective R & D programs, coordinate them, harmonize national R & D budgets, and synchronize these with the Communities budget. It thus stands as the key to successful sequencing of the Communities' R & D policy. This, however, is yet to happen, since CREST's time is taken up with single proposals and projects for cooperation.

Basic Research. The same concerns which led the Communities to push for the coordination of R & D also led it to suggest certain areas of scientific and technological research in which priority ought to be given to collective over national efforts. The objectives included a definite Parkinsonian impulse, namely, rescuing the extensive nuclear research facilities built up earlier under the EURATOM program. These facilities faced an uncertain future with the dismantlement of EURATOM and the rapid growth of national nuclear energy programs in several member states. Hence this portion of the program sought to identify aspects of European technology in which sustained and collective research efforts would go some way toward making the corresponding European industries competitive with their American counterparts while also giving the E.C. joint research center a new lease on life. Hence, the plan proposed joint work on certain industrial materials, reactor safety, fusion, geothermal and solar energy, and their associated environmental protection problems. It also took the initiative in the creation of a European Science Foundation to provide private expert advice on such projects.[6] To what extent these measures will or will not be subordinated to a common scheme which also includes national activities is again something which CREST is to decide eventually.

Collective Sectoral Programs: The Environment. In its effort to mesh collective with national efforts, the Commission naturally sought to build as much as possible on research activities for which it already had some responsibility. It therefore proposed to expand the research program on biology and environmental health and medicine. More importantly, it took advantage of the energy crisis to branch out even further into an ambitious research program on conservation. Europe first evidenced its concern with the "quality-of-life" question in 1972, at the Paris Summit Conference, which had called on the Communities to prepare an environmental action program by July 31, 1973. This action program, in which the Commission made a serious effort to transcend item-by-item regulation and to subordinate the entire range of issues to an overarching concern with the quality of life, contained some twenty separate projects, ranging from the continuation of specific measures to deal with single pollutants and nuisances to comprehensive research on urban planning and the improvement of the working environment.[7] Had the proposal been accepted as a package, it would have constituted an instance of holistic and rational planning. Like the Dahrendorf plan, it would have provided for a reciprocal division of labor among the national, private, and E.C. institutions in the marshaling of new knowledge prior to the adoption of common and single policies for the collectivity. Like the Dahrendorf plan, however, the proposals were dismembered and acted on piecemeal in an effort *not* to disturb an earlier consensus on older objectives as these came under challenge from the new environmental concerns.

In November 1974, the Council unanimously adopted the "Polluter Pays Principle" as the single policy to govern the financial aspects of European environmental degradation.[8] It also adopted regulations governing water purity, ruling that both national and international surface waters should be of equal quality but stopping short of setting deadlines or specific standards. It committed the Communities to respecting environmental concerns in developing new energy policies and sources without yet calling for specific measures. In 1975, the Council adopted a program of action for dealing with radioactive wastes.[9] However, the program is dependent on the furnishing of initiatives by national administrative authorities and is far from constituting an E.C. set of regulations for nuclear waste disposal. Separate directives were issued for dealing with the sulphur content of gas-oils, limiting the discharge of dangerous substances into water, and assuring the purity of water for bathing.

The Commission returned to the fray by submitting a Second Action Programme in March 1976. It proposes to (*a*) ensure that policy followed since November 1973 be continued; (*b*) emphasize measures for setting up common machinery for preventive action, particularly in regard to pollution and the physical planning and generation of wastes; (*c*) give special attention to nondamaging uses and the rational management of space, the environment, and natural resources; (*d*) reduce pollution and nuisances, with priority given both to measures for protection of fresh water and sea water and to noise abatement; and (*e*) add an environmental dimension to the Communities' policy for cooperation with the developing countries.[10] However, there was no serious evaluation of the First Action Programme. In fact, the content of the Second Programme reflects the degree of disintegration which had befallen the Commission's attempts to transcend item-by-item regulation and to subordinate the entire range of issues to an overarching concern with the quality of life. Repetition of old items of business, such as the reduction of pollution or the rational management of the environment, illustrates the failure of the Commission to push a single environmental package during the first four years of the program, and it hints at the competition for attention which the "quality-of-life" concern met. Links among all of the parcels may have been demonstrated, but they failed to sell. The reaction was not so much to seek new knowledge, then, as it was to seek a political *modus operandi* capable of generating consensus by designing compromises on an issue-by-issue basis.

Collective Sectoral Programs: Energy. If the energy crisis spawned major efforts by the Communities in the area of environmental protection, it gave birth to an even greater number of new proposals, debates, concerns, and programs in the energy sector itself. Most of 1974 was spent in trying to dissolve the differences among the member states regarding the very nature of an E.C. energy policy. The British opposed a coherent policy and sought only a vague formulation aimed at simple coordination of national energy policies; the Danish and Dutch delegations had serious reservations concerning the call for speedy development of nuclear energy production; and the French, who were the only ones among the E.C. Nine who had refused to join the International Energy Agency (IEA), sought reassurance that the Communities would adopt a single, or at least a common, policy. Compromise was finally reached by the end of 1974.

The Nine agreed to act in concert in discussions with the oil-producing states and in prior consultations with other consumer countries.[11] The British gave up their objections after they had received assurances that the Communities would not attempt to develop a common external policy for energy: The external decisions to be reached by the Nine were to be closely coordinated, with the possibility—but not the mandate—of arriving at a common policy vis-à-vis third countries.

The establishment of commonly agreed production and consumption targets can be considered an indispensable first step in the adoption of a common policy among states. Such a policy was indeed adopted by the Council in 1974. It demanded, first of all, that the conflict over the amount of nuclear energy to be generated be eliminated. Denmark and Holland, for ecological reasons, had held out for a maximum installed capacity by 1985 of 160 GWe, whereas others preferred the target of 200 GWe. A compromise target was found. Other agreements included adoption of target figures which reduce the per annum increase in energy consumption from 5 percent to 3.5 percent, and to reduce dependence on imported oil from 63 percent to 43 percent, through a program of maintenance of a prescribed level of hard coal production, an increase in the Communities' production of natural gas, development of hydrolic and geothermal energy, and an increase in North Sea oil production. All energy consumption was to be reduced, by 1985, to a level 15 percent below that which would have resulted from normal development at that date. In addition, medium-term guidelines were established for both coal and electricity.[12]

However, while these targets were accepted by the Council, many of the specific tactical measures proposed to attain them were not. The Commission had called for supervising the investment plans of oil companies, gearing coal pricing and coal imports from third countries to the planned level of reliance on imported oil, using the North Sea deposits in the planning, accelerating the development of nuclear power plants, financing the importation and reexportation of oil, Communities-wide rationing and price control regulations, and collective negotiations with OPEC. All failed to be adopted as means of reaching the new objectives. Thus, the Commission's attempt to impose rational planning on the energy-economic growth-dependency syndrome was dismembered according to the rules of pragmatic decision-making.

Meetings held since have not sought to build a comprehensive policy anew. The Commission has discussed and then proposed to the Council a number of the components from the original plan, and the Council has picked and chosen according to its ability to build a consensus around any given point, in line with parallel efforts being undertaken within the IEA. Consequently, the Council has issued directives limiting the use of gas and of oil products in electric power stations; but no agreements on coal price supports or on a coal disposal guarantee have been forthcoming; nor has there been developed any real program for the development of alternative energy resources.

Establishment of genuine solidarity among the member states in the event of oil supply difficulties, encouragement of energy conservation, and adoption of measures to protect or encourage the development of Communities' energy resources remain to be acted on. The member nations have found it difficult to reconcile the new demands for systematic energy planning with their prior commitment to the operation of their customs union. The tension between the two sets of objectives is illustrated by the five principles for international cooperation on energy questions adopted by the Council in March 1975: (1) The Nine recognize the right to free access to energy sources to be developed; (2) discrimination on price and access to energy sources is prohibited among the Nine; (3) all energy production targets will be established by way of joint action; (4) a consultative mechanism for assessing joint action is to be created; (5) in the development of alternative energy resources, the Nine shall share the effort to be made in proportion to the benefits to be obtained.[13] The first two principles seek to protect the common market and the principle of unfettered competition; the third and fourth attempt to link the common market to centralized decision-making for European R & D measures and imply the need for coordination in negotiations with third countries. The final principle hints at insulating national energy markets from the full logic of the customs union.

Collective Sectoral Programs: Industrial Policy. The vague field of "industrial policy" should be the obvious and immediate beneficiary of a number of E.C. efforts. The Commission argued in the Dahrendorf plan that the aircraft, shipbuilding, communications, and electronic industries and the chemical industry were most in need of collective help; and it proposed a series of coordinated steps in national and collective planning, research, and investment to bring about the technological innovations held desirable.

Action has been attempted only in the aeronautics sector. In its March 1975 meeting, the Council formally adopted a resolution compelling all E.C. governments to share information regarding new civil aircraft programs and propulsion systems for such aircraft before procurement decisions are made. Such cooperation is to consist of consultations, but without an obligation to achieve agreement. Further, in October 1975, the Commission proposed to put the aeronautics sector under tutelage, that is, political control by a Communities authority. The action program for the aircraft industry calls for *(a)* a common program for development, production, and marketing of large civil aircraft; *(b)* Communities financing to support development, production pooling, and sales financing of aircraft; *(c)* a common fund for basic research; *(d)* a common external policy in regard to industrial collaboration with non-Community countries; *(e)* a common market for civil transport through a common policy for civil air transport procurement; and *(f)* an ad hoc agency concerned with the procurement and development of airborne weaponry.[14]

However, no action has been taken. The entire industrial policy has been hampered by problems with CREST (which must approve all of the preceding projects), by overlapping areas with COST, and by private firms which seem most reluctant to engage in consultation and patent-sharing. The entire effort is complicated by the fact that the customs union makes it simple for non-European firms to benefit from industrial coordination, a condition which could change only if the Nine governments were able to arrive at a common policy with respect to multinational corporations. Hence, this aspect of the plan remains to bear fruit.

Only the field of information technology seems to be an exception. The Communities succeeded in making operational an ambitious computer network and data bank for scientific information (CIDST), as well as a number of sector-specific data banks from which European private industry is expected to benefit. The plan calls for the continuation and intensification of this effort under E.C. management.[15] This has been among the few joint projects planned by COST and PREST which had progressed well enough to be taken over under the new dispensation of CREST. It involves a computerized system for handling import-export data for the management and financial control of agricultural market organizations, systems for retrieval of legal documents, real-time systems for processing of air traffic control data, and studies on computer-aided design.[16] Finally, the plan called for and implemented an unprecedented effort at systematic forecasting. A consortium of national systems analysis institutes was given the task of projecting the character and needs of European industrial society as a whole after the turn of the twenty-first century, the "Europe + 30" project carried out in 1974–1975.[17]

Toward a Pragmatic Order

Do these pieces fit together? Have goals expanded and become more interconnected? Is background knowledge more consensual? Has any learning taken place? Does the plan and its commitments amount to a scheme to subordinate regional political processes to insights and techniques derived from a scientific view of order? It would be an exaggeration to answer with a flat yes. No single institutional or decision-making style prevails. Inconsistencies and incongruities abound. The mixture becomes clear from the summaries presented in Tables 13 and 14.

A similar summary of the E.C. program in the late 1960s would have disclosed the dominance of the skeptic model. The decision-making characteristics would have been incremental, based on a shared commitment to keep and perfect the common market. No call for new knowledge was made. Learning consisted of working out small accommodations to satisfy members who appeared dissatisfied with some aspect of the common pro-

TABLE 13
Decision-Making Characteristics of the E.C.: 1976

Program Activity	Characteristic				
	Knowledge	*Learning*	*Tactics*	*Objectives*	*Bargaining*
R & D	deliberate search	scanning	new tasks added to old	sudden addition	cooperative constant-sum
Energy	deliberate search	incremental	new tasks added to old	sudden addition	cooperative variable-sum
Environment	deliberate search	scanning	new tasks added to old	sudden addition	cooperative constant-sum
Industrial Policy	incremental search	incremental	old tasks prevail	slow accretion	competitive zero-sum
Information/ Basic Research	deliberate search	fixed— formal routines	new tasks prevail	slow accretion	cooperative variable-sum

TABLE 14
Institutional Characteristics in E.C.: 1976

Program Activity	*Characteristic*			
	Purpose	*Instrumentality*	*Division of Labor*	*Institutions*
R & D	maintain capability	common policy	sequential	Problem recognition in hands of centralized expert bureaucracy.
Energy	create capability	common framework	pooled	Decisional power in hands of instructed national delegates.
Environment	cope with consequences	common policy	sequential	
Industrial Policy	maintain capability	joint facility	pooled	Power to implement decisions shared by national governments and central bureaucracy.
Information/ Basic Research	maintain and cope with consequences	joint facility	pooled/ sequential	

gram. Today things are very different, though far less tidy institutionally. Even though the Commission's holistic proposals have suffered the fate of dismemberment typical of decision-making based on issue-by-issue bargaining, the sum of the bargains still represents a step toward a more comprehensively linked set of policy objectives and tactics. The sum of the decisions, and the cluster of institutions devised for implementing them, represent marked movement in the direction of a pragmatic order for issues raised by high industrialism.

However, as will be seen further on, the views and experiences of the participants do not confirm our interpretation, because they see the European Communities as first and foremost an economic undertaking. Its purpose is to contribute to the economic welfare of the member states by increasing opportunities for economies of scale and a more efficient division of labor. Hence its core tactics are the perfection of the customs union and its evolution into an economic union. True, many groups and individuals, and especially the Commission and its staff, consider all this a necessary stepping stone for the achievement of a political union, an orientation which is even shared in somewhat diffuse fashion by many key politicians. Questions dealing with redistribution, the quality of life, the role of research, science policy, and the reordering of social processes are a *secondary* set of objectives which have recently gained acceptance as desirable goals, but which remain to be integrated with the first set of E.C. aims. Some deliberate search for the links between primary and secondary sets of goals is being conducted by some individuals in charge of these programs; but they have yet to succeed to the point where it can be stated that learning is becoming cumulative. Most decisions are made on the basis of bargaining characterized by variable-sum rewards, side payments, and complex package-dealing among the old and the new goals. In recognition of the fact that there is some momentum for change, however, we have included in our study a number of respondents whose major responsibility lies in the economic sphere, but whose work is on the margin of the secondary issues which preoccupy us. Thus, we have included officials whose work lies in medium-term economic planning, agricultural policy, industrial policy, and industrial relations with third countries. In each case we questioned these persons on how the technological and research plan of the Communities impinges on their work. Moreover, the delegates we interviewed usually have responsibility for economic as well as technological questions.[18]

How Do Scientists Perceive the Communities Plan?

There can be no doubt that the scientists, engineers, and economists involved in these plans are a very cynical lot. Two-thirds of them show up as skeptics in our typology of attitudes toward the nature and use of science in public policy; eclectics account for 8.3 percent, and only 16.7 percent proved to be determinists. Their impressions with respect to their organizational and programmatic experiences are even more striking: 82 percent of the respondents are eclectics on the organizational experience scale; 18 percent are social forecasters. The combined scale gives us 18 percent pragmatists and 82 percent eclectics. The Communities plan, in short, is in the hands of people with elaborately structured personal attitudes not matched by organizational experiences consistent with their preferences. This finding reflects accurately the very real buffeting of national and group interests to which these officials are exposed routinely, and among which they try to chart a course. We now show how this eclecticism manifests itself in responses to specific questions.

By an overwhelming margin, the E.C. respondents failed to identify *any* undesirable implications of the continued introduction of technological innovations. They see themselves as representing the organization as such and the interests of industrial society as a whole. The target of their action is identified as the main international policy-making organs and specific national agencies having responsibility for science and technology. Again, this identification corresponds most accurately with the targets we would select if we were pragmatically and instrumentally motivated. Do the plans of specialists influence the perceptions of politicians with respect to links between scientific knowledge and policy? Half of the sample is doubtful; the other half believes that the organization's program has shown old issues to be no longer relevant, or demonstrated the existence of new issues.

Information, Planning, and Bargaining. A clear majority of respondents feels that the E.C.'s program *has* succeeded in showing the member governments that sectors of public policy are interconnected and demand comprehensive rather than ad hoc policy solutions. In other words, this positive assessment of the action program is offered *even though* most of the people making this judgment are not rationalists in their organizational experience or determinists in their personal beliefs. A further look at the range of comments we received underscores the detached sophistication of these officials, their capacity to separate short-

range from long-range features, their confidence in their manipulative abilities.

There was wide agreement that E.C. will be permitted to include in its program only sectors which national governments
consider appropriate for collective action. A "commitment to
priorities" means only that there happens to be a (temporary)
political consensus on computers, airplane engines, fusion
power, and pollution, not on major philosophical and moral
principles with respect to the role of science and technology in
the regional order.[19] All agreed that, whatever language might
have been used in resolutions and declarations, a sectoral emphasis would prevail in practice. Those who thought that governments had learned to link knowledge with action, however,
also thought that in the longer run the sectoral emphasis would
be pushed aside in favor of a holistic thrust. All agreed that the
program of collective solutions to environmental problems illustrates the high point of governmental learning. All agreed that
CREST was a huge improvement as a joint problem-solving technique over the previous institutional mechanisms, *because* it relies
on instructed officials with real responsibility instead of experts
speaking only for themselves; but some also felt that this solution
was late and marginal to evolving national policies. Moreover, a
large majority (69 percent) felt that it was *not* getting easier to
achieve new agreements on the role of science and technology in
collective policy-making, although they also welcomed the CREST
innovation. The paradox is explained by one respondent (a delegate):

> Governments clearly learned something from E.C. work on Euro-
> pean environmental and pollution issues, but the lesson could not
> become regional policy until after the Gaullist influence had been
> eliminated. PREST/COST corresponded to Gaullist preferences; CREST
> may well be an improvement. Also, the key to E.C. success may be in
> stressing specific issues and avoiding general definitions and com-
> prehensive solutions. The more elaborate, general, and unified the
> bundle of program proposals, the less disposed governments are to
> take them seriously, a lesson the Commission has yet to learn. Gen-
> eral solutions trigger more opposition from entrenched commercial
> and bureaucratic interests, no matter how well founded in science.
> There is no cumulative learning process. Things go easier when
> there is indifference and ignorance at the national level. The better
> informed people are, the more opposition develops, and things will
> get harder in the future.[20]

These very mixed projections of organizational experiences
are quite consistent with the kind of planning familiar to E.C.
officials. Our respondents divided half and half with respect to

objectives underlying their planning, between those who simply wish to raise living standards and others who subordinate planning to the achievement of political union in Europe. Very few felt planners can make politicians introduce coherence into their rival and clashing objectives by the use of formal models, scientific forecasting methods, and multivariate analysis using cost-benefit techniques. More thought that less formal methods have been successfully used to demonstrate to politicians which objectives can or cannot be attained simultaneously because of resource constraints. A strong minority (33 percent) felt that none of this is as effective in making decisions as is ordinary coalition-building based on bargaining. The more deterministically minded officials prefer formal methods; the eclectics point out that the Council of Ministers is incapable of understanding—or being persuaded—by the scientifically based techniques of analysis. Moreover, the fragile character of the consensus on technological questions means that the scope left for bargaining and coalition-building is quite restricted.

This detached cynicism is also reflected in the assessment of whether the availability of scientific information in E.C. decision-making has made it possible to resolve conflict more easily. The responses are as follows:[21]

Did not make conflict resolution easier	45.5 percent
Issue never arose	9.1
Conflict grew less intense	45.5
Conflict grew more intense	18.2
Factual character of information made for change	27.3
Normative impact of information made for change	36.4

There was general agreement that conflict had been moderated through factual information on environmental issues. There was also general agreement that the opposite was true on energy questions and the coordination of industrial and R & D policies in the aircraft, reactor, and computer industries. Here, facts had the effect of making the parties conscious of the commercial and management *losses and costs* they were likely to incur as a result of joint planning. The normative significance of the science and technology syndrome was mentioned only by the few pragmatists; they saw in the Paris Summit the affirmation by Pompidou, Brandt, and Heath that post-industrial society faced an entirely novel set of challenges.

How Influential Is Knowledge? Unlike the majority of the international programs analyzed in this study, the work of the European Communities speaks to issues which have percolated toward the top of the national and the regional agenda. Moreover, this political organization enjoys more legal power and a stronger mandate for action binding on its member states than any other program or organization we studied, regional or global. Therefore, the decisions made, postponed, and aborted reflect something serious, a commitment and an obligation to implement *if* something concrete is decided. We found, however, that there seems to be an inverse relationship between the potential to act meaningfully and organizational experiences which stress rationalism, consistency, and scientific-technological determinism. In short, the more powerful the organization, the more "political" its *modus operandi*. We doubt that this can be explained on the basis of Communities weakness in technical skills, good information, access to national and regional clusters of influential actors, public and private. Compared with other collective efforts, the E.C. is strong on all these dimensions. We think that the explanation is correctly sensed by the majority of E.C. officials who recognize that decisions on scientific and technological issues, being part of a nexus of core allocational choices, remain deeply embedded in a bargaining process in which the stakes for future national prosperity are very high indeed. Whether this bargaining process is now moving from the extreme of the confrontation of raw and immediate interests toward a more computational model of choosing remains a matter of disputed and varying perceptions.

The contrast can be illustrated in an imaginary dialog between officials conscious of such a movement and those who fail to see it. Each, obviously, carries a cognitive map which implies a particular regional "order." The map contains several components. Should sectors of action be considered separately and incrementally (nationally or regionally), or should they be combined in deliberately linked issues subordinated to a vision of the future? Should the separate perceptions of national needs be permitted full reign, or should they be subordinated to a regionally defined set of overarching priorities? Should the specialized knowledge of the scientists-technocrats be permitted fuller scope, or should bargaining among more-or-less informed politicians be accepted as the norm? Eclectic and pragmatist now compare their experiences.[22]

P: "Well, my dear colleague, we finally have a candid statement of the mess we are in. Did you see Mansholt's statement?[23] He puts it on the line. We can't go on just lowering tariffs, setting prices for hogs, and protecting the widows and orphans of migrant workers. Listen to this; he tells us what the real task ought to be:

What can we do as "Europeans" and what should we do to keep the machine from breaking down? The problems are so fundamental, so complex and so tightly linked that we should ask ourselves: is there really something to be done? Can Europe intervene? Isn't this a job for the whole world? . . .

If Europe does not follow a clear policy but remains at the mercy of events and fails to take the initiative I think the battle is lost, because, in my opinion, the U.S. does not have the necessary political power to guide the world toward a solution of this great problem. The U.S. is declining and it will be very difficult for us to keep it from foundering. . . .

To begin with, we should no longer orient our economic system toward the search for maximal growth, toward the maximization of the GNP. It could be suggested to replace GNP with "gross national utility". . . . It would be desirable to study in what way we could contribute to the installation of an economic system no longer based on maximal growth per capita. Therefore, we must stress the problems of planning, of fiscal policy, the distribution of raw materials and perhaps also of certain essential end products."[24]

E: "So what? Just more of the Club of Rome nonsense. So everything depends on everything else? How does that help us? Even if he is right, we can't persuade the Council of Ministers of this if all they're worried about is the rate of unemployment and keeping the lid on inflation until the next election. That's the trouble with you scientists. You think a little causal modeling is enough to persuade a politician."

P: "Yes, if it's done right. Say what you will, science is systematic and factual, a lot better as a way of choosing options than bargains made by politicians. We, together with our colleagues in the national ministries of education and research, and some private think-tanks, have been modeling technological innovation, economic growth, and various futures since 1969. We can show how much money will buy what kinds of benefits. We can also show which social costs will be generated. Our network of specialists can tell politicians how to think and thereby preempt their choices. That's why we commissioned Europe + 30, as an exercise to show how things are interconnected, to demonstrate how the values by which Europeans live will trigger trends over the next thirty years, and raise the question as to whether we want these trends or not."

E: "You really think that you can outflank industry and governments and the concrete interests they defend by marshaling scientific knowledge. Let me tell you a few homely truths. Sure, scientific knowledge can make governments choose a little more rationally because, in some sectors, you can demonstrate that certain options won't work. But that doesn't mean that science is superior to sorting out interests as a way of making a decision. How can I tell? Because we both know that there is no single instance in the history of the Communities in which conflict among governments was moderated or resolved by our introducing scientific information. On the contrary. Did EURATOM go down because of an absence of technical information, or because there was too much contradictory data which each government could use to defend its interests? We can get the ministers to agree only when we demonstrate that with a given budget you can do this or that, and sometimes a few things together. When they see the printout from your models they tune out."

P: "That's the trouble with you. You think only of surviving the next meeting of the Council of Ministers or of CREST. Are we building Europe, or do we standardize the wiring on toasters? When are you going to start thinking of the whole system as your target?"

E: "What system? Where do you find that governments, corporations, labor unions, or even planning agencies in our governments focus on a system? They focus on electronics, airplanes, computers, water pollution, and breeder reactors. Some of them, if they worry about fission, make a fuss over finding unconventional sources of energy. Many even agree that we ought to work harder on fusion. They stress single sectors of Communities action because they rightly see in this the way to compensate for what they cannot hope to accomplish by national R & D efforts alone. You can present all this in a plan which talks about the whole system of industrial society and its future. But as soon as the real work starts they will just take it apart again and treat things in terms of the sectors that interest them most."

P: "Then why did the Council accept our plan?"

E: "Because there was no real consensus on where European society ought to be thirty years from now, or twenty. Everybody except the Dutch and the Danes still just wants more technology and more economic growth. The Council took you seriously only after the energy crisis broke. The progress we made on protecting the environment came only piecemeal, as single nuisances got on people's nerves. Our comprehensive action plan on the environment was taken apart when the real work started."

P: "You're wrong. Maybe there is no consensus at the political level. But we are agreed, here, that what we have to do is make clear that the laws of nature put a limit on what politicians can opt for. We have to identify the most remote social and political

consequences that can be brought about by technological innovation. We have to help them get to a consensus on these things."

E: "If you do that you just scare them."

P: "Oh no. We are in the business of building Europe, right?"

E: "Yes. But we can't even get them to harmonize countercyclical policies."

P: "But we have a terrific opportunity right now. We succeeded in showing Pompidou, Brandt, and Heath that the future
of industrial society can be pretty dim. Now everybody is worked
up over oil, nuclear power, information technology, and pollution. If we pick out the right sectors of action, we can trigger a
process through which the politicians will be forced to confront
the whole system eventually. That's why it is so important to pick
your allies among the experts and present the information in
appropriate form."

E: "How can you get at the whole by picking a few parts?"

P: "Like this. You select for attention a few sectors on which
they all agree, for whatever reasons. The only thing these sectors
have in common is that they are linked to technology and to
economic growth, and that they cannot be dealt with adequately
through national action alone because of the benefits expected
from the common market. You then tie them in a package which
each government thinks can be exploited item by item. But they
are wrong. In a few years it will become clear that the items are
connected, and that you can't have the benefits of one without
joint action on the other. There is nothing automatic about this,
though. We have to help this along step by step. That's why it is so
important to set up our integrated information network and
data banks. The industrial policy implications, the social services
we'll need, and the economic coordination will become pretty
obvious then."

E: "Your scenario assumes that you can accelerate incremental
processes that are embedded in economic policy by feeding new
concerns into them. Eventually, the incremental activity will
stop, and you will be at a point at which policy has to be made for
all our member governments by linking together all sorts of
issues which they are in the habit of treating separately."

P: "Yes."

E: "Well, it won't work. At least, it won't work in such a way as
to give you a stronger legislative and executive authority in the
Communities, though possibly you will get more harmonization
of policy among the governments. Take CREST. Until this year we
never succeeded in getting issues linked with each other in the
way you suggest. We wanted them to consider technological in-

novation together with industrial development and energy issues and economic policy as a whole. We wanted them to stop considering each piecemeal and tie them together instead. We had a little success. PREST and COST refused to do the linking. CREST may yet do so, but if it doesn't, I am not willing to rock the boat even more by throwing science and technology into the bargaining when they can't even agree on the economic policies for which we have direct responsibility."

P: "But why not? We can show that these are crucial to economics."

E: "Because there is not even the minimum common denominator of agreement among our governments on the post-industrial issue package that you find on common market matters. This stuff has low visibility. If anything has to be sacrificed in some negotiating package, it is the science stuff. It goes first. Why? Because our industrialists are not so eager to share their trade secrets and coordinate their planning as long as they can get what they want from their national authorities."

P: "I guess you are right about that. That's the limit in building a new consensus. Still, I believe that we can gradually build a wider consensus by showing how the issues are all linked. Look where we are now as compared with 1970. We have a policy for the environment for the whole Communities, and an energy program. We can build on that in CREST, just because it represents the experts in governments with whom we have our special ties, to link the issues more tightly. We'll get there."

E: "Maybe. But not until the air gets a lot fouler, oil prices climb some more, or a breeder blows up. Until then I think we'll just muddle through some more."

DEVELOPED COUNTRY SCIENCE POLICY

From the relatively focused concerns of the European Communities, we now turn to international programs of a much more diffuse character. This set of scientists is concerned with making science applicable to the solution of problems besetting industrialized countries, as in the case of E.C., but *without* access to the legislative and executive means of implementation available in Brussels. In contrast to the E.C. pattern, these scientists are also deeply involved in making collective policy *for* science and technology, quite apart from using scientific methods and concepts in fashioning social and economic policies. In practice these two analytically different concerns tend to overlap because the same individuals are active on both questions. Our subsample is therefore an amalgam of three separate programs which share a concern with these issues. The bulk of our respondents is associated with the Organization for Economic Cooperation and Development (OECD), whose science program is analyzed further on at some length.[25] A much shorter description is devoted to the International Council of Scientific Unions (ICSU) and to the European Center on Nuclear Research (CERN), with which only three of our respondents are affiliated.[26] No description is given of two additional organizations from which we had respondents.[27]

Our analysis leads us to the conclusion that the decision-making characteristics of the programs are eclectic; they do not consistently follow any of the patterns associated with the world order models. On the other hand, the institutional characteristics are consistent with the pragmatic model. It follows that we cannot be very confident about predicting a clear line of future development for these organizations and their efforts at collaborative international action. Our lack of confidence is consistent with the fact that our respondents display a wide variety of incongruent perceptions concerning their work.

CERN and ICSU

CERN is devoted to the acquisition of a capability in basic nuclear research. It carries out high-energy physics experiments of research interest, unconcerned with their applications in technology. The raison d'être of the international laboratory is simple: The experiments and the equipment are too costly to be financed singly by the member nations. Hence they have merged their talents into a joint facility which is entirely financed from public funds. The operational details of CERN's program thus need not detain us, since they are not immediately related to the social use of knowledge. The activity is highly collaborative and even sequential. Its social relevance is marginal.

The same also tends to be true of ICSU, though things are changing. The council is the "peak organization" of seventeen international unions of physical, biological, earth, and mathematical scientists. Sixty-two states were "national members" through their academies of science in 1972. The role of national governments in decision-making, however, is sharply restricted, because the council's general committee contains representatives of all unions, whereas only eleven national academies of science are represented at any one time.[28] ICSU's central staff is confined to five elected officers and an appointed executive secretary. Until the council's charter was amended in 1972, its activities were clearly confined to the facilitation of research for its own sake; it constituted no more than a common framework to create a capability for ad hoc collaboration. Since 1972, however, there has been an overt commitment to subordinate research to the anticipation and control of unwanted side effects, at least in the physical realm. There has also been a more cautious commitment to attempt to make scientific research more relevant to the development needs of Third World countries. The shift in emphasis is illustrated by the beliefs of the two presidents who have served since 1972, Jean Coulomb and Harrison Brown.

It is the pure research function which concerns us in this chapter, since it serves the overwhelming majority of Western scientists affiliated with the council's work. Research applied to world environmental protection and to economic and social development will be taken up in the subsequent chapters. The aspects of the ICSU program included in the present discussion are confined to the research interests of the scientists active in member nations of OECD, who clearly dominate ICSU.[29]

What is the ICSU program? ICSU does not "do" research. It organizes commissions and working parties, in response to requests from member unions and academies, to plan and coordinate large research projects which call for joint efforts on the part of more than one national group in order to be successful. But the actual work is done by multinational consortia of institutes, unions, laboratories, and individuals. ICSU is also called on for expert advice on scientific questions by certain intergovernmental organizations, notably UNESCO, with which it has a close relationship. These organizations frequently make financial contributions to multinational research projects planned and coordinated by ICSU. Some of these projects are limited in duration, such as the International Year of the Quiet Sun, the International Indian Ocean Decade, and the International Geophysical Year. Others are more open-ended and relate directly and indirectly to larger programs mounted by intergovernmental organizations. These also tend to be more relevant to the environmental and developmental concerns added since 1972.[30] We take up these programs in the following chapters. Here we are concerned only with "pure research" interests and with certain statistical, monitoring, and data bank activities sponsored by ICSU in furtherance of pure research. Clearly, there is no question of an overarching organizational purpose here, other than to advance knowledge. These activities are not tied to any core international or national governmental programs. They are not intended to have a direct and visible impact on social policy; but they imply choices and alternatives in planning for science itself.

Science Policy in the OECD

The Organization for Economic Cooperation and Development, unlike the European Communities, lacks major operational capabilities and mandates. Its purpose is not to be instrumental in the introduction of a new economic or political order, but to be a communications link among its twenty-three member governments for the discussion and possible harmonization of national policies. OECD is not expected to make "decisions," but to recommend to member governments measures on which prior discussion has disclosed a consensus on a common need. Originally, this consensus was confined to economic questions: how to sustain optimal levels of national growth and how to fashion multilateral trade, monetary, and countercyclical policies to attain this aim. Additional items in the original consensus included the harmonization of foreign aid policies among the members and the operation of the European Nuclear Energy Agency. OECD continues to deal with these matters. However, the range of tasks has gradually been expanded to include more and more topics on the periphery of economics. Slowly, the organization's program has moved toward coping with the consequences of its original activities; this includes environmental concerns, education, housing, urban problems, industrial R & D, manpower training, social services, and, most recently, energy development and oil allocation measures. "Science policy," while clearly overlapping many of these topics, has come to be recognized as a distinct task area, because it is regarded as a means for attaining other objectives while also being thought of as a master concept for identifying and planning the contours of the future of industrial societies.

It would be a mistake to think of this nexus of recognized issues as a firm programmatic consensus. Because OECD lacks an operational mandate and does not make decisions binding the governments on most issues, its staff and experts are free to indulge in studies which are not directly tied to national policy.[31] A word about the institutional characteristics of OECD is necessary to explain this point. The supreme organ of OECD is the Council of Ministers, meeting at ministerial level. It also meets at the level of permanent representatives, and on these occasions it is chaired by the secretary-general. However, the nature of the ministries represented at any one council meeting is determined by the subject to be discussed: In this case, it is the ministers of science (or environment, education, and so forth) who attend. Below the Council, specialized committees composed of senior national civil servants seek to supervise the work of the secretariat: In this case, it is the Committee for Scientific and Technological Policy and the Environment Committee. They assemble three or four times a year and examine the program of the secretariat. The secretariat directorates of interest to us are "environment" and "scientific affairs," the latter headed for over a decade by Dr. Alexander King (until 1974). These directorates are of course subject to instructions from the secretary-general, the committee, and the Council, but in fact have considerable latitude to undertake studies and launch ideas on their own. In doing so, they are able to appoint consultants who serve exclusively in their individual capacities and expert committees made up of representatives of national bureaucracies.[32]

What, then, is OECD's science policy program? We use the 1971 guidelines for defining the focus:

> Expansion of research, development and innovation *to meet social needs*, such as environmental quality, health, education and urban development;

> continued stimulation of technological innovation in the economy to achieve *qualitative* as well as quantitative growth;

> more effective *management* and *control* of technology in the public interest.[33]

To attain these objectives the Committee for Scientific and Technological Policy was instructed to promote the exchange of information among member countries, to launch new studies to assist in the formulation of new policies for science and technology, and to promote multilateral efforts to improve coordination of international research. However, the ministers of science also noted that "it is of growing importance to harmonize national efforts, as distinct from the creation of centralized international institutions."[34]

Before commenting further on this program and its effectiveness, we must explore the working methods of OECD in greater detail. If a "program" lacks a permanent consensus and focus, and if it is not binding on the members, in what way can it be considered authoritative? The typical sequence of events, though far from inviolable, runs something like this. The initiative for reexamining, and hopefully redirecting, the ongoing policies of member governments comes from the directorate in the secretariat.[35] Under Dr. King, the Directorate for Scientific Affairs prided itself on being a "look-out institution," an advance warning system which seeks to identify and explicate problems facing industrial societies but which are not yet on any public agenda. Occasionally, the secretariat launches such an initiative after being prodded by a national delegation; France and Sweden played such a role on occasion. Having decided that something new should be done, the secretariat appoints an outside consultant and/or a group of private experts to do a "study" on the problem. If national or collective action is contemplated in the near future, such committees of experts tend to be composed of representatives of national bureaucracies. Throughout this procedure, the Committee for Scientific and Technological Policy is kept informed, and diffuse support for the studies is given, even though this committee rarely asserts any initiative or control over the secretariat. Once the studies are completed, a meeting of the Council (usually at ministerial level) is convened. A mandate for the harmonization of national policies, or for a collective policy, is then extracted from the representatives of the governments and a "work program" or an "action plan" becomes official. After that point, the permanent committees of experts are called on to inform the secretariat of the extent to which actual harmonization is proceeding, what problems are being encountered, and what new remedial steps might be called for.

If the program takes hold, the secretariat will seek to routinize review and implementation by means of the "confrontation procedure." This involves the periodic examination of national policy and programs under OECD auspices. With the consent of the government in question, a group of "examiners" is appointed by the secretariat. These people serve as uninstructed experts to look into national policies, basing their study on a prior report dealing with that country, compiled by the secretariat. When they complete their investigation, they, together with the secretariat staff, will "confront" the national officials responsible for the programs being investigated and make suggestions for reform or improved performance. The permanent representative of the country being "confronted" will be present at the meeting, but the chairmanship is assumed by the permanent representative of another state. A successfully routinized program will then recommence the same cycle as new issues come to the fore and new studies will be completed.[36] No consensus is final, and the process never ends.

Since 1971, the emphasis has been placed squarely on making science and technology useful to meeting social needs. But it was not always so. At the first OECD ministerial conference of ministers of science (1963), the emphasis was put equally squarely on economic growth, on planning efficient resource allocation at the national level, with international cooperation only in areas which seemed to require a pooling of personnel and costly equipment. The same theme was endorsed at the second conference (1966), with explicit attention to the links between technological innovation and economic progress. The job then was to overcome the "technology gap" between Europe and the United States. The emphasis changed at the third conference (1968). In 1966 national action alone had been demanded; now joint measures were proposed, particularly in the information technology and computer sector. Moreover, the third conference came to grips with the relationship between fundamental research and applied technology and social development. Since innovation was desirable, special efforts had to be made in the field of education to produce appropriate skills. Reforms had to be instituted in higher education and in the funding of research in order more effectively to innovate. The interest of OECD in research and information management stems from that time, both with respect to stimulating appropriate national reforms and to complementing them with international action where needed.

The interest in research, information, and information management was retained at the fourth conference (1971), but it was here linked to the problems of post-industrial society: The task now became to manage technological innovation and basic research so as to improve the quality of life, particularly with respect to education, health, urban decay, transportation, and environmental protection. Technology assessment now became a key activity. Although the core themes overlapped from conference to conference, the focus shifted appreciably each time. Thus, new knowledge was deliberately sought, and new objectives suddenly were added to old ones. This could be considered a case of collective learning, but such an interpretation seems farfetched if we recall that efforts at implementation remained sporadic and that a certain faddism dominated the discussions each time. The special studies done to provide the new foci did little to diminish this sense of the episodic.

At the 1975 ministerial meetings, the leading theme was "science and technology in the management of complex problems." Science and technology, if only pursued more systematically and energetically, were once more praised as the cornucopia of knowledge necessary to assure a higher standard of living and a better quality of life. The ministers "called on" the member countries (that is, on themselves) to intensify all the activities recommended at previous meetings. But two major new themes were superimposed on the familiar ones: the need for public involvement, and the call for new patterns of extra-OECD international cooperation in the field of natural resources.

Having in mind, one suspects, recent European popular protests against nuclear power plants and other high technology, the ministers "expressed the wish that the OECD should review the experiences of member countries regarding public participation in science and technology. It was hoped that this initiative would materially *assist member governments to devise effective means of informing the public* of the implications of new technological developments, soliciting their reactions, and engaging them in the decision-making process."[37] The ministers also "agreed on the necessity" to alter and intensify the mode of technology transfer to developing countries, but they only invited further study of how this might be done. They committed themselves to "the urgent need for a better husbanding of the world's natural resources," but they merely suggested intensified international cooperation, bilateral as well as multilateral.[38]

The OECD Program. What is the idea of "science policy"? The secretary-general appointed a group of experts under the chairmanship of Harvey Brooks in 1969 to make suggestions to OECD on how to adapt scientific research and innovation to a society in which both economic growth and "scientific progress" were increasingly subjected to doubt and attack. The experts were asked to make science safe for society as well as safeguard science from society's wrath. The result was a set of recommendations designed to subordinate applied science and technological innovation at the national level to systematic social goals and to adapt government planning machinery to the implementation of such goals. Internationally, more basic social science research into the causal linkages among environmental degradation, economic growth, social discontent, and education were to be launched and joint efforts at technology assessment were to be strengthened. International social indicators were to be worked out. Basic science was to be strengthened financially and left to its own devices after that. "Science policy" became somewhat of a magic wand for doing everything more rationally and systematically. The fad soon passed, and what evolved in its wake is an ill-defined and overlapping set of efforts at harmonizing national practices. What are they?

1. *Improving national R & D capabilities.* While the dangers of unplanned growth are more appreciated, the publication of the Brooks report obviously does not mean an end to industrial innovation. On the contrary, such innovation is to be accelerated in the areas of acute social need, channeled, made safe for the quality of life, but not stopped. Hence OECD is undertaking systematic surveys of national R & D planning practices and priorities. Which sectors are favored and which needs ignored? In addition, inquiries are being launched into the planning methods employed by governments, their efficiency and their gaps. How, in essence, are governments using scientific methods in planning? Finally, the art of technology assessment is to be furthered by appropriate studies and publications in order to provide the improved national R & D planning institutions with the capability of forecasting wanted and unwanted side effects.[39]

2. *Improving national research systems.* True to the recognition that higher education and its funding are directly tied to the rate of social innovation, the OECD continues to inquire into the functioning of the research systems of its member states. Studies and discussions are conducted in how research is organized and financed, who sets goals and priorities. There is particular interest in ascertaining how the social sciences are used (or ignored), and how they may be better employed. In addition, special sectoral programs are featured in the field of materials science to aid in the modernization of specific industries held to be crucial for environmental reasons, for transportation, and for halting urban decay. These programs are a continuation of efforts started in the 1960s when the objective was to bridge the technology gap, an aim which is no longer stressed.[40]

3. *Improving information systems.* The information industry—at the public and the private levels—is of particular interest to member states and the secretariat. Studies are being made of the kinds of data banks to be created, on their use and their possible abuse in terms of violations of privacy. Efforts are also devoted to familiarizing potential consumers of data retrieval systems in government agencies with the benefits of this technology. Finally, the wider use of computers is linked by OECD to the automation of management systems used by governments, and therefore to public sector planning in general.

4. *Environmental protection.* Efforts to promote joint measures for protecting the environment differ from the programs just described because they may include binding commitments by

member states, or at least a commitment to continuing joint study of problems and harmonizing national measures for their solution. In other words, in the environmental field OECD has something approaching an action program in a more literal sense, even though this program overlaps heavily with similar activities of the European Communities which have the effect of legally binding the nine member countries of E.C. who also belong to OECD.

OECD commitment to environmental protection measures was institutionalized in 1970 following ten years of technical studies of pollution in various sectors of the economy. In that year the Council authorized a program

> to investigate the problems of preserving or improving man's environment with particular reference to their economic and trade implications;
> to review and confront actions taken or proposed in member countries in the field of environment together with their economic and trade implications;
> to propose solutions for environmental problems that would as far as possible take account of all relevant factors, including cost effectiveness;
> to ensure that the results of environmental investigations can be effectively utilized in the wider framework of the Organization's work on economic policy and social development.[41]

While the emphasis is on study, review, confrontation, and proposal, the effort is clearly to be part of a holistic perspective of the totality of economic and social life, in marked contrast to the sector-specific economic approach of the earlier European Communities program. The most recent authoritative mandate on environmental matters was issued by the ministerial meeting on the environment of November 1974. The ministers recommended that (1) governments continue to study and review the deleterious effects of chemicals prior to their being manufactured and marketed; (2) governments institute technology assessment procedures for evaluating the unwanted environmental consequences of all significant public and private projects; (3) governments issue noise emission standards; (4) governments plan urban transportation systems in such a way as to ease urban congestion; governments take measures to reduce emissions into the air of sulphur oxides, nitrogen oxides, and hydrocarbons and to institute appropriate monitoring systems; (5) governments take measures to control water eutrophication, especially on international waterways. These recommendations are sector specific. In addition, however, the ministers adopted two rec-

ommendations which address the economy as a whole. In view of
the increasing importance of energy policy and energy planning, the governments were asked to integrate environmental
considerations into their plans for energy, including conservation, new operating procedures for power plants, and public
environmental impact discussions prior to the installation of new
equipment. Finally, the ministers *affirmed* that "the Polluter-
Pays-Principle constitutes for Member countries a fundamental
principle for allocating costs of pollution prevention and control
measures introduced by the public authorities in Member countries."[42] All recommendations were qualified by phrases admit-
ting the continuing importance of economic growth and the
maximization of social welfare as well as the necessity of taking
costs into account. In all cases, the OECD was asked to report on
the progress made by member governments in implementing
the recommendations.

What has actually been done? Member governments voluntarily notify one another of anti-pollution measures they are con-
templating and discuss complaints of a government which feels
that a given measure tends to affect its exports adversely. The
"early warning system," in short, is a consultative procedure for
minimizing the trade costs of anti-pollution measures, not a system for improving environmental protection. Since the uncoordinated introduction of controls may have serious trade consequences for several members, this provides some incentive for
harmonizing national legislation. So far, this has been done only
for products using PCB's, for which an OECD-wide set of regulations was adopted. Efforts to use this incentive to standardize
air and water quality standards through emission controls have
so far failed, because of the deleterious trade consequences anticipated by several governments or by significant national industries such as automobile firms. A group of economic experts
has worked out a set of analytic methods to evaluate the
economic consequences of pollution controls and applies them
to specific sectors of the economy. It also has worked out the
Polluter Pays Principle. Its approach is essentially based on the
application of cost-benefit calculations to systematic measurement of pollution control costs.[43]

While no overall mandatory regulations have come out of the
environmental effort (except in the case of chemicals), the process of study by the secretariat, soliciting proposals from experts
and consultants, holding seminars with national officials and
seeking to persuade them to accept the secretariat's recommen-

dations, are continuing. The fact that in 1974 the ministers managed merely to recommend some very general, and not necessarily standardized or uniform, guidelines to their governments does not suggest that the acts of persuasion were very successful.

5. *OECD and the New International Economic Order.* A program launched by OECD in 1976 may presage an unprecedented effort at linking economics, trade, technology, and environmental concerns with the desire of some member states to take steps toward inaugurating the New International Economic Order demanded by the developing countries. The secretariat, following an initiative of the Japanese government, succeeded in persuading the Council of Ministers to approve a three-year research project on "the future development of advanced industrial societies in harmony with that of developing countries." The description of the project stresses the interdependencies between prosperity and growth in the First and Third Worlds and notes that these have not been systematically considered by governments. While emphasis is to be placed on economic factors, industrial, technological, environmental, agricultural, demographic, and sociocultural aspects are to be included in order to enable governments to plan beyond the short-range span to which they are accustomed. Four separate assessments are envisaged: relationships among industrialized countries; relationships between industrialized and developing countries; physical constraints on growth (energy, raw materials, environmental concerns); the evolution of international economic structures and institutions (market forces, multinational corporations, management strategies for common property resources).[44]

While the intent is conceptually holistic, the institutional and decision-making features associated with it leave unclear whether the commitment meets the requisite of the skeptic or the pragmatic model. Financing is based on voluntary governmental and private contributions. By no means do all member states evince equal interest. Research is to be coordinated with what is already being done by private agencies at the national level. Direction will be given by a steering committee consisting of representatives of the participating governments, even though the research will be done by scholars engaged by the secretariat. Progress will be evaluated by means of the OECD "confrontation procedure," as well as by the customary system of outside panels. In short, the approach does not guarantee an impact on policy any more than do other and similar aspects of the OECD's program.

How Influential Is OECD? There is evidently a very wide gap between holistic professions of intention and the implementation of programs. Ten years ago, OECD was committed to increasing the utilization and effectiveness of specific technologies considered vital to economic growth. So was the E.C. Today both are persuaded that the purpose of their science and technology programs is to anticipate and control unwanted side effects of technology *so as to deal with these* in the context of employment, trade, family life, urban quality, and even social harmony and change. Whether all of the member governments share this commitment, however, is a different question.

We have evidence from officials, advisers, and delegates that some member governments react very differently to the program. Most advisers feel that they have been successful in demonstrating to most governments the increasingly complex linkage of scientific, technological, and economic issues. Delegates from smaller industrial countries (for example, Belgium, Sweden, and Holland) maintain that they find the OECD program useful because it supports the policy initiatives taken by some groups at the national level, and compensates for shortages of skilled personnel available nationally. This view is not shared by delegates from the larger industrial countries, who consider the value of the OECD programs to be marginal. OECD officials share this impression, but add that their programs are taken most seriously in partially industrialized countries such as Austria and Spain now becoming aware of the linkage of issues implied in a "science policy." The impacts of the program are not experienced in the same way in all sectors. Computer and information technology specialists feel that their impact has been great. Environment specialists and technology assessment personnel are bitterly disappointed with their impact. One OECD official felt that collective decision-making was getting simpler when technology assessment and environmental protection first became major questions of public policy, only to realize later that these were apparently temporary expressions of concern which did not lead to a lastingly holistic conception of the links among sectors of policy. Governments lost interest quite soon. The overall impression is that with the introduction of scientifically validated data and methods of analysis, decision-making among government officials becomes *more difficult* as the costs of the decisions become more apparent.

The same conclusion emerges when we examine the implementation of some of the major science policy studies endorsed by the OECD. The Brooks Report was taken seriously in very few member countries as far as the reform of governmental science planning machinery was concerned. Only in Holland and Sweden could effects be pinned down, and then only because there was a preexisting disposition to do the things the report recommended. The Japanese liked the tone of the report but did not dramatically change their administrative procedures as a result. France, Britain, and the United States ignored it. Data released by the Directorate for Scientific Affairs on social and quality-of-life objectives in R & D planning confirm this impression. Even though OECD programs were, after 1971, to foster such a reemphasis, the study shows that government funding practices as of 1972 had not changed much, despite the availability of a set of OECD-devised social indicators for measuring and assessing shifts:

> To date there has been very little research on the social objectives and what there was concentrated on the technological factors. . . . The main characteristics of R & D for these objectives were fragmentation of responsibility, absence of major programmes and low "R & D intensity." . . . Until such time as governments reform their administrative structure to give greater coherence and political weight to social needs, this fragmentation will probably remain. . . . With the possible exception of health, there are as yet no major R & D programmes for the new objectives of comparable size to those financed for defense, nuclear energy or even civil aviation or computers. . . . To date the major programmes have all been in "high technology" areas and such programmes may not be the answer to social needs. . . .[45]

The final piece of evidence comes from a close textual analysis of the declarations of the first four ministerial conferences on science policy. We compared the strength of the predicates used to link the major sectors of policy to be considered together in the future. We also counted the number of such sectors in order to get an impression of the "complexity of the universe" requiring policy coordination as it evolved in the minds of the ministers concerned. We found that the primary or core theme addressed by each conference does indeed become more complex in the sense that more ancillary themes are added to the original emphasis. However, the strength of the predicates linking the themes declines over time. Instead of saying that A demands B, or that B is necessary to achieve A, more elusive phrases, such as B is desirable for A, become more prominent. Moreover, the particular acts of international cooperation or joint action called for also decline over time, with increasing emphasis being put on appropriate actions on the part of national governments aided by OECD studies.[46]

We can now summarize why the decision-making characteristics of the OECD's program of science for developed societies are highly eclectic according to our typology. Certainly, the organization is animated by a commitment to the deliberate search for new knowledge, perhaps more so than any other international effort. The commitment, however, is typical of the secretariat and its associated panels of experts, rather than of the governmental delegations. The mode of learning which prevails in the secretariat is formal-rational; it stresses cost-benefit analyses of environmental, R & D, and educational policy questions; it relies on computer models and simulations; it features the dissemination and standardized use of these techniques in the member countries. Nevertheless, the goals of OECD do *not* reflect the pragmatic and rational thrusts of the learning and knowledge patterns of the staff. Goals are volatile. Economic objectives of old standing remain always in the foreground of activity. Social issues associated with highly developed industrialism gain prominence and fade into obscurity with bewildering rapidity. They do not seem to leave a permanently visible imprint on the goal structure of OECD. To be sure, there is increasing activity on environmental, energy, quality of life, and industrial innovation questions without, however, it resulting in an agreed view of the future or a coherent set of priorities. Goals, therefore, are *not* periodically refocused in line with learning patterns, thus resembling the helter-skelter process of goal expansion we associate with the skeptic model. Bargaining among the governments proceeds on an item-by-item basis. There is no package-dealing. Issues are not linked. The process resembles a constant-sum game (sometimes a zero-sum game) based on variable minimum winning coalitions which do not offer side payments to their negotiating partners.[47]

The institutional characteristics of the OECD program nevertheless meet the requirements of the pragmatic model. The overriding purpose of the program is clearly the maintenance of an industrial and innovative capability which has existed for a long time. Additionally, the activities in the environmental and R & D fields are clearly aimed at coping with consequences of industrialism which were found to be undesirable, either in their physical or social effects. The instrumentalities adopted for achieving these purposes approximate what we call a "joint facility"; in addition to calling for the standardization of routines of collecting and sharing information, OECD actively seeks to persuade member countries to harmonize their policies so that, whatever specific measures a government may adopt, the commonly defined targets of action may be attained. This applies to environmental regulation, investment in R & D, institutions for fashioning a coherent science policy, energy conservation and innovation, and urban policy. On the other hand, the *modus operandi* of IEA is closer to that of a common framework than to a joint facility. The resulting division of labor among the governments, and between the governments and the OECD, however, remains very loose. It calls for pooling rather than sequencing, for sharing information rather than for re-arranging the timing of decisions. The institutional nexus meets the criteria of successive efforts at centralization followed by splitting tasks into segments and spawning new institutions with specific mandates. It also conforms to the pragmatic pattern in that it features the uneasy coexistence of governmental representatives wielding ultimate authority with groups of experts and secretariat departments exercising considerable influence —and enjoying some autonomy—because of their specialized knowledge.

Perceptions of Actors in All Science Policy Programs[48]

Given the diversity of programs and institutions, it is not surprising that the attitudes of our respondents with respect to the character of knowledge and its use in policy-making are quite as varied. Eighteen percent are determinists and 24 percent skeptics. Instrumentalists and eclectics account for about 30 percent each. Their reflections on their organizational and program experiences result in an equally scattered breakdown:

Deterministic planners	40.0%
Social forecasters	6.7
Physical controllers	33.3
Random appliers	6.7
Eclectics	13.3

The combined typologies then give us a strong minority of rationalists (33.3 percent) and a plurality of eclectics (40.0 percent); pragmatists and skeptics account for 13 percent each. Unlike the distribution of attitudes and experiences in the European Communities, where the clustering into two poles tended toward nondeterministic combination of perceptions, the two dominant clusters here occur at opposite ends of the continuum: A strong minority of planners-rationalists-determinists faces a majority of complete eclectics and appliers of knowledge. Eclectic, in a world order dialog, would have to face rationalist, not pragmatist.

With what kinds of clienteles do these people identify? Over a quarter feels they represent nobody; another quarter identifies with the home country. Twenty percent each identify with mankind and their professional disciplines, respectively. The rest are scattered. Their commitment to holistic organizational goals in the use of science is startling: Well over half identifies comprehensive international planning and overarching ecological objectives as their programmatic aims. Are they successful in influencing politicians? Very few report negative experiences. Over two-thirds thinks that they succeeded in showing politicians how fields of action are linked in terms of a comprehensive and overarching logic, or at least demonstrated pragmatically how fields of action must be joined. And two-thirds also identifies national governments and specific national agencies as the proper target of their efforts, while also pointing to international conferences and secretariats as groups to be influenced.

Do they see themselves as successful in demonstrating to national governments how fields of action ought to be linked in policy-making? Half of them do, a lesser percentage than their colleagues in the European Communities. The same contrast in perception between the two groups emerges in their use of scientific methods and assumptions in planning. The European Communities people all feel that this poses a real issue; several of the science policy respondents state the issue never arises! Most of the European Communities group felt that rough cost-benefit demonstrations, together with bargaining, can be used effectively in planning international programs; the science policy group opts more heavily for formal models and careful demonstrations based on good data.

The conclusion is inescapable: Eclectics expect little and thus can live with their programmatic disappointments; rationalists have a harder time of it. Their belief in methods and principles capable of circumventing political bargaining and short-term calculations of advantage, even though often translated into specific programs, nevertheless falls short of rapidly and visibly altering the practices of national and international bureaucracies, as many admit. On the other hand, rationalists can find a more congenial home in organizations which do not have many operational powers and which are conceded to be think-tanks rather than regulatory or planning agencies. No wonder that

OECD is more hospitable to dissatisfied rationalists, and the E.C. remains the laboratory of pragmatic and eclectic activists who have learned to live with incorrigible politicians. We can add to our imaginary dialog by letting Rationalist express his views. Rationalist is an adviser to OECD; he faces Eclectic, an official of OECD.[49]

R: "I tell you, you fellows give in too easily. We do one report after another for you. Each time we lay it on the line. The carrying capacity of the biosphere is limited, and we *know* what the limits are; the internal combustion engine is the main threat; we have to have uniform emission standards now. Do you want us all to choke? So what if VW and Renault don't like it? Science is not the servant of industry."

E: "We had to give in. Once you scientists demonstrated so scientifically to the government officials how much it would cost in new equipment, you made them realize that environmental protection and R & D to achieve it will mean that somebody will sell fewer cars. Once they saw they really had a choice only between no standards or uniform standards—given our commitment to not distorting trade—they went for the Polluter-Pays idea as a way of equalizing the costs, while leaving so many loopholes as to commit them to nothing for the moment."

R: "Well, does it have to be that way? I believe that science is better than political bargaining; it is systematic, neutral, and factual. Politics is just jockeying for momentary advantage. I believe that science should be used systematically to educate politicians on the right way to make policy. I take you seriously when you say that OECD is a shop which seeks to anticipate unwanted consequences of technology and work for a better society. And I expect you to take seriously what I find and recommend to you. If you did, you would find that gradually your politicians would change their minds and go along. Remember that fellow who did a causal model of the innovation process in the petrochemical industry? . . ."

E: "Sure, I remember him. I commissioned the study. You know what happened, too. Nobody could understand the model except the fellows from the multinationals. They picked it to pieces because this or that variable was missing and some others were not estimated correctly. By the time the committee got through listening, they told us to go back and make some more studies. And you got another contract."

R: "And I did the work, and you still have no agreement from your politicians."

E: "That's right, and you know why, too. For every scientist I hire I get a different scientific conclusion. If you fellows are so cocksure of your methods, why is it that your forecasts are so far apart? Of course we have to bargain, because there is nothing else left to do after the politicians realize that the education you provide leaves all the most important questions unanswered. They still have to choose among alternatives, and your methods don't seem to make it easier. All you do is to make the costs evident to them. And who are you anyway? Prometheus Unbound, to proclaim the truth to one and all? There is no international community of science, just as there is no international community of man. There are good and bad interests, always in conflict. And you scientists pick your side and decide which interest to further with your objectivity and your superior knowledge. The only thing I hope for from all this is that enough of the truth does seep through this fighting and bargaining to narrow the range of options at the end. That's the only reason I work with you."

Notes

---

1. *Bulletin of the European Communities,* supp. 14/73, "Scientific and Technological Policy Programme," p. 7 (hereafter cited as *Bulletin*). This is the Commission's text submitted to the Council on January 14, 1974. For a general summary of the Communities' nuclear energy programs, see Jean Touscoz, *La Coopération scientifique internationale* (Paris: Editions Techniques et Economiques, 1973), pp. 203–46, and "Colloque sur la politique technologique de la Communauté Européenne," special issue of *Revue du Marche Commun* 153 (April 1972).

2. The plan was drawn up by the Commission's Directorate-General for Science, Technology, and Education and the cabinet of Commissioner Ralf Dahrendorf, in consultation with many expert committees. This version of the plan was a substitute for an earlier proposal prepared in the cabinet of Commissioner Altiero Spinelli, which was not taken up by the Council of Ministers. See *Bulletin,* supp. June 1972, "Objectifs et moyens pour une politique commune de la recherche scientifique et du développement technologique," transmitted to the Council on June 14, 1972. The two proposals differed with respect to the extent of centralism and sociotechnological holism which inspired them. The Spinelli proposal had the backing of the governments of Italy, Belgium, and the Netherlands. It stressed the organic links among the various technologies and branches of knowledge, and it favored a centralized approach to making decisions about these matters, focusing on E.C. institutions. This approach was opposed by Britain, France, and Germany, who favored the Dahrendorf proposal because it seemed to permit separate decisions by sectors, left open the question of what would be financed and managed nationally, and put the Communities in the position of coordinator rather than ruler. Those who backed the Spinelli proposal were looking for collective measures to make up for what they considered their lack of national capability; France and Germany simply sought to supplement by collective means what they could do less well nationally, without having to give up such natural advantages as they thought they possessed.

3. The history of this evolution is presented and analyzed by Henry R. Nau in "Collective Responses to R & D Problems in Western Europe," *International Organization*, summer 1975.

4. *Bulletin*, February 1976, p. 44, and *Agence Europe*, November 22, 1975, p. 8; January 29, 1976, p. 6; and February 4, 1976, p. 9.

5. *Bulletin*, October 1975, p. 44, and *Agence Europe*, February 4, 1976, p. 9.

6. For an account of the vicissitudes of the EURATOM program, see Henry R. Nau, *National Politics and International Technology* (Baltimore: Johns Hopkins University Press, 1974). The foundation groups the national academies of science of fifteen European countries, including the nine of the Communities.

7. Ernst B. Haas, *The Obsolescence of Regional Integration Theory* (Berkeley: Institute of International Studies, 1975), pp. 44–50.

8. PPP emerges as something less than a firm institutional device, suggesting that much ambiguity will dominate the application of E.C. environmental protection policy. The principle is merely a "resolution"—not a directive or a regulation. Moreover, the form of management adopted by the Council continues to permit a great deal of national diversity. Exceptions to PPP can be legitimated by claims that the uniform application of the formula will cause special problems to certain industries, regions, or social groups. State subsidies and tax breaks, therefore, continue to be acceptable. These exceptions were spelled out by the Commission in December 1974 in the form of a sliding scale of permissible subsidization—to become illegal after 1980. Ibid., p. 49.

9. The Commission contributed 19,160,000 u.a. for a five-year indirect program, the aim of which is a joint management plan to deal with the mounting quantities of radioactive waste. The program is to solve certain problems arising from the processing, storage, and disposal of medium- and high-activity waste and from the separation and recycling of long-life waste. It is also to define an overall legal, administrative, and financial framework for the management and storage of waste, and to lay down a first set of guiding principles. *Bulletin*, June 1975, pp. 48–9.

10. *Bulletin*, March 1976, pp. 17–19, and *Bulletin*, supp. June 1976, "Environment Programme: 1977–1981."

11. In February 1975, this concerted action was extended to include deliberations within the IEA meetings, except when the Nine fail to reach a joint position; at such a time, the Eight who were members of the IEA were free to resume their independent maneuvering. *Agence Europe*, February 15, 1975, p. 6, and *Bulletin*, February 1975, pp. 14–17, 46–7.

12. The target figures and the policy measures designed to attain them are given in *Bulletin*, May 1974, "Energy for Europe: Research and Development," April 5, 1974. See also *Bulletin*, November 1974, pp. 27–9, 64–8; *Eighth General Report*, pp. 190–3; and *Agence Europe*, December 18, 1974, pp. 4–5. For details regarding the debates and proposals relating to the hydrocarbon industry, the coal industry, and the electricity industry, refer to *Bulletin*, November 1974, pp. 69–71, and December 1974, pp. 14–17, 65–6; and *Agence Europe*, December 16–17, 1974, p. 5.

13. *Agence Europe*, March 5, 1975, p. 6. Also see *Bulletin*, January 1976, pp. 9–12; and *Agence Europe*, March 20, 1976, p. 4, and March 24, 1976, pp. 4–6. Germany altered this "fifth principle" in such a way that no mention was made of development actions directly or indirectly benefiting all countries concerned. This was clearly related to the issue of coal. Germany stressed—using the example of indigenous coal—that if a country develops such sources and markets them, it diminishes the demand for energy on the market and thus benefits the other member states.

14. *Agence Europe*, December 21, 1974, p. 8; *Bulletin*, October 1975, pp. 13–14; and *Bulletin*, supp. November 1975, "Action Programme for the Aeronautical Sector."

15. *Eighth General Report*, pp. 141–3.

16. *Bulletin*, June 1974, p. 55, and February 1975, pp. 18–20.

17. The project was under the direction of Lord Kennet and used research centers in Heidelberg, Milan, Paris, and the University of Sussex. *Eighth General Report*, p. 180.

18. Thirteen respondents make up this subsample. Eight are E.C. officials, four are national delegates to E.C. (and some to OECD), and one is an OECD official with responsibilities similar to those of the E.C. officials.

19. However, the Belgian and Italian delegates pointed out that the OECD's work on these issues *had* influenced their governments to consider such linkages. Contrast this to the opinion expressed by the OECD official in this program, who felt that no cumulative impact had been scored on national governments because there was no generally accepted model of industrial innovation and economic growth. If there were such a model, international programs could influence national policy, he thought.

20. Another delegate noted that while things in general will not get easier, his country will benefit from CREST simply because the total size of the pie to be carved up will be larger—let the pie be justified with holistic argument and centralized decision-making organs; as long as the national sectoral programs to be supported gain access, this is a secondary matter. Still another delegate thought that decisions will become easier because the CREST formula means that the ambition of the Commission has been cut down to size. Many Commission officials, who also think that it will become more difficult to make decisions in the realm of collective R & D choices, accept this reading of the future. A minority of Commission officials (those associated with the Dahrendorf plan) feels that decisions will become easier in the future because of centralized management of information, models, and projections through "Europe + 30" and CIDST.

21. Since the question could appropriately be answered differentially for various sectors of action and since we were interested primarily in obtaining concrete instances of our respondents' experience with these issues, multiple answers were possible

22. The dialog is imaginary, but the opinions expressed are not. Each "speaker" is a composite of several respondents. "Pragmatist" speaks for Commission personnel identified with the elaboration of the Dahrendorf plan; "Eclectic" speaks for national delegates, a high Commission official with general responsibilities, and several Commission officials responsible for economic and industrial policy.

23. The "Mansholt letter" suggested reorganizing the E.C. program so as to tackle head-on the issues of population growth, exhaustion of natural resources, environmental degradation, and food shortages. It was directly inspired by the Forrester and Meadows models, and for the first time introduced into E.C. discussions the notions of controlled economic growth, closed-circuit production processes, and the systematic improvement of the quality of life. The letter was dated February 9, 1972, addressed to the E.C. Commission, of which Mansholt was then a vice-president. We translated appropriate passages from the text given in Commission document SEC (72) 596/2, entitled "Note à l'attention de MM. les Directeurs Généraux," April 17, 1972. Even though the Mansholt initiative was endorsed by Commissioners Spinelli and Barre, the Commission as a whole did not take action on it. The Dahrendorf plan, however, is consistent with the proposals.

24. In the discussions which followed the Mansholt initiative and the subsequent preparation of the Dahrendorf plan, close contact apparently existed between the Commission and the Club of Rome.

25. Our OECD respondents included four advisers, five officials, and three delegates. All were associated with the Directorates for Scientific Affairs and Environment. This group also includes one UNESCO official with responsibility for mathematical modeling of industrial societies.

26. Two officials of ICSU, an adviser to CERN. On CERN, see Touscoz, *Coopération*, pp. 190–202, and Robert Jungk, *Le CERN: Une Internationale de savants* (Paris: Le Seuil, 1968).

27. One adviser to the Conference Committee on Disarmament and one to NATO.

28. National academies of science have varying degrees of subordination to their governments. Such subordination is minimal in most Western countries, but it is considerable in the socialist bloc. The situation in most Latin American, Asian, and African nations varies greatly from time to time and from place to place, though the linkage is tightest in countries with a consistent commitment to development planning.

29. We identified the Western-industrial impact on ICSU by determining the national and institutional attributes of the 832 individuals who served on all committees associated with ICSU, as well as the officers and committee members of the scientific unions which belong to ICSU. We used the year 1972 and relied on the information given in International Council of Scientific Unions, *Yearbook 1973*. The results are as follows:

Nationals of:
OECD member countries	661	(79.4%)
Eastern Europe	117	(14.1%)
Latin America	23	(2.8%) (mostly from Argentina)
North Africa/Middle East	4	(0.5%)
Africa	5	(0.6%)
South/Southeast Asia	19	(2.3%) (almost all Indian)
Far East (other than Japan)	2	(0.3%)

The fifty-five presidents and secretaries-general of these organisms were distributed as follows:

Nationals of:
OECD member countries	50
Eastern Europe	4
All others	1

30. These programs are the Scientific Committee on Oceanic Research (SCOR), Committee on Space Research (COSPAR), Special Committee for the International Biological Program (SCIBP), Scientific Committee on Water Research (COWAR), Committee on Science and Technology in Developing Countries (COSTED), and Scientific Committee on Problems of the Environment (SCOPE). A case could be made for including SCOR and COSPAR in the present chapter because, originally, these programs were largely of concern to developed countries, Western and socialist. Since oceanographic research has become closely tied to environmental policies and development-related concerns, however, SCOR is discussed in Chapter 8. Since the applications of space research to resource satellites have become a prominent issue, we include COSPAR in Chapter 9. On ICSU generally, see Touscoz, *Coopération,* pp. 45–56; H. Jones Spencer, "The Early History of the ICSU, 1919–1946," *ICSU Review,* October 1960; W. Sullivan, "The International Geophysical Year," *International Conciliation* 521 (January 1959).

31. Binding decisions are made on occasion, usually in adopting a multilateral convention by which all or some of the member states seek to regulate a problem area. Examples include the European Monetary Agreement (and its successors) and the International Energy Agency. Binding understandings also emerge from the discussion of certain perennial issues in committees of the Council, notably those referring to the reform of the international monetary system.

32. Permanent committees of experts reporting to the Committee for Scientific and Technological Policy and working with the secretariat directorate include the Information Policy Group, Computer Utilization Group, Group for the Development and Utilization of the Social Sciences, Group on Innovation in Social Sectors, Group on Industrial Innovation. None of these has a statutory basis, and each can be abolished by the committee.

33. OECD Fourth Ministerial Meeting on Science, October 12–14, 1971, as reported in *OECD Observer,* no. 55 (December 1971), pp. 22–6. The summary here quoted is taken from *OECD at Work for Science and Education* (Paris: 1972), pp. 16–17. Emphasis added.

34. *OECD Observer,* no. 55 (December 1971), p. 23. On OECD generally, see Touscoz, *Coopération,* pp. 174–88.

35. We stress that these working methods are typical of the directorates and programs of concern to us. They do not apply to all activities of OECD, and most particularly not to the discussion of core economic and monetary issues, where initiative lies firmly with the member governments.

36. The results of confrontations are published as "reviews of national science policy." The following have been completed: France (1966), Japan (1967), United States (1968), Italy (1969), Canada (1969), Norway (1971), Austria (1971), Spain (1971), Switzerland (1972), Netherlands (1973). For a description of a recent confrontation (the use of social science in France), see *OECD Observer,* no. 72 (October-November 1974), pp. 2–33.

These confrontations can take place only when there is a consensus on basic objectives and when the government in question welcomes criticism. Moreover, there is a general feeling in the secretariat that these confrontations accomplish little because every effort is made to avoid controversy. It is far from clear that any concrete changes occur as a result of the exercise, an uncertainty which is exacerbated by the fact that OECD conducts *no* follow-up investigations! New issues are discussed without ascertaining what was done about the old ones. Hence some secretariat members feel that work with committees composed of official experts is not very useful and that results are obtained only from the more diffuse method of circulating new studies among private experts and the media. For instance, even though the secretariat initiated the systematic compilation of national R & D statistics (which are considered authoritative) and continues to publish them, it had no very firm ideas on how to use this information to influence national policy. When some of the larger member states wanted to stop the publication for budgetary reasons, the secretariat sided with them and was deterred from ending the program only because the Scandinavian delegations insisted that the material was useful for them.

37. "Science and Technology in the Management of Complex Problems," *OECD Observer*, no. 76 (July-August 1975), p. 24. Emphasis added. Georges Ferné, a member of the secretariat, argues in this context that the rapidly changing nature of knowledge puts a special burden on processes of consultation because of the tendency of our mastery of means to overtake the definition of the social ends to which the means, ideally, ought to be applied. He calls for the invention of new forms of political dialog, not otherwise described, to overcome this condition. Ibid., pp. 28–9.

38. Ibid., p. 24. Only the food sector was singled out for real action. The secretary-general of OECD was asked to prepare plans for intensifying food research in member countries in order to assist in alleviating the global food crisis. The secretariat, in a separate paper, proposed launching a formal systems study of natural resource supplies and demand and drawing up a regional plan. This was to be done by "centers of scientific and technological expertise" whose apolitical scientific standing should put their findings above political confrontation. "Science, Technology and Natural Resource Policy," ibid., pp. 25–7.

39. The most authoritative statement on the methods of technology assessment is François Hetman, *Society and the Assessment of Technology* (Paris, 1973). This excellent "state of the art" presentation is the *only* systematic service in the field of technology assessment performed by the OECD.

40. The Directorate for Scientific Affairs takes credit for having demonstrated to the member states which aspects of the so-called technology gap were real and could be dealt with by harmonizing R & D policies, and which were spurious. This accomplished, the directorate feels that the episode is over.

41. *OECD at Work for Environment* (Paris, 1973), p. 7. Pursuant to this mandate the Environment Committee was created, with these subsidiary sector groups of national officials: air management; water management; unintended occurrence of chemicals in the environment; urban environment; economic experts for analysis and evaluation; waste disposal. The 1974 recommendations were the result of the deliberations of these groups.

42. OECD Press Release, November 14, 1974, "OECD Environment Committee Meeting at Ministerial Level," p. 23. Adoption of the Polluter Pays Principle is *recommended*, while the same principle was adopted mandatorily in the European Communities the same year. The two initiatives agree in putting the cost of pollution control into the context of preventing cost and price distortions in international trade and therefore oppose contributions from tax funds to such measures, except in unusual circumstances and for limited periods. The ministers also suggested close intergovernmental cooperation and review to limit the cases in which public assistance will be provided to polluters, while in the E.C. the Commission acquired the power of review over such practices.

43. The various sector groups have been meeting but have not agreed on many common measures. The water management group has examined the ways in which member governments seek to purify water and control effluents and has broken down into subgroups of governments coordinating their activities for *monitoring* water pollu-

tion. These groups include an alpine project, a reservoir project, a North American project, and a Nordic project. The group also studies collective measures that might be taken for the control of international waterways and river systems. The air management group investigated the polluting character of a few chemical compounds. It made some recommendations which simply reaffirmed the conclusions made by earlier private studies but was unable to recommend stringent uniform standards, especially for automobiles and oil, for fear of introducing trade-distorting effects. The urban environment group is fertile in generating scenarios on improving the quality of life in cities but has made no visible impact on the actual policies of governments.

44. OECD Press Release, January 28, 1976, doc. PRESS/A(76)2. See also doc. C(75)204, November 28, 1975, especially pp. 8–11.

45. OECD doc. DAS/SPR/73.35, pp. 450–7. A later study came to the same conclusion: "R & D Trends in the OECD Area since 1971," *OECD Observer*, no. 76 (July–August, 1975), pp. 30–2.

46. For further details on the methodology of this analysis, see Ernst B. Haas, "On Systems and International Regimes," *World Politics*, January 1975, pp. 160–4.

47. We remind the reader that this summary applies to OECD programs in science policy. It is not quite accurate when applied to monetary and trade negotiations. Moreover, the OECD negotiations in the energy field since 1973 constitute a possible exception to the summary. The definition of new objectives, the refocusing of goals, and the manner of bargaining may amount to a pragmatic pattern, though the use of knowledge and the mode of learning do not quite fit. In any event, the agreement establishing the IEA resembles a constant-sum game involving considerable packaging-dealing across a wide variety of issues, and it did evoke side payments. For a description of IEA arrangements, see *OECD Observer*, no. 73 (January–February 1975), pp. 20–5.

48. Recall that this subsample is made up of eighteen individuals, representing six different organizations and their programs. All programs are devoted to dealing with issues of science planning and high technology in industrialized countries. Twelve of the eighteen individuals are associated with OECD.

49. For two articulate eclectic views on the utility of science in shaping public choice expressed by OECD officials in their private capacities, see J. J. Salomon, *Science and Politics* (Cambridge, Mass.: MIT Press, 1973), and François Hetman, *La Maitrise du futur* (Paris: Le Seuil, 1971).

Chapter 8

Science and Technology for Environmental Management

> The earth is a spaceship. We should have known this for the past two thousand years, and in a sense we have—in a coldly intellectual sense, as a mere fact of physics, the human implications of which almost completely eluded us. Before we can make "decisions for survival" wisely we must see these implications clearly. We must feel in our bones the inescapable truth that we live on a spaceship. From now on no major political decisions can safely be made without taking into consideration this basic fact.[1]

Environmental management, as a concept of political action, is the totality of knowledge which goes into understanding the causative mechanisms of the degradation of nature *and* the measures to be taken to halt this degradation. Because of the complexity of the physical chains of causation among the agents and organisms involved, the informing image underlying management is the notion of the ecosystem: The measures of control and rectification must be as complex and interconnected as the whole to be safeguarded.

And that is the trouble. Pollution controls affect costs of production. Shifting to new sources of energy interferes with world trade, payments, investments, employment, consumer demand. Conservation of natural resources implies rescheduling of production, exports, and imports. Recycling may benefit the industrialized countries, but it reduces the earning capacity of the poorer nations. What is good for one passenger on spaceship earth may be very bad for another. What do we manage? Resource use in industrial countries only? Global exploitation of resources, and therefore trade, investment, and technological innovation? A better quality of life in terms of clean air and water? Or do we give a more extended meaning to that popular term and equate it with the eradication of poverty?

"Eco-development" is the new slogan under which total environmental management is to unfold. In the words of Maurice Strong, eco-development aims at respecting both the "inner" and the "outer" limits of the environment. The "inner" limits are the basic needs of good health and minimum welfare of all human beings; the "outer" limits are given by the physical carrying capacity of the biosphere. "We recognize the threats to both the 'inner limits' of basic human needs and the 'outer limits' of the planet's physical resources. But we also believe that a new sense of respect for fundamental human rights and for the preservation of our planet is growing up behind the angry divisions and confrontations of our day."[2] It is the purpose of this chapter to discover whether the beliefs and experiences of scientists working on eco-development in the United Nations system bear out the advent of such a sense of respect. Environmental management ought to be the province *par excellence* of our rationalists.

We shall examine first the overall organizational pattern of U.N. efforts to cope with environmental issues. We then go on to investigate programs for mapping ecological systems, the management of water resources, efforts in oceanography and meteorology, and programs in public health. We omit in this chapter examination of the interaction between environmental and economic development objectives, but this theme will reappear in the following chapter. No effort is made to survey the entire range of United Nations activities relating to science and technology.[3]

THE ORGANIZATIONAL PATTERN OF ENVIRONMENTAL MANAGEMENT

The First Steps

Formally, the U.N. and the world recognized the existence of an environmental issue with the holding in 1972 of the U.N. Conference on the Human Environment (UNCHE) in Stockholm. Piecemeal concern, however, had been expressed before and had begun to crystallize in a series of fragmented programs which UNCHE was, among other things, expected to coordinate. One of the pioneer organizations was the International Union for the Conservation of Nature (IUCN), whose history illustrates the unfolding of the notion of eco-development.

IUCN, though technically a nongovernmental organization, is partly financed by government contributions. It was founded in 1948 as a common framework for the purpose of establishing a capability in the field of conservation. Its activities, limited both by design and by lack of funding, primarily involved the collection of information on "facts, ideas, literature, persons, organization, or institutes" and their transmission through correspondence and bulletins.

However, throughout the ensuing years, the organization's scope widened as the growing popularity of ecological issues attracted financial support and as its legitimacy was strengthened with the introduction of more environmental organizations which pressed for the IUCN's cooperation: first ICSU's International Biological Programme and UNESCO sought the expertise of the IUCN; then the Food and Agricultural Organization and UNESCO's Man and the Biosphere program followed. In addition, in 1961, the World Wildlife Fund was begun as an international charitable foundation whose purpose was saving the world's wildlife and wild places, and it immediately established itself as a major source of funding for the IUCN.

Thus, while there was no deliberate search for new knowledge or new areas of interest, the IUCN, in an effort to build and support the growing consensus on ecological issues, witnessed among its programs a gradual accretion of new subgoals and a concomitant change in organizational tactics. IUCN programs came to be tied more and more to strategies of rational exploitation (or nonexploitation) of resources in the context of economic development. The criteria for justifying the organization's concern for conservation issues grew from the "ethical," the "aesthetic," and the "scientific," to include the "educational," the "recreational," *and* the "economic." It was realized that "to fulfill the objectives . . . IUCN must concern itself deeply with the conservation of wildlife and wildlife habitat, but not solely with this objective. While it is not IUCN's intention to become deeply involved with the direct economic aspects of conservation, misuse of these resources can adversely affect . . . species and their habitats and so become a part of the Union's concern."[4] In other words, while the IUCN recognized its limitations and did not attempt to extend its goals too far beyond their original intent, the organization did place these goals into a new, more comprehensive framework and adjusted its strategies accordingly.

Internationally coordinated research on environmental matters had also been undertaken under the auspices of the International Council of Scientific Unions. While IUCN activity was concerned with practical measures of conservation, ICSU sponsored three major programs which were to establish the scientific links among the elements in natural ecosystems. The International Biological Programme (IBP) sought to do this without special emphasis on the role of man, as did the Special Committee on Oceanographic Research (SCOR). But the Special Committee on Problems of the Environment (SCOPE) in 1969 took as its mandate the investigation of man's impact on natural ecosystems, and it was SCOPE's first report which provided the scientific basis for the discussions of UNCHE.[5]

From the scientists' point of view, the first capability to be sought in environmental management had to be the observation and measurement of agents considered critical in the maintenance or deterioration of environmental quality, the activity now universally referred to as "monitoring." Partly as a result of ICSU activity, many U.N. agencies had already committed themselves to monitoring programs prior to 1972, and several of these were operational at the time of UNCHE.[6] Thus the World Meteorological Organization (WMO), through the medium of forty-five stations in seventeen countries, was monitoring atmospheric turbidity, the gaseous constituents and solid particles in the air, and the chemical constituents of precipitation. The World Health Organization (WHO) sought to create a network of stations and laboratories to monitor pollutants in urban and industrial locations. It also maintained a global information network on communicable diseases, adverse drug reactions, and food contamination by chemicals, as well as participating with IAEA in monitoring radioactivity in the environment. The International Atomic Energy Agency (IAEA) was doing the same with respect to the concentration of certain isotopes in precipitation. Discussions were underway with respect to launching several cooperative monitoring programs for the oceans: for meteorological data (IGOSS), for fish (FAO), and for ascertaining levels of marine pollution (GIPME), planned jointly by WMO, WHO, IAEA, FAO, the Intergovernmental Oceanographic Commission (IOC), and the Intergovernmental Maritime Consultative Organization (IMCO).

Environmental Protection: What Is It?

A monitoring capability, however, is a far cry from an environmental management capability, and on the eve of UNCHE, impatience with approaches that singled out the monitoring of pollutants as the most important issue facing the world was widely manifested. Many scientists in industrial countries and the majority of the governments of these nations did consider this the priority issue, but many other scientists, again predominantly from industrial countries, wished to extend the issue in order to impose a more holistic view of the environment on the world's consciousness, a view which also stressed economic growth and nongrowth, population, food and resource use. Scientists from developing nations, on the other hand, expressed the fear that the concentration of scientific and technological knowledge related to environmental issues in the developed countries made participation by the developing countries all but impossible. And most importantly, many of the governments of these nations professed the view that pollution is a problem for the polluters, not for the poor. If environmental management were to be attempted, it would have to address the issue of poverty.[7]

Consequently, even before an institutional arrangement had been designated, the number of fields of knowledge perceived to be contained under the rubric "environment" had proliferated considerably. How could the interdependencies among these fields be mapped? Would the mapping lead to an agreed program of action? In order to demonstrate the relevance of environmental issues to nonindustrial countries, a formula for expanding the concept of the environment had to be found.

This effort caused some U.N. specialized agencies to fear that UNCHE would become "too rational." A number of U.N. agencies charged with aiding economic development felt threatened by the impact of the new interest in environmental protection and wished to avoid the creation of a new agency with superordinate authority in the field. Consequently, internal measures were taken in several agencies to reorganize their programs in order to protect their budgets and preserve the integrity of their mandates.

The attempt to demonstrate the relevance of environmental issues to nonindustrialized countries took the form of the Founex report, which sought to redefine the environmental issue for the benefit of the poor.[8] The report recognized that two different kinds of environmental problems face developing countries: poverty and the inadequacies of current development policies to eradicate that poverty, *and* the development process itself. As desired transformations come about in agriculture, industry, networks of transportation and communication, and the growth of urban areas, undesirable and frequently unforeseen environmental side effects result. In particular, the Founex report named five categories of potential environmental side effects of the process of development: (1) resource deterioration; (2) biological pollution (agents of human disease, plant pests); (3) chemical pollution; (4) physical disruption (including thermal pollution, noise, and silting); and (5) social disruption (congestion and a loss of sense of community). The target for concerted national, regional, and international action must be the aggregate of these interconnected issues. National action, the Founex Report recommended, should therefore include a "selective attack," within the context of national development planning, on the "worst manifestations of poverty," including malnutrition, disease, illiteracy, squalor, unemployment, and inequality. Emphasis was placed on the provision of a sociopolitical "good," not simply on physical ecosystemic improvement. But such action still requires data collection for basic information on the current state of the environment as well as the formulation of guidelines for project appraisal.[9]

Obviously, the "environment" was beginning to mean something more than the chemical and biological properties of ecosystems and their preservation in a state of equilibrium. Much the same result came about in UNESCO's initiative to carve a major niche for itself in the environmental field. UNESCO in 1971 devised its "Man and the Biosphere" program (MAB) in an effort to safeguard its role as an agency working for economic and social development while also committed to work in the natural sciences. In MAB the concept "biosphere," much as that of the "environment," assumed a wider meaning than had its strictly scientific predecessor, the International Biological Programme. The scientific content remained: The biosphere is a superstructure under which are contained a number of natural and man-modified ecosystems (sometimes also referred to as "biomes").

> [Ecosystems] are distinguishable portions of the biosphere functioning to some extent independently of one another. Each ecosystem consists of the plants, animals and micro-organisms occupying a definable portion of the earth's surface, together with the relevant features of their abiotic environment; it is usually in some sense homogeneous at the scale considered. Landscape units—a drainage basin, a mountain range, a town and the rural area associated with it—generally are at a higher level of complexity again, and may be considered as a mosaic of different types of ecosystems arranged in a definable spatial pattern. These mosaics combine at a still higher level of complexity to form the biosphere, the tenuous shell surrounding spaceship earth within which man moves and has his being.[10]

This definition of the biosphere and its component ecosystems is inherited directly—and intentionally—from IBP. However, the purpose of studying the biosphere is comprehensive and far-reaching: It is to create a capability for the rational management of natural resources as they relate to greater productivity in the economic sense and to a better quality of life in a social/cultural sense—and particularly as these are relevant to the developing countries. There arose an explicit commitment to remedial action in addition to scientific analysis. A new ideology was being expressed: The entire international community is collectively responsible for the economically fruitful and scientifically rational exploitation of resources.

The U.N. Environmental Program

The conceptual redefinition of environmental matters which resulted from these events was a fortuitous outgrowth of political and bureaucratic dynamics illustrating the *lack* of consensus on the nature of the problem to be solved. The marriage of developmental and environmental issues in the Founex report and in the many resolutions adopted at UNCHE was an effort to combine a set of political purposes which, at first blush, seemed to be mutually antagonistic. Whether this amounts to more than a temporary marriage of convenience remains to be seen. The institutional formula adopted at UNCHE—the United Nations Environmental Program (UNEP)—was an effort to retain the autonomy of the specialized agencies *while also* subjecting them to joint programing with a focus on world ecosystemic issues.[11]

The program which took shape after 1972 constitutes a first test of the finality of the marriage. But it also constitutes a test of the hypothesis underlying our study. If the convergence of initially antagonistic political and bureaucratic purposes is to become permanent, it must be based on some degree of conceptual reorientation, on learning. It must imply that governments come to redefine their initial objectives in response to demonstrations that the character of the physical world does not permit them to attain all their objectives simultaneously, at least not without eventually paying an exorbitant price in the deterioration of the quality of life. This demonstration must be the work of scientists. In short, the analytical significance of UNEP is its ability to shed light on whether "politics," understood as the confrontation and resolution of conflicting demands, is yielding to "science," or to the use and acceptance of a set of overarching concepts derived from nature and from the methodology used for studying nature.

UNEP's work to date illustrates the tension; it does not suggest its resolution.[12] To be sure, holism is implicit in the definition of UNEP's approach to the protection of the global environment; the program is

> an attempt to maximize the number and kinds of relevant contributions and to attempt to ensure that the relevant complications are all at least considered before the problem is simplified in an attempt at solution. Such a task implies a considerable amount of inter-agency, intergovernmental and inter-organizational action in plan-

ning, and indeed UNEP's principal line of work will be setting up such interactions and carrying them through to co-operative action.[13]

UNEP's official task is to *coordinate* the separate environmental activities already carried out by other agencies, to *introduce* into the work of such agencies and of governments environmental themes and concerns not now considered, and to *initiate* new studies and programs of its own when these cannot be accommodated under the tasks of coordination and introduction. UNEP's funds are to be disbursed to stimulate these activities.

Toward what end? Is the purpose comprehensive eco-development or simply an improvement of our understanding of how global pollution comes about? Is the purpose *monitoring* the quality of the environment or is it intersectoral programs of *changing* the environment while respecting its "outer limits" and upgrading its "inner limits"? While UNEP wants to have it both ways, the bulk of its activity has gone into the study of organic and inorganic processes, into monitoring. Most of its energy has been devoted to creating the program called Earthwatch, an effort to coordinate, integrate scientifically, and expand the separate monitoring activities already carried out by national governments and other international agencies. UNEP has added to the preexisting structure the concept of impact, regional, and baseline observation stations.[14]

But what pollutants are to be monitored? Are all of equal significance to all member states? The fact that the list has been revised four times since 1971 suggests the controversiality of the issue. Earthwatch, far from being only a scientific program devised according to scientific criteria, is part and parcel of the unresolved dispute over the *priorities* which UNEP is to serve. At first these were confined to pollutants and pollution patterns of primary interest to the industrialized members. However, the very first meeting of UNEP's Governing Council showed a lack of consensus on this issue, which led to an expansion of the list of pollutants and of the interaction patterns considered important.

The list of priority subject areas of UNEP reads as follows, though the order of the items is not an official ranking; all six priorities are "equally prior": (1) Human settlements, human health, habitat, and well-being; (2) land, water, and desertification; (3) trade, economics, technology, and transfer of technology; (4) oceans; (5) conservation of nature, wildlife, and genetic resources; (6) energy. The last three are of primary interest to the industrial countries, while the expansion of the focus to the first three items reflects the much broader concerns of the developing nations. It would seem that, in principle, the "management of the environment" has become coterminous with all human planning of welfare in general. The more holistic the area of priority, the less concrete the consensus on how to manage the interdependencies implied. The largest of these areas is the trade/economics/technology nexus, which so far has not been tackled by UNEP at all in terms of an operational program. The human settlements/health/habitat nexus is almost equally ambitious in scope.

UNEP has neither preempted nor eliminated the programs of other U.N. agencies; it has arrived at a position of coexistence with them, giving UNEP a superordinate role only insofar as its financial contribution can shape the programs of the other agencies. The management of global environmental affairs thus remains fragmented and our discussion of the participating scientists must respect that fragmentation. We divide our discussion into four "programs" and indicate the organizational affiliations of the respondents associated with each.

The first program analyzed here is devoted to the identification and monitoring of ecological systems, largely but not exclusively defined as natural systems. The organizations participating in such studies include UNESCO, WHO, IBRD, and ICSU's SCOPE and IBP, among the ones we singled out for attention. A second program is concerned with the properties of the oceans and of weather systems as constituents of strategies of environmental management. Affiliated organizations studied by us include WMO, IOC, IMCO, and ICSU's SCOR. A third program deals with the rational management of water resources, which includes WHO, UNESCO, and ICSU's Committee on Water Resources. Finally, environmentally related public health programs provided some of our respondents, who were affiliated with WHO, FAO, IAEA, and ICSU.

ECOLOGICAL SYSTEMS

International Council of Scientific Unions (ICSU)

International Biological Programme. A combination of social, technological, and scientific pressures spurred the organization of the Special Committee for the International Biological Programme at the Tenth General Assembly of ICSU, in 1963. The committee was prompted by a concern for the existing and potential problems created at the intersection of increased population pressures, unscientific exploitation of natural resources, and the delicate balance of ecosystems. The International Biological Programme was set up to promote "basic knowledge relevant to the needs of man,"[15] and establish a scientific foundation for predictive analysis of development, management and conservation procedures.

The program was divided into three major categories: biome studies of such ecosystems as grassland, forests, and deserts; comparative studies of ecosystems with emphasis on understanding basic chemical processes; and ecosystemic studies focusing on man. Each category, in turn, was subdivided into seven functional sections. Coordination between sections was undertaken by intersection working groups. The ensemble eventually added up to eighty-three separate research themes and two thousand separate projects. In organizational terms, the IBP was a common framework for pooling the varying research interests and capacities of the participating scientific units. However, insofar as its participants also contributed to the creation of the UNEP system of global monitoring, its work shaded into the evolution of a joint facility which sought to preside over a sequential division of labor.

The Scientific Committee for the IBP (scibp) set up a central office, staffed by two scientists and an executive officer, sectional offices, with either a whole or a part-time scientific coordinator, and country offices to correspond to the country committees, which were the actual workhorses. There were fifty-eight participating countries in IBP, and an additional forty countries established contact through correspondents or through project-specific contributions. The committee then established an agenda for sequencing the program into three phases: Phase I, termed the "preparatory phase" and scheduled from 1964 to 1967, was devoted to detailed planning at the international level, with specific attention to methodology. During this time participating countries were able to form their national committees and organize projects. One outgrowth of this preparatory phase was the formation of regional IBP federations separate from the scipb. In Scandinavia representatives from Denmark, Finland, Norway, and Sweden met regularly to arrange a division of labor among their national programs. Kenya, Tanzania, and Uganda organized an East African IBP federation. In addition, a number of Latin American countries met in various Pan-American arrangements to discuss IBP matters of mutual concern, and the U.S., Canada, France, and the Scandinavian countries collaborated in circumpolar studies.[16]

Phase II was designated the operational phase, and was to run from 1967 to 1970. This phase was earmarked officially for data collection, a function which soon made evident the need for biological data centers for sorting the data in a comparable manner. The third and final phase, termed synthesis and transfer, ran from 1970 until 1972. This phase included a two-year extension offered for those national committees which had not yet had time to synthesize the results of their operational phase. This synthesis was limited to integrating the physical and biological properties of ecosystems, not linking them with issues of development, economics, or quality of life. The methodologies which had been developed permitted the study of ecosystemic scientific processes only. It was left to future programs to link these processes to economic and social issues. Consequently, the third phase also served to transfer unfinished IBP work to other organizations. Many of the IBP's objectives were easily fulfilled by the collection and analysis of data through the data banks. Others required follow-up. Thus, environmental biology and conservation activities were transferred to IUCN, and marine productivity to SCOR. The Programme for Analysis of World Ecosystems and Global Monitoring was given to SCOPE. This last transfer was particularly important, because continuity was ensured between these committees simply by placing all of the SCIBP people on the SCOPE.

SCOPE. Although the IBP had looked at a number of issues which lie at the interface of the "social and natural systems," the primary purpose of the program was to lay a methodological basis upon which other programs could build. In addition, the duration of the IBP had always been limited: It was to be only temporary, and any long-term outgrowth from its work would necessarily have to be bequeathed to a permanent committee.

SCOPE, born out of the Twelfth General Assembly of ICSU in 1969, was just such a committee. It began its existence by asking the following questions:

> In what qualitative ways and by how much quantitatively is the global environment of man being adversely affected by the technological revolution begun during the 19th century? The growth of population and the per capita capability of modification and exploitation of the environment are accelerating at such rapid rates that unforeseen and often unwanted side effects are continually arising. How serious are the consequences of these *for the future life of man on earth?*[17]

SCOPE, therefore, was the first of the environment-oriented organizations to zero in on *homo sapiens* in a changing ecology as *the* focus of attention. IUCN had certainly been concerned with the effects of conservation and exploitation of resources on man, but as a species, or as an ecological phenomenon, man got no more attention than did his less sapient kin. Similarly, IBP had emphasized ecologies in which humans participated no more than those in which the human was entirely absent. IBP research had gone forward on the assumption that research is good in itself, because a fuller knowledge of the natural world is a prerequisite to rational governmental action. IBP had no more elaborate social objectives than that; its purpose was to devise a methodology of ecological research which would be universally acceptable. Hence the committee never encountered the need to convince politicians and administrators of the import of its work with respect to social choices. But scope focused on man for two reasons: his welfare in the face of depleted or damaged resources is of ever greater concern, *and* man's unique ability to fashion tools causes him to alter his environment, thus making man the catalyst of ecological disequilibrium. The making and misuse of technology defined the boundaries of the problem.[18]

scope was to advise its parent organization, ICSU, on policies concerning the interaction of man with the environment. It was to advise and cooperate with the United Nations, U.N. agencies, regional and nongovernmental international organizations. And it was to coordinate research relevant to both environmental quality and the rational exploitation of resources. Like ICSU, scope's organization is a common framework in which the contribution of individual scientists are pooled through four commissions. These commissions deal with (1) biological assessment of materials which might significantly alter the biosphere and the environment; (2) the toxicology of chlorinated hydrocarbons; (3) a quantitative basis for the creation (that is, model-building) and management of artificial ecosystems, including, in particular, ecosystems pertaining to problems in developing countries; and (4) the logistics of global monitoring systems for comparative data on the atmosphere, waters, soil, and biota.

The emphasis on exploring alternatives for the developing countries was not always present. Originally, the ideology was better captured by this statement:

> It should be the special responsibility of developed countries to ensure that any industrial enterprise which they may finance should have a high degree of ecological control. In the absence of local legislation, a situation may develop which is far worse than would be tolerated at home by the industrial nations; man simply cannot af-

ford to repeat mistakes of this kind. Properly qualified ecological
advisers should be consulted before technical assistance is granted.[19]

However, by 1971, we saw that the climate of opinion on both the
environment and development—and their interrelationship—
had changed considerably. A separate SCOPE working party of
natural scientists from Asia, Africa, and Latin America was set
up to define the major areas of concern to developing countries.
Rational environmental policy is now seen to require the inclusion in development planning of national policies on the "improvement of human settlements"; this is to involve planning for
population density, the careful siting of new industries and the
relocation of older industries, the improvement of facilities in
rural areas surrounding an area in the process of industrialization. Various efforts at stimulating informal organization are
proposed in order to promote a sense of community among
migrants to urban areas. While SCOPE scientists continue to advocate the "control of pollution and environmental hazards," they
now add that before a developing country can consider controlling pollution, it must conduct or have access to practical research
aimed at alternative solutions. The choice for developing countries cannot be polluting industry versus no industry; the choice
ought to be between polluting industry and alternative industry.[20] Thus, within the short period of two years, 1969–1971,
SCOPE had expanded its concept of the environment, had articulated a more comprehensive objective, and had designed a more
complex strategy in pursuit of this objective.

SCOPE is today recognized as the major nongovernmental actor
in international environmental affairs. Scientists affiliated with
its network are prominent in advising UNEP, the specialized
agencies and governments involved in GEMS, and its research is
institutionalized under ICSU auspices in its Chelsea laboratory.
Yet, SCOPE's impact on government policy remains modest. Our
respondents were quick to point out that scientists from industrialized and nonindustrialized countries continue to disagree
over priorities and that SCOPE's work illustrates the fragmentation of the scientific world along north-south lines. Scientists
from the industrialized countries attach more importance to the
anticipation and control of the unwanted side effects of technology in the physical realm, whereas their colleagues from underdeveloped countries are interested in identifying the more remote effects on employment, trade, and social stability. The first
group believes that politicians can be made to see the underlying
logic of interconnectedness; the second does not and puts its

faith in political bargaining and coalition-building, not formal demonstration. Both groups agree that their actual impact on governments has been minimal. Their impact on parallel work going on under UNESCO's auspices is our next concern.

UNESCO: *Science and Environmental Research*

"Since wars begin in the minds of men," we are told by the UNESCO constitution, "it is in the minds of men that the defenses of peace must be built." This lofty commitment may make an impact on the activities of UNESCO in the fields of education, social science, communications, and the humanities, but its effect in the natural sciences is not easily discernible.[21] Our programs and our respondents are concentrated in the division of natural sciences. The division is headed by the assistant director-general for science, and it includes departments which deal, respectively, with science policy, scientific and technological education, and the environmental sciences and natural resources. In 1973/74 the total share of the UNESCO regular budget taken by the division amounted to 12.5 percent; its share of the technical assistance budget was 35.0 percent. Our concern in this chapter is with the environmental sciences and natural resources.

In recent years almost the entire programmatic effort of UNESCO has been subordinated to the overriding objective of aiding in the economic and social development of Third World countries, an obvious result of the demands made by the delegates from these nations. Since these demands, however, are rarely specific with respect to the organization's program and are filtered through a number of additional fora and institutions, we must first say a word about the working methods commonly used in UNESCO. Programs are worked out by the Secretariat, packaged as independent promotional activities or included in the technical assistance budget, approved rather routinely by the General Conference, and then left to the national governments for action and to such implementing activities as the Secretariat is able to mount. The number of such activities is very large, a great many discrete projects are underway at any one time both at headquarters and national levels, some field operations are undertaken jointly with other specialized agencies, and the funds earmarked for any single activity are extremely modest. In short, the principle of scatteration and fragmentation rules supreme. Not a single one of our respondents expressed satisfaction with the impact of these programs. Many expressed reservations on the techniques used. Most felt that the contradiction between the strong emphasis on national development and the desirable international role of science is becoming more acute. Many delegates complained that their governments do not take UNESCO seriously.

UNESCO, more than any other intergovernmental organization, relies on independent experts and nongovernmental organizations to realize its objectives. Much of the program consists of holding colloquia of experts in Paris, publishing these as special reports or as part of regularly issued series, and occasionally using them as the basis for requesting a resolution from the General Conference. The publication of bibliographies often results from such encounters. It is difficult to discover any thematic coherence and continuity emerging from these convocations, though undoubtedly the fact that people talk to one another about something constitutes a species of international communication, even if it resembles the Tower of Babel. It is difficult to find traces of these discussions in the field work done by experts engaged for technical assistance operations, more difficult than in the case of other U.N. agencies.

The main nongovernmental ally of UNESCO's program in science and technology is ICSU, which holds "consultative and associate status," the most comprehensive kind of relationship UNESCO is able to establish with nongovernmental bodies. The relationship is administered by a coordinating committee which meets every six months, presided over by the president of ICSU and the assistant director-general for science. The coordination may take several forms. ICSU may propose a new research program involving the need for a great deal of international collaboration, and, on being approved by UNESCO, funds will be granted to ICSU. Such efforts as the International Geophysical Year and the International Year of the Quiet Sun illustrate this method. Other programs may involve UNESCO financing for research activities requiring a longer period, such as in IBP and SCOPE. In short, international scientific associations are able to draw on UNESCO for the furtherance of their interests. It was just such efforts which brought aspects of the IBP under the purview of UNESCO's natural sciences sector with the new title Man and the Biosphere.

MAB. When the first session of MAB's Intergovernmental Coordinating Council (ICC) met in Paris in November 1971, thirteen project themes were chosen for development. The overriding purpose of these projects was to establish a capability to cope with the consequences of ineffective or harmful environmental management:

. . . . to develop the basis within the natural and social sciences for the rational use and conservation of the resources of the biosphere and for the improvement of the global relationship between man and the environment; to predict the consequences of today's actions on tomorrow's world and thereby to increase man's ability to manage efficiently the natural resources of the biosphere.[22]

In MAB emphasis was put squarely on thematic definitions, methods of data collection, and modes of influencing national governments and scientists so as to encourage the rational planning of policies for preserving ecosystems *and* for adapting them to human needs. Thematically, this commitment is reflected in the projects adopted by MAB.[23] Tactically, the program is flexible as to local methods of implementation favored and economical in focusing only on subjects of major regional or global significance. The criterion of significance chosen favors the needs of the developing countries in their attempts to industrialize and modernize.

The key to successful implementation of these projects lies primarily with the national committees, which, though loosely joined into a common framework, are voluntary and independent of any international machinery. In 1974, there were seventy-three such committees in operation. Many existed before the advent of MAB.[24] In such cases, the main function of the MAB international secretariat has been to contact these groups, link them with an international network of similar or newly created committees, and urge them to continue their research in a manner relevant to the MAB projects and consistent with uniform methodologies. This stress on a common methodology, inherited from the IBP, has been one of MAB's successes. Thus, countries without the resources of a strong national committee have been able to participate—sometimes vicariously and sometimes directly—through a regional division of labor made possible by comparative research methods.

This has led to greater regional cooperation. A regional project emerges when a national committee decides that its own project has regional merit and presents its plans to other countries. If these states are interested, then all concerned are to apprise the secretariat; the proposed cooperative projects are then submitted either to the MAB ICC or to the MAB bureau, and finally to UNESCO, to obtain funds. This procedure has been followed primarily in situations in which some regional collaboration existed independently of and prior to MAB. Examples include mountain ecosystem studies among Alpine countries and coastal ecology studies among Mediterranean countries.

Moreover, by 1974, after each project area had been given the attention of expert panels and sufficient basis for project implementation had finally been achieved, the MAB secretariat began to take a more direct role in organizing regional cooperation.[25] Thus it attempted to push MAB toward the level of a joint facility, at least at the regional level. Cooperation among participating scientists and government agencies was now infused with suggestions and foci generated by MAB itself. The division of labor among the participants began to resemble a schedule of tasks requiring more elaborate coordination for successful execution. The task itself was made more elaborate by including the social sciences as an important component. Evolution toward a joint facility is attained through the regionalization of research. We illustrate one such venture.

MAB, UNEP, and FAO jointly organized a meeting on the ecological management of arid and semi-arid rangelands in Africa and the Near and Middle East.[26] Pilot projects were proposed and adopted, and a regional division of labor was established. Each ecosystem variant and each process variant in the region was to be analyzed and the results shared among all participants. Egypt is conducting a project among coastal dunes and nonsaline depressions on the potential agricultural uses of the land; Libya is carrying out essentially the same project, only in a more arid bioclimatic zone. Tunisia has a project on animal breeding, phyto-ecology, and the economics of water management and agro-meteorology; Morocco has one on the development of forestry and grazing land to rangelands for crop-farming; and Algeria has a project on the eco-types of semiarid zones which could be used for fodder production. In summary, the "meeting's main achievement was that it placed ongoing national projects in a regional context, thus making it possible to avoid duplication and to use the resources available to the best possible advantage. Some of the proposed pilot projects are complementary as regards ecosystems while others complement each other in using different procedures and involving different fields of study."[27]

Activity has also been taking place between the social science division of UNESCO and MAB. The social sciences have always officially been a key component of MAB, but, in fact, they have been segregated and subordinated. This changed in 1974, with the convening of a task force on the contribution of the social sciences to the Man and the Biosphere program. The main thesis proposed at this conference was that man is simultaneously part of the environment and—with his awareness and capacity for deliberate action—responsible for its stewardship. Thus, man should not be seen merely as an 'actor' on the environmental 'stage.' The 'man *in* the biosphere' aspect should be stressed, and a systemic, holistic view taken of the interrelationships between man and other components of the biosphere.[28]

The social scientists sought a slight shift in emphasis by stressing "the increasing scale and complexity of the interactions of humans with the natural environment, the increasing differentiation and greater integration (or interdependence) within and among natural and social systems, and the increasing pace of change."[29] While none of the recommendations demanded revision of the content of any single MAB project, they did set questions of ecosystems management within the context of social complexity and political decision-making. This should have greatly altered the program's tactical decisions, but, in general, MAB has managed to side-step these issues.

As will become clear in the next section, our overall assessment of MAB's development does not quite match that of the participating scientists. What can we say about the evolution of institutional practices? The purpose which inspires the whole effort is a clear commitment to the methodological capability for *coping with the consequences* of economic and social policies resulting in environmental degradation. This has been true from the beginning and continues to be true today. The collaborative effort at first involved the definition of a division of labor such that each national and regional group would concentrate on research of interest *to it,* with the results being pooled under UNESCO auspices. Later, however, this decentralized mapping of variables gave rise, in some MAB projects, to a division of labor in which findings in one area or on a given topic would become the basis for the next collaborative step, thus moving toward the pattern we call "sequencing." The instrumentality provided by UNESCO and the national committees was, at first, simply a common framework for determining the rules of pooling. As efforts were made to superimpose priorities and man-centered concepts on the research, the central staff began to resemble what we call a "joint facility," even though its success in making its priorities prevail remains very much in doubt. One may argue whether the institutional ensemble should be described as diffuse or decentralized. Looked at from the vantage point of the participants on single projects or committees, it appears to be very diffuse; the self-confidence of some UNESCO staff members, however, suggests a gradual integration among themes which comes closer to the pragmatic norm of decentralized-but-converging action. We think the local practitioners' perception is accurate.

Decision-making procedures clearly conform to the pragmatic norm, though some of them approach the rational. MAB is dedicated to the deliberate search for new and socially relevant knowledge. It self-consciously prefers rational-analytic modes of learning; but we believe that the lack of a consensual and systematic body of ecological knowledge today, despite IBP and scope efforts, proves that the commitment to rational-analytic modes has *not* resulted in the acceptance of its primacy in international program-making. Partial scanning, therefore, more accurately describes the process of accumulating and interpreting the results of scientific research. Seen in the context of the totality of United Nations program commitments, the advent of the ecological program certainly represents the sudden addition of a new set of goals. However, the older goals, far from being abandoned, received new impetus and support from the developing countries. The attempted refocusing and integration of environmental and developmental objectives remain incomplete: The U.N., UNEP, and UNCTAD, since 1974, have wrestled with the issue of refocusing and have so far come up with nothing better than a rhetorical sum of everybody's demands and a practical commitment to continue the sector-specific programs of the specialized agencies. In UNESCO, the bargaining process has been simplified by the ability of member governments to opt in and out of environmental programs, depending on their urgency in national perspective. The agreements represent variable-sum bargaining since the nature of the pie differs from country to country. Package-dealing is possible among countries with regionally congruent interests. Side payments, in the form of technical aid to developing countries, can be readily offered as long as UNEP pays for them. While the MAB *research program* is the result of such cooperative behavior, the *policy implications* of the research continue to be treated by most governments as a zero-sum game.

Views of the MAB Sample.[30] Our sample was about evenly divided between UNESCO officials and members of national MAB commissions who serve as delegates to UNESCO-sponsored MAB meetings. We now describe the characteristics of all affiliated persons. In terms of personal attitudes toward science, the picture is as follows:

Determinists 9.1%
Instrumentalists 18.2
Skeptics 45.5
Eclectics 27.3

Our MAB respondents tend to fear the dominance of technique over values in the application of scientific knowledge and show great concern over the rapidity of social change due to technological innovation; only about a quarter of the sample is indifferent to over-reliance on the application of scientific knowledge to problems of social choice. No less than 70 percent identify national professional associations as their natural clientele! There is no very marked difference between delegates and officials, though the incidence of eclectics among the delegates is a little higher.

MAB personnel are quite unusual in identifying their organizational experiences in very holistic terms:

Determinist planners 45.5%
Social forecasters 36.4
Physical controllers 0
Random appliers 18.2
Eclectics 0

The random appliers are all delegates, the majority of national representatives are social forecasters, and almost all the planners are UNESCO officials. The organizational commitment, in short, is to comprehensive ecological planning on a global scale, and the expectation that science can infuse this planning with a methodological and conceptual core is great. This, however, does not mean that these expectations have been realized. Almost all agree that, to the extent anyone has been influenced by MAB projects, it is specific national agencies charged with an environmental protection mandate. Nevertheless, 70 percent of the respondents do not believe that the work has succeeded in demonstrating the complexity of cause-and-effect links to governments; almost two thirds suggested that bargaining and coalition-building among politicians was the only means to obtain programmatic agreement and that more formal scientific methods of demonstration do not work. Given the highly decentralized nature of MAB's working methods, it is hardly surprising that the effectiveness of the program varies greatly from country to country.

In terms of organizational ideology, finally, the MAB group

displays a greater commitment to the rationalizing role imputed
to science than do most of our programs:

> Rationalists   27.3%
> Pragmatists   9.1
> Skeptics   36.4
> Eclectics   27.3

The only difference between delegates and UNESCO officials is
the absence of eclectics from the latter group. But we also saw
that the dominance of rationalists and pragmatists in UNESCO is
far from guaranteeing a coherent global program. In fact the
split between the more holistically inclined officials and the more
skeptical national commissions is one of the key weaknesses of
MAB.

Views of All Respondents

Our sample of respondents involved in research on ecological
issues includes another eight individuals whose organizational
and programmatic affiliations varied widely.[31] Hence it makes
little sense to tabulate their organizational experiences and
ideologies. We now incorporate the views and experiences of
these respondents with the MAB group to obtain a profile of
organizational ideologies for all of our scientists engaged in international action on ecological problems. The distribution of
personal views on the role of science is as follows:

> Determinists   15.8%
> Instrumentalists   15.8
> Skeptics   36.8
> Eclectics   31.6

Clearly, the wider sample does not share the MAB group's beliefs in the special quality of scientific knowledge with the same
degree of commitment. Nor do the respondents from other
agencies and environmental programs display the same kind of
organizational experiences with respect to the goals of their programs, as shown in the breakdown of these experiences:

> Determinist planners   31.6%
> Social forecasters   42.1
> Physical controllers   5.3
> Random appliers   15.8
> Eclectics   5.3

While the number of committed planners and social forecasters
is much greater than in most other international scientific programs, thus reflecting the growing programmatic emphasis on

the role of man in environmental matters, this trend is muted when we combine personal and organizational commitments in our typology of organizational ideologies:

Rationalists	21.0%
Pragmatists	15.8
Skeptics	31.6
Eclectics	31.6

The combined sample evinces no clustered perceptions with respect to any unwanted effects of the prominence of science and technology. Only a quarter feels that science increases the fragmentation between developed and developing countries and triggers undigestible social changes; a third feels that technique is being stressed at the expense of values; very few, however, feel that no untoward consequences at all are implicit in the application of science to social choice, in marked contrast to other scientific programs we analyzed. Nor does the combined sample show any special attachment to a single group of clients, though half identifies national environmental agencies as the units to be influenced by the programs. Unlike the MAB group, the combined sample divides about equally between those who affirm and those who deny that their work had influenced governments to see the complexity of cause-and-effect linkages; but the great majority still feels that consensus is achieved through bargaining and not through formal scientific demonstration of truth.

METEOROLOGY AND OCEANOGRAPHY

The attempt to manage the environment presupposes that we understand how and why the physical components of the environment interact to produce the effects to be managed. In this section we examine some international programs in meteorology and oceanography which are designed to obtain this knowledge. In the field of meteorology the chief actors are the World Meteorological Organization (WMO) and ICSU. Oceanographic research, to the extent that it is designed to deal with environmental issues, is closely coordinated with meteorological research through the International Decade of Ocean Exploration (IDOE) and the Integrated Global Ocean Stations System (IGOSS), both of which are managed by the Intergovernmental Oceanographic Commission (IOC). Marine pollution studies are carried out through the Global Investigations of Pollution in the Marine Environment (GIPME) program, managed by the IOC and the Intergovernmental Maritime Consultative Organization

(IMCO). The IOC is, in turn, advised by ICSU's Special Committee on Oceanographic Research (SCOR) and IMCO by the Group of Experts on Special Aspects of Marine Pollution (GESAMP). Our sample of respondents is drawn from these programs and organizations.[32]

This multiplicity of programs, organizations, and advisory groups of experts is, in turn, brought under a single roof by UNEP: This roof is best visualized as a jumble of gables and turrets of unequal height which have a tendency to leak. The great bulk of the actual measurements and observations, the largest number of experiments and models, the personnel and funds which mount these activities, the ships, sounding rockets, buoys, computers, teletypewriters, and balloons are deployed by national government laboratories, universities, and research agencies. The international machinery seeks only to define a division of labor for the national efforts and to provide for a standardized methodology; it is designed to accelerate and make more useful the collection of data needed to attempt environmental management eventually. No such management is now evident under international auspices.

Meteorological Research

The roots of international cooperation in meteorology go back to 1873, when the first International Meteorological Congress was held. Six years later, a nongovernmental group, called the International Meteorological Organization (IMO) was established to further collaboration among meteorological scientists. The nongovernmental status of this group, however, was already coming under scrutiny at the end of the First World War when the advent of weather forecasting as a public service suggested the need for governmental representatives in the organization. Thus, in 1935, the inclusion of such government representatives, and particularly of directors of national meteorological services, was made formal.[33] Even greater change, though, was needed after the Second World War. Meteorological technology was advanced by the war to an unprecedented level of sophistication, and the political-military relevance of meteorological data was being acknowledged. Clearly a new capability was needed. Consequently, in February 1946, the IMO became the WMO, a fully intergovernmental organization. In 1951 it adopted a program which was limited to the establishment of uniformity in observational practices through the preparation of technical regulations.[34] In our terms, it provided a common framework.

During the first decade of the organization, the efforts to achieve this uniformity were overriding and significant. Having pooled their data-gathering talents, the members were able to agree on technical regulations, and these became binding on all members, with formal notification required for any deviations. Further, during this period, WMO began systematically to collaborate with ICAO, UNESCO, FAO, WHO, IMCO, and ICSU, and thus it expanded its concern from providing weather forecasts for aviation and shipping to include agriculture, atmosphere pollution, and water resources.

However, little was accomplished during this period in the way of technical assistance. The first two WMO congresses virtually rejected a separate WMO technical program, and the third congress, although it increased financial support for assistance, failed to provide sufficient funds for a full program. It was not until the fourth congress, in 1963, that a firm commitment was made with WMO funds (called the New Development Fund, or NDF), allocated specifically for development purposes not provided from other services.[35]

Meanwhile, tremendous changes in technology were taking place. Of most relevance to meteorology were discoveries in electronics, statistics, and numerical analysis, the routine use of computers, progress in dynamic and physical meteorology, and the introduction of space techniques—particularly in the form of data transmission by satellite—into meteorology. So revolutionary were these developments that their consideration consumed most of the agenda of the fourth, fifth, and sixth congresses, culminating in sweeping programmatic changes within the WMO. The most important of these changes was the creation of the World Weather Watch (WWW) and of the Global Atmospheric Research Program (GARP). Furthermore, priorities were redefined and divided into four areas of "main activities": technical cooperation; interaction of man and his environment; education, training, and research; and the World Weather Watch.[36]

Technical cooperation primarily involves assistance in the form of expert missions, equipment, and some special projects geared either to provide meteorological and hydrological infrastructure to less developed countries or to promote research and training in the scientific aspects of natural disasters. Training in general meteorological and hydrological services is also conducted as a part of technical cooperation, both through individual fellowships and through regional training centers. Funding for all technical cooperation comes from the WMO regular budget, the WMO Voluntary Assistance Programme, and the United Nations Development Programme. UNDP is by far the most important donor.[37]

"Interaction of man and his environment" provides a focus for the application of meteorology to agriculture, aeronautics, operational hydrology and disaster relief. Data are collected through the WWW, GARP, and ocean observation stations, and are made available to scientists working in these fields. For example, since the 1974 World Food Conference, WMO has given agrometeorological information daily to experts and to national governments for assessing crop production and studying crop/weather relationships. WMO also prepares hydrological forecasts to promote research which might mitigate the effects of the Sahel droughts. Access to data for marine and aeronautical meteorology and for forest-fire prediction is provided. Cooperation between WMO and UNEP takes the form of WMO technical support and advice when requested by UNEP. UNEP gives financial support to WMO projects on background pollution monitoring, climatic change, and tropical cyclones.[38]

Research activity is exemplified by the Global Atmospheric Research Programme (GARP) to study physical processes of the atmosphere necessary for understanding large-scale weather fluctuations (in order to forecast on a long-term basis) and normal atmospheric circulation. GARP was conceived by ICSU and launched with WMO in 1967. It represents the largest and most complex international scientific research project ever initiated. GARP undertakings thus far have included the Atlantic Tropical Experiment (GATE), whose purpose is to pinpoint primary energy sources for atmospheric circulation; and the GARP Global Experiment, an attempt to define the circulation of the entire atmosphere, up to a height of thirty kilometers, and to develop a mathematical model for long-range forecasting.[39]

The WWW is a modest example of a joint facility. It requires, in addition to pooled labor, some standardization and harmonization of behavior among its multinational participants. Its essential components are a global observing system, consisting of observational networks; a global data-processing system, the global telecommunications system, consisting of facilities for rapid exchange of observational data; a research program; and a program in education and training.[40] WMO *coordinates* all but the last; the people and the equipment involved in these activities are the national meteorological services.

Oceanographic Research

SCOR. In oceanography as in meteorology, nongovernmental scientific cooperation eventually became subject to governmental interest and participation. SCOR was the first of the ICSU interunion commissions; it was established in 1957 when a number of ICSU unions expressed interest in a coordinating body on marine science. SCOR is responsible for the original conception and planning of the International Indian Ocean Expedition. In 1960 members of SCOR were invited by UNESCO to organize an expanded UNESCO program in oceanography. This meeting resulted in the creation of IOC and the appointment of SCOR as the main scientific advisory body to the IOC.[41]

The purpose of SCOR is to create and further an international capability for scientific activity in all branches of ocean research; it identifies areas of ocean research which can benefit from an international division of labor, and then arranges for obtaining the information. SCOR discharges its functions through the vehicle of a common framework, broken down into two major types of activities: planning international collaboration in oceanography by means of its working groups, and advising the IOC. The committee's membership is of three kinds: (1) scientists nominated by national committees for ocean research; (2) officers of affiliated organizations, the chairmen of all SCOR subsidiary bodies, and nominees of other ICSU committees; and (3) marine scientists who have no national committee with which to affiliate. There is an executive committee of all present officers, all past presidents of SCOR, and all current presidents of each affiliated ICSU organization. The executive committee is responsible for SCOR's work between general meetings.

SCOR's general meetings are held every two years, and its executive committee meets every eight months. The executive committee may respond directly to a request for advice posed by IOC, but it usually does so only when the advice is required immediately. When broader scientific opinion is needed, the question is put to the more than thirty SCOR national committees, or to a number of specific scientists with the appropriate expertise. When the answer requires a period of time and study, expert working groups within SCOR, or jointly between SCOR and other international and nongovernmental organizations, are formed in order to pool their expertise. These working groups examine problems related to international ocean activities and the marine environment, including the design of critical experiments and measurement programs. All reports from working groups, national committees, or individual scientists are reviewed by the executive committee and then passed on to the IOC.

The process is cumbersome and results in a proliferation of committees of experts with overlapping mandates. New projects are added helter-skelter; older projects are rarely abandoned. When marine pollution became a topic of international concern in the mid-1960s, SCOR was requested by IOC to make suggestions for dealing with it. A bewildering group of international committees was thus spawned, some with advisory and others with operational responsibilities.[42] The research program, rather than being comprehensive, is essentially an aggregation of distinct sectors of interest, gradually put together by oceanographers affiliated with national marine research institutions (public and private), predominantly in developed countries. The most active national SCOR committees are in Britain, the United States, Canada, France, and the Scandinavian countries.

SCOR, as an organization and in its interaction with IOC, is dedicated to the principle of making the world safe for oceanographic research. This commitment has increasingly brought it into conflict with the developing countries who look on oceanography as an investment in exploring their own natural resources and who are most reluctant to internationalize the activity.

IOC. The Intergovernmental Oceanographic Commission was created in 1960 as an integral part of UNESCO. However, with the advent of environmental concerns at UNCHE, other U.N. specialized agencies and some governments launched a campaign to separate IOC from UNESCO and make it into an interagency marine environmental operation. In the wake of UNCHE it was decided to make IOC an autonomous unit within UNESCO, jointly managed and financed by FAO, IMCO, WMO, WHO, and UNESCO.[43]

Before 1972 it would have been accurate to consider the IOC the public side of the private scientific network which is SCOR; since 1972 matters have become more complicated with the assertion of a nationalistic distrust of international oceanography on the part of the developing countries, which resulted in a loosening of links between SCOR and the IOC. At one time, the IOC relied heavily on using SCOR to build a programmatic consensus among the national committees and delegations which made up IOC's constituency. Now the IOC is trying to work out its own direct links with working groups of national experts in the earliest stages of program preparation, with the hope that these national experts will, in turn, be successful in influencing their respective national delegations.

No serious effort to link the sectors of research under a core idea was made before 1966. In that year the U.N. General Assembly adopted a resolution which called on the secretary-general to bring about a "comprehensive survey of what was being done by various governments and organizations in the fields of marine science and technology, and to formulate proposals on improved national arrangements for undertaking such a work."[44] Under the impetus of the 1966 resolution, the United States proposed an International Decade of Ocean Exploration. The overall program of the IOC—the Long-Term and Expanded Programme of Oceanic Exploration and Research (LEPOR)—is the result. It is to increase knowledge of the ocean, its contents, and its interfaces with land, the atmosphere, and the ocean floor, with the ultimate objective of enhancing the use of the oceans for peaceful purposes and for the application of rational planning and management of ocean resources. LEPOR is scheduled to run from 1971 to 1980, with programs in four major areas: (1) environmental forecasting, including the long-range prediction of weather and climate; (2) quality of the marine environment; (3) resources of the sea floor and sea bed; and (4) living resources, including the relationship between marine life and the marine environment. These activities are carried out by means of cooperative expeditions and other investigations and a network of national marine observation and monitoring posts for meteorologists, navies, and oceanographers. IOC seeks to cater to developing countries through its Training, Education, and Mutual Assistance (TEMA), primarily for the purpose of evaluating the needs in marine sciences of the developing countries, and of providing the needed facilities, training courses, and expertise through national committees. Does this program constitute a consensual, integrated approach to ecological management?

As oceans have become a major international issue in their own right, and as marine environmental issues have been directly and indirectly linked to broader environmental debates, the IOC has come under severe political pressures as the developing countries dispute the primacy of work on pollution. Even though the IOC has made an effort to provide both increased and improved technical assistance in response to the demands of the developing countries, the debate continues. Moreover, another ocean-related issue has since been interjected. The new issue pertains to the study of the seabed and to the collection and dissemination of data regarding resources in the area of "national waters." Attempts at designing the research program in such a way as to emphasize resources relating to development have not led to an agreement because any solution now depends on the Law of the Sea Conference, where the developing countries, and particularly the Latin American states, are "holding oceanography hostage to their claims on the territorial sea." In addition, the developing countries continue to seek a reduction of "IOC programs and expenditures . . . in areas they define as primarily the interest of industrial states, e.g., pollution studies and monitoring."[45] It is highly indicative of continued distrust that the IOC was systematically excluded from the Law of the Sea negotiations: The resource issue is too important to the developing countries to make them receptive to the expert advice of oceanographers.

Summary of Program Development

The experiences of meteorologists and oceanographers, as they relate to world order concerns, are not identical. Oceanography, because it has collided with the ongoing world debate on resource allocation and redistribution, is becoming a victim of a hostile political environment. It has been weakened by the differences in basic objectives which characterize the industrialized and developing members. Industrialized countries show increasing concern over pollution in the oceans and over the trade-offs between pollution and exploring for natural resources. Developing countries are more interested in controlling research off their shores and reaping the economic benefits of new discoveries. The only clear overlap in objectives relates to research on the living resources of the oceans. Oceanography will continue in its present state of fragmentation until the question "Who benefits from research?" is answered consensually.

Meteorology has managed to avoid this issue because of the noncontroversial nature of its research in a medium which is considered a public good.[46] More predictable weather is readily translated by any policy-maker into better crops and more effective storm warnings. Even though the actual work program of WMO is not systematically linked to the production of social benefits—these are promised but remain to be produced—the organization and its program of research are given the benefit of the doubt by governments. Meteorological research, unlike the case of oceanography, is left to the researcher and his invisible colleges.

Despite these differences, the two programs share many institutional characteristics. In terms of their underlying purposes, both are dedicated to the *acquisition* of a capability, to forecast weather more effectively, to understand the oceans better, to map atmospheric and oceanic conditions relating to pollution. The instrumentalities considered necessary for this by governments are a reflection of the consensus on purposes. In oceanography the stage of a common framework for negotiating minimal ground rules for research has never been transcended, and the division of labor remains a pooling of separate efforts. In meteorology, however, what started as a common framework for standardizing measurement and reporting has evolved into a joint facility. WMO, prior to the launching of the World Weather Watch and its associated research activities, did no more than seek to standardize and improve national methods of weather observation. WWW and GARP, however, have become more ambitious as collaborative enterprises. WWW, because of the technologies associated with it, calls for more than standardization: It demands the creation of new norms and practices specifically designed to fit into the central scheme. GARP, because of the nature of the scientific collaboration involved, implies a sequencing rather than a pooling of effort: Experiments conducted by one group or laboratory must be concluded and interpreted before the next experiment by another group becomes feasible. The institutions associated with oceanography were diffuse at the beginning and remain diffuse today. In the case of meteorology, however, the trend has been toward a pattern of institutionalization which resembles decentralization rather than diffuseness.

These differences disappear once we examine the evolution of decision-making processes. Both activities clearly exhibit the characteristics of the skeptic world order model, and not much change can be discovered. The search for new knowledge has been highly fragmented. New research commitments have grown up around very specific themes and concerns. Moreover, these themes have been defined in terms of the interests of scientists rather than with reference to social and economic demands. The pattern of learning is best described as the incremental accretion of new pieces of knowledge, a situation which might conceivably evolve into scanning in the case of meteorology, depending on the success of the model being elaborated in GARP. Objectives are added slowly in the case of meteorology. The process of addition is largely a function of the invention of new technologies in space exploration, data processing, and tele-communications, *not* the consequence of a serious reconsideration of overall goals. When technology makes possible the expansion of research, WMO and ICSU will attempt to formulate new goals which do justice to the possibilities. These goals, however, represent only an incremental increase over the prior goals. In oceanography, it is difficult to discover any new objectives; what has happened is that conflict over the old ones has intensified without giving rise to a new commitment. A tactical refocusing of end and means arrangements occurs, without giving rise to new master designs or a new consensus incorporating the knowledge gained with new social objectives. In oceanography, new demands are simply thrown onto the existing agenda without being integrated with it. In meteorology, it is taken for granted that man will be better served by more knowledge of atmospheric conditions. Ends and means in research are not systematically refocused at all. Bargaining patterns also differ slightly. In oceanography, what started out in 1960 as a constant-sum game among a few interested countries and professions, and which called for very little bargaining on the distribution of benefits from research, has now developed into something resembling a zero-sum game as the number of interested parties has increased. In meteorology, however, a constant-sum game continues to be acted out, characterized by package deals on substantive items which are closely related to one another, facilitated by inexpensive side payments offered by the governments most concerned to developing countries interested in better weather forecasting. This pattern is made possible by the fact that, while consensual knowledge may not be increasing rapidly enough to infect social goals, the degree of scientific consensus is already great enough to legitimate the programs actually carried out.

Views of Participating Scientists

A majority of our sample is doubtful that science is qualified to work for larger social goals, as shown in the distribution of personal attitudes toward the social role of science:

Determinists	0.0%
Instrumentalists	36.4
Skeptics	63.6
Eclectics	0.0

However, organizational experiences show a confidence in using oceanography and meteorology to translate science into social control. While there is no commitment to ecosystemic wholeness, there is a clear recognition that science can serve social needs:

Determinist planners	0.0%
Social forecasters	54.5
Physical controllers	27.3
Random appliers	9.1
Eclectics	9.1

The combined typologies provide us with a similar picture— no rationalists and only one eclectic—but with an averaging effect which lowers the overall anticipation of comprehensiveness. The skeptics clearly dominate these programs:

Rationalist	0.0%
Pragmatist	27.3
Skeptic	63.6
Eclectic	9.1

Who is the constituency for these pragmatists and skeptics? Just over half identifies the organization concerned and the professional discipline. A strong sense of internationalism is also indicated both by the number (44.4 percent) of respondents who named world interest as its clientele, and by the fact that no one referred to the home country as a source of identification. However, when asked to identify the clientele to be influenced, almost two-thirds named various national agencies and another third named national governments. Apparently we have a group of international scientists strongly identified with their professional disciplines and seeking to make their programs effective by collaborating with their professional counterparts in appropriate national agencies.

Were our respondents successful in convincing these national groups of the complexity and the logic underlying their program? Two-thirds of the respondents answered no. However, this should not necessarily be taken as a sign of failure, because few of the respondents themselves perceived the programs to be very comprehensive. A number of them felt that they should aim at goals which are simple and sectoral.

Were oceanographers and meteorologists able to apply the scientific method to reduce conflict in program planning? Forty percent stated that the issue does not even arise, that they are not called on to fulfill such a role. However, of those who do have an opportunity to use science in such a way, half preferred to use a method based on careful analysis of good data, and 40 percent relied on less sophisticated forms of argument based on reliable data. No one was so deterministic as to employ formal models, but neither was any one so skeptical of scientific methodology as to ignore it altogether and resort only to political coalitions.

The shape of the programs in oceanography and meteorology largely reflects the expectations of their framers. Work is directly relevant to the needs of states who initiate the programs. It makes few challenging cognitive demands on either the scientists or the decision-makers. The one major exception is the part of the program which runs head-on into allocation and resource issues. Here our respondents have met with less success, partly because most of the participants were unable, by virtue of their personal attitudes and professional commitments, to translate a rhetorical acceptance of a social forecasting role into a program palatable to the entire United Nations membership.

In short, the relative success of these programs is clearly associated with their sectoral specificity and the tight professional network of the participants, which encompasses a commitment to a common research methodology of considerable sophistication and an acceptance of standardized formal models. At the same time, interdisciplinary work is rudimentary, and the commitment to comprehensive social and ecological definitions of resource issues is more rhetorical than real. The mismatch between personal skepticism regarding the unifying role of science and the growing organizational commitment to integrated research and planning is too striking to be overlooked.

WATER RESOURCES

UNESCO *and the International Hydrological Decade*

The international importance of water resources was officially recognized by UNESCO's general conference in 1965. An International Hydrological Decade (IHD) was proposed for the purpose of promoting international cooperation in water research and in the training of experts and teachers in scientific hydrology. The intent was to generate improved and new hydrological infrastructure at the national level so that individual countries might make a fuller assessment of their own water resources, more rationally exploit their resources in view of changes in population, industry, and agriculture, and coordinate water development at a regional level.

The IHD was designed to operate through a coordinating council composed of twenty-one member states selected by the general conference of UNESCO. The council met at least once a year at UNESCO headquarters. Secretariat services were provided by the secretariat of UNESCO. The actual work of the IHD was accomplished through the pooled efforts of one hundred seven national committees. The only regions in which governments did not respond fully by creating such committees were in Africa (only twenty-three states participated) and in the Pacific. These committees ranged in size from over thirty members to three or four. They were typically composed of representatives of all government agencies having some responsibility for water, from meteorology to agriculture, and of professional hydrologists associated with universities and research centers. Nongovernment members were more prominent and numerous on the committees functioning in industrialized countries.

The scientific program of the Decade encompassed all aspects of hydrology, but primarily emphasized water within land areas. Five major categories of activities comprised the IHD program: (1) collection of basic data; (2) inventories and water balances; (3) research; (4) exchange of information; and (5) education and training in hydrology. The first three were the responsibility of the national committees, although assistance was provided by the international IHD secretariat. Much of this assistance was directed to developing member states. Some monies were budgeted for the IHD from UNESCO funds, though the lion's share was donated by UNDP.[47]

Collection of basic data included not only the actual gathering of information on water balances and hydrological processes, but also efforts to improve hydrological measurement techniques. Once basic data had been collected, participating countries established water balances in all geographical zones in order to allow hydrologists to plan for the rational utilization of water and related resources. A number of projects were created at the global, the regional, and the national levels. Global projects included inventories of snow and ice, estimates of the total world water balance, and measurements of glacier variations. National projects were designed to determine national water balances, including levels of precipitation, evaporation, river discharge, sediment discharge, groundwater reservoirs. Regional cooperative hydrological projects were encouraged in the Central American Isthmus and the La Plata Basin, at the Great Lakes, for the Danube and Rhine basins, the Baltic Sea Basin, the Mekong Basin, the Niger, Senegal, Taoudeni and Nubian Sandstone basins, and the Mediterranean Basin.[48] But there was no attempt to provide systematic links among the projects. States and regions had their own pet plans to which they devoted their research and for which they were willing to share their data.

In 1974, the Decade officially came to an end. When a survey of the Decade's achievements was carried out, it was felt that the main contribution had been the establishment of an infrastructure, of a capability, and the provision of an impetus for hydrological research and cooperation. Consequently, it was decided at the sixteenth session of the UNESCO general conference to launch a long-term intergovernmental program in order to carry through the momentum initiated by the Decade. This new program, of indeterminate length, is called the International Hydrological Programme (IHP).

UNESCO's *International Hydrological Programme*

The IHP is considered not only an extension but also an expansion of the IHD. This expansion includes more emphasis on the impact of man on hydrology, and the direct linking of this impact to complex problems of water management and the environment. It also includes a major concentration on eight scientific projects, but this concentration represents no more than a decision regarding priorities; these eight projects are not linked to a single comprehensive program. While there has definitely been a slow addition to the original IHD objectives, understanding of cause-effect relationships has not altered so as to suggest a conceptual switch to a new overriding set of means. IHP projects include studies on water balances, research into hydrological regimes and development of methods for hydrological computations for water planning, investigations in representative and experimental basins, the study and long-term prediction of the groundwater regime. The projects which specifically deal with the influence of man on the hydrological cycle are just beginning. These include the investigation of water regimes of river basins as affected by irrigation, study of self-purification processes, investigation of the effects of thermal discharges, the effects of urbanization on the hydrological regime of surface and groundwater and on the quality of water, and the development of hydro-ecological indices for the evaluation of water projects. New stress is also placed on cooperative activities between the IHP and MAB, WMO, FAO, and the IAEA.

Furthermore, although the IHD does not face the same north-south divisiveness as has the IOC, pressure has been exerted on the new IHP to strive for more direct relevance to development needs. Thus, the Eighteenth General Assembly of UNESCO, which included in its agenda deliberations on the new international economic order, gave the new IHP a specific mandate to concentrate on projects directly applicable to the needs of the developing countries, and to attempt to complete these soon. In addition, priority has been given to hydrological problems which, though they are not exclusive to developing countries, tend to be of considerable importance to them. These include droughts, floods, tropical storms, and problems peculiar to arid and semi-arid regions.

The International Hydrological Programme is to be executed through successive phases, each of six years' duration. At the end of each phase an evaluation will be made by the UNESCO general conference and the content of the next phase determined. A thirty-member Intergovernmental Council for the IHP, elected by the general conference, guides and supervises the implementation of the program. The council, in turn, established two advisory committees: one on the influence of man's activities on the hydrological regime, and a second on education, training, and technical assistance. The committees were encouraged to continue the interorganizational cooperation with COWAR, MAB, the IOC, WMO, and the IAEA that had been begun by its parent, the IHD. However, the real burden for project initiation and implementation remains with the national committees. A general plea was issued by the IHP to UNESCO's member states either to establish new national committees at the earliest possible date or to make use of the existing IHD committees for the IHP.

UNESCO's scientific advisory body for water questions is ICSU's Committee on Water Resources (COWAR). COWAR was established by ICSU in 1964 as a result of a proposal from the International Union of Geodesy and Geophysics. The committee's functions have always been closely tied to the IHD/IHP topics, although they have expanded beyond this in more recent years to include all aspects of water problems. In particular, COWAR's tasks are defined as analysis of problems in international water resources, and translation of this analysis into research programs; establishment and coordination of networks of international organizations interested in water problems; and carrying out scientific advisory activities for UNESCO, WMO, FAO, and WHO on matters relating to the IHD/IHP.[49]

In its role as scientific advisor to the IHD/IHP, COWAR participates in the plenary meetings of the Programme's coordinating council, and it frequently places a number of people on Decade and Programme working groups. It was also responsible for reviewing the work of the first half of the Decade, for preparing proposals for the second half of the Decade, and for submitting views on a long-term program in various fields of hydrology. COWAR's interests and activities are rather loosely linked under the general label of water resources. It does not have, nor seek to have, an integrated program.

It is difficult to assess the full merit and impact of the program in water resources, because it has been so inextricably inter-twined with previously existing national policies and plans for hydrology. For example, one respondent from the French IHD committee pointed out that the French committee's membership is composed almost entirely of scientists and representatives of the government's various hydrology-related departments (elec-tricity, water pollution), and consequently it is hard to differ-entiate the work of the government from the work of the com-mittee. Thus, while there is no question that a large amount of constructive hydrological work—especially of a cooperative na-ture around river basins[50]—has been carried out during the program, it is not always clear to whom or to what this work is responsible. Many of the programs had already begun before the Decade and have continued in operation separate and dis-tinct from it. Similarly, in many of the developing countries, there existed plans, independent of the Decade, to improve or to construct hydrological infrastructures.

While all of these activities may well have proceeded even in the absence of an international program, the water resources program has served as an extra "push," an extra impetus for decision-makers in priority planning for hydrology, and for sci-entists to pool and analyze hydrological data of a comparable nature. Furthermore, there is no question but that new research methods have been more rapidly diffused by the program, and that new networks of scientists have been established. These networks are composed almost exclusively of hydrologists and administrators of water resources and thus fall far short of true interdisciplinarity. Consequently, the success of such new emphases as the relationship between man and water, or the linking of water resources to development needs, will depend largely on the ability of those in the water resources program to cooperate with sister programs.

The conclusion is inescapable that, both with respect to decision-making and institutionalization, the program in water resources was and remains in the pattern we call skeptical. Its purpose is the acquisition of a capability to make better alloca-tional choices in the future. The instrumentality has not evolved beyond the stage of a common framework to recognize and de-limit the problem through appropriate research techniques, based on a pooled division of labor among national participants. The overall pattern is highly diffuse; very little evidence of any centrally accepted procedure or scheme can be discovered. The trend toward a more focused, but still decentralized, plan of action—as in the case of MAB and meteorology—is hardly discernible. Knowledge is being sought in a highly sector-specific fashion and the accumulation of knowledge is incremental. Its linkage with social and economic needs is left to decision-makers in other professions and lower levels of action. Objectives change slowly, if at all, and the meshing of ends and means in such a way as to reorder goals is episodic and rare. In some countries it is attempted, but in others it is not. The highly diffuse character of the activity and the modest amount of international financing all but precludes the need for any bargaining.

Perceptions of Scientists in Water Resources[51]

Given the low level of interdisciplinarity displayed by the scientists in water resources, it is not at all surprising to find that the personal attitudes of our respondents to the application of knowledge in policy-making cluster toward the skeptical:

Determinists	10.0%
Instrumentalists	10.0
Skeptics	60.0
Eclectics	20.0

Organizational experience, however, suggests considerable commitment to social and ecological goals—a finding which could be evidence of the programmatic shift toward greater interdisciplinarity noted earlier:

Determinist planners	14.3%
Social forecasters	28.6
Physical controllers	28.6
Random appliers	14.3
Eclectics	14.3

Organizational ideologies resemble those of the program on oceanography/meteorology: There are no rationalists, and over half of the respondents are skeptics:

Rationalists	0.0%
Pragmatists	14.3
Skeptics	57.1
Eclectics	28.6

Fully 70 percent identify their professional discipline as their main constituency; half mention a world interest and only 20 percent identify their organization. This is certainly consistent with our assessment that most of the real work done under the auspices of water resources is actually carried out, planned, coordinated at the national level. Moreover, influence appears to flow from one national government sector to another: Asked whom they seek to influence, 70 percent of the respondents named various national agencies, and 30 percent named national governments.

Were our respondents successful in convincing these national groups of the complexity and the logic underlying their program? Fifty percent said yes, and 50 percent said no. It is difficult to assess precisely what this might mean, but one may conjecture that, since most clients and targets of influence were at the national level, this is a reflection of varying country experiences.

Were they able to apply the scientific methods and assumptions implicit in their program to reduce conflict in program planning? Very few said that this issue does not arise in their program, but over two-thirds stated that conflicts are best handled through either careful analysis (57.1 percent) or formal models (14.3 percent). When asked to specify what some of these conflicts might be, most respondents referred to problems of environmental degradation due to industrial pollution. When these scientists were given an opportunity to advise policymakers on difficult choices to be made, 60 percent considered themselves successful in changing the perceptions of the politicians to reduce conflicts.

PUBLIC HEALTH

Our sample of scientists active in international programs relating to public health was drawn largely from the World Health Organization (WHO). Moreover, a large number of the respondents were consultants to that organization rather than officials of it.[52] This is a virtue in terms of eliciting impressions of program-making because WHO relies heavily on the services of consultants organized into standing advisory panels, both at the global and the regional levels. Members of our sample were associated with a variety of programs, but they do not represent a cross-section of WHO activities, nor do they fit into the core responsibilities of IAEA or FAO. Their work deals with applied radioactivity, intersectoral modeling and design of country health services, maternal and child health services, determination of toxic content in food, study of the genetic composition of populations, control of brucellosis, plague, and coccal diseases. We therefore give a brief overview of WHO to show where these activities fit in.

The World Health Organization

WHO is dedicated to "the attainment by all peoples of the highest possible level of health," and health is defined as "a state of complete physical, mental and social well-being and not merely the absence of disease or infirmity."[53] However, this commitment, no matter how holistic and interdisciplinary it appeared to be, soon gave way to a program which was geared to the control of individual diseases and based on a tight professional network of medical personnel. Major attempts at health planning and preventive medicine which encompass nonmedical considerations as well were not made until the late 1960s. Moreover, global planning in WHO is difficult because of the organization's commitment to decentralization.

It is WHO's decentralization into six regional organizations which makes it unusual among U.N. specialized agencies and facilitates its direct access to states. Each region has a regional committee and a regional office, headed by a regional director; such organizations are presently provided for Southeast Asia, the Eastern Mediterranean, the Western Pacific, the Americas, Africa, and Europe. The post of regional director is always important. "All communications from the field must pass through the appropriate regional office; they cannot be sent directly to WHO headquarters in Geneva. Thus the regional director occupies a crucial point in the organization's communications network. Acting on behalf of the director-general, regional directors have authority over all appointments of field personnel in their region."[54] In addition, although the regional budget must pass through review by the entire regional committee, the regional director puts together the budget. His primary constraint is that he is elected by the regional committee and is "thus unlikely to take action that would alienate its members."[55] The overwhelming majority of WHO's funds—approximately 90 percent—is expended in activities which directly benefit the states, through, for example, epidemiological services and research, technical assistance projects, and fellowships. Approximately 16 percent of the budget is spent at the Geneva headquarters, while the remaining 84 percent is used by the regional offices.[56]

Decisions on, and priorities among, program items are determined by the biannual World Health Assembly; their implementation is supervised by an executive board, but program initiatives seldom originate in these organs. Ideas and proposals tend to originate in the secretariat's divisions, where they are discussed at the regional and global levels in conjunction with the large number of standing panels of experts associated with each division. These same panels often monitor the programs. With the significant exceptions of the issue of population planning and birth control, and an early disagreement over WHO's role in

making available medical supplies to member states, major controversies had been excluded from the WHO agenda until the
Arab-Israeli issue became prominent in 1976.[57] In general, the
work of the secretariat and its expert panels has been severely
"technical"; the scientists associated with WHO take pride in
their professionalism and are self-conscious in considering public health a nonpolitical matter to be dealt with in medical terms.
To what extent this devotion to technical criteria also militates
against the definition of health as a multidisciplinary matter
which overlaps with conflicting approaches to development policy remains somewhat ambiguous.

Major WHO programs can be described in ascending order
from the most self-contained and "technical" to the more open-
ended program commitments which depend on contributions
from other disciplines. The more interdisciplinary the commitments, the more doubtful it becomes that the public health profession can treat as "medical" and "factual" questions which call
for allocational choices in a setting of scarcity. In short, the self-
contained items in the program are of long standing and largely
beyond controversy; the open-ended ones provide the source of
the ongoing controversy over the relationship of public health to
development and environmental protection in general. It is relatively simple, for instance, to stipulate that malaria should be
eradicated; it is more difficult to find consensus on such themes
as community health planning with public participation, or the
subordination of supplementary food programs to eco-development planning.

The criteria of medical professionalism continue to rule in the
WHO program for eradicating malaria, tuberculosis, yaws, tra-
choma, smallpox, leprosy, syphilis, gonorrhea, and influenza.
Similar principles prevail in the research WHO sponsors in the
field of veterinary diseases which can be transmitted to man, as
well as in the fields of cancer and heart disease. WHO also maintains advisory services for population planning, maternal and
child health, and supplementary feeding programs providing
protein-rich foods. In all of these areas, field projects are undertaken with UNDP funds and through the budgets of the central
and regional offices which pay for the training of local personnel, the improvement of medical education, and the creation of
local administrative services.

In addition to these activities, WHO maintains certain international public health services which also respond to a sector-
specific definition of health and which have long been administered according to stringent medical principles of quality. Thus,

WHO coordinates the world effort in standardizing the content and labeling of drugs through the International Pharmacopaea. It maintains advisory services on the adverse effects of drugs and certifies the addictive qualities of new drugs. WHO is the nerve center of the world's warning system on the spread of epidemics through its epidemiological intelligence service.

What about health as a state of "complete physical, mental and social well-being"? True, WHO quickly expanded its services to developing countries beyond attacks on specific diseases when its membership more than doubled after 1960. After some hesitancy the organization launched a program in social psychiatry and the epidemiology of mental disorders. Its entry into the field of population planning took place after the advent of the developing countries. A broadening of the spectrum took place again after UNCHE, when joint programs with other specialized agencies were launched in the fields of water and air quality, the evaluation of new insecticides and of pollutants as public health hazards. In adding these activities, WHO in effect entered the area of development planning, a long step from a commitment to the eradication of specific diseases.

But such a commitment does not assure that a professional concern with specific sectors has in fact been transcended. The difficulties in superimposing a comprehensive approach on an established capacity to cope with specific problems are illustrated in the abortive WHO effort to apply a model for comprehensive health planning. Long-term programs arranged according to a hierarchy have been discussed in the World Health Assembly, but in fact priorities continue to be established piecemeal. Attention has also been called to the need to link the numerous health-related projects within a single country into a national health plan and relate this plan explicitly to development. Such a program, called intersectoral modeling, was begun in 1970. Its purpose was to construct a model of the "health" of national populations with health care as the core, and then to apply it in specific countries through Country Health Programming. Country Health Programming was to aid a country in setting up an entire health program, taking into account the socioeconomic variables which are thought to interact with illness. By employing its model as a theoretical framework for Country Health Programming, the intersectoral modeling group hoped not only to test its own work, but also to provide a foundation for broadening the concept and publicizing the full implications of a health care system. However, in practice, Country Health Programming did not make use of the intersectoral modeling.

There was a lack of interaction between the modeling team and the regional WHO team which administered the program. Perhaps the model was inapplicable once it was transferred from computer to field. As matters turned out, even Country Health Programming was a failure. However, it is not clear whether this was the fault of the program's logic or approach, or of the personnel involved, or of the fact that the states where it was applied were interested more in the WHO imprimatur (which would allow them to qualify for outside aid) than they were in WHO planning techniques.

The international collaborative effort in public health remains institutionally diffuse, even though most of the activity is carried on by WHO. Diffuseness, despite organizational concentration, is due to the evident satisfaction associated with the pooling of information and data-gathering methods which characterizes the division of labor among governments and between governments and WHO. No more than a common framework seems to be required to make the actors happy. Their purpose was and is confined to creating a capability for better policy at the national level and for a more effective sharing of consensual information at the international level. The garnering of new knowledge is defined by medical definitions of illness. This will continue to be true as long as governments and professionals resist the effort to redefine public health objectives in terms of economic and social development concepts. Hence the learning process remains incremental. Goals change in the sense that new objectives are added piecemeal, without leading to any successful integration of the new with the old, or any systematic reconsideration of the appropriateness of ends and means linkages. As long as the professional consensus on the adequacy of this pattern continues to prevail, there is little call for bargaining over the allocation of resources and skills.

Views of Respondents

Scientists affiliated with the public health programs clearly do not share our view of such a lack of integration. They consider medical and biological knowledge to be an authoritative guide to policy:

Personal Attitudes

Determinists	33.3%
Instrumentalists	50.0
Skeptics	16.7
Eclectics	0.0

Obviously, their understanding of the importance of intersectoral linkages and comprehensive thinking in the field of public health is different from our assessment, since these findings suggest a confidence about the potential of scientific knowledge which we do not find in the manner in which segments of the WHO program are connected with one another. The differences in perception are explained by the type of organizational experiences which dominate:

Organizational Experience

Determinist planners	8.3%
Social forecasters	16.7
Physical controllers	58.3
Random appliers	8.3
Eclectics	8.3

The task of public health programs, then, is to deal with medical conditions which sap *physical* welfare. The purpose of the program is to cope with these physical problems; the number of public health experts who seek to subordinate these to a view of social and ecological planning is relatively small. Thus, if the definition of one's mission is confined to coping with physical implications, with a pathology whose causes are understood and for which relief is possible, a self-perception which suggests satisfaction with the professional knowledge at the basis of public action is to be expected.

The combined typologies give us a very high number of pragmatists. The participants have a high level of certainty regarding the usefulness of their expertise; they differ only slightly in their conceptions of how broadly this expertise may be extended in terms of goals.

Organizational Ideologies

Rationalists	9.1%
Pragmatists	72.7
Skeptics	18.3
Eclectics	0.0

Also unique to this program is the prevailing perception of who the clients are. There is a relatively strong sense of identification with "world interest" (45.5 percent) *and* with the respondents' professional disciplines (54.5 percent). Since most of our respondents are advisers, we do not find a strong identification with either home countries (9.1 percent) or the organization (18.2 percent). Detached professionalism prevails. Another 41.7 percent felt that they were influencing the international secretariat, and 25.0 percent, an international political body; 41.7 percent also named national governments, but only 25.0 percent named national agencies as targets of their work.

Were our respondents successful in convincing national target groups of the complexity and the logic underlying their program? The answer is an overwhelming no (72.7 percent), but this must be taken as lack of satisfaction with program *integration,* not disappointment with sector-specific activities.

In conclusion, we repeat that the key to the success of this program lies in its decentralization, sector specificity, and medical professionalism. Although there have been a number of attempts at comprehensive program planning, most respondents seem to be satisfied with a more fragmented, project-by-project approach. This is, however, by no means a unanimous and final opinion, and the malaise regarding this question is clear in the respondents' answers. One might expect that, as isotope tracers, nutritional planning, community health programs, and other approaches which transcend conventional medicine are introduced, there will be even greater pressure to incorporate interdisciplinarity and integration into the program.

ENVIRONMENTAL PROGRAMS: HOW CLOSE TO ECOSYSTEMIC PLANNING?

Commitment to a holistic perspective is striking among scientists affiliated with United Nations and ICSU environmental activities. The distribution of organizational ideologies of the entire group looks like this:

Organizational Ideologies
(N = 48)

Rationalists	10.4%
Pragmatists	31.3
Skeptics	39.6
Eclectics	18.8

The combined figure for rationalists and pragmatists among scientists associated with programs of global economic development is 25 percent (see Chapter 9); the corresponding figure for personnel in international science programs of the industrialized countries is 35 percent (see Chapter 7). Can we conclude that the world is on the way toward the acceptance of an ecosystemic perspective? Can we infer also that the combination of scientific knowledge and scientific decision-making implied by such a perspective is propelling us toward a rationalist world order?

The answer is no. While the aggregate of the four programs may seem to justify such a conclusion, it would be a serious mistake to regard the four programs as constituting a single approach and a single commitment. Our discussion showed that the commitment to focusing on man and his works as the crucial cause of environmental disequilibrium is *not* matched by projects of research and regulation that would subordinate man's activities to a comprehensive plan. Within the overall commitment to single out man and his works, the sector-specific preoccupation of professionals and government agencies continues to hold sway.

Moreover, we cannot claim that our respondents shared or accepted our definition of ecosystemic holism and integrated planning: Some did and some did not. The single focus— environmental connectedness—is our construct, not the respondents'. Each of the four programs contained its own dependent variable, its own notion of connectedness among independent variables, and therefore its unique standard of what constitutes a successful program. Scientists associated with MAB and SCOPE may come close to sharing our concept of the crucial dependent variable, but the same cannot be said of oceanographers, hydrologists, and public health specialists.

Hence an aggregate appreciation of these programs would be artificial. It would mislead us in pinpointing links between science and future world orders. A comparison of the four programs must respect the different conceptions which prevail among the participating scientists. Since there is no common dependent variable—not even at a rhetorical level of commitment—comparable to the principle of making science and technology the servant of a more perfect industrial society, there is no point in constructing an imaginary dialog; our respondents, considered across the programs, do not have enough in common to engage in the appropriate conversation. Most of them remain too remote from any application of science to policy-making in the economic and social sectors to give point to their discussion.[58] The situation is otherwise, however, when, in the next chapter, we take up the same nexus of concerns in a setting of economic and social development.

We now compare the four programs in terms of their implications for new world orders. We believe that a commitment to regarding man's activities as the core concern is a crucial indication of the extent to which living "in" and "with" the physical environment is coming to be considered as a field for rational analysis and deliberate social engineering. Such a commitment implies that man's activities, after being "understood" on the basis of good data, can be changed and rechanneled so as to be compatible with an ecological objective (preservation of the environment) and a social goal (a higher quality of life equitably distributed among all countries). Discovering and demonstrating the "truth" will provide the rational focus for future policy; it will suggest the rules and institutions needed by man to fashion that policy.

How "whole" is the environment and how successful are international scientists in demonstrating this "wholeness" to national governments? The distribution of organizational ideologies across the four programs and the impressions regarding the complexity of linkages provide some answers. (We recall that the construction of organizational ideologies highlights the role attributed to science in working out government priorities and stresses the extent· to which a concern for social and economic objectives is self-consciously incorporated into science policy planning; rationalists and pragmatists are the types of scientists who opt for a special role for science and who are concerned with the social and physical implications of science and technology.)

With the exception of the program in public health, there is *no* overwhelming commitment to enthroning science as the font of wisdom in public policy. Moreover, as we have argued, the finding for public health specialists must be interpreted with caution because of the tendency of these professionals to associate the control of specific diseases with social planning and forecasting; their conception of the whole is smaller than ours. However, it also appears as if participants in programs with very modest social and economic aims tend to regard their work as more successful in demonstrating scientific complexity to national governments. Hydrologists, who score lowest on organizational ideologies, do best on success; medical personnel show the greatest disappointment. Scientists associated with ecosystemic research in MAB, scope, and unesco have a marked, but not dominant, commitment to comprehensive organizational ideologies and also show a modest degree of satisfaction with their impact on governments. Perhaps their experience suggests that a totally new world order is not required?

Before we can entertain this possibility, three further tests can

TABLE 15
Key Characteristics of Global Environmental Programs (percentages)

Characteristic	Environmental research	Oceanography/ meteorology	Water resources	Public health
Organizational ideology: Rationalists + Pragmatists	36.8	27.3	14.3	83.3
Personal attitudes: Determinists + Instrumentalists	31.6	36.4	20.0	83.3
Organizational experience: Planners + Social forecasters	73.3	54.5	42.9	25.0
Organizational experience: Physical controllers	5.3	27.3	28.6	58.3
Most important client is professional discipline	41.2	55.6	70.0	54.5
Most important target is national administrative agency	52.6	63.6	70.0	36.4
Complexity of linkages successfully demonstrated to national governments	43.8	33.3	50.0	27.3
Conflict reduced by use of formal models and good data	30.8	50.0	71.4	insufficient data

be applied to our four programs. In terms of personal attitudes, determinists and instrumentalists believe that science is either superior to, or at least different from, other modes of thinking; they also favor interdisciplinary modes of analysis and associate the progress of these methods with more rational priorities for government action. It seems reasonable to suppose that such thinking would be *hostile* to identification with one's own profession. Determinists and instrumentalists might prefer to influence important global and national decision-making fora rather than functionally specific national agencies. What, then, do we find?

1. Public health specialists, indeed, do not see in national agencies their primary target group, but they still identify with their professional peers to a greater extent than with any other group of possible clients.

2. Oceanographers and meteorologists come next in opting for determinism and instrumentalism (though only a third of the sample does so), and they overwhelmingly identify national administrative agencies as their target while also identifying with their professions.

3. Ecosystemic researchers tend not to be determinists and instrumentalists, identify less with their professional peers than do other scientists, only half selects national agencies as their target, and they are reasonably self-satisfied.

4. Hydrologists, finally, are overwhelmingly skeptics and eclectics; they identify strongly with their professional peers and with specific national agencies, *and also consider themselves more successful than any other group.*

In short, there is no consistent and strong association between success, professional and administrative specialization, and a commitment to interdisciplinary thinking. The water resources program suggests that the key to success lies in fragmented thinking, high professional identification, and access to specific national agencies. Yet the ecosystemic research program contains a clue that no such sweeping conclusion is warranted.

A similar test is possible if we compare organizational experience to professional identification and national target groups. The contrast is between organizational goals which stress overall planning and social forecasting as opposed merely to controlling the physical manifestations of environmental factors. Among public health personnel, lack of success goes hand-in-hand with a commitment to physical control and significant identification with professional peers. Hydrologists profess moderate identification with social forecasting and planning, while over a quarter identifies with physical control; yet their satisfaction coexists with great professional and administrative specialization. Meteorologists and oceanographers are more committed to social forecasting than hydrologists, identify less with their professional disciplines, but seek out national administrative agencies as targets almost as often as hydrologists—and see themselves as considerably less successful. Before we conclude that the key to success is the combination of professional and administrative specialization with a moderate endorsement of social forecasting, we should recall that ecosystemic research again proves this inference to be misleading. Ecosystemic researchers overwhelmingly opt for planning and social forecasting, identify less with their professional peers than do any others, and look to national administrative targets less commonly than do hydrologists and meteorologists. And yet they see themselves as moderately successful.

Since neither of these tests discloses a clear pattern of association, we attempt a third one. Is success associated with a commitment to the scientific method as a device for preempting or avoiding political bargaining as a way of making decisions? It evidently is in the case of water resources planning, a conclusion which also strengthens the impression that success goes hand-in-hand with professional, administrative, and disciplinary specialization. However, ecosystemic research personnel profess some satisfaction, and less than a third of the sample thought that success goes together with reliance on formal models and good data! Most of our respondents instead called attention to the incidence of major environmental catastrophes as the triggers of consensus among governments. Meteorologists and oceanographers, finally, did point to the importance of formal models as builders of agreement, though they are not particularly happy with their impact on governments.

No single variable is clearly associated with success. The experiences of the four programs are diverse, and they tell no single story. Knowledge is not the sole key to political agreement, and the sharing of knowledge among disciplines has not produced an evenly overarching consensus on ecological wholeness even among scientists. Some programs get along fine without consistently paying obeisance to the goddess of connectedness; others could not get off the ground without making sacrifices at her altar.

No tidy future world order can be projected from such a pattern. Global programs of environmental research, mapping, and regulation are certainly major innovations in terms of methods, commitments, and institutions. They do imply a way of looking at interdependence which could not have come into being without dramatic changes in consensual scientific knowledge. Science has heavily influenced the means considered appropriate for action. It is undeniable that it has also affected the definition of goals and objectives, though less significantly. Whether these findings can be used to speculate about future world orders will be examined in the concluding chapter.

Notes

1. Garrett Hardin, *Exploring New Ethics for Survival: The Voyage of the Spaceship Beagle* (Baltimore: Penguin, 1973), p. 16.

2. "The Cocoyoc Declaration," adopted by the participants in the UNEP/UNCTAD symposium on "Matters of Resource Use, Environment, and Development Strategies," October 8–12, 1974. *International Organization,* summer 1975, p. 901.

3. For a complete survey of U.N. activities in science and technology, see R. M. Lees, "Institutional Arrangements for Science and Technology within the United Nations System," U.N. doc. ESA/S&T/Misc. 2 and ESA/S&T/Misc. 2/Annex and Add. 1, January 13, 1975.

4. *Proceedings* of the IUCN Eighth General Assembly, p. 83.

5. *Man's Impact on the Global Environment,* Report of the Study of Critical Environmental Problems (SCEP) (Cambridge, Mass.: M.I.T. Press, 1970).

6. The situation before UNCHE is described in "Current Activities and Plans in the United Nations System on Monitoring or Surveillance," doc. A/CONF. 48/IWGM.1/Inf. 1, July 1971. We are indebted to Dr. Branislav Gosovic for leading us to these sources.

7. The issues are analyzed from these viewpoints in "Environment and Development: The Founex Report," *International Conciliation* 586 (January 1972).

8. The Founex report was written by a panel of twenty-seven senior experts from all parts of the world, meeting in Founex, June 4–12, 1971. The panel was chaired by Gamani Corea, then consultant to the secretary-general of the U.N. on environmental and development planning matters and deputy-governor of the Bank of Ceylon, and soon to become secretary-general of UNCTAD. Even though the report was "unofficial," the character of the participants went a long way toward preparing a consensus for the upcoming UNCHE session.

9. Text of the Report in U.N. Conference on the Human Environment, doc. A/CONF. 48/10, Annex I, December 22, 1971. While the emphasis was put on national action, the panel also recommended that regional organizations assume a training and technical assistance function in this area and that global agencies assume responsibility for compensating poor countries for special costs incurred in attempting environmental management. Global programs should assume responsibility for devising nonpolluting industries and for financing their introduction into poor countries through appropriate research.

10. MAB-ICC, First Session, Paris, November 9–19, 1971, p. 40.

11. Most specialized agencies with responsibility for development programs anticipated UNCHE by redefining their ongoing activities so as to make them appear congruent with the environmental emphasis, thus marrying environmental concerns with an unchanged commitment to economic development. The agencies expected the new environmental funds to be made available for specific projects, much like the UNDP formula. Projects would be worked out jointly by several agencies, but one agency would be designated as the "lead agency" and given responsibility for administering the projects.

12. For UNCHE, see the summary of Lars-Goran Engfeldt, "The United Nations and the Human Environment—Some Experiences," *International Organization,* summer 1973, pp. 393–412. The issues debated at Stockholm and the divergence of approaches which were to be accommodated in UNEP can be gleaned from David A. Kay and Eugene B. Skolnikoff (eds.), "International Institutions and the Environmental Crisis," *International Organization,* spring 1972. UNEP is included in our study only insofar as its activities are reflected in the work of other U.N. agencies. We present this summary of activities to set the scene, not to offer a systematic analysis of UNEP.

13. Doc. UNEP/GC/32, March 7, 1975, p. 31.

14. Earthwatch consists of three separate activities: (*a*) Global Environmental Monitoring System (GEMS), (*b*) International Referral Service, (*c*) International Register of Toxic Substances. The referral service is a global data bank of existing knowledge regarding pollution and its control. GEMS is the heart of the operation. It is the sum of existing monitoring activities plus UNEP's effort to coordinate, integrate, and expand

them. This involves ten major UNEP-financed projects for the period 1973–1978. The total cost is $5,556,000, of which the UNEP share is $3,424,000, distributed as follows:

Lead agency	Number of projects	Total cost	UNEP contribution (%)	Activity
WHO	2	865,000	57	air and water pollution
WMO	2	321,000	61	pollution of atmosphere
IAEA/IOC	2	448,000	39	intercalibration for trace metals
WMO/IOC	1	336,000	80	IGOSS
FAO/Unesco	1	1,005,300	54	soil degradation
UNEP/FAO	1	1,450,565	86	Mediterranean Pollution Program
ICSU/SCOPE	1	1,129,700	45	Chelsea Laboratory

SOURCE: Docs. UNEP/GC/14/Add. 2, pp. 100–2; UNEP/GC/32, pp. 36–7; UNEP/GC/62, pp. 26–8; UNEP/GC/68, Annex. Courtesy of Branislav Gosovic.

Note: The budget figures represent the share contributed by international organizations in the U.N. system. The bulk of contributions comes from national governments directly.

15. International Council of Scientific Unions, Special Committee for the International Biological Programme, *1970 Review*, September 1970, p. 2.

16. Ibid., p. 5.

17. Emphasis in original. International Council of Scientific Unions *Bulletin* 19 (November 1969), p. 25.

18. Ibid., chap. 6 ("Problems of the Human Environment").

19. Ibid., p. 28.

20. Doc. UNEP A/Conf./18/10, Annex 2, pp. 6–13.

21. For a description of UNESCO's work in the social sciences, humanities, culture, and in the field of communications, see John E. Fobes, "UNESCO: Management of an International Institution—Facilitating and Understanding Economic and Social Change," in Robert S. Jordan (ed.), *Multinational Cooperation* (London: Oxford University Press, 1972), pp. 110–50; and James P. Sewell, "UNESCO: Pluralism Rampant," in Robert W. Cox and Harold K. Jacobson (eds.), *The Anatomy of Influence* (New Haven: Yale University Press, 1973), pp. 139–74.

22. UNESCO, "International Coordinating Council of the Programme on Man and the Biosphere," first session (Paris: November 9–19, 1971), *MAB Report Series no. 1*, pp. 7–8.

23. MAB's thirteen projects can be ranked in terms of the level of complexity they seek to cover. Projects dealing with natural ecosystems only are at the lowest rung; next come projects which study the impact of human activities in specific biomes; the effects of technology constitute the next level; the highest level is sought in the project entitled "perception of environmental quality," because it is designed to sketch perceptions as catalysts or retardants of environmental action. The projects are as follows:

Group 1: conservation of natural areas and genetic material; interactions between environmental transformations and genetic and demographic changes.

Group 2: Effects of human activities and management practices on tropical and subtropical forests, temperate forests, grazing lands, arid and semi-arid zones with emphasis on irrigation; lakes, marshes, rivers, and coastal zones; mountains; islands.

Group 3: Pest management and fertilizer use in terrestrial and aquatic ecosystems; effects on man of major engineering works; energy utilization in urban and industrial systems.

Group 4: Perception of environmental quality.

The perception project was to permeate all of the other MAB activities. In 1973, four more areas of emphasis were added to it: the effects of pollution on ecosystems; the long-term influence of human economic activity on the energy resources of the biosphere; the effects of various land tenure systems on the biosphere and on the immediate environment; and the effects of war, and particularly of chemical warfare, on the biosphere. "International Coordinating Council of the Programme on Man and the Biosphere," Second Session (Paris, April 10–19, 1973), *MAB Report Series no. 10*, pp. 9–10.

24. Developed countries account for the majority of these national committees. The MAB international secretariat has had to work more directly with the developing countries in order to establish national committees. In 1973–74, 41.8 percent of the budget went to direct assistance to national committees and regional groups; in 1975/76, the figure was 31.5 percent. Expenditures rose from $181,460 to $191,000. See UNESCO, *Approved Programme and Budget for 1973–1974*, doc. 18 C/5 (Paris, February 1975), pp. 210–14.

25. It is unclear how much of this role was precipitated or even dictated by UNEP. We do know that by the middle of the decade, MAB began to look toward UNEP for major financial support. Thus, in the 1973/74 budget, MAB was allocated $432,990, with no recorded additions from UNEP. However, in the 1975/76 budget, MAB was allocated $606,707 by UNESCO and an additional $446,000 from UNEP. This led to a much heavier concern in MAB projects with environmental pollution than previously. UNESCO, *Approved Budget for 1973–1974*, pp. 211–16, and UNESCO, *Approved Budget for 1975–1976*, pp. 210–14.

26. UNESCO, "Regional Meeting on the Establishment of Co-operative Programmes of Interdisciplinary Ecological Research, Training and Rangeland Management for Arid and Semi-Arid Zones of Northern Africa," organized jointly by UNESCO, FAO, and UNEP (Sfax, April 3–12, 1975), *MAB Report Series no. 30*.

27. Ibid., p. 25.

28. UNESCO, "Task Force on the Contribution of the Social Sciences to the Man and the Biosphere Programmes" (Paris, February 28–March 2, 1974), *MAB Report Series no. 17*, p. *iii*.

29. Ibid.

30. The MAB sample was made up of thirteen individuals, eleven of whom provided us with codeable information. Six respondents were UNESCO officials and seven were members of national MAB commissions, who were counted as delegates in our breakdown of roles. Among the eleven we count ten biological scientists and one physicist.

31. This group was composed as follows: three officials of nongovernmental organizations, two of whom were concerned with general environmental issues, and one who specialized in the human settlements area; two advisers on human settlements questions, one of whom worked with UNESCO and the other with IBRD; three officials of intergovernmental organizations dealing with general environmental questions, one each affiliated with FAO, WHO, and UNESCO. The number for all environmentally related programs was nineteen.

32. Our sample included eleven persons. Five were affiliated with IOC, four with WMO, one each with IMCO and SCOR. Nine were officials of intergovernmental organizations, one was an official of a nongovernmental organization, and one was an adviser.

33. Edith Brown Weiss, "International Responses to Weather Modification," *International Organization*, summer 1975, pp. 809–10.

34. "One Hundred Years of International Cooperation in Meteorology (1873–1973)—A Historical Review," *WMO Bulletin*, vol. 22, no. 2 (April 1973), pp. 180–2.

35. Ibid., p. 185.

36. WMO/WWW, "Planning Report No. 30: Scope of the 1972–1975 Plan, with Particular Reference to Meteorological Sub-Systems" (Geneva, 1969), p. 2.

37. WMO, *Annual Report of the World Meteorological Organization 1974* (Geneva, 1975), pp. 58–68.

38. Ibid., pp. 44–9.

39. WMO/WWW, "Planning Report no. 30," pp. 193–5.

40. David Arthur Davies, "Man and His Environment," in R. Symonds (ed.), *International Targets for Development* (New York: Harper Colophon, 1970), pp. 39–40. The observing system is composed of a combination of surface stations, merchant ships, ocean

weather ships, commercial aircraft, and meteorological satellites, collectively called IGOSS. The data-processing system functions through three world meteorological centers (which process global data), regional meteorological centers (which prepare more detailed analysis and forecasts for their regions), and national meteorological centers (which operate according to their respective levels of sophistication). Likewise, the GTS processes data at global, regional, and national levels of organization. Most of the research activities are part of GARP: WWW provides GARP with observational data, and GARP translates this data where possible into mathematical models.

41. Warren Wooster, "Interaction between Intergovernmental and Scientific Organizations in Marine Affairs," *International Organization*, winter 1973, p. 105. There are four permanent science advisory groups to the IOC; the other three are the Engineering Committee on Ocean Resources (ECOR), which represents the World Federation of Engineering Organizations; the Advisory Committee on Marine Resources Research (ACMRR); and the Advisory Committee on Oceanographic Meteorological Research (ACOMR).

42. ACMRR is a group of independent experts attached to the Department of Fisheries of FAO. GESAMP has become the main body of international expertise for identifying marine pollutants and proposing methods for assessing them. While GESAMP reports to a number of U.N. specialized agencies, its main patron is IMCO. For a discussion on the relationship between the IOC and ACMRR and GESAMP, see Michael Brenner, "The Inter-Governmental Oceanographic Commission and the Stockholm Conference: A Case of Institutional Non-Adaptation," *International Organization*, summer 1975, pp. 779, 781–2, 785, and 793. For a discussion of the relationships among SCOR, IOC, IMCO, ACMRR, and GESAMP, see Wooster, *International Organization*, winter 1973, pp. 11–12.

43. For the details of this struggle and the subsequent redefinition of the IOC's program, see Brenner, *International Organization*, summer 1975, pp. 771–804.

44. Wooster, *International Organization*, winter 1973, p. 107.

45. Brenner, *International Organization*, summer 1975, pp. 793–4.

46. Informal rules have been developed which allow the WWW to continue operations uninterrupted even in times of war. Because meteorological data become strategic information in combat, there was some fear that limited and regional wars could disrupt the system. However, a tacit agreement has evolved whereby states at war may temporarily discontinue transmitting without fear of reprisals and without irreparable damage to the entire program.

47. Financial support was as follows. The UNESCO share included funds for hydrological work not technically part of IHD.

Year	UNESCO Contribution	UNDP Contribution
1965–1966	$226,000	—
1967–1968	187,966	$1,527,966
1969–1970	215,475	1,848,000
1971–1972	268,000	1,254,000
1973–1974	378,490	1,700,000

See UNESCO, *Approved Programme and Budget, 1965–1966*, doc. 13 C/5, para. 707–25; ibid., 1967–1968, doc. 14 C/5, pp. 225–30; ibid., 1969–1970, doc. 15 C/5, pp. 282–8; ibid., 1971–1972, doc. 16 C/5, pp. 221–3; and ibid., 1973–1974, doc. 17 C/5, pp. 235–44.

48. UNESCO, *Nature and Resources*, vol. 1, no. 3 (September 1965), pp. 1–4. See also UNESCO, International Hydrological Decade Coordinating Council, *Final Reports for the IHD Coordinating Council* (Paris, August 20, 1965), doc. NS/198; ibid. (June 24, 1966), doc. NS/204; and ibid. (September 12, 1967), doc. SC/CS/75/64.

49. COWAR's task of coordinating international organizations in the field of water research has expanded to include nongovernmental as well as governmental organizations. Further, it participates in both GARP and WWW, particularly in regard to problems of chemical transport in the oceans and in the entire hydrological cycle, and the chemical composition of rain water.

50. One member of the IHD international secretariat expressed the belief that IHD's greatest successes were promoting or strengthening regional cooperation for research and the rational exploitation of waters in the Rhine River, the Baltic, and the Danube

Basins. Social and economic policies, however, were solely under the jurisdiction of the national committees, although the international secretariat was in a position to provide such hydrological help as might lean toward social and economic side effects. Thus, he claimed that, as an outgrowth of IHD research in Tunisia and Algeria, these two countries, with the help of FAO, had formulated plans to tap groundwater and to set up numerous small desalinization plants in order to tap the safari tourist trade. In fact, he continued, research locating useable saline water had been one of the most important sources for data of immediate economic importance.

51. Ten respondents make up this sample. Three were officials of IHD/IHP, two associated with UNESCO, and one with WHO. Four were members of national IHD committees, considered as delegates in our analysis. One was an adviser on water research to WHO, and two were officials of COWAR. All but one were engineers.

52. Thirteen respondents make up this sample, nine of them advisers and four officials of intergovernmental organizations. Three officials were affiliated with WHO, one with FAO. Seven advisers were consultants for WHO, one for IAEA, and one for ICSU. Professionally, four were physical scientists and nine were biological and medical specialists.

53. Constitution of the World Health Organization, Article 1 and Preamble.

54. Cox and Jacobson, *Anatomy of Influence*, p. 201.

55. Ibid.

56. Ibid, p. 181.

57. During the height of the Cold War, the socialist states did withdraw from WHO participation, but "they were entreated to return and were welcomed when they did." Further, since their return to "active participation, tensions between Communists and anti-Communists have occasionally arisen in WHO, but their total effect on the organization can only be described as trivial." Ibid., p. 213.

58. This is not to say that it would be impossible to construct such a dialog. While our respondents, whom we consider to be representative of influential scientists in international organizations, showed no uniform commitment to a single overarching concept, other participants in the ongoing international confrontation on these issues certainly do. For a prominent example of such a concern we call attention to the concept of "another development," development policy which respects the redistributional demands of Third World countries while also mindful of considerations of limits to growth in a global environmental and resource setting. "Another development" is the slogan of the Dag Hammarskjold Foundation and its affiliated research centers in Geneva and Mexico City. For discussions of how the concept can be applied to ongoing international negotiations, see "What Now: Another Development," *Development Dialogue*, 1975; and "Another Development and the New International Order: The Process of Change," ibid., 1976, no. 1. In our opinion, this commitment remains rhetorical and devoid of any specific ideas as to what a different world order would be, other than to endorse the entire package of demands included in the program for the New International Economic Order.

Chapter 9

Science and Technology for Economic Development

Not very long ago it would have been considered naive to ask how science and technology could best be managed and organized to spur economic growth. The answer seemed obvious: The normal operations of the international division of labor, in science and in trade and investment, *automatically* result in spreading the appropriate knowledge and funds to areas which enjoy the natural and human advantages for best utilizing them. When automaticity seemed to lag, it could be helped along with loans, tax incentives, licensing agreements, and technical assistance, without fundamentally challenging the rules of competition and the market. Since the early 1960s this view has been strongly challenged because it stressed a single developmental goal: increasing the gross national product through reliance on the classical division of labor in the international economy.

There is no difficulty about enumerating the new goals. The trouble begins when a government is forced to choose among goals which cannot be obtained simultaneously, because of costs or because they are perceived as antagonistic in terms of their potential results. These goals still include raising the gross national product, but also call for (1) achieving more equitable distribution of growth through more egalitarian consumption, income, health, and housing patterns, (2) maintaining social stability and traditional values, (3) spurring national pride and self-confidence. The first is almost certainly incompatible with the second. If national pride is achieved by dint of efforts to develop an indigenous scientific elite and technological capability, as is the professed aim of almost all developing countries and of international organizations, it is most likely to interfere with the goal of equality and delay the optimization of aggregate economic growth. The incompatibility of goals tends to be fudged by stressing the argument about economic and cultural dependency and the imperative need for ending it. The international division of labor must be modified so as to create incentives in developing countries for the evolution of an indigenous capacity to innovate technologically.

What technologies does one select to meet these goals? The international organizations and their programs of concern to us have *not* developed an approach for answering this question. Repeated efforts to elaborate "strategies" do not come close to settling the issue. Hence the question remains: Does the sum of these efforts conduce toward the evolution of a different world order? If there were a *substantive* agreement among the various agencies on which goal ought to be singled out, or which mixture of goals, some order other than the present one would indeed be implied. But suppose that there is a *procedural* agreement on the methods appropriate for eventually deriving a substantive consensus, for taming the debate on dependency, growth, national pride, and the sanctity of traditional (that is, nonscientific) values? If we could identify such a consensus among the experts we studied, a case for the evolution of new world order could still be made.

The answer may already be coming clear. Two major international developments have given a distinctly political thrust to a debate which might have developed along purely "technical" lines if the world setting had been different. In 1970 the U.N. General Assembly adopted a scheme for world economic development which in some ways resembles an "indicative plan," the "strategy" for the Second Development Decade (which is to end in 1980). Science and technology were introduced into the plans as potentially crucial triggers of progress. The Advisory Committee on the Application of Science and Technology to Development (ACAST) was the body charged with preparing appropriate proposals, and its work will be examined in this chapter. In 1974, the overall dissatisfaction of the developing countries with the pace of global redistribution of wealth and welfare reached crescendo proportions, resulting in the declarations for a New International Economic Order. Because this development also called into question the previous pace and kind of international activity designed to use science for economic development, it resulted—among other things—in a new U.N.-ECOSOC Committee on Science and Technology composed of governments challenging the utility of ACAST's work. The use of science for development has become part of the global confrontation over wealth and welfare: It is now part of the struggle for rearranging the international division of labor.

How does all this concern our programs? With respect to *ag-*

ricultural development and *fisheries* the crucial role of science had been recognized for a long time. It grew acute as new technologies became operational and as the promise of these technologies was linked by developing countries to their demands for redistribution. The Food and Agriculture Organization (FAO) was and remains the main institutional vehicle for international programs. We shall examine it as a separate topic within the overall discussion of science for economic development. Research and use of *outer space*, similarly, acquired great prominence because of the potential relevance of satellite technology for education, training, communication, and remote sensing of environmental and resource conditions. Organizationally, international programs are in the hands of ICSU's Committee on Space Research (COSPAR) and the U.N. Committee on the Peaceful Uses of Outer Space (COPUOS). Both will concern us here.

Apart from ACAST, the major organizations having responsibility for the use of science and technology in *industrial* development are UNESCO, the U.N. Industrial Development Organization (UNIDO), and the International Bank for Reconstruction and Development (IBRD). UNESCO has programs in scientific and technological manpower training and education, satellite communication, scientific data storage and retrieval, and in sensitizing the consumers of technology to the social and ethical implications of technological innovation. UNIDO's mandate calls for the collection of information on technological innovation in industry and the dissemination of that information among developing countries. The IBRD's work, of course, overlaps with this concern on a broad front, and indeed with agricultural technology and its application as well.[1] These programs, though they do not exhaust the catalog of participants, constitute our sample of activities collectively labeled "science and technology for industrial development."

Unsuccessful efforts have also been made by the International Council of Scientific Unions to partake of this approach. Respondents from its program are included in our sample, though their impact does not warrant extensive discussion. Originally committed to coordinating research which lacked any applied component, ICSU in 1966 indicated interest in the social and economic implications of science and technology by creating a Committee on Science and Technology in Developing Countries (COSTED). Under the leadership of Lord Blackett, COSTED sought to aid Third World countries in organizing national associations for the advancement of science and in the teaching of young scientists. It produced several manuals describing techniques for achieving these goals and made itself available for missions to countries requesting its assistance.[2] Since these activities did not cause any visible ripples of accelerating development, COSTED in the early 1970s was taken over by a group of Indian scientists who use it as a source of fellowships for training young researchers from developing countries. It remains unclear whether this effort results in the internationalization or the nationalization of science and its values.

What, then, do we wish to know about the programs of these organizations?[3] We have to recount as much of the work as is necessary to put the opinions and impressions of our respondents into a context of action. We have to know the extent to which these programs cohere in a single form which expresses a goal commitment with respect to the role and purpose of technology in development. The point can be made by showing how one prominent plan would link pieces of knowledge and action in a coherent whole. The Club of Rome, in its recent work "Reviewing the International Order" (RIO), postulates that the purpose of international action for development is to assure everyone a life of dignity and every state internal stability. This demands an annual increase of 5 percent in global per capita GNP. In order to assure that the developing countries obtain most of this benefit, there must be an integrated global policy linking money, trade in manufactured goods, commodity management, food, minerals, ocean resources, national and international technology planning, and the conduct of multinational corporations.[4] Our discussion, then, will indicate the extent to which such an ideal is being approximated.

SCIENCE AND TECHNOLOGY FOR INDUSTRIAL DEVELOPMENT

As well as judging its approach to an ideal, we will be discussing the development of the program over time and juxtaposing our evaluation of this program with the perceptions of our scientists and technologists—much as we have done in Chapters 7 and 8. To do this, we concentrate first on programs which seek to mobilize the resources of science and technology for spurring the *industrial* development of Third World countries. Among this group movement has occurred from an eclectic to a skeptic model, in institutional and decision-making terms. The skeptic model now dominates; there is some flow toward a more pragmatic model as well. Thus, even though a consensus on knowledge relevant to industrial development is far from being achieved, decision-makers have begun to conduct a deliberate search for new knowledge which can provide the missing links among the plethora of issues already assembled. Similarly, decision-makers are moving from a total reliance on the catch-as-catch-can learning of incrementalism to at least some reliance on partial scanning and a recognition of the need to reconsider goals. However, these changes have by no means permeated the entire program, and sector-by-sector search, as well as sector-by-sector "learning," still prevail. In addition, zero-sum, unit-veto bargaining continues, with some exploitation of package-dealing. The extent to which these packages might become more comprehensive will not be known until the projected 1979 conference on science and technology is adjourned. Institutional purposes remain at the level of acquiring a capability, but the program's common framework, with its pooled division of labor, is being partially replaced by joint facilities, organized around a sequential division of labor. Action is taken in decentralized fora, based on discussions in intergovernmental conferences, and influenced both by international agencies and by intergovernmental committees with varying mandates.

Views of Participating Scientists

Most of our respondents see their work in very similar terms. The bulk of this sample consists of persons associated with UNESCO, UNIDO, and ACAST.[5] Over one-third are physicists by profession; over one-half are officials of these intergovernmental organizations. What are their personal beliefs? Do they propose to let the process of technological diffusion through private corporate and scientific activity hold sway, or do they opt for planning and steering the process in a centralized fashion?

Personal Attitudes

Determinists	14.8%
Instrumentalists	25.9
Skeptics	44.4
Eclectics	14.8

More than 40 percent are unwilling to let unplanned diffusion dominate the industrialization process, but an even larger number seems unwilling to attribute a special role to science as a cognitive device for focusing a planning effort. When examined in terms of their organizational experiences, moreover, the bifurcation in regard to planning is even more pronounced:

Organizational Experience

Determinist planners	8.7%
Social forecasters	26.1
Physical controllers	4.3
Random appliers	21.7
Eclectics	39.1

Scientists who are reluctant to plan and forecast comprehensively, or who feel unable to articulate consistent impressions of their work, account for over 60 percent of the group. We therefore arrive at this breakdown in terms of organizational ideologies:[6]

Organizational Ideologies

Rationalists	9.5%
Pragmatists	9.5
Skeptics	33.3
Eclectics	47.6

When personal beliefs and organizational experiences are matched in individual cases very little of a commitment to a world order devoted to planning industrial development systematically seems to remain intact. It appears as if there were a strong hiatus between personal beliefs and organizational experiences. Relatively few scientists who opt for the systematic planning of industrial development feel that their work in international organizations actually gives scope to such a commitment. Some who identify their programs as oriented toward planning or forecasting nevertheless have doubts concerning the scientific basis for such activities. *The result is a resounding lack of thrust toward a new world order in the task setting of industrial development.*

Nor are the personal attitudes expressed particularly consistent among themselves. Two-thirds of the respondents identify fragmentation between developed and underdeveloped countries and the unleashing of undigestible forces of social change as undesirable consequences of technological and industrial diffusion processes; one-third complains about the dominance of technique over values in these programs; only 15 percent expressed indifference to such undesirable results. Yet when queried about who was the clientele for the work of international organizations, only 24 percent pointed to the consumers of technology and a mere 16 percent identified with developing countries. The largest single group referred to as a client was the employing organization itself. Self-preoccupation is also suggested by the responses as to who is influenced by the organizational programs. Sixty percent identify the international secretariat. Only a third thought specific national administrative agencies or national governments were successfully influenced. No wonder that a large number feels that this never even touches on the issue of whether or not international conflict is lessened; an equally large number thought that conflict had been reduced by scientific programs. These scientists have little faith in systematic analysis and formal modeling as international planning techniques; over half feels that political methods of persuasion and coalition-building are more significant. Are they satisfied with their work? Three-quarters replied that governments do *not* appreciate the complexity of cause-and-effect links embedded in these programs, and an even greater number testified that it is *not* getting easier to achieve agreement on the role of science and technology in overall program-building.

UNESCO

The main working methods of the organization and the character of UNESCO's division of natural science have already been described in Chapter 8. Here we are concerned exclusively with the division's work on science policy and science education, and with the role of UNESCO in coordinating scientific research done by others, notably nongovernmental organizations.[7]

The natural science division described its mission in the field of science policy by saying that

> science policy is indispensable for the development of national scientific and technological potential on the one hand, and for the adequate orientation of national research effort on the other. . . . As regards aid to Member States in the planning of their national science policy, the objectives of the programme coincide both with the ultimate ethical aims of the Organization and with the most profound desire of the developing Member States, that is, for *independent national development.*

Toward that end the program undertakes the diffusion of all scientific knowledge through international exchanges and communication, technical assistance, and "the promotion in the national science policies of Member States of such motivations and measures as are conducive to the peaceful uses of science and technology."[8] Science and technology education are to result in the training of persons able to integrate modern science into traditional cultures while also creating a modern society able to live and progress by itself.

UNISIST. As we saw in Chapter 8, UNESCO's work relies heavily on institutionalized forms of collaboration with nongovernmental groups, and especially with ICSU. This is as true in the area of science policy and science education for development as it is in the environmental field. The United Nations World Science Information System (UNISIST), proposed by UNESCO and further developed by ICSU, illustrates the form of collaboration. The General Conference adopted resolutions in 1966 and 1968 authorizing the director-general to study the feasibility of creating such a resource. René Maheu then contracted with ICSU to conduct a study under the supervision of a joint central committee, but the actual work was done by independent experts chosen by ICSU.[9] In 1971, a report was issued confirming the feasibility of creating the system, and by 1973 the General Conference authorized the first of many long steps needed to make the system operational.

What is UNISIST? It is described as a "world network of interconnected referral services, using similar standards."[10] The aim is to establish a capability which would facilitate rapid and universal access to the latest scientific information by creating major focal points for identifying the information, and international coordinating units for distributing it. One of the main objectives is to make this information available to developing countries and thus increase their ability to profit from modern research in making technological choices. The information would remain decentralized in the libraries and data banks where it now is. UNISIST would seek to standardize methods of storage, retrieval, indexing, natural and computer languages, and telecommunications methods in order to ease both access and use. The task is obviously enormous considering the wide variety of methods and standards now in use even within single countries and disciplines. It would require a major reorganization in order to establish a joint facility which would permit standardization, first by identifying the available sources and existing referral and abstracting services, then by socializing their managers into using similar or identical techniques, and finally by combining all of this into a single world information network. Work has begun on the process of identification, but it is confined to materials in the basic sciences represented.

Science Policy and Planning. We now focus on two key—but mutually antagonistic—components of the UNESCO program in science: efforts to improve science policy-making in terms of economic and social planning; and activities designed to warn the consumers of science and technology of flaws in the merchandise. Science policy has long been on UNESCO's agenda. But early efforts were concentrated on improving the teaching of science, on identifying manpower availabilities and needs in developing countries and on building up such Western-derived science institutions as academies of science, professional associations, professional schools, and libraries.

The Second Development Decade and the creation of ACAST added a new dimension to this effort: Science policy was now seen as a key component in overall economic and social planning, not just an end in itself. Moreover, many staff members of the natural sciences departments came to accept a very holistic view of the nature of knowledge, the links between disciplines, and the implication of this with respect to methods and techniques to be used in fostering science and economic planning in the Third World. Cybernetic models of the process of innovation were in vogue, and the institutions recommended for developing countries were designed accordingly. Structural-functional concepts were increasingly used in the analysis and description of science policy institutions in the development process, and PPBS was accepted as the way to translate a systemic understanding of the process into recommendations for policy. All of this could be interpreted as a rationalist thrust, if it had not been for the simultaneous and equally marked disenchantment with science, the emphasis on its "dehumanizing" qualities, its abuse and misuse for military and anti-ecological purposes. Among our respondents, several spoke in favor of continuing the systemic-integrative work on science policy and its diffusion, while at the same time they expressed strong fears of science and its eventual results. They personally hoped for a cognitive integration which would subject the diffusion of science to an appreciation of its shortcomings, but judged that neither UNESCO nor the Third World member nations were interested in anything other than the most rapid diffusion of technique alone.

The emphasis on formal techniques of analysis and planning was demonstrated by the recurring surveys of manpower and institutional needs sponsored by UNESCO. Each professional discipline represented in government staffs was to be analyzed in terms of relevance to development plan targets, social mission, and scientific content. The categories were derived from PPBS experiences in developed countries which, as it turned out, failed to make the system work.[11] Science policy planning structures were described and recommended in terms of cybernetic flowcharts derived from computer science manuals, but the data to which they were applied consist of observations derived from cryptic governmental responses to crude questionnaires.[12]

Formal modeling was used in attempts to put the planning of scientific manpower training in Asia on a systematic footing, in line with the commitment to the systematic building of science policy planning institutions. The CASTASIA model

> ... seeks to show how the future supply of qualified scientific and technical manpower in the Asian region can be estimated quantitatively.... Special attention is given to identifying the potential manpower available for R & D activities. ... Thus the Castasia Model does not attempt to predict what the future situation will be, but is rather a quantification in manpower and cost terms of the application of a set of science policy variables and parameters.[13]

On the basis of this model a number of specific recommendations were made as to who would be trained where for what kinds of jobs in Asia. However, the model is limited by its built-in assumptions about demographic features, pay and promotion, labor utilization, and the proportion of technical to scientific personnel employed. The demand side of the problem is left to government planning with respect to the rate and kind of industrial development desired. The model only addresses the supply side. In any event, despite the solemn adoption of the CASTASIA model by the assembled ministers, and regardless of the recommendations they made with respect to using and perfecting it, UNESCO staff members feel that its impact on planning has been minimal.[14]

In the case of Africa, work began with a very similar survey and model. As the application also failed to match the initial expectations, the working methods were shifted toward seeking to attain the same results without reliance on the model. Staff members feel that results improved somewhat as bargaining with crucially placed local officials and scientists was undertaken to improve the forecasting of needs and supplies of scientific manpower. The emphasis here, however, remains on simply increasing the quantity and quality of "science" available for potential economic development. No direct link to the *use* of scientific manpower in the context of *specified* economic and social goals has yet evolved. Nor has the ambivalence toward science itself made itself conspicuous in this program.

However, the CASTAFRICA effort deserves a more extensive description because of its attempt to quantify the demand side of the scientific manpower issue and to link the findings to institutional recommendations. It is also interesting because it marks the substitution of Delphi methods for systems analysis and makes its peace with the need for political bargaining as the only way to secure implementation. The occasion for the effort was the Conference of Ministers of African Member States responsible for the application of science and technology to development, held in January 1974. In preparing for the conference, the UNESCO secretariat did an enormous amount of preliminary work, justified by the commitment to improve the management of science and technology policies, promote research "as an essential element in the cultural, social and economic development of nations," "stimulate technological innovation with a view to increasing productivity," as well as examine the position of science within overall government policy and encourage international cooperation.[15]

UNESCO research sought to identify and quantify these elements: technologically feasible futures for Africa, barriers to the success of these futures, scientific disciplines relevant to these futures, national development goals dependent for their realization on the adequate representation of these disciplines, and institutional innovations needed to overcome the dependencies. The technologically feasible futures were identified as a result of a Delphi exercise in which variable numbers of African and other international experts participated.[16] The exercise resulted in a rank-ordered list of technologies which could be implanted in Africa within the next ten years if a special effort to overcome manageable economic, technical, and cultural barriers were made. A second survey was then made of national experts and government officials in African countries. These respondents were asked to rank-order the importance of some 122 scientific disciplines in their countries with respect to their role in helping to realize economic and social goals. There were 12 such goals, described only as "agriculture," "public health," "mines," "education," and so forth. The juxtaposition of the disciplines and goals yielded a "dependence profile" for each country, determined by the respondents' judgment of how important each goal was and to what extent its realization is a function of the further development of a given scientific discipline. Institutional needs were then computed by the secretariat on the basis of a "shortfall index," that is, a determination of the lack of scientific manpower, given the dependence profile. The aggregate results for Africa indicate that needs are greatest in most branches of engineering, hydrology, and climatology, with ecology, public health, agriculture, and chemistry being far less relevant to perceived needs.[17]

How did UNESCO combine these findings in order to lead the ministers to an agreed strategy?[18] After a discussion marked by ambivalence over whether cybernetic models of the interaction between R & D institutions and economic growth should determine the choice of a strategy, the secretariat recommended quantitative targets for investment in training, and R & D facilities for achieving "reasonable" growth objectives. In short, the demand side was still treated in terms of assumptions unqualified by any specific social objectives regarding the welfare of populations; the calculations only addressed the supply of manpower. The preservation of indigenous cultural values was also commended, while the primacy of economic development via science was stressed. Self-reliance‧ was praised, but the attainment of the targets was made dependent on the acceleration of technology transfer from abroad. No reference to the economic questions of the utilization of new technologies in productive processes occurred. No thought was given to a country's position in world trade, to the balance between industrial and agricultural development, to the division of gains in productivity among strata of the population. But the ministers were asked to *choose*, not simply to submit to a technological imperative. They were reminded that while science and technology may trigger human evolution, some technologies may still be more appropriate to their needs—which remain undefined—than others. The results of the Delphi exercise were then presented as the reasonable choices.

The secretariat then went on to discuss various ways in which the feasible technologies might be implanted. A strategy of horizontal transfers reduces dependence on indigenous R & D efforts and relies on the creation of proper links with developed countries. While it may be cheaper, it does have disadvantages as compared to the vertical transfer of technology, because of the sacrifice of indigenous science and the overreliance on technologies which may not be appropriate. A judicious mixture of both procedures is recommended. This, in turn, requires the intensification of international cooperation in Africa. The global and regional plans drawn up by ACAST established priority areas of action which could be used for determining where cooperation should take place.[19] In addition, the relevance and dependence profiles established by the UNESCO survey can be used to specify the modes of international cooperation. The combination indicates that efforts should be concentrated in increasing cooperation in R & D with respect to agriculture, health, animal breeding, and water. Who should cooperate? The African states were divided into clusters on the basis of geographical location and language affinities to constitute eight centers of cooperation. This mode of clustering is identified by UNESCO as "the matrix method."[20]

While no strategy for science and technology for the economic development of Africa emerged from this effort, some results of the thinking which went into the exercise made themselves felt in new UNDP projects at the national level. Technical assistance projects incorporating aspects of this approach were launched in Kenya, Tanzania, Senegal, and Cameroun. UNESCO staff members feel that the data can be effectively used in influencing national policy through discussion with appropriate national officials. If so, the attempt to be scientific in the marshaling of options is significant, even if the components of the preparatory studies are fitted together haphazardly, and even if the specific recommendations owe little to them. And the attempt is also significant because it shows the continued sway of the science-for-development ideology in the face of growing disenchantment with science.

The Danger of Science. Ambivalence toward the application of science remains very much part of the scene. It was given full expression by the adoption in 1974 of the "Human Implications of Scientific Advance" program (HISA), which we now analyze because of its diagnostic significance for the exploration of alternative world orders. What is HISA?[21]

The program consists (1) of a series of studies to be undertaken, (2) the appointment of an international committee of experts to review the thrust of the studies and advise the director-general on future work, (3) cooperation with the leading non-governmental organizations of scientists and humanists to spread the impact of the studies, and (4) technical assistance to developing countries wishing to develop similar programs. The substance of the studies is central to the program since the core idea is to promote a new and more critical attitude toward science and technology. The studies are to provide assessments of trends in science and technology with respect to society in general, and in the context of developing countries in particular.[22] They are also to include assessments of the cultural, ethical, and esthetic issues posed by scientific and technological advance. Sci-

ence and technology, HISA seems to be saying, are on balance
progressive forces which should be fostered and treasured, provided they are purged of certain bothersome side effects: the
reckless exploitation of nature and its resources, their misuse for
military purposes, the perpetuation of inequality and dependency in the Third World due to the importation of the wrong
technologies, the destruction of privacy, and the fostering of
alienation among workers and the young. A proper understanding of science and technology, HISA argues, is a more
rational—even a more scientific—way of understanding human
progress. A more perfect world society can still be fashioned if
we use a critical and humane scientific spirit to correct these
misapplications which flow from a partial and mechanistic understanding of science. A better science can rescue the world
from a bad science. The program is the embodiment of a
rationalist organizational ideology. If it were fully implemented,
it would be a step toward the construction of a rationalist world
order. How did it come about?

HISA evolved in response to the secretariat's concern over
random diffusion of Western attitudes and techniques, as first
illustrated by the growing criticism of science and technology in
the West, and later by the neo-Marxist antidependency arguments voiced in parts of the Third World. These thoughts resulted in the adoption by the General Conference in 1972 of
several—not wholly consistent—resolutions authorizing the
director-general to mount the program which became HISA. He
was told to start work on the ethics of science, explore science in
the contemporary world, improve public understanding of science, as well as investigate how to prevent the misuse of science
by society. This mandate, however, was no more diffuse and
heterogeneous than the preparatory work for HISA done by
three separate sets of experts convoked in special colloquia by
the secretariat. The members of the first colloquium split sharply
into two groups, one defending the progress of science as the
perfection of human rationality and better control over nature,
the other seeing in science the key to a new humanism critical of
purely rational determinism. The second meeting agreed that
science and technology are indeed Janus-headed, but it concentrated on examining how developing countries could be made to
profit more from technological progress without simultaneously
losing their cultural souls and their economic independence.
These experts opted for a notion of intermediate technology as a
possible solution. They also advocated programs for better understanding of science among the public as a way of mobilizing

popular opposition to technological innovations which might spell ecological disaster. The third meeting ranged widely over the same issues, including esthetic and ethical matters, but the tenor of the papers suggests that two extreme schools of thought have now been excluded: Nobody argued that unguided and unfettered scientific and technological innovation is desirable, and nobody suggested that science and technology should be frozen, banned, or ostracized. The participants sought to articulate various principles for having it both ways: human progress through science without incurring the catastrophes evoked so often.[23] The proof of the rationalist pudding will be in the skeptical eating.

ACAST *and the Committee on Science and Technology*

Optimism in global fora over the promises of scientific-technological achievements for lifting the southern nations out of poverty perhaps reached its height in 1963 with the convening of the U.N. Conference on the Application of Science and Technology for the Benefit of the Less Developed Areas (UNCAST). The institutional legacy of that conference is the U.N. Advisory Committee on the Application of Science and Technology to Development (ACAST), a body of distinguished experts, twenty-four strong in 1976, who act in their personal capacities. ACAST functions as a standing committee under the Economic and Social Council and has its own secretariat in the Office for Science and Technology of the U.N. Department of Economic and Social Affairs. Its ambiguous terms of reference embody supervising and coordinating functions. ACAST is assigned responsibility for keeping an eye on the entire work of the U.N. in the field of science and technology. This includes reviewing the programs of other organizations, helping to define priorities, and rendering advice on practical measures and institutional arrangements.

ACAST came to the conclusion relatively early in its career that it had neither the authority nor the resources to perform such a role. Instead, it decided to concentrate, in its own words, "upon those activities of the various organizations that are directly relevant to specific problems which the Committee has itself selected as being of major importance for the application of science and technology to development."[24] In effect, this has meant that ACAST has devoted its efforts largely to producing its own studies on these problems, ranging from relatively specific sectors such as computer and space technologies to broader concerns of science and technology policy. The latter include LDC access to world science and technology, the development of national and regional science structures, research and development for industrial needs, appropriate technology and appropriate education, the scientific-technical manpower implications of development planning, and the relationship of technological breakthroughs to human rights and environmental decay.

World Plan of Action. These efforts culminated in the preparation of a blueprint for a global campaign to put science and technology at the service of economic development with the goal of bridging the gap in scientific-technological capability between north and south. The "World Plan of Action" is ACAST's principal contribution to the planning of the U.N.'s Second Development Decade (1971–1980) and perhaps its most tangible achievement to date.[25] On the basis of the world plan, more specific plans geared to regional priorities have been worked out for Africa, Asia, Latin America, and the Middle East. However, insofar as much of this achievement has yet to transcend the realm of paperwork, ACAST's efforts to instill a sense of urgency toward the task of integrating science and technology with going concerns of development planning have been largely abortive. As ACAST frankly admits,[26] none of its "plans" is anywhere near to being accepted, either inside or outside the U.N., as a guide for action. The planning endeavor is little known among scientific communities or public officials in either developing or developed countries. The specialized agencies have seldom bothered to consult ACAST and have for the most part ignored the recommendations it has made over the years. On the other hand, the core approach of ACAST has largely been a response to UNESCO initiatives. Nor has ACAST had any greater success in bringing a significant amount of new resources to bear within the U.N. on areas which it has selected for priority. Two proposals to which it has devoted considerable attention—involving the establishment of special funds for the world plan and for protein and calorie malnutrition—have received short shrift in policy-making organs of the U.N.

Views of ACAST Members. ACAST has been in existence since 1963; fifty-six scientists have served as members.[27] What do they believe? How do they link science to economic development? How concerned are they that science and its diffusion may spread the flaws now recognized in UNESCO's program? We will review the work of ACAST, and especially the world plan, in the search for clues. First, however, we summarize the expressions of opinion we obtained from our respondents.[28] They see themselves as influencing the General Assembly and international secretariats, *not* national authorities with responsibility for using science in development. They also see themselves as successfully showing politicians *at this level* how fields of knowledge are linked by science, though only on the basis of obvious factual demonstrations and not by conveying an understanding of systemic connections. They believe that careful analysis of data *and* the use of political bargaining are effective in planning. As one distinguished member of ACAST told us, the proper mix of technological knowledge with an understanding of social anthropology and sociology is necessary to avoid triggering overly rapid change and the victory of technique over social values in diffusing science. Insofar as a knowledge of nutritional habits, for instance, can explain differential learning patterns, the introduction of new agricultural techniques can be linked to industrialization. Social science is a help when it can demonstrate that a culturally validated local value system is friendly or hostile to the reception of a new industrial technology. Science itself can inform the proper diffusion of science. The "appropriateness" of the technologies can be defined accordingly.

To ACAST, advances in science and technology in the Third World are not merely an imperative of social and economic development. Scientific and technological progress, rather than being one of the means or ends of development, is equated with evolutionary development itself. As the World Plan puts it: "Every nation can be positioned somewhere along [a] spectrum of stages of technological development. . . . In fact, the process of socio-economic development is the movement from one stage to another of greater technological complexity."[29] However, the laws governing the transition to higher stages of complexity are subject to manipulation. How? Through more and better use of science and technology. "[T]he scientific approach offers the best hope for assisting the developing nations to speed up the process of their all-around development."[30] The "selection and development of those technologies which will allow developing nations to skip one or more decades in the development process has barely started."[31] But the poor countries should immediately prepare to seize the opportunities that already exist or are likely to emerge in the near future. Thus, LDCs are urged to acquire third-generation computers in order to "leap-frog" plateaus of development not only in science and technology but also in national planning in general.[32]

Investment in science and technology, according to ACAST, can yield effective results only if made on a scale that is vastly greater

than that to be found today. It warns that without a "more pur-
poseful and more systematic use of the powerful tool of applied
science" the dependence of the South on the North "will become
all but final and complete."[33] The gap in levels of technology
between developing and developed countries is seen as a major
reason for the gap in their living standards. The acquisition of
modern technologies becomes a *sine qua non* of development.
"[T]he process of world development consists partly (but not
wholly) in bringing about a wider sharing of these benefits not
only through trade and aid but also through the transfer of
modern technology to the developing countries."[34] Redressing
the international inequalities in science and technology would
also require that the rich divert a greater proportion of their
research and development effort away from defense and space
and toward the specific problems of development, and that
LDCs acquire a greater capacity to do their own scientific and
technological work. That each country must have an indigenous
capability in science and technology is the major premise—and
one of the cardinal goals—of the World Plan.[35] Thus, despite the
frequent exhortations on behalf of international cooperation,
international science is conceived of largely as a means to the end
of *national* science.

Evolution of ACAST *Thinking.* Soon after it came into existence,
ACAST stated it had reached the conclusion that "the wider and
more intensive application of existing knowledge, suitably
adapted to local conditions, provides the best prospect of secur-
ing rapid advancement in the developing countries."[36] Such a
conclusion notwithstanding, the experts stressed the creation of
new knowledge rather than the application of existing knowledge. Thus they embarked on a quest for research capable of
yielding a "'breakthrough' . . . if a massive, world-wide attack on
the problem is made."[37] The committee nominated for special
attention twenty-seven "problems" in eight "sectors" (food, industry, natural resources, transportation, housing and urban
planning, health, population and education). The accent was on
research that is clearly beyond the reach of most developing
countries. While aware of this, ACAST's misgivings were over-
shadowed by strong faith in "a potential development effect of
extraordinary dimensions" inherent in each research problem.[38]
A professed purpose was to nail down a vital agenda of problems
which would gain consensus within international organizations
and, with that, the "critical mass" of effort—including the finan-

cial support—necessary to "break the vicious circles" of under-development.

Essentially the same priorities and proposals are served afresh in the World Plan. Once again, ACAST highlights areas in which knowledge to be gained through basic and applied research—though it stresses more than before the better and wider use of available know-how—can make what it terms "a resounding impact."[39] However, the plan differs from ACAST's earlier work in two fundamental respects: (1) it focuses on the tasks entailed in building up scientific and technological capabilities in LDCs through the manpower training and institutional development schemes favored by UNESCO, and (2) it sets up specific financial targets for carrying out the measures spelled out for these tasks. The concept of a world plan was initially described as an effort "to develop a world programme in the sense of a planned international campaign to strengthen existing programmes and to add appropriate new arrangements to round out the total effort."[40] More recently, ACAST has spoken of an "ultimate objective [of evolving] a science and technology policy for human society as a whole."[41]

As an adjunct to the World Plan, ACAST proposed a series of quantitative targets, to be met by the end of the Second Development Decade (December 31, 1980), for restructuring the international division of labor in science and technology. These targets call for (1) the developing countries to boost their R & D expenditures from an average of about 0.2 percent to at least 0.5 percent of their GNP and their total spending in science and technology to a minimum of one percent of GNP; (2) developed countries to (a) step up their aid for the direct international support of science and technology to reach an average level equal to 0.05 percent of their GNP, and (b) channel 5 percent of their nonmilitary R & D outlays to development problems, to be selected through consultations with LDCs, with priority for problems earmarked for "concerted attack" in the World Plan.[42] These proposals are still the object of fierce wrangling within the U.N.[43]

While links between the proposals and the avowed objective are rarely demonstrated, ACAST shows varying degrees of sensitivity to the social and economic consequences of the application of science and technology for development. It warns of the dangers of environmental degradation and destruction; of the perpetuation of inequalities through the monopoly on the benefits of knowhow in the hands of a limited sector of society; of the aggravation of unemployment through further technological breakthroughs by industrial countries in synthetic substitutes; of the infringements on personal privacy posed by the proliferation of data banks. The World Plan calls for more attention to the human rights of squatters and slum dwellers and to the health and safety problems of industrial workers. It cautions against the facile use of technical fixes, noting that "[e]ven technological advances such as the Green Revolution may have frustrating economic and social consequences unless the technological implementation is guided by concern for converting the scientific advance into improvements for the broad masses of the population."[44] ACAST therefore appeals for a systemic approach to development that integrates science and technology with socioeconomic concerns in development planning. "This entire process involves the application of systems analysis to decision-making. There is an important need for further development of the methodology involved . . ."[45]

The foregoing commitment however is belied by the instrumental view of technology in the World Plan. Ecosystemic considerations do *not* constitute an integral part of the programs under discussion. Caveats about the second order consequences of technology usually appear as fleeting afterthoughts; more often, they are deferred to national policy-making. Unwanted consequences are seen as factors which merely complicate the acquisition of modern technology by developing countries; they do not invalidate the promise inherent in it. The advisory committee has surprisingly little to say about the unfolding of technology. The overriding concern is the exploitation of, not the monitoring or regulating of, technology. Be it forestry or fisheries, the declared objective is the same: "to improve the level of utilization of existing resources, while at the same time building up technology to permit unconventional resources to be more effectively exploited."[46] ACAST is only now placing on its agenda the integrated approach to development which it urged upon others in the World Plan. As it explained ten years after its founding: ". . . most of its own past work had been concerned with the application of natural sciences and technology to the problems of development; it now felt that its work would be more balanced if it also gave due attention to the social and human factors in development."[47]

Yet there is a profound ambiguity in this work: Should progress occur by the rapid—if selective—diffusion of knowledge already available in the developed countries, or should the developing countries invent their own road to salvation via technology? ACAST's endorsement of the concept of "appropriate" technologies is ambivalent.[48] Support is often given to the proposition that the developing countries must acquire the full panoply of their own scientific institutions and gain full citizenship in the world through independent scientific efforts and technical invention. Thus excellence in science will be attained and with it pride and self-confidence, even though the fruits of this research may very well prove to be irrelevant to the requirements of science applied to economic development! At the same time, however, ACAST calls attention to the fact that for many years it will be cheaper and easier for the developing countries to rely on technology transfers.

Disillusionment with ACAST. It is hardly surprising, therefore, that even though a science-technology-development nexus has been defined in the United Nations, the governments of many developing countries have come to the conclusion that this work is too important to be left to the experts acting as individuals. In 1971, LDC pressure led to the creation of an intergovernmental committee for science and technology in the U.N. The new Committee on Science and Technology for Development (CSTD), a subsidiary body of ECOSOC, is addressing itself largely to the more overtly political issues which have eluded ACAST. Its sweeping mandate covers all the activities ever pursued by ACAST. CSTD has been declared "the focal point in the United Nations system for policies and activities related to the application of science and technology to development, including their effects on economic, social and human welfare concerns in all nations."[49]

The meaning behind the creation of CSTD is clear: Science and technology, like trade and industry, are to be employed as another prong in the South's redistributive thrust against the North. CSTD's abortive early meetings, pitting DCs and LDCs against each other in UNCTAD-style encounters, have dealt largely with the financial targets for science and technology in the 1970s. CSTD is also doing the spadework for the international Conference on Science and Technology to be held in 1979. The developing countries have already gone on record that they do not wish another "science fair," as they now reflect back on UNCAST.[50] Rather, if they have their way, this would be a ministerial meeting, an action-oriented dialog, with specified provisions for follow-up, that is to be seen as another round in the "new international economic order" diplomacy.[51] CSTD is also the focus of a debate on proposals for a full-fledged U.N. "science and technology program." The debate is centered round the issue of whether this is to be a program in the sense of a set of closely

related and well-coordinated activities—a program with a small
p—or a Program in the institutional sense à la UNDP or UNEP.[52]

As far as ACAST's organizational interests are concerned,
CSTD may prove to be an instrument capable of giving programmatic flesh to some of its thoughts in the World Plan. However, there is no doubt that the intergovernmental committee
has eclipsed ACAST's position in the U.N. In deciding to retain
ACAST, ECOSOC placed it firmly under the wings of CSTD. ACAST
no longer reports to ECOSOC but to CSTD itself. While ACAST has
been instructed to "furnish expertise" to CSTD and to receive
from it "such instructions . . . as will be necessary to provide . . . scientific, technical, and innovative advice and ideas in
this field,"[53] it has not yet been presented with many requests to
do so. CSTD has bypassed ACAST even in areas where ACAST had
done considerable work.

U.N. Industrial Development Organization

UNIDO was born in 1967 after years of clamoring by the developing countries for more help in their pursuit of industrialization.
Its establishment represented a compromise between the poor
and the wealthy: the former, their appetites whetted by the creation of UNCTAD, were more than ever before bent on asserting
control over the activities of multilateral organizations in the
field of economic development. Hence, they fought for a fully
independent specialized agency for industrialization. The West
(particularly the United States), anxious in the wake of UNCTAD
to thwart the proliferation of new bodies, fiercely opposed the
idea. A new organization in the field of industrialization, the U.S.
predicted, would, like UNCTAD, turn into a forum for Third
World demands against the rich. The compromise, in the words
of UNIDO's executive director, spawned an "unwanted child."[54]
The developing countries gained "their" organization for industrial assistance, but they failed to secure for it either the autonomy they wanted or the commitment of the major donors.
The compromise has left deep scars on UNIDO. Its first decade of
existence has been dominated by wrangling over its status and
functions. In the absence of anything remotely resembling a
consensus on what these functions ought to be, and with hostility
toward the newcomer by established agencies in the United Nations, the organization's attempts to carve out its own sphere of
action in economic development have been far from successful.

Purpose and Structure. UNIDO's purpose, as defined by the General
Assembly, is "to assist in, promote and accelerate the indus-

trialization of the developing countries, with particular emphasis on the manufacturing sector." Its sweeping, "action-oriented" mandate stresses assistance to developing countries in the transfer, adaptation, and development of technology; application of modern methods of industrial production and planning; enhancement of administrative, training, and research capabilities; formulation of industrial programs and projects, including preinvestment and feasibility studies, as well as obtainment of external financing for specific projects; and reform of the international rules governing industrial property in order to accelerate the diffusion of technical know-how. In addition, UNIDO has been assigned "the central role in and . . . responsibil[ity] for reviewing and promoting the coordination of all activities of the United Nations system in the field of industrial development."[55]

UNIDO is structured closely after the model of UNCTAD. It is a subsidiary organ of the General Assembly, functioning formally as an autonomous organization within the United Nations, with its own secretariat and budget. Its principal policy-making body, the forty-five member Industrial Board, has a majority of developing country members, who occupy twenty-five seats. Moreover, although there are no provisions for such, UNIDO has been holding general international conferences à la UNCTAD every four years. The parallels with UNCTAD end there, however, for its often militant impulse notwithstanding, UNIDO has never enjoyed the freedom of maneuver of UNCTAD. UNIDO, in fact, has so far been little more than an executing agency of the United Nations Development Program. At present, more than four-fifths of its operational expenditures comes from UNDP, the U.N.'s principal source of allocations for development assistance which is financed largely by donations from the developed countries.[56] Accordingly, while the Industrial Development Board is formally required "to formulate principles and policies to achieve the purpose of the Organization" and "to consider and approve the programme of activities of the Organization,"[57] UNIDO's field activities are circumscribed by UNDP's established country programing procedures. "UNIDO implements the projects that have been requested by Governments, approved by UNDP, and assigned to UNIDO for implementation."[58] UNIDO does not have any more budgetary control over its administrative and research functions, for these "supporting activities" are financed from the U.N. regular budget. "Again, while the Board considers, approves, or comments on the programme, the final budgetary decision is taken by the General Assembly on recommendation of the Advisory Committee on Administrative and Budgetary Questions."[59]

Work Program. Nonetheless, UNIDO claims that its role in coordinating the U.N.'s work on industrial development "is being increasingly accepted not only by the organizations in the United Nations family but also by the organizations outside the United Nations system."[60] These claims are belied by more sober assessments by UNIDO itself. UNIDO acknowledges that it cannot exercise a coordinating function because it lacks the authority to do so. The working links established with other organizations, notably the specialized agencies, are more often than not designed to sort out conflicting territorial imperatives. This effort, according to an expert group, may have "created a sense of cooperation and co-existence," but it "adds up to a disappointingly small achievement. UNIDO has not become a unifying, organizing centre within the United Nations system for formulating industrial strategy and joint programmes of action."[61]

This negative assessment of UNIDO's work, as judged from a vantage point which stresses integration of knowledge, planning, and implementation in industrial development, is not only ours and that of other observers cited. Our respondents did not see things much differently.[62] Their personal attitudes and their organizational experiences made *each one* an eclectic. Half of them thought that their work influences politicians by demonstrating the existence of new possibilities and areas of choice, but *none* felt that the work was successful in the sense of triggering appropriate integrated action at the national level, even though their work is directed to the attention of national ministers, specific administrative agencies, and industrialists. Almost all told us that their work is so fragmented as not to merit being considered as a planning exercise. Nobody felt that it is easier now than earlier to achieve agreement on the role of technology in policy-making and nobody suggested that the work has anything to do with using knowledge as a means of reducing conflict. The reasons for these perceptions of institutional despair will become clearer as we describe the program of UNIDO.

The alternatives for an organization such as UNIDO are to do either a little of many things or a great deal of one thing. UNIDO, hedging its bets, has so far opted to do a little of many things. Its program, despite its meagre resources, roams across the gamut of current concerns of developing countries in the area of industry. That none of these concerns is actually touched with anything more than pinpricks is thus hardly surprising.

Substantively, UNIDO's program centers on the delivery of technical assistance in its pre-investment phase. UNIDO activities are devoted largely to feasibility studies and advisory services. It does not engage directly in capital investments projects; assistance for the establishment of complete industrial units has been limited to a few pilot and demonstration plants. Emphasis is on project identification, preparation, and evaluation; programs and policy development; investment promotion; institution-building; training and upgrading of skills and the transfer of know-how. Three-fifths of the technical assistance expenditures is poured into the supply of expertise; one-fifth goes to fellowships and training; and the remainder is spent mostly on equipment and subcontracts.[63]

Almost one-half of the substantive program of technical assistance is directly concerned with industrial technology in the developing countries. Priorities have gone overwhelmingly to three sectors: (1) engineering industries, including metal products, machine tools, electrical apparatus, transport equipment, machinery, and repair; (2) metallurgical industries, with special focus on iron and steel production; and (3) light industries, including food, textiles, leather, and printing. Sectors receiving second priority are petrochemicals, fertilizers, and pesticides; building materials and industrial construction; chemical, drug, pulp and paper industries. This order of priorities is not expected to change significantly in the near future despite the declared aim of directing more assistance to the production of fertilizers and pesticides and, in general, of emphasizing the achievement of a balance between agriculture and industry through the establishment of agro-industrial complexes.

An area which has recently crept into the industrial technology program, and one singled out for increased attention in the current medium-term plan, is industrial pollution. UNIDO is working with the United Nations Environment Program on a long-term program (so far devoted mainly to the drawing up of case studies) on the incorporation of environmental considerations in industry. The program is stated to reflect the need for demonstrating "the very real possibilities" of preserving and enhancing the environment "at very little or zero cost to the polluter and with a net gain in the wealth of the nation as a whole."[64] UNIDO plans to use the data as a basis for developing the concept of integrated industrial complexes with minimal pollution. It has worked in environmental themes in several of its in-plant training programs, but the professed effort to heighten awareness of governments is not perceived as a success.

Of more central concern in the UNIDO program are activities related to industrial infrastructure. The activities so far have included assistance and advice on formulation of national requirements in applied research and establishment of industrial research institutes; product standardization and quality control; industrial legislation, including licensing and patents; industrial estates and fairs; management and consulting services; and training of engineers and administrators. Estimates of future demand for operational projects in these areas are considered "far beyond" the delivery capacity of UNIDO.[65]

UNIDO regards one of its main functions as "that of the middleman, who encourages direct contact between the financial and business communities in the industrialized world and their counterparts in the developing countries."[66] This role entails bringing together potential buyers and sellers (typically from LDCs and DCs respectively) for negotiations on joint ventures, marketing and licensing agreements, management contracts, and project financing. The objective in sponsoring such contacts is stated to be "to liberate—on a business-to-business basis—vast reserves of technology, skills and finance that are not normally available through an international organization."[67] As direct foreign investment came under attack from many quarters, delegates from developing countries came to express a dim view of much of this program. The Industrial Development Board's response so far has been to adopt a recommendation that promotional activities be given "third priority" by UNIDO.[68]

In-house research, though not in the mandate for UNIDO, has also been part of its fare all along. Recent work has included a simulation of multilevel, multisectoral information-gathering and decision-making processes. The stated aim is eventually to produce a prototype industrial planning model which can be used to spin off "custom-tailored versions for individually requesting countries."[69] This type of work has drawn fire from both the developing and developed countries. UNIDO's overall research work on industrial strategies and policies has been described as "too abstract and academic to meet the practical needs of the developing countries."[70] Appeals that the organization concentrate on operational activities and leave general studies to others have been voiced at every session of the Industrial Development Board.

Search for a Strategy. The secretariat once claimed: "What in the early years of UNIDO's work appeared as a fragmented programme of field activities composed of seemingly disconnected individual projects is gradually turning into a more discernible framework of individual country programmes, reflecting integrated development policies. . . ."[71] Yet where is the glue to hold together the organization's two-thousand-odd projects in more than one hundred countries? Helping Bolivians to analyze asbestos fibers, Mexicans to transform algae into edible protein, Upper Voltans to discover the uses of plastics, Egyptians to process electronic data, Nepalese to distill better alcohol and Mongolians to make cashmere out of camel and goat hair[72]—such endeavors, even when multiplied a thousandfold, do not add up to a strategy for the industrial development of the poor countries. And it is largely on the lack of an explicitly formulated strategy, with clearly defined priorities, that UNIDO has foundered.

Such a strategy is not to be found in several recent exercises of self-criticism undertaken by the group of experts mentioned earlier and by an ad hoc committee of official delegates for implementing the strategy. UNIDO is called on to assist the developing countries in formulating and executing industrial policies and strategies by "bas[ing] itself, as a major new element in its activities, on a broad and permanent programme of action-oriented studies and analyses at the sectoral, national, and regional levels and on a study of world trends both in the development of specific sectors and in the industrial development process as a whole."[73] But it is also enjoined to let operational activities "continue to constitute a major task" before it and to "continuously seek the most appropriate and comprehensive methods of technical assistance that conform to the complex nature of industrial projects from the planning to the investment, start-up and production stages."[74] The sum of the suggestions amounts to a continuation of the scattered approach which is being criticized. The ad hoc committee singled out "alternative technologies" as one type on which information should be provided by UNIDO. This is added almost as an afterthought. There are few hints as to what these technologies are. Moreover, the fundamental question of how information on them should be used in the organization's own operational activities is altogether ignored.

To say that UNIDO does not have a strategy for the developing countries is not to say that the developing countries do not have a strategy for UNIDO. The LDCs would like to see an "UNCTADized" UNIDO—another instrument in their struggle for a restructuring of the rules of the game between North and South. The UNIDO Second General Conference (Lima, March 1975) brought the organization directly into the negotiations for a "new international economic order." The Lima conference adopted a "declaration and plan of action on industrial development and cooperation" calling for the establishment of a system of consultations within UNIDO for a transformation of the present division of labor in world industry to increase the developing countries' share in industrial production from the present 7 percent to 25 percent by the year 2000. To achieve this end, the conference recommended that UNIDO be converted into a full-fledged specialized agency with increased representation on its policy-making organs for the developing countries. UNIDO would no longer be an operational arm of UNDP but would receive for the first time the major share of UNDP funds in the field of industry. In addition, an Industrial Development Fund would be created to enhance the autonomy of UNIDO.[75]

It is hard to imagine that conversion into a specialized agency with more generous funds would make a fundamental difference as far as the mobilization of knowledge for action is concerned. The widespread rethinking in recent years of intersectoral economic development appears to have produced only a few weak echoes in UNIDO. True, the organization now officially subscribes to a development doctrine under which industry and agriculture are regarded as mutually supportive. Since a major push in one sector at the expense of the other has little chance of success for most countries, it maintains, a primary task for development policy is to promote mutually reinforcing patterns between the two. However, the holistic approach to development suggested by official rhetoric is not of a piece with UNIDO's view of industrialization. Whatever the intersectoral relationships might be, in the final analysis it is industrialization which is held to be the mainspring of development, the key to economic progress. UNIDO gives short shrift to attempts to link rural decay, mass migration, and urban unemployment in the Third World to industrialization. It considers manufacturing to be "the largest single source of urban employment in developing countries in the 1970s."[76] And it maintains that the rate of absorption of labor into industry would have been greater "(w)ith higher growth rates of output and changes in industrial and other policies."[77]

The leitmotif of UNIDO has been the wholesale transfer, not the adaptation or indigenous development of technology. Its attitude toward the issue of appropriate technology, like ACAST's, is one of ambivalence: technology is considered appropriate if the country using it feels it is appropriate. The Lima Declaration called for a greater degree of world research expenditures to be directed to develop appropriate technologies for

LDCs. However, UNIDO was not asked to give any programmatic commitment on its part toward such measures. UNIDO is eager to stress the *limits* of applying labor intensive technologies. Such technologies, it states, "may be socially feasible" in some countries in the sense that economic growth need not be sacrificed in order to generate additional employment. But, it hastens to add, "there is not much room for change as the advocated labour-intensive techniques imply."[78]

A singularly ambivalent attitude is also displayed toward the type of information that is to be passed on to LDCs. Technological information, UNIDO correctly points out, is biased toward a narrow range of techniques and products. Hence, the pressing need for information on technological alternatives. But alternatives to what and for what ends? UNIDO skates over the issue. Knowledge, it says, is "needed to make technological choices; the fuller the information available as to possibilities, the better the choice is likely to be."[79] As with technology, so with information: the assumption is that more is better and will inevitably be used for better purposes. Any kind of information—so long as it is desired by someone—appears to be the operating rule. Hence, UNIDO can rightly claim to be working for the creation of an international market for the flow of technical and financial resources to LDCs whom it assists "to enhance their capabilities to negotiate and formulate their own decisions without overburdening UNIDO's own capacity."[80]

A Skeptical World Order? Summary

We can now summarize why we have characterized the decision-making attributes of the program on science and technology for industrialization as being skeptic, even though there appears to be some movement from this model to the pragmatic model. The roots of the "skeptical" character of the program are obvious: Decision-makers have often failed to find common ground with the experts, and the experts, attempting both to create an acceptable program, and to retain what they have sometimes considered to be the scientific integrity of their programs, have been little more than groping for answers. More often than not, the result has been inconsistent, sometimes contradictory, proposals thrown together piecemeal. Less frequently, the result has been an integrated proposal which has suffered from lack of direct relevancy. However, these failures have been symptomatic of the more general international debate regarding the entire development process. Experts have attempted to respond by creating theories, but no theories of development have found general acceptance for long. It is little wonder, therefore, that the program has come to mirror the disjointed incrementalism of its environment.

Yet the program's decision-making characteristics are undergoing the kind of change which might lead from a skeptic model to a pragmatic model. With the exception of UNIDO, which suffers from the absence of any strategy sufficient to direct search and interpret potential learning experiences, the industrialization program has begun to engage in deliberate search for new knowledge. ACAST's early plan for giving special attention to twenty-seven problems in eight sectors, later revised and elaborated upon in the *World Plan of Action*, was a deliberate attempt to provide a framework within which new knowledge could be sought and fruitfully applied. Within UNESCO the development of both UNISIST and of HISA marks a movement toward deliberate search for new knowledge. UNISIST, though it is not meant to search for new *data*, is meant to systematize and improve access to existing data and thus to place new *knowledge* at the disposal of more experts and decision-makers. HISA is an attempt to search deliberately for knowledge which deals with the first- and second-order consequences of science and technology. Further, it is both a reaction to new learning and an institutional response geared to conduct partial scanning of the environment. These are just beginnings; the skeptic mode still prevails. Thus, ACAST opted for partial scanning through its *World Plan of Action*, but so far this has made little impression upon its most crucial audience, the CSTD. Further, UNIDO and most of the science for industry program within UNESCO continue to rely upon incremental modes of learning, picked up haphazardly from the design and application of their various individual programs.

The objectives and goals of the program have not yet begun to reflect the pragmatic thrust evidenced by the knowledge and learning patterns. UNIDO officially claims now to be subscribing to an integrated and interdependent process of development whereby industry and agriculture are no longer to be considered in dichotomous terms, but the continued use of tactics which stress primarily urban industrialization contradict movement toward more comprehensive goals. ACAST, on the other hand, has come gradually to accept for itself the integrated approach to development which it advocated earlier for others, but it is presently suffering from ambiguity and dissent regarding the way in which tactical changes can be made to realize this comprehensive objective. UNESCO is in a similar situation in regard to HISA. The recognition that the act of applying science and technology often carries with it disastrous unforeseen or unintended consequences has led to an acceptance within UNESCO that objectives must be more complex and that tactics must reflect this complexity. However, no agreement has yet been reached on precisely what this means within the context of the program. Consequently, the refocusing of the program constituents will depend on the 1979 international conference on science and technology.

The scheduled conference should have some effect on the type of bargaining which will characterize these programs. Recent efforts in CASTAFRICA, for example, and the creation of the CSTD have brought home to the program's designers that more sophisticated methods of bargaining are needed if the experts are to influence the political decision-makers. Comprehensiveness requires movement from a zero-sum game to a variable-sum game, from package-dealing over a small range of issues to package-dealing over a wider range of issues. Such a change depends on a conference decision on what, if any, issues will be linked and what kinds of packages can be assembled.

The institutional attributes of the program also remain within the skeptic model. The overriding purpose of the program clearly is the acquisition of a capability sufficient to bring about industrial development in developing countries. HISA and parts of ACAST, it is true, are concerned with coping with the first- and second-order consequences of science and technology, but these goals are not strikingly salient in the minds of LDC governments. The instrumentalities adopted for achieving this purpose rely on a common framework; separate national capabilities have been pooled in the attempts to establish a common capability. However, there have been recent attempts to move toward a joint facility, toward the harmonizing and sequencing of national policies for commonly-defined targets of action. This has particularly been true of UNESCO efforts through the CASTAFRICA program. It could be true of ACAST, if that body were able to establish regular channels of communication and influence with the CSTD. The program continues to be managed by decentralized international agencies and intergovernmental committees with varying mandates. The 1979 conference is seen by some to be a thrust in the direction of centralization of all U.N.-related science and technology for development, but we can draw no conclusions at this time.

SCIENCE, AGRICULTURE, AND FISHERIES

Science has for a long time been a major constituent of man's efforts to increase agricultural production and to improve the quality of food. Biochemists and soil chemists, nutritionists and plant geneticists have been major participants in fashioning international and national programs ever since these branches of science came of age. They have been joined more recently by agricultural economists and fisheries managers in efforts to arrive at socially determined principles of adjusting supply to demand, or to alter patterns of demand. More recently still, specialists on resource mapping and resource planning have joined the ranks of the experts, including practitioners of the science of remote sensing, systemwide forecasting, and indicative planning. Ecologists are the most recent recruits to the field.[81]

Our subsample of agricultural and fisheries experts includes representatives of all these professions.[82] Most of them are associated with the Food and Agriculture Organization of the United Nations (FAO). Some work at the interface between economic and biological approaches to the management of fish stocks. Some deal with methods of pest control and others with manipulating the genetic characteristics of crops. A few are concerned with commodity policy and trade. Others work on mitigating the unwanted consequences of productivity increases by addressing such questions of rural development as land tenure, cropping practices, and diets. The "environment" is an increasingly important concern to many. The interest ranges from the total management of ecological systems, including full-scale resource and soil surveys conducted by satellite, to the ad hoc regulation of pollutants in the soil and in the water. We shall see to what extent these points of emphasis and pieces of programs add up to a single approach, or an overarching strategy of development. We argue that the program on science and technology for agriculture and fisheries is characterized best by the eclectic model in both its institutional and its decision-making properties. In other words, some attributes of the program are decidedly skeptic; others fall within the pragmatic model; neither is sufficiently dominant to determine a consistent theme.

Where do the program's experts fall with respect to our typologies of personal attitudes and organizational experiences? They tend to cluster toward the deterministic end of the scale on personal attitudes:

Personal Attitudes

Determinists	22.2%
Instrumentalists	22.2
Skeptics	22.2
Eclectics	33.3

A tendency toward a holistic perception of organizational activity is also apparent:

Organizational Experience

Determinist planners	15.8%
Social forecasters	31.6
Physical controllers	10.5
Random appliers	21.1
Eclectics	21.1

If over 57 percent of the group profess some commitment to the application of scientific expertise to the shaping of social goals, one would expect an organizational program which puts heavy stress on ecological and environmental concepts as a master strategy for ordering more concrete programs in agricultural and food production. But while individuals certainly express appropriate views and sometimes even attempt to shape organizational programs in accordance with this view, the combined typologies show just how limited their impact is:

Organizational Ideology

Rationalists	0.0%
Pragmatists	33.3
Skeptics	22.2
Eclectics	44.4

Certainly the organizational context provides the opportunity for the pragmatists to confront the skeptics and eclectics, but this access does not suffice to convert them even when the pragmatists are to be found among the highest ranks of the FAO bureaucracy (as they are). There are other factors at work here, and we can only come to grips with them by looking more closely at the content of the program in question.

FAO

The motto of FAO is *fiat panis*. The predominant programmatic thrust in FAO, since its origins in 1945, has been the increasing of the world food supply. The study of plant and animal health, of soil conditions, of water, of cropping and land tenure, and of fishing methods was seen as instrumental toward raising the supply of food to meet the growing world population, to improve diets, and to avert famine. With the advent of environmental concerns, a more ecosystemic view was superimposed on this commitment. Somewhat earlier, the United Nations commitment to a form of indicative planning had sought to channel these activities so as to include employment, rural life and rural income, land reform, and the maintenance of the foreign exchange earning capacity of poor countries. By using a conservative measure for determining the portion of the FAO regular budget devoted to the activities of interest to us, we arrive at 28.2 percent in 1976/77.[83] The chief components of the FAO program have remained the same over years, as have the working methods; it is the manner in which the components interact that may have been influenced by the twin emphasis on the environment and on social planning. It is our task to discover whether interaction has been fostered as a result of the recent emphasis on environmental matters—which involves physical control— and the commitment to "plan"—which evokes notions of social forecasting.

What are the components of the program? The most spectacular, and probably the least successful, portion of the FAO program is to oversee the world trade in agricultural commodities in order to assure adequate supplies and to provide emergency aid in the case of famine. Closely linked to this activity is the provision of supplementary food supplies to poor countries through the World Food Program. Four major proposals by various directors-general to institutionalize, centralize, and manage the equitable distribution of basic foodstuffs have been turned down by the FAO council; the 1973 proposal gave rise to the World Food Conference of 1974 and to the halting efforts at global management which have been undertaken since then. With the exception of certain measures for famine relief and food intelligence-gathering in specific crisis situations, it is fair to say that past FAO efforts to manage food had faltered on the determination of the major food-exporting nations *not* to subordinate the forces of the market to demand considerations based on stable prices and nutritional needs. The marginal role of FAO is confirmed by the evolution of a world food policy since 1974; the limited measures for world food security, emergency stocks, surveys of need, and more ambitious investment plans for food production in developing countries are all being implemented under the aegis of the autonomous World Food Council, a United Nations grouping in which all interested agencies participate under the direction of thirty-six state-members elected by the General Assembly. The emphasis remains on increasing the food supply, even though the dominance of market principles may now be eroding.[84]

FAO personnel agree that little effort has been made to link this aspect of the program to systematic research which seeks to bring under one roof the concerns of economists, agronomists, geneticists, technologists, and ecologists. Formal modeling is not used; the core of the technical work consists of simple demand and supply projections for single commodities. Even the substitution of synthetics (and their social consequences) is not consistently taken into account. For our purposes this aspect of the program has one lesson to teach: Knowledge is considered the enemy of the free market.

Another portion of the program which has never gathered momentum toward a systematic view of forecasting is research and training to improve the quality of rural life by dealing with rural education, housing, rates of urbanization and rural depopulation, more effective management of small farms, and land reform. Small programs designed to include knowledge of these features are included in the technical assistance operations of FAO, provided the recipient governments are willing to have them! But compared to straightforward physical and biological measures designed to increase food supplies, these activities are stepchildren. Considerations of employment and distribution of national income do appear in the aggregate calculations of the Indicative World Plan, but they have little discernible impact on the highly disaggregated field operations which are to serve the goals of the Plan.

Research and research coordination with respect to improving and increasing the food supply in the physical sense is the activity of greatest concern to us, in agriculture and in fisheries. It is here that the commitment to planning and forecasting and the impact of environmental concerns should manifest themselves as an indication of a more holistic cognitive trend. An organizational commitment toward such a view clearly exists. How it is perceived and implemented by the scientists who animate the programs, however, remains to be demonstrated.

Finally, the field operations of FAO—financed largely by the

U.N. Development Program, often in conjunction with bilateral programs and funds—provide the core of routine activity. They matter to us because they constitute one of the chief media whereby the approaches and principles of research can be translated into social results. The question is to what extent do technical assistance operations go beyond the most concrete and pinpointed efforts to increase and improve the supply of a *specific* food or commodity in a *single* locality? To what extent is the activity closely geared to a comprehensive national development plan?[85]

FAO Working Methods. The working methods of FAO with respect to the last two types of activities now require attention. Overall guidelines and budgetary allocations, of course, are provided by the biannual conference and the council. But the details of the programs are set by the secretariat, even though these must conform to the overall emphasis set by the governments in the conference. That emphasis is eloquently simple: Do everything possible immediately to raise and improve the supply of food for the Third World, and do so in the context of overall demands in the United Nations. Thus, if these demands include—as they now do—the emphasis on global forecasting and environmental improvement, FAO must take such commitments into account. A specific work program is determined by the secretariat division in question through a process of intimate and formalized consultation with standing panels of outside experts, usually serving as individuals. Research priorities on soils, fertilizers, pollutants, or genetic pools are then fixed, but the actual research is done by national institutes, universities, ad hoc panels of experts, special consultants, and by such special programs of the International Council of Scientific Unions as SCOPE, COWAR, and IBP. FAO "coordinates" and commissions the research; it does not carry it out. What is done with the completed research? Routinely, it is published in one of the many specialized scientific publication series sponsored by FAO. But what if the research is supposed to be linked to urgent action?

One routine and three extraordinary channels are then available. Routinely, the results of scientific research are supposed to be communicated to the experts and consultants employed by FAO to carry out field operations. They are also supposed to tender their technical assistance in the context of whatever principles FAO has adopted as a result of prior research and directives of the political organs. Hence, briefings and discussions between regular secretariat personnel and field staff are an important link in this chain. But often this is not enough. The secretariat may then convene a special conference of experts who are to be impressed with the importance of the conclusions. Such experts typically are the chief national administrators of research centers in the field of concern and in the geographical region singled out for attention.[86] But what if this is too leisurely a process? The results of research previously undertaken can also be fed into the intergovernmental process of negotiation. If, after a series of meetings of key national administrators, sufficient concern has been aroused, the results of the work can be made the basis for an intergovernmental conference, which may eventually agree to a common program by way of a treaty. Technical support for implementing the terms of the treaty may then be mandated back to the FAO secretariat.[87] Finally, much the same process may also lead to negotiations for a common approach among intergovernmental organizations in the U.N. system, which in turn can lead to an agreed program among governments. How long does all this take? Five years is a reasonable period when the scientific findings are relatively straightforward.

How Integrated is the Program? What characterizes an agency's program as "holistic"? Put negatively, a program which self-consciously addresses itself to the narrow boundaries of a single discipline is contained, specific, sectoral, nonholistic. Improving the design of trawlers, perfecting measures for monitoring soil erosion, creating germ plasma banks, and specifying the pesticides appropriate for given species are instances of nonholistic programs: They rarely include attention to unwanted physical first-order consequences, and they altogether fail to be concerned with the social and economic second-order effects. Inclusion of either first- or second-order consequences may move a program toward holism; inclusion of both as permanent constituents is the *sine qua non* of holism.

Hence the identity of the unit which is the subject of research is *not* the defining characteristic of holism; the purpose underlying the research is. A research project which aims at determining the physical and biological characteristics of a lake or a crop area is "specific" or "sectoral" if no effort is made to link the findings to a set of additional concerns. The same activity becomes more "holistic" if it seeks to link the characteristics of the lake to an environmental program for greater water purity, increased crop production through irrigation, improvement of potability, fishing, and transportation. The key is the concern for first- and second-order consequences having to do with an improvement of human living standards.

A holistic concern can be pinpointed more acutely in terms of the human element: What is *the range of potential beneficiaries* of a program? A holistic program explicitly addresses the question of who stands to gain or lose. Here, holism is "extended" to the degree that the program attempts to distribute benefits to a broad stratum of the population for a combination of physical, social, economic, political, and often moral reasons. It implies a preoccupation with the issue of *for whom* and *by whom* goods and services are produced which goes beyond the usual concern with *how much* is produced. In the context of rural development strategies, it obviously entails a focus on a wider set of clientele than most developing countries and international organizations have recognized so far. Access to productive inputs, technical know-how, and financial credit would go primarily to those who have been traditionally bypassed—small holders, tenants, sharecroppers, landless and near-landless laborers. This dimension of holism addresses the fundamental reorientation in development strategies in the 1970s, a reorientation to which most international development agencies, including FAO, have publicly pledged to dedicate their efforts. Consequently, this focus deals head-on with a full recognition of the intricate interdependencies among the physical, the scientific, the social, the economic, and the political.[88] We now return to the FAO program with these distinctions in mind.

From Fragmentation to the Search for Links. FAO began its life with a highly respected scientific staff and a commitment to applying scientific research to improve and increase the world food supply. It acquired its technical assistance responsibilities five years later, at the very time when the key governments decisively turned down proposals to make of FAO an agency for managing the economic as well as the scientific aspects of food distribution. Field operations, therefore, naturally acquired the item-by-item, local-project-by-local-project characteristics already typical of the scientific staff, and indeed of most experts at the national level. Despite growing criticism that the fragmented approach to technical assistance accomplishes little, things are changing very slowly.

Take the field of genetics. At first FAO scientists joined with others in opting for the "package development" formula represented by the wholesale introduction into traditional low-producing agro-ecosystems of the genetic strains of wheat, maize, and rice associated with the "green revolution." However, FAO also realized,

> On the one hand, [these developments] have given encouragement to plant breeders, agronomists, governments and technical assistance organizations to strive for similar "package developments" on a broad front. On the other hand, the success of the new varieties and the rapidity of change has threatened the survival of the traditional local varieties or landraces which, as is generally recognized, are invaluable genetic resources for the world at large, and more particularly for the countries in which they have evolved.[89]

Hence, FAO scientists now seek to combine work on increasing the food supply with systematic attention to the preservation of crop genetic resources by having member states adopt appropriate research and management policies. Ecosystemic considerations have been included in the program.

Similar concerns appeared in the field of fisheries. For over twenty years the emphasis had been placed on improving the capability of under-developed countries to increase their fisheries and thus add to their food supply and earning capacity. Emphasis on fish conservation and management developed later. By 1971 concern for environmental questions was added to this objective. Conservation of fish stocks alone was no longer good enough; systematic monitoring of marine pollution *in relation to* fish population dynamics was now called for, requiring the integration of discrete monitoring systems. This implied the abandonment of a laissez-faire approach to fisheries development.

> The immediate challenge is for humanity to define its long-term objectives for the aquatic environment and its communities as part of a steady and balanced economic development. National governments, industries, and international agencies must look critically at plans that conflict with environmental values and must strengthen existing programmes and allocate resources to maintain these values. Ecologists, economists and workers in other sciences must clarify and extend the relevant theories and models from which are derived the efficient variables to be monitored in order to judge whether society's objectives are being met.[90]

The emphasis was then placed on devising appropriate monitoring systems *without* similar efforts being made to accomplish the prior intellectual and cognitive integration called for in this declaration. FAO field programs thus far remain largely unaffected by the new commitment.

The emphasis on monitoring was also evident in the evolution of the program relating to soils. With the development of the remote sensing technology, the earlier work on soil surveys was extended to include closer monitoring of grasslands, forests, locust movements and water resources. Again, the emphasis was put on the intercalibration of a variety of monitoring networks thus calling for extensive interdisciplinary cooperation.[91] Pest control programs also reflect the environmental concern. Following a period of encouraging the use of chemical pesticides, the idea of "integrated pest control" gained currency. It stresses a crop-specific mixture of techniques, including biological pest control approaches, and a more careful selection and monitoring of chemical agents. Stress is put on the development of methods of integrated pest control which can be generalized among countries and regions. Some field programs are designed with this object in mind.[92]

Adding environmental dimensions to policies designed to increase the food supply is one thing; translating the policy into systematic economic development planning is quite another. Well before the advent of environmental policies FAO developed a macro model of the world agricultural economy through which it generated a massive forecast to 1985 called "Provisional Indicative World Plan for Agricultural Development." The variables included aggregate food supply projections based on assumed growth rates as well as demand forecasts based on various assumptions concerning population growth. Diet was considered insofar as the supply-demand picture varied as, for example, between commodities. Supply was disaggregated among countries in terms of their participation in world trade and their exchange-earning capacity. Land use and employment (as an indicator of income-earning capacity) were also included. A serious food crisis was predicted unless a variety of remedial steps were taken in time.[93] What matters to us is that the Plan was never implemented in the sense of leading to qualitatively different and more holistic field programs or commodity management. It remained a planning exercise FAO was unable to apply to its operational activities. Five years after its presentation to the conference, FAO was beginning to devote serious attention to the difficulties involved in combining economic, sociological, dietary, agronomic and genetic research so as to be able to offer integrated advice to developing countries. Whether and to what extent the existing planning machinery at headquarters and the scientific capabilities of the various international food research centers can be brought into a coherent intellectual framework remains on the agenda of technical discussion.[94]

Economic and social policies remain poorly linked to a stated holistic commitment. But environmental policies do not fare very much better. Approaches to a redefinition of objectives continue to stress biological and physical components over social welfare and even nutritional and crop-economic ones. An FAO consultant pointed out that land use planning continues to be *use*-oriented instead of addressing upcoming issues of overall resource planning as the demands for increasing the food supply will put pressure on farmers to put land into cultivation which ought to be regarded as part of a more encompassing ecological space.[95] Such a view would put heavier stress on the role of water resources in a total environmental concept rather than regard water only as a source of irrigation. The hydrological cycle would thus become a core concept in soil management and land use planning. The inclusion of such considerations would then lead to agricultural planning based on environmental quality standards. But, speaking concretely, these proposals largely advocate increased FAO competence to stimulate proper research methods and monitoring under the umbrella of financing provided by the U.N. Environmental Program. While there is an intellectual commitment to combining environmental holism with economic and welfare considerations, little of this evolution can be discerned in the programs devised to deal with agriculture and food as a planning issue.[96]

This conclusion is strengthened by a look at the official program called "Natural Resources for Food and Agriculture," which was approved by the seventeenth session of the FAO conference.[97] One part of the program is devoted to the *assessment* of the state of natural resources for food and agriculture through the continuation of ongoing surveys, information exchanges, and the design of additional monitoring networks. This calls for the continuation, under UNEP funding, of collaborative programs with ICSU, UNESCO, WHO, WMO, and the International Union for the Conservation of Nature and includes the continuation of international standard-setting activities, such as upgrading the *Codex Alimentarius*. Another part of the program advances the notion of overall "ecological management." What is it? For the most part, the program merely regroups activities already carried out with respect to the collection and dissemination of the kinds of technical studies we have examined. Certain large-scale field operations are included, e.g., fighting salinization in irrigated areas and desertification of arid grasslands, as well as the conservation of endangered crop genetic resources. "Eco-development" is advocated as a master concept, but it is described merely in terms of increasing production in presently marginal agricultural lands.[98] In short, the integration of food supply goals with environmental and economic planning considerations remains very superficial.

Nutritional Planning and Analysis: Toward Integration?

One development triggered by the World Food Conference deserves special attention because it illustrates the slow convergence of expert knowledge focusing on an increasingly holistic goal *and* the linking of policy objectives by governments and international organizations: the evolution of intersectoral nutritional planning and analysis. Malnutrition, until very recently, was considered a condition defined by the lack of minimum caloric or protein intake by a given population. It was dealt with by means of supplemental feeding and food fortification programs, with small children and nursing mothers the primary targets. While there is plenty of data concerning the relationship between the incidence of various diseases and the lack of proper food there is a dearth of data relating nutritional deficiencies to incomes, prices, productivity and rural development. Nevertheless, there has evolved a consensus among nutritionists, public health specialists, and certain economic development planners that there must be a dynamic relationship between overall social betterment and dietary patterns which cannot be adequately mapped or planned if the emphasis is placed solely on increasing agricultural productivity and keeping food prices low, while using supplementary feeding programs to give marginal aid to the most disadvantaged.

The existence of such a relationship, and the need to make it the focus of national and international planning, has been recognized by the World Bank.[99] IBRD committed itself in 1976 to conduct systematic research, in cooperation with national and private food research agencies, to map the link between nutritional deficiencies and overall economic underdevelopment, and to take the findings into account when financing nutritional intervention programs. The Bank lent Brazil $19 million, as the first step in implementing the commitment, to rationalize food production, marketing and distribution, support of small agricultural and industrial producers, and aid to food planning agencies in Brazil. The Bank explained the approach in this way:

> The project will help to establish the information base necessary to formulate longer-term policies and programs to combat malnutrition. An innovative aspect of the project is the establishment of a mechanism in the Ministry of Agriculture to analyze the nutritional

consequences of price policies and other agricultural programs. As part of a test of four alternative delivery systems to reach people with better nutrition, the project introduces a novel concept for nutrition interventions—the combined use of agricultural and social extension to improve simultaneously the nutrition and productivity of low-income farm families.[100]

Within FAO and WHO, moreover, a consensus is developing among expert consultants that the concept of "malnutrition" had been given an overly restricted meaning. Because it was made to refer to physiological conditions amenable to diagnosis and treatment by public health specialists on the one hand, and by specialists in agricultural productivity on the other, nutritional policy was effectively separated from efforts to plan national agricultural income and production patterns. When malnutrition was linked to economic growth policies, these experts argue, the issue of food was approached mainly in terms of increasing the overall supply to feed the burgeoning urban population, to the detriment of the development of the larger rural sector, and sometimes at the cost of actually decreasing rural welfare. How, then, should food and nutrition be linked to economic planning as a whole? The redefinition of malnutrition has become the key to a new approach to development planning:

> A new approach to nutrition in national planning is required, because old approaches have failed in situations far less serious than those now faced and because, if they are continued, they will lead to more rather than less malnutrition. They might well lead also to less rather than more "development." In any case, the magnitude of the problem that now threatens many countries demands a reexamination of past strategies and a search for a more effective approach to nutrition in national planning. . . .

> It is now clear that development strategies pursued according to the policies and criteria that have guided past efforts have often failed to have a significant impact on the poverty of the world's poorest 40 percent and have commonly had the effect of aggravating malnutrition. Sustained reduction in nutritional deprivation will depend on the success of development efforts which give high priority to food and nutrition strategies that are designed to have a major impact in improving the health and nutrition of the large segments of the population that have been by-passed under previous development strategies.[101]

Field Programs and Holism: Summary

In January 1975, FAO was engaged in some 1,700 field projects, involving an aid allocation totaling $567.5 million, in 126 countries and territories. FAO's participation in these projects was limited to technical assistance or "pre-investment" activities: (1) institution-building, emphasizing training and research; (2) feasibility studies and development schemes, focusing on fisheries and forestry; and (3) soil and water resource surveys. Well over one-half of the projects were of small scale, entailing outlays of not more than $150,000. The input mix has been fairly consistent over the years, with expenditure on personnel—experts and consultants—continuing to account for three-fifths of the total.[102]

In evaluating the field programs along the criteria of holism suggested previously, it is important to bear in mind that FAO is usually no more than a junior partner in these operations. Whatever distinctive approach the organization may have to offer, it is severely constrained by the prerogatives of national governments and the dictates of more influential multilateral agencies on which it is dependent for support. In both content and focus, its field activities are still largely shaped by the resolutions of UNDP and the investment criteria of the World Bank. For these activities to have a more effective and distinctive impact, FAO maintains that it must be in a position to treat field and regular programs as an integral whole, which implies a greatly diminished reliance on extra-budgetary resources for funding program development. FAO also wishes to acquire an in-house investment and development capacity for helping Third World countries to design projects through all their phases, ending the present distinction, which FAO regards as arbitrary, between pre-investment and investment or development follow-up. Such a capacity, it insists, must not be "unduly influenced by links with the World Bank or any other institution."[103]

We believe that FAO nevertheless has an ability to influence the direction of the flow of aid to agriculture that is more than marginal. The crucial questions are whether FAO has been able to articulate new policies for technical assistance which embody a more holistic thrust, and whether such policies are reflected in the types of programs and projects to which it lends its backing. The answer to both of these questions, based on our assessment as well as FAO's own evaluation of its field programs over the last ten years, is negative.[104] On the basis of its participation in UNDP-financed activities, FAO notes,

> There does appear to be movement towards more "integrated" or "multi-disciplinary" projects, of longer duration and with a larger allocation of funds. Rather than concentrating on surveys, feasibility studies or research per se, such projects seek to integrate these ele-

ments within a pilot development or action programme, dealing not with a single crop or specific activity as in the past, but incorporating all the major inter-acting elements contributing to the development of a "farming system." . . .[105]

Such progress, however, by no means characterizes its overall program. A survey by FAO country representatives in 1975 attests to the fragmented nature of the large-scale projects executed by the organization. As many as one out of three were rated poor or fair in design, the main shortcoming being "the absence of clear links between project activities and activities outside the immediate scope of the project."[106] The consequences of the attempt to promote more integrated approaches to development programs, while catering to demands for "bankable" projects leading to a high volume of production within a short period of time, are best described by FAO itself. It notes

the growing tendency to carry the coverage of the project up to the stage where the final product, which may in many cases be processed, will reach the consumer. As a consequence, preference is given to multidisciplinary projects concentrated on a single subject matter area, or crop or region. In other words, integrated projects are given priority but are concentrated on specific fields and aim at achieving precise goals. Any decline in the number of projects covering a large number of agricultural projects on a monodisciplinary basis, i.e., from a purely production angle, is paralleled by a tendency to select a product such as rice, and cover every facet, from rice breeding through disposal.[107]

If FAO's progress is mixed on the spatial dimension of holism, it is elusive along the human dimension. Here is most apparent the failure to impress on either its clients or on itself the need for a reorientation of development policy that would systematically attempt to estimate the probable winners and losers in programs and projects. FAO points out that "[w]hile there is general support for 'integrated rural development' projects with special emphasis on the poorest and vulnerable sections of the population, *requests for new projects do not in any way reflect this concern.*" FAO argues that "the main inhibiting factor . . . is the extreme difficulty of formulating or implementing such projects."[108] But it is clear that such projects would require a conceptual recommitment which FAO has so far not made. This conclusion emerges from FAO's evaluation of a series of "area development projects" in which it has been involved with UNDP and the World Bank.[109] Area-specific, sector-specific, and crop-specific projects all qualify under the rubric. The degree of participation by the local population in the implementation of project activities is included as a criterion in the assessment of the *impact* of the projects, but it does not uniformly enter as a criterion in their *design*. FAO's conclusion is that area development projects which have received the support of the major donors—for example, the programs in the drought-stricken area of Sholapur, India, and the semi-arid region of Central Tunisia—"do not appear to be turning out well."[110] The reasons given run the gamut of constraints which have bedeviled development everywhere in the Third World—ranging from confusion about means and ends to the lack of government support and interest.

But FAO's less than sanguine attitude toward the notion of "area development" goes far beyond the recognition of and misgivings about such constraints. FAO suggests that the concern with rural unemployment and income distribution in the seventies may be a policy fad like the Green Revolution in the sixties. It all but rejects the utility of the notion of a target population:

> Considering the present level of development in the rural areas which encompass practically the entire land surface in the vast majority of the developing countries, the relatively small proportion of non-rural population in many of them, the pattern of agricultural holdings and the general level of agricultural incomes, it would be difficult for most governments to conceive of a traget population other than the entire population of the area concerned.[111]

FAO's plea is for a limit to holism in development planning.

We, as authors, conclude that the portion of the FAO program which is linked to science and technology is heavily skewed in the direction of the relatively *disaggregated* application of new scientific techniques in the hope of improving the quality and quantity of food. Verbal formulations which seek to link this emphasis to overarching environmental and economic welfare considerations are too superficial to merit a finding that the organization is seriously striving toward a program which would be described as committed to social forecasting. On the other hand, there is evidence that the scientific aspects of the program show an increasing determination toward the *physical* control of the undesirable consequences of pesticides, marine pollutants, and high-yielding varieties of cereals. If the overall program cannot be fairly characterized as the *random* application of scientific and technological discoveries, it certainly is not designed for their integrated utilization either.

The program, in short, does not point to any single-minded approach toward a different world order; rather, it presents a highly eclectic model, confused by the number of different approaches taken in fisheries, agriculture, genetics, nutrition, pest control, and agriculture-related environmental policies. Deliberate search for new knowledge is conducted, and partial scanning has been institutionalized, but little seems to be done with the results of these procedures. Thus, there is ample evidence that FAO is aware of important links among, for instance, the food supply, population growth, diet, nutrition, world trade, land use, the environment, and exchange-earning capacity, and that comprehensive policies have been formulated, but there is equal evidence that these policies are rarely translated into action programs. Consequently, while there is a refocusing of goals from time to time, the absence of a comprehensive framework makes it difficult to reevaluate the cause-effect links. Thus, experts are slow to remold tactics, reluctant to redesign strategies, and incapable of broadening the bundles which comprise package bargaining.

The institutional attributes of this program are also eclectic. The program's purpose is to acquire a capability in applying agriculture and fishing to development needs. Commitment to coping with the undesired and unintended consequences of science and technology is minimal, if present at all. Both a common framework, employing a pooled division of labor, and a joint facility, relying on some deliberate sequencing, are found within this program. The instrumentality seems to vary according to the major financing institution involved, the comprehensiveness of a specific project, and/or the urgency of the work program. Largely because of the diverse agencies and organizations on which FAO must rely for much of its funding and research, the program's decisions are taken in a diffuse organizational setting. UNDP, UNEP, SCOPE, COWAR, IBP, national institutes, universities, and foundations all share directly and indirectly in the making of agricultural and fisheries policy with FAO. Yet the pattern is not based on strong links among these organizations. It is diffuse, not merely the decentralization of separate but coordinated pursuits.

Views of FAO Respondents. How does our conclusion square with the finding that half of our respondents exhibit personal attitudes which stress the role of science in furthering the evolution of a better world order, and that almost half describe FAO as striving for a world order committed to social forecasting and rational planning for welfare? These findings are deceptive. When asked to identify undesirable consequences of technological innovation, 41 percent of our respondents answered "none";

they scored well below our total sample in pointing to specific problems associated with technological innovation, thus suggesting tolerance toward the unintegrated application of new knowledge. The majority describe themselves as serving a general world interest; only 33 percent mentioned the consumers of technology as their "clients." We believe that a systematic adherent of holism would have evoked a more pinpointed clientele. Their organizational experiences are sufficiently diverse to suggest that the expressed programmatic commitment toward holism is overstated. Only half feels that their work has succeeded in demonstrating to governments the complexity of cause-and-effect linkages. When asked to describe their experiences with formal planning methods as opposed to political bargaining in making programmatic decisions, well over half opts for the informal and political mode. Those who feel that their work has indeed sensitized governments to the complexity of links among variables also note that conflict over these issues has declined because the more obvious and nonsystemic factual connections among natural phenomena have been successfully demonstrated. But the experiences these respondents have in mind are confined to the control of unwanted physical consequences of innovations.

Another reason for the hiatus between a modest program and the ambitious claims made for knowledge resides in the way these attitudes are matched in the case of many of our respondents. Many score toward the holistic end of the continuum on one dimension and toward the disaggregative end on the other. We illustrate this perfectly plausible phenomenon.

An adviser on pesticides and an official dealing with soil resource mapping feel that science is not superior to politics in making decisions, but different in that it provides a factual limit to the kinds of decisions that could be made. In so doing it can help make decision-making for welfare more rational. The soil specialist also believes that his group can aid in introducing global planning by providing unambiguous factual information on the biophysical characteristics of soils. The pesticides specialist entertains similar notions about the potential role of integrated pest control approaches. But the combination of the two dimensions—one cautious and the other ambitious—yields an *eclectic* organizational ideology. In terms of their personal attitudes, a specialist on remote sensing and a research coordinator agree that science is far superior to politics and can infuse the organization with a holistic cognitive thrust toward welfare questions. But they characterize their organizational programs as the ad hoc application of specific scientific and technological techniques to narrowly defined problems of information gathering. The combination of the two dimensions gives us the personal attitudes of determinists and organizational experiences of random application, resulting in a *skeptic* organizational ideology.

We arrive at a picture of an organizational commitment to the use of science at a very low level of integration with nonscientific goals. A majority of our sample feel that it is becoming easier to achieve agreement on the role of science in program-making. But 80 percent also say that the proper target for operationalizing this growing consensus is provided by specific national governmental agencies, that is, by the highly specialized and issue-specific counterparts of the international officials. How sophisticated is the growing consensus? Forty-one percent of the respondents feel that it is due to simple factual persuasion on demonstrable linkages, as opposed to 24 percent who feel that a truly systemic-cognitive consensus is growing and 29 percent who deny any increase in consensus. We conclude that the integration of scientific with nonscientific goals is remarkable only with respect to controlling the degradation of the environment, a field in which the consensus in question is shared by the various specialists who work on biological and physical controls and improvements.

ECONOMIC DEVELOPMENT AND THE OUTER SPACE PROGRAM

Why is the scientific exploration of outer space a matter of international concern? More pointedly, what does it have to do with a commitment to economic development? Space exploration as an enterprise of basic research is all but monopolized by the United States and the Soviet Union. But the respective government agencies and professional groups are compelled to work in cooperation because high costs make a minimal division of labor appropriate and therefore suggest the desirability of sharing data. Data sharing, in turn, demands a certain amount of standardization of measurement and equipment. It also calls for agreement on certain basic rules with respect to radio communication frequencies and noncontamination by alien biological organisms of the earth and other celestial bodies. Coordination of basic research is the responsibility of the nongovernmental program known as COSPAR, an activity of the International Council of Scientific Unions. The "rules of the road" are spelled out in intergovernmental agreements negotiated within the United

Nations system, preeminently the United Nations Committee on the Peaceful Uses of Outer Space (COPUOS). These two agencies provide the focus for our discussion.

It is the results of basic research which, through technological application, acquire relevance to economic development in the form of three major activities, all based on the same technological innovation, space satellites: (1) improved and cheaper telecommunications, (2) improved weather forecasting, and (3) vastly improved knowledge of global resources obtained by remote sensing. The last of these will concern us most because of its prominence in influencing a possible future world order in terms of access to resources, prices, and trade. Weather forecasting as an international activity is the province of the World Weather Watch and WMO, and is discussed in Chapter 8. Broadcast frequencies for communications satellites are assigned by the International Telecommunications Union, a story which does not concern us here; commercial space communications are the responsibility of INTELSAT and INTERSPUTNIK. Neither of these activities is likely to trigger processes moving us to a different type of world order.[112] However, the massive use of direct broadcast satellites could exert such an influence because of the relevance of communication techniques to policies of nation-building. Hence, we will treat it in our overall analysis of the work of COPUOS.

As it exists now, the decision-making attributes of the program on economic development and outer space are eclectic. No search—either sectoral or holistic—is being undertaken on a regular basis, but partial scanning, during periods in which issues are being refocused, or during which there have been sudden additions of new issue areas to older ones, does take place, followed by periods during which there is simply a continued disaggregated pursuit of specific policies within the whole. Further, although tactics have been modified and objectives added, there has been resistance to reconsidering prevailing goals. Bargaining is zero-sum, with side payments made by the strongest actor.

Institutional attributes, on the other hand, fall within our skeptic model. The purpose of the outer space program being discussed here is to acquire a capability to aid in the economic development of developing countries. A common framework is the primary instrumentality, but there is a growing tendency toward the establishment of a joint facility and the utilization of some sequencing among the participants. The institutions for decision-making are decentralized, relying mainly on intergovernmental conferences with few links among interested agencies and concerns.

Our subsample of outer space specialists is evenly divided between respondents associated with the United Nations and with nongovernmental organizations.[113] Most of them are physical scientists by profession. In terms of personal attitudes toward the use of science, 50 percent are instrumentalists, 20 percent skeptics, and 30 percent eclectics, a very high commitment to the unifying role of science compared with our total sample. But in terms of organizational experiences, almost 55 percent are random appliers of the technology! Eighteen percent are physical controllers and social forecasters, respectively. There are no planners and only one eclectic. The combination of high personal commitment and modest organizational program experiences gives us this picture for organizational ideologies:

Organizational Ideologies

Rationalists	0.0%
Pragmatists	22.2
Skeptics	44.4
Eclectics	33.3

We now show how these characteristics are distributed among the respondents identified with the two organizations of concern to us as we describe the content of the programs in greater detail.

ICSU's Committee on Outer Space Research (COSPAR)

ICSU's Committee on Space Research is more than just a global coordinating body for national space research programs, though it is that as well. COSPAR is officially recognized by the United Nations as the main consultative organization for the international implications of space research and COSPAR representatives attend meetings of COPUOS.[114] Representatives are important participants in the discussions of WMO and ITU. In short, the group functions as the main international source of expert advice to intergovernmental deliberations on the regulation and use of space technology. It is a federation of twelve international unions of scientists and of thirty-four national academies of science. Work is assigned to seven groups which deal, respectively, with tracking and telemetry, interplanetary experiments, astrophysical techniques, upper atmosphere experiments, space biology, meteorology and earth surveys, and studies of the moon and the planets. Primarily, these groups seek to standardize equipment, work out a division of labor on experiments to be conducted, and arrange for the sharing of data.

Since the actual research is done largely by the Soviet Union and the United States, these working methods in effect provide the main channel for achieving bilateral cooperation in space research.

In addition, COSPAR working groups seek to orient their efforts toward helping the United Nations in attaining declared development and environmental objectives. Thus COSPAR conducts workshops on the economic and social applications of space research, as in the fields of remote sensing and communications satellites. It works with UNEP and with nongovernmental cooperative efforts in contributing to the design of hardware and instrumentation needed in setting up meteorological and environmental monitoring networks, in designing large-scale weather experiments, and in aiding developing countries that wish to establish rocket-launching facilities.

At one point it looked as if COSPAR could become the scientific community's early warning system for anticipating harmful effects of space exploration. ICSU requested in 1962 that the committee play such a role. Only two instances arose to test COSPAR's capability in technology assessment: Its opinion was solicited when objections were voiced to Project Westford—which was carried out by the United States despite warnings that it might interfere with astronomical observations—and its services were used unsuccessfully in working out procedures for sterilization and decontamination of spacecraft.[115] In each case the interests of the two governments engaged in space research prevailed over COSPAR's and over the concerns of scientists not closely identified with the ongoing cooperative research programs.

Such is the official position and the official program; how do the participating officials evaluate the work in terms of its relevance to world order issues? Those most concerned with using the committee as a framework for sidestepping the Soviet-American ideological and military confrontation are quite satisfied with their work and consider COSPAR a prime example of how scientific collaboration can bring about a politically relevant consensus; they consider their work a major contribution to the use of science as a means to resolve conflict. Others disagree. Some feel that the technical work is trivial and the consensus achieved is quite irrelevant to any larger economic or political goals. Some others hold that if the main objective was the initiation of countries lacking the capability for space research into the community of researchers this objective has been attained in fact, though without any discernible effects on a cognitive linking of separate disciplines or the evolution of a socially relevant consensus. Several prominent respondents felt that COSPAR may no longer be needed. There is widespread agreement that when the committee was established in 1958 its mission was simply to advance research for its own sake. Most of our respondents still feel that progress will continue to come from the politically unguided pursuit of research. Now, it is true, the programmatic consensus has shifted toward stressing the applications of space research to meteorology, communications, and earth surveys, with remote sensing the most prominent part of the program. But there is disagreement within COSPAR on relative priorities and on the role to be accorded to social forecasting in the context of the use of earth resource satellites. The minimum common denominator remains the generalization and widespread application of the techniques themselves. In our scheme of things, COSPAR officials are overwhelmingly random appliers.

Very few see themselves as artisans of a different world order.[116] At a purely technological level they concede that their work has succeeded in demonstrating to politicians the complexity of cause-and-effect links and they feel that, at this level at least, it has become simpler to achieve agreement on the role of science in policy-making. However, most of them identify national and international professional associations as their primary target groups, and only secondarily identify specific national administrative agencies as receptive clients. And there is widespread agreement that, at a more political level, the impact of COSPAR advice to COPUOS has been minimal. The United Nations has all but ignored its primary scientific consultative group, though the impact on UNEP, WHO, and European regional space organizations has been much more significant. Our nongovernmental scientists, then, emerge overwhelmingly as skeptics and eclectics who do not see themselves as critical contributors to a world order significantly informed by scientific approaches and concepts.

U.N. Committee on Peaceful Uses of Outer Space (COPUOS)

Concern that outer space constitutes mankind's new frontier, and therefore should be treated as a planning issue under United Nations control, was voiced almost as soon as Sputnik I was orbited in 1957. At first, attempts were made to give such a mandate to the International Civil Aviation Organization, an attempt which failed in large measure because the Soviet Union is not a member. In 1959 the U.N. Committee for the Peaceful Uses of Outer Space was set up with the expectation on the part of many governments that it would become the key regulatory agency on space matters, to be advised on technical questions by COSPAR.[117] This expectation was soon disappointed as the more functionally specific aspects of standardization and rule-making with respect to equipment and its utilization were given by governments to ITU, WMO, ICAO, and UNESCO. The commercial use of telecommunications evolved entirely outside the U.N., primarily in the form of INTELSAT. The logic of transgovernmental relations explains the evolution: Most national officials having direct responsibility for aviation, meteorology, telecommunications, and education preferred to deal with their opposite numbers in devising rules of the game in their appropriate international agencies. Only the Soviet Union preferred a centralized regulatory approach. In the face of uncertainty regarding the pace and type of technological development most governments sought to hedge their bets and hesitated before committing themselves to a global pattern of regulation. There was one notable exception: Each major space power did have an immediate interest in not permitting the other to acquire a military advantage from space achievements; thus they had a common interest in making space safe for peaceful national exploration. The achievement of this objective became the first task of COPUOS.[118] It was only toward the end of the 1960s that COPUOS also acquired a major task in mobilizing the new technologies in the service of economic and social development, while the overall global system of regulation and planning remained diffuse and devoid of a center.

Working Methods. The working methods of COPUOS consist of efforts to devise new rules of international law with respect to the use of outer space; this is the task of its legal subcommittee. Additionally, COPUOS is to explore the application of space technologies to economic and social development, a task given to its scientific and technical subcommittee, which, in turn, gave that task to its working parties on direct broadcasting and remote sensing. Finally, COPUOS undertook the task of actively promoting the use of these technologies by developing countries through demonstrations, workshops, manuals, fellowships, and special training sessions. This is done by the U.N. Secretariat. A traveling salesman of these techniques—entitled United Nations Expert on Space Applications—was appointed in 1970 and has been active since that time.

Four major legal instruments have been completed; three more are being considered. The completed agreements provide for the nonappropriability by any state of the moon and other celestial bodies, the prohibition in outer space of military activities, equal access to outer space of all states, cooperation in the rescue of astronauts, and rules governing liability for damages caused by objects launched into space. In addition, the General Assembly in 1961 adopted a resolution asking for the voluntary registration with the United Nations of all space launchings. A treaty making such registrations compulsory was completed in 1974. Finally, work has been underway on a treaty for the moon which would establish detailed rules for exploiting lunar resources as the "common heritage of mankind." Full agreement on the issue of resources has not been achieved, as the two space powers continue to oppose a sweeping definition of "common heritage."[119]

The promotional activities of COPUOS began with a massive effort to acquaint the developing countries with the relevance of space techniques for resource and communications planning and a large U.N. Conference on the Exploration and Peaceful Uses of Outer Space was convoked for that purpose in 1968.[120] Shortly thereafter the Secretariat began to promote the use of the same technologies through submissions to ACAST and ECOSOC's Committee on Natural Resources in which the promise of vastly expanded understanding of available natural resources was presented in glowing terms.[121] In addition, the Secretariat made itself the vehicle for establishing collaborative arrangements for promoting the technologies by initiating bilateral contacts between technology-supplying and -importing countries and by encouraging similar activities on the part of the International Astronautical Federation. Finally, it appointed the expert on space applications as its chief promoter. The scientific and technical subcommittee drew up an elaborate questionnaire to inquire of member governments whether they understood the potential of remote sensing and how they planned to use the technology. The subcommittee hoped that the responses would aid in developing a more coherent policy of technical assistance, while also going along with the open-ended training and proselytizing mission of the expert.[122] For our purposes, COPUOS activities relating to direct broadcasting and remote sensing are the focal points of interest.

Direct Broadcasting. Direct television broadcasting by way of satellites is a technology of particular international concern because it dispenses with the need for numerous ground stations and makes possible the beaming of broadcasts over long distances.

Moreover, one of its variants has no need for special receiving sets; its broadcasts can be seen on any commercial set. Thus the technology is attractive to large countries whose populations live in isolated areas and which lack the capability to install many sending stations and home receivers. It is equally attractive to any governmental authority which may wish to reach a large and semiliterate or illiterate audience. The technology can be easily adapted to beaming broadcasts designed to reach the population of another country directly into the target population's receivers. The relevance of the technology for nation-building became obvious almost immediately. Its potential role in multiplying intercultural contact and the universalization of values relating to world peace did not escape UNESCO. That organization's aggressive mass communication division entered the field of propagating the new technology in 1968.[123]

India in 1970 entered a program of acquiring a direct broadcast capability and therefore decided to orbit a national Indian instructional television vehicle as well as build one ground station. The satellite was launched in 1974. What was the purpose? To teach family planning, agricultural methods, rural public health practices, literacy? To overcome linguistic and geographical autonomy and isolation, to "integrate" the nation, to build a national culture? To create a specific Indian technological capability and thus be able to inculcate values which would free India from dependence on imported technology and the values it carries? To demonstrate methods of participatory planning at the village level?[124] All of these were put forward as explanations. Moreover, these many and often mutually contradictory purposes were all justified in terms of a "systems perspective on planning," as if intellectual harmony could be introduced among purposes which simultaneously stress indigenous culture (as well as its integration into a national culture), novel technologies in agriculture and family life (as well as resistance to alien technologies), democracy and centralized planning. The program, then, raises the familiar question: *instructional television for what social end?*[125]

While the use of systems thinking may legitimate the application of the direct broadcast technology in the sense of linking it to social and economic development objectives *and* to scientific methodology, the drawing of boxes and arrows cannot obscure the fact that the technology pits against each other the principles of privacy and engineered social integration, planned modernization and preservation of traditional cultures, broadcasting peaceful messages and propaganda designed to discomfit one's enemies. In the Indian case the last issue does not arise because the system is entirely national. But that need not always be the case. After three years of actively promoting the new technology, both UNESCO and COPUOS began to encounter some second thoughts. This has triggered a debate which remains unresolved: Should the technology be extended and promoted further or should its use be restricted?

In 1972 the UNESCO General Conference passed a controversial declaration on this subject and the Soviet Union introduced in the U.N. General Assembly a demand that a treaty be drafted to elaborate international principles governing the use by states of artificial earth satellites for direct television broadcasting. The Soviets explicitly deny that there is an international norm assuring freedom of information, but they "have no intention at all of hampering progress in this sphere of technology." Hence their proposal for restricting use of broadcast satellites is prefaced by the assertion that all states enjoy equal rights in sending and receiving broadcasts. The restrictions are these:

> (*i*) recognition of the rule that direct television broadcasting may be carried out to foreign states only with the express consent of the latter; (*ii*) even in the case of such consent, certain types of broadcast should be regarded as illegal and as incurring the international responsibility of states; (*iii*) the recipient state has the right to counteract illegal television broadcasting by the means at its disposal.[126]

Unlike the Soviet draft convention, the UNESCO declaration did assert freedom of information as the fundamental principle which ought to govern the exclusive use of satellites for broadcasting accurate and unbiased news, programs furthering peace and international understanding, and programs accelerating the spread of education in all forms. The restrictions suggested are much weaker: "Satellite broadcasting shall be apolitical and conducted with due regard for the rights of individual persons and non-governmental entities, as recognized by states and international law"; the needs and rights of audiences should be respected in programing; bilaterally determined programs must feature the free and equal cooperation of both parties; the preservation of diverse cultures is "part of the common heritage of mankind."[127]

While the enthusiasm of the experts remains alive, the governments are beginning to worry. The Soviet Union presented its initiative as a measure to limit the use of aggressive propaganda and pornography in international life. It was supported by all the socialist countries, Chile, Syria, Mexico, Indonesia,

Iraq, and Afghanistan. The United States opposed the initiative because it would interfere with freedom of information. This view was at first supported by most Western countries. However, Brazil, Argentina, France, and Sweden wanted it both ways: freedom of information *and* restraints on broadcasts threatening national sovereignty. COPUOS and its legal subcommittee were instructed to prepare a consensual text. But so far the consensus is confined to generalities. No draft agreement had been adopted by COPUOS as of 1976, though agreement was reached on such principles as the applicability of all existing international norms to the subject, the responsibility of states for their actions, the rights of states to participate in programs affecting them, and the need for international cooperation. There is a great desire to arrive at a reconciliation of the concepts of prior consent to programs and freedom of information. The Soviet Union continues to stress the first and the United States defends the second principle. A Canadian-Swedish draft proposes that the direct beaming of broadcasts to another country can be done only on the basis of consent and participation of the receiving states but that no restriction be placed on broadcasting within the zone of "unavoidable spill-over" of the satellite signal. "Technically unavoidable spill-over" beyond that zone, however, is also to be subject to the consent-and-participation rule. It cannot be said that the future application of the technology is entirely clarified by the debate thus far.

Remote Sensing. Nor are questions of open as against restricted use resolved with respect to the remote sensing technology. Is ERTS a spy-in-the-sky or an unprecedented source of information vital to environmental monitoring and resource mapping? Since it can, of course, be both of these things, the question of who controls the technology and who will benefit has acquired enormous significance. The United States, well before the civilian aspects of the technology were made operational by NASA, realized this and in 1969 offered to make the United Nations a repository for access to information obtained by American resource satellites. The offer was motivated "by the fact that the inherent sensitivity of the issue must be neutralized by some form of international legitimation and this means U.N. sponsorship."[128]

For several years it appeared as if this preemption of the issue had been successful and that the road was cleared for general application of the technology under the auspices of bilateral agreements for acquiring and sharing data, masterminded by

NASA and monopolized by the United States. The U.N. responded to the United States initiative by creating the working group on remote sensing within COPUOS, with a mandate to "promote the optimum utilization of this space application including the monitoring of the total earth environment for the benefit of individual states and of the international community" and to "review all of the factors relevant to the problems of establishing, operating and using such systems in order to have an adequate basis for making recommendations . . . to solve specific environmental and resource problems . . .".[129] The group was to *promote and review*, to assess the virtues and drawbacks of various systems *before* a firm United Nations role was defined. It turned out to be the review function which the working group's chairman, Italy's Franco Fiorio, has stressed ever since.

Promotional activities were soon launched by the Secretariat and the expert on space applications. They included demonstration resource surveys in various African countries, attendance at workshops and meetings for national delegates, hosted by NASA and by Brazil for the U.N., arranging access to NASA's data bank of ERTS and airplane-obtained imagery, and inducing developing countries to include systematic resource surveys in their development planning process. In the views expressed by the working group, however, restraint was in evidence. The group sought to discover, by way of questionnaires mailed to governments, what was expected of national and international remote sensing programs and which systems were likely to prove most useful. Caution was advised in opting for systems prematurely even though the full implications of the technology for planning were constantly stressed.

The wholesale promotion of the technology encouraged by the United States, coupled with the huge benefits which the new information could provide, was bound to raise the issue as to whether the activity would be increasingly internationalized in order to weaken the prominence of the United States or whether the opposite would occur, demands for restrictions on sensing and the safeguarding of territorial secrecy. No final resolution is in sight, but in the meantime both trends became highly visible.

The secretary-general of the U.N., in 1973, submitted to COPUOS a proposal for internationalizing remote sensing. He proposed three schemes: (1) a new organization to undertake remote sensing on behalf of the world community primarily for environmental monitoring and resource surveys; (2) giving the U.N. the power to store, process, and make available to consuming nations data obtained by satellites owned by other countries; analysis of the data could also be provided for countries lacking the skilled manpower; (3) strengthening the U.N. as the "focal point" of an international remote sensing system through coordination of national activities, making these activities more relevant to the needs of developing countries, giving technical aid, and working out global legal regulations. The secretary-general did not indicate his own preferences.[130]

Early in 1974 Brazil submitted a draft treaty on remote sensing to COPUOS which consummated the worries expressed by many developing countries and by the Soviet Union. It would prohibit remote sensing undertaken without the consent of the state being overflown and empower the states denying consent "to take measures . . . to protect their territory and maritime areas under their jurisdiction." Consenting states must be able to participate in sensing activities and are entitled to full access to the data obtained. Moreover, such data cannot be released by the state owning the satellite to any other state, party, or international organization without consent, nor can it utilize the information for its own purposes. Finally, states owning satellites *must* permit others to participate in sensing activities outside areas of national jurisdiction and take active measures to diffuse knowledge of the technology.[131] The fat was in the fire. How did COPUOS react?

The legal subcommittee in 1974 reported agreement on the same general principles already stated in our discussion of direct broadcast satellites, with the addition of the proposition that remote sensing should be used for the protection of the natural environment. It was instructed to continue its search for a consensus on the broader questions raised by Brazil and others, while the scientific and technical subcommittee was instructed to seek "technical criteria relevant to the definition, for purposes of remote sensing, of the terms 'natural resources of the Earth' and 'data on the natural resources of the Earth acquired by means of remote sensing.' "[132] If knowledge is power, can we assume that technical knowledge will have the power to settle the issue of how to use knowledge of resources?

At the same time the scientific and technical subcommittee took up the secretary-general's suggestions, albeit in very muted and cautious forms. Like its working groups, the subcommittee advised against any premature exercise of options with respect to remote sensing systems and urged more detailed studies of the costs and benefits of various systems in conjunction with a better assessment of probable demand for remote sensing services than was revealed by the earlier surveys. The secretary-general is to study the feasibility of establishing a United Nations-operated center for teaching the skills required for interpreting data obtained from remote sensing. Finally, the financial requirements of an internationally operated, owned, and financed "operational space segment for global coverage" are to be ascertained, even though the subcommittee expressed a distinct preference for regarding the bilaterally operated receiving stations in several countries as potential regional receiving and storage centers, not necessarily under U.N. control.[133] In short, neither the nationalization nor the internationalization of knowledge is foreclosed. The evident satisfaction of COPUOS officials with their work further supports this conclusion.

Views of Participants. Our COPUOS respondents included two delegates and four high Secretariat officials with primary responsibility for making the remote sensing and direct broadcast technologies available to developing countries. Neither delegate, though by profession a physical scientist, expressed deterministic opinions about the social use of science while *all* the officials proved to be instrumentalists. The delegates are satisfied with the evolving consensus on controlling physical damage and on generally applying the technologies. But they feel that scientific methods of demonstration add very little to persuading politicians, though they certainly persuade the experts in these areas. While tending toward the skeptical organizational ideology, they seem to be satisfied with this state of affairs. The officials, however, tend to be social forecasters in their programmatic commitments and pragmatists in terms of organizational ideology. Undesirable social consequences of the technologies are blamed on the overall "dependency" of developing countries, not the technologies. These officials feel that they *have* been successful in influencing the U.N. General Assembly and that formal and technical methods of planning are important techniques in bringing about a growing consensus. Technical information *has* been useful in resolving conflicts over these technologies and improved factual understanding *has* come about. Whatever the pace and scope of the program, then, those who are involved in it feel they are contributing to a more rationally designed world order.

We cannot agree with this assessment. In their eagerness to satisfy the aspirations of the developing countries the members of the U.N. Secretariat have opted for a breakneck policy of applying technologies dependent on outer space, a commitment reinforced by the staffs of FAO, UNESCO, and the experts serving on ACAST. The commitment was also strengthened by the prose-lytizing policies with respect to these technologies adopted by the United States. The less desirable consequences which can be associated with direct broadcasting and remote sensing have become prominent foci of international debate since 1972 as Brazil, Canada, Mexico, and the Soviet Union have developed second thoughts and their efforts to impose restrictions on the use of these technologies are clearly gaining ground in U.N. political debates. A cautious attitude with respect to the wholesale application of remote sensing has also characterized the work of the COPUOS delegates. It appears as if opposing factions within the program were attempting to meet two purposes simultaneously: the acquisition of a capability and the ability to cope with the consequences of that capability. The result thus far has been that capability creation has been slowed down until the issues of coping have been decided. Efforts to cope, while they must deal directly with the multidisciplinary and systemwide implications of the technology, have not yet yielded a very holistic view of the total "system." So far they have resulted simply in demands for further study and deliberation, not in a commitment to the total planning of global resource mapping. Other institutional characteristics suggest additional skeptic features. In the absence of international consensus on either the direct broadcasting or remote sensing technology—both of which would push the program in the direction of a joint facility largely dependent on or ordering and scheduling national behavior which does not now exist—the program relies on a common framework. Furthermore, contrary to the original expectations of COPUOS, decisions are made in a highly decentralized institutional arrangement, in which most scientific expertise is provided by COSPAR outside the U.N. and issues of standardization and rule-making, particularly with respect to the satellite technology, are handled separately by WMO, ITU, ICAO, UNEP, and UNESCO.

The decision-making characteristics of the outer space program are eclectic. The search for new knowledge is conducted without an overarching purpose or design as far as the social application of the technology is concerned. In COPUOS there is no search at all; in COSPAR and in the specialized agencies the search is confined to matters of engineering. To the extent that the desire to improve hardware, information storage and retrieval, and the sharing of broadcast channels to minimize interference relies on the coordination of separate organizational activities the learning pattern resembles a form of scanning: The process is far from random. Learning by way of partial scanning, however, has not made itself felt in the deliberations of COPUOS; systematic learning among the space experts in COPUOS working groups remains to be assimilated by the delegates who must ratify the findings of the specialists. Objectives have changed dramatically over the years, but the change has taken the form of the sudden addition of new objectives to the preexisting ones. At the same time there has been strong resistance to reconsidering tactics of action—technical assistance, bilateralism, attention to hardware questions—and the effort to marry the new and the old objectives in a single scheme has so far failed. The impulse to add objectives without integrating them into the mandated program is largely due to the rapidly changing character of the technology and the desire of some to apply it as soon as possible, while others experience equally strong needs to forestall the application. The confrontation may eventually produce a new consensus on goals and tactics, and when it does it would imply the acceptance of a pragmatic order. In the meantime the bargaining pattern is of the zero-sum variety. Each major space power wields a veto. Each is able to win allies in the debate by offering appropriate side payments to other countries desirous of acquiring some aspect of the technology.

Thus the scientific experts working in the outer space programs, in their profession of a pragmatically oriented view and their commitment to social forecasting, face an increasingly skeptical political clientele. Thus far, the experts have been satisfied; 67 percent feel that their work has demonstrated the complexity of cause-and-effect links to governments; 75 percent feel that the scientific content of their programs is getting more consensual. Most feel that international conflict has been reduced by the factual character of their demonstrations to governments and, overwhelmingly, they feel that they are serving mankind with their work, even though they recognize that undesirable consequences are also released thereby. We suspect that the growing caution of governments will soon dampen the enthusiasm of the experts.

TOWARD WHICH NEW WORLD ORDER?

We now attempt a synoptic summary of these fragmented organizational experiences in seeking to apply science to economic and social development. We begin by listing a number of suggestions already on the U.N. agenda, though not yet part of any operational program. In the aggregate these ideas and the reasoning on which they are based imply a rationalist organizational ideology; they call for the systematic and deliberate subordination of research and its application to social forecasting and social planning; they insist on a methodology of candid and full confrontation among bits and pieces of factual knowledge which is visualized as being on a course of continual self-improvement.

The 1979 U.N. Conference on Science and Technology, for all its uncertainties, does represent the commitment to a more holistic approach. Random selection and application of technologies "taken off the shelf" are no longer considered acceptable. Technical assistance of the familiar kind is no longer adequate, because it is too dispersed and unintegrated. Instead, the U.N. should provide services involving "research and analysis, the dissemination of information, development projects, experiment and innovation, and the services of intermediaries to rally cooperative efforts, bringing to the task a comprehensive catalogue of resources and techniques."[134] ECOSOC and its Committee on Science and Technology should engage in systematic technology assessment: provide the means to enable Third World planners to study and assess the costs and benefits of alternative new technologies, with emphasis on the identification of social costs.[135] The results should inform the funding practices eventually adopted by UNDP and IBRD, and avoid the continuation of the kind of uncoordinated technical assistance activities which seem to bring short-term benefits at the cost of long-term disaster.[136] Such a commitment, which also involves endowing the U.N. with an explicit mandate to act as an "early warning system" for anticipating the unwanted consequences of innovation, requires a much stronger capacity to provide appropriate information to negotiators and thus calls for more reliance on panels of independent experts.[137] Moreover, such an approach necessitates the adoption, as part of the new division of labor now being discussed, of a code of conduct regarding technology transfers and the rights and obligations of multinational corporations.[138] If "global planning" is too strong a term to describe these suggestions, "managed foresight and responsibility" is not.

The sum of these thoughts resembles a world order which is close to what we described earlier as a *pragmatist* stance. It puts great weight on the role of knowledge as conditioning choice, but it does not claim that action is easily derivable from knowledge: The link between objective information and proper social choice is real but elusive. The management of information and choice suggested implies the need for new international institutions which are likely to depart from the familiar pattern of slow—if not always sedate—intergovernmental negotiation. We stress that the pragmatist view does not come close to representing the pattern of organizational ideologies we mapped in our survey of scientists engaged in the three programs devoted to economic development in the Third World:

Organizational Ideologies:
All Economic-Development-Related Programs
(N = 48)

Rationalists	4.2%
Pragmatists	20.8
Skeptics	31.3
Eclectics	43.8

We now illustrate the implications of this distribution by summarizing the current international discussion of the future of the technology of remote sensing from satellites.[139] The core issue of a restrictive as against a widely permissive application of the technology was discussed previously. The issue is the readily visible part of the cognitive iceberg: The hidden portions include concern over the role imputed to increased knowledge as such; the link between this knowledge and the organization of programs for human betterment; the kind of global planning or management called for; and the institutional and legal implications of collecting and disseminating the information.

Five persons concerned with these matters encounter one another by chance at the elevator in the U.N. building and get into a heated discussion. Their conversation ranges over the scientific findings made available through NASA's Earth Resource Satellite (ERTS) program and the state of the remote sensing technology. They consider how the knowledge can be put to practical use and estimate the likely demand. And they worry about the planning and institutional implications by contrasting the proposals now being put forward by various governments. Rationalist, a former U.N. official, is now a high-level adviser and a distinguished scientist; he sympathizes strongly with the position of the Club of Rome. Pragmatist is a U.N. official active in promoting the use of the remote sensing technology; he identifies strongly with the demands of Third World countries and professes a socialist stance. Skeptic is a delegate from an industrialized country who avoids any overt ideological ties. Two eclectics join the impromptu conference.

One, a delegate from a developing country committed to the quick application of the technology, professes no systematic beliefs about science, knowledge, or international order. The second, however, identifies with a strong organizational commitment to systematically managing the remote sensing technology, though he does not believe in the absolute superiority of science or in any special role for it. He is an official in a specialized agency charged with using remote sensing data; we shall refer to him as rationalist-eclectic.

R: "Did you see this? The boys put together some reports from governments on what they got out of the ERTS data that NASA gave them."

S: "Probably more raw data that nobody can understand."

R: "Not at all. The Bolivians discovered some new earthquake faults. The Brazilians realize that their maps of the Amazon tributaries are off by 20 kilometers and they found some brand new islands, 200 square kilometers big. The British showed the Saudis where the locust breeding grounds are. Iceberg movements in the Arctic are now understandable. Pakistan is assessing flood damage along the Indus. And the Egyptians found out that the seepage from Lake Nasser is caused by an earthquake fault under the lake! Now maybe you fellows are convinced that we have something here."

P: "It does show that if proper training arrangements are made, people like the Brazilians can interpret the data they get. But who else has the digital computer set-up you need?"

S: "That makes my point: Unless Third World countries get their own set-up, NASA will always pull the strings. 'Interpretation is the transformation of an assemblage of remotely sensed data into useful information. Such interpretation may comprise preliminary study, manual reduction by a skilled interpreter or automated analysis,' we said in our report.[140] Should everybody really have this capability? Or only NASA?"

E: "Everybody should have it. We also said in our report that 'information is the aggregate of facts, deductions and hypotheses that can be inferred from the analysis of all the remote sensing data, including as necessary other supporting data from ground or aircraft-based observation and measurement.' And 'application of remote sensing system means the use of that system for practical purposes, including scientific, economic and/or socially beneficial goals.'[141] So what are we waiting for?"

RE: "We are waiting for a little more certainty on what the system can deliver. And we have to be certain that we choose the proper components. Satellites aren't the only possibility in the space segment. We might also include sounding rockets, manned spacecraft like Skylab, lunar observation posts. We still have to decide how to combine polar orbiting and geostationary satellites to get complete coverage."

R: "I believe that science contains the key to a better life all around, if we make proper use of science and stop abusing it for the wrong ends. I want to say a few things about the technology of remote sensing. Right now resource mapping is done only by NASA. The maps we get depend on the kinds of sensors they use on the satellites. They say they will freely share not only the raw data but the interpretation as well. We are in the business of training people to translate the interpretation into information and applications, especially the fellows in WMO and FAO. Meteorology and the soil sciences are being revolutionized because of all this. That means we are in the business of using the information only for progressive and peaceful purposes. But how do we know NASA doesn't hold back on data or information? Maybe the Brazilians are right to worry about who has knowledge about their resources and the information can be used to exploit them. We all know about the military uses of the same technology. I am saying that this constitutes an abuse of science. We owe it to the world to make science safe for social progress and to manage remote sensing so that nobody can continue the abuse."

RE: "You overstate the case. Science tells us about the limits to political choice. In my job, science tells us what you should *not* do if you want rational land use that considers productivity as well as ecological needs, and remote sensing gives us the information to stipulate the 'don'ts.' But you don't need a full-fledged technocracy of the pure at heart to pull this off."

P: "That's right. Before we start arguing that only the Kingdom of Science can save us from our collective follies I want to remind you people of a few things. The ERTS system and its ground receiving stations are still experimental. NASA has no plans yet to orbit any vehicle after LANDSAT. Receiving stations run the gamut in complexity, from fancy libraries to completely automated operations that reduce the satellite signal to soil maps, photos of the cloud cover, and registers of underground mineral deposits. Some require big crews. The Canadian station has a 'quick look' capability that seems especially useful for economic development planning and disaster forecasting. The complexity of the station determines what kind of data inputs it can handle. It also determines what kind of information can be laundered out of the final maps."

S: "Let's talk about costs. One operational satellite costs NASA $100 million for launching, controlling, monitoring from the ground. It costs another $4 million annually for tracking and data acquisition support. We don't know yet what the ratio of costs to benefits is going to be. Canada and Brazil paid a lot less for their access to the data because they only had the expense involved in creating the ground receiving facilities. Even so it cost Brazil an initial investment of $7.5 million and an annual maintenance outlay of $2 million. But this is a lot of money for a developing country, even a big one. Sure, science can help us make more rational economic and social choices, but we have to know more about the trade-offs first."

E: "Don't forget something else. Cost-benefit calculations have to include the capability of the sensors. Brazil would be happier if the data contained only Brazilian territory. A cost-effective satellite can't operate that way. It has to take in a wide sweep. Science doesn't have any answers for a problem like that. That's a practical problem of talking among governments. In fact, science is a trouble-maker. It creates expectations that can't be met, it triggers change that can't be controlled, and it makes the rich even richer and gives them even more power to kick the poor countries around. I don't count on any technocracy of scientists to solve these problems for my country. If we're not very careful, you scientists just make things worse. I think the Brazilians have a very good point."

R: "There you go disregarding what science teaches about the connectedness of natural processes. Politicians always worry about the wrong things. You have to cope with the whole system: ecology, economics, population, and the arms race. You want to develop your country, but you know how we are wasting our resources now. You are going to make it much worse. Remote sensing is a blessing because it can *prove* how things are connected and why you can't just grow and grow and grow. You are going to abuse science even more the way you talk."

RE: "You overstate the case again. But I agree with you that this kind of talk about science will discredit what remote sensing can show about the connections between ecology and economics. I'll tell you something else. We can show you how and where erosion patterns can undo the Green Revolution. But we can also show you how the indicators we can work out from remote sensing data can give you the planning tools to decide where to plant and where to protect the run-off with scrub."

S: "I don't trust all this talk about the connectedness of things. Anyway, no matter what you scientists say, politicians will take it all apart and try to deal with problems in pieces. You just have to do the best you can in demonstrating what you think you know, and then let politics take its course. Maybe the bit about agriculture and water and ecology will take hold."

P: "I think it will. A few years ago six countries had coordinated their national administrative services to deal with remote sensing data; now twenty have done it. Some say they want continued monitoring but some say they think they know enough for a while. A lot of them don't know what to do with the data, but they suspect it is valuable. There isn't any absolute trend in consumer demand, and it may well be that demand will peak at a certain point, and then slough off. But we don't know. EROS handled 13,000 requests from outside the U.S. in 1973. The Canadians handled 220,000 requests for information within Canada. Also remember the regional applications in the Sahelian zone, the Mekong basin, and in the Bengal area. That suggests that the demand for restricted use and tight controls will undermine the benefits of the technology. The regional concept is crucial, though it doesn't argue against a national monitoring system for very large countries."

E: "I would put the emphasis at the national level. Science in the abstract can't do a thing for my people's needs. But if we tell these scientist chaps what we want to do with their information, we may be able to get a few things done. The American delegate told us that NASA will continue to share all the data and even interpret it, and he said he saw no need for any regulations restricting the free flow of the information. But information is never free. And even if it were, I am not so sure I want that feudal-reactionary neighbor of ours to have it."

S: "Then you think that the whole idea of managing technology diffusion and utilization in the U.N. makes no sense? My government certainly has no great expectations. Look at the waste of effort in ACAST. UNESCO just talks, and UNIDO is in the retail hardware business."

E: "I don't believe in anything like a world plan and neither does my government. We Third World countries believe in power, not the power that flows from the barrel of a gun, but the collective weight that we can mobilize to force the rich countries into the New International Economic Order. The model we have in mind is that of global collective bargaining: Each side mobilizes its energies and negotiates as a bloc with the other. The more cards our side holds the better the deal we will get. When you fellows in the West worry about resource depletion, pollution, population growth, and famine our cards get better. You worry more about these things than we do. That's why I don't take our organizational mandate very literally as far as it suggests a 'plan.' We are supposed also to 'make recommendations for possible development, provision and operation of data collection and utilization systems in the United Nations or other international framework, taking into account the economic, social and legal implications for the international community that might arise as a result of selecting any particular system.'[142] That leaves it wide open and anything we come up with, plan or not, my government will use in its overall effort to get our own technology and our own science."

S: "My government doesn't believe in a plan either, but I don't agree with you that you can just get your own technology and your own science. You depend on the kind of analysis we do here. You won't know which system to use unless we sort the alternatives and assess their potential. You've got to make up your mind whether you want maximum information on the alternatives or whether you want to keep the information just for yourself. If you opt for restrictions on knowledge about technology, and remote sensing is just a current example which could apply to other things in the future, you may be cutting yourself off from the free flow of ideas. I don't believe in a world knowledge plan, like ACAST's or UNESCO's, but I do think that economic development will come sooner if we permit all relevant information to circulate widely, so that it can be taken up by governments as they choose, and by private business."

R: "If we don't have some kind of plan, the misuse of science and technology will escalate. ACAST and UNESCO are too uncritical, but the new UNESCO program on the ethical implications of science is a step in the right direction. So is FAO's use of remote sensing data. Our mandate is 'to promote the optimum utilization of . . . space application including the monitoring of the total earth environment for the benefit of individual states and of the international community.'[143] That means that the U.N. should work out a plan for remote sensing systems which deals with economic and environmental problems."

RE: "That's right."

P: "No, it isn't. Our mandate also says that we should take into account 'the sovereign rights of states and the provisions of the Treaty . . . on Use of Outer Space.'[144] You know what that means when read together with the duty to evaluate the potential of remote sensing systems? It means that the marshaling of knowledge has to be done in such a way that the Third World can overcome its dependence on the West and the socialist bloc. Collective bargaining is just a temporary technique, not a view of a future order. It must lead to an order in which each region, if not each country, is autonomous economically and culturally. Third World autonomy is what the Brazilians have in mind. Any planning we do has to be oriented toward realizing the goal of autonomy, and that may involve some restrictions on the use of the knowledge. If the West had secrets before, it is now time for the Third World to have some secrets too. So I am not so sure that the FAO's use of remote sensing data is so good because they go ahead and prepare soil maps of every place in the world and distribute them freely."

R: "You fellows will not see the whole forest. You always get side-tracked by one clump of trees or another. We are not just talking about satellites and sensors and receiving stations. We are talking about finally harnessing science and technology to the totality of human needs. And we are doing it so as to use science responsibly for the benefit of mankind. That means screening out, anticipating, and deflecting the bad things science has done too. If you leave things to governments and private business, that won't happen. We must create a global remote sensing system, owned and operated by the U.N., managed according to the best scientific information, with receiving stations that can interpret the data according to rules we have to work out here. There is no other way by which you can make the knowledge available and also reassure countries fearful of losing control over the natural resources. And we have to do both. Once we do it for remote sensing we will have set the precedent on how to manage other global technologies for the common good of mankind. ECOSOC would work out and supervise the rules of the system. Regional centers can specify what data they want and in what form. And they will then pass it on to the individual countries."

P: "I don't like the centralization you want. I prefer the creation of several autonomous regional centers for receiving, interpreting, storing, and diffusing the information according to national requests. I am not sure you want the U.N. to do any managing. The regional centers would be more cost-effective than a proliferation of national efforts, even if the space segment continues to be nationally owned. There may even be more than one space segment. But we have to have some rules as to what can be sensed and how the information should be distributed. NASA's position is not acceptable for the future. We don't have to go as far as Brazil with this, but the suggestions made for the negotiation of new ground rules somewhat more restrictive than the Outer Space Treaty must be followed up. Then you can build gradually toward sharing more and more information, as trust develops. But instead of relying on the U.N. I would much prefer to build up toward trust by relying on informal networks of scientists and national officials."

RE: "I prefer the 'focal point' plan. It would increase and centralize the information without creating an internationally owned system, and it could have the same benefits as the regional center approach."

S: "I agree with that. And I also agree that a more decentralized approach would set a much better precedent for bringing other areas of technology under international scrutiny. The U.N. would become the 'focal point' of the system in the sense that it would seek to coordinate the separate sensing programs promoted by WMO, UNEP, FAO, and IOC, though the actual sensing would be done by nationally owned systems. It would carry on promotional and technical assistance operations to enable all countries to make use of the data, but it would not tell them *what* use to make of it. And it would be the place where we negotiate new operating rules. If new uses suggest themselves we can amend the rules as we see fit. The U.N. should establish a facility or a center to which states with sensing systems would voluntarily submit data. The center would be a reference service, a library, or an indexing operation, not a full-fledged ground receiving station."

E: "Except for the center, you would essentially continue to do what we are doing now? You wouldn't want to work self-consciously toward a new technological world order?"

S: "That's right. Except for one thing. My government, along with the Soviet Union, Argentina, Sweden, Mexico, and France, wants more restrictive rules on sensing than the United States is willing to accept. We don't know yet what form these rules should take, but we don't want to go as far toward restriction as does Brazil."[145]

E: "Okay. But my government wants one more thing. We want the U.N. to establish a training center for our people who want to learn the techniques of data interpretation, and we want the rich countries to pay for it. The promotional activities the U.N. has carried out so far are just not good enough for our needs."

R (with a heavy sigh): "That's always what happens. When we get through talking over the issue, we arrive at a consensus which simply calls for more technical assistance."

Notes

1. IBRD's role in the use of science and technology for industrial and agricultural development is not fully discussed here, for we had very few respondents affiliated with the bank and the focus on technology *as such* is not clear in the bank's work. Loans often include a scientific and technological component in the context of specific project needs. Technological innovations are often brought to the attention of borrowers by the bank's staff. Efforts are also made to demonstrate the planning principles by virtue of which technological R & D can be incorporated into national planning. Despite these commitments, however, there seems to be no bank policy or approach on the use of science and technology for development. Instead, a modified laissez-faire attitude to the diffusion of skills and techniques appears to prevail. IBRD personnel argue that private entrepreneurship remains very important as the transmission belt between R & D and economic growth and that private and parastatal lending institutions should be included in the transformation process and its planning. Multinational corporations are singled out as key actors, but they are cautioned *not* to seek arrangements which aim at implanting developed country manufacturing capacity. Instead they should work out joint venture agreements of limited duration through which technologies modified for local use are jointly developed.

2. COSTED's efforts resulted in five requests for assistance, none of which involved any follow-up. The manuals were generally regarded as useless, with the exception of a Russian version of Graham Jones's *The Role of Science and Technology in Developing Countries* (New York: Oxford University Press, 1971), which drew on Central Asian experiences. See also J. M. Robertson, *Associations for the Advancement of Science* (ICSU-COSTED, 1970).

3. For an up-to-date and exhaustive description of all U.N. and specialized agency activities relating to science and technology, see Committee on Science and Technology for Development, "Institutional Arrangements for Science and Technology, Report of the Secretary-General," doc. E/C.8/29/Add. 1, October 3, 1975 (hereafter, doc. E/C.8/29/Add. 1). The activities of various United Nations bodies described in this and the preceding chapters are far from exhausting the programs relating to science and technology. Some United Nations activities relate neither to environmental protection nor to economic development. Many of the activities cannot be easily linked to the larger political themes of interest to us.

4. Jan Tinbergen (coordinator), *RIO: A Report to The Club of Rome* (New York: Dutton, 1976).

5. This subsample consists of thirty respondents. Their organizational affiliations are as follows: UNESCO ten, UNIDO nine, ACAST five, ICSU two, IBRD one, IAEA one, miscellaneous advisory panels two. There are six advisers, fifteen IGO officials, two NGO officials, and seven delegates. In terms of professions we have ten physical scientists, three biological scientists, seven engineers, four social scientists, and six diplomats.

6. The response pattern varied among the three typologies listed here. For the personal attitudes we had an N of twenty-seven, for organizational experiences twenty-three, and for organizational ideologies only twenty-one.

7. Our UNESCO respondents in this program included five officials of the division, three delegates, and two advisers. Seven are physical scientists, one a biologist, and two diplomats.

8. Quoted from chapter 2 of the program and budget requests submitted by the director-general to the general conference in 1969, p. 108. Emphasis supplied. Budget figures from UNESCO, *Approved Programme and Budget for 1973–74*, doc. 17 c/5 Approved, pp. 5, 165. The regular budget was $119,954,000 and the UNDP contribution was $100,000,000. The expenditures reported by UNESCO for 1975 are somewhat higher, but include the operations of six regional offices and of certain statistical services. See doc. E/C.8/29/Add. 1, p. 45. The fragmented nature and lack of focus in UNESCO's policy is

analyzed by James P. Sewell, "UNESCO: Pluralism Rampant," in Robert W. Cox and Harold K. Jacobson (eds.), *The Anatomy of Influence* (New Haven: Yale University Press, 1973), and James P. Sewell, *UNESCO and World Politics* (Princeton: Princeton University Press, 1975).

9. *UNISIST: Study Report on the Feasibility of a World Science System* (Paris: UNESCO, 1971). The central committee was chaired by Harrison Brown, as president of the ICSU, and a single UNESCO representative, Dr. A. Wysocki. The other members served as experts in their individual capacities, though some occupied high positions in their respective national governmental science machineries.

10. Ibid., p. 91.

11. "Outline of a Methodology for Determining Institutional Needs of Developing Countries in the Field of Science and Technology," doc. UNESCO/NS/ROU/211 Rev. 1, March 1971.

12. Y. de Hemptinne, "Governmental Science Policy Structures," doc. UNESCO/NS/ROU/234, July 24, 1972. De Hemptinne has been for many years director of the Science Policy Division.

13. Conference on the Application of Science and Technology to the Development of Asia, New Delhi, August 1968, *Science and Technology in Asian Development* (Paris: UNESCO, 1970), p. 164.

14. The exception may be the case of Indonesia. See UNESCO, "Indonesia: Science, Technology and Research: Policies and Programmes for the Second Five-Year Plan (1974–1979) of Indonesia," report no. 1, serial no. 2960/RMO.RD/SP, August 1973. Eleven additional reports in the series discuss specific sectors of the R & D situation.

15. UNESCO, *Science and Technology in African Development,* doc. SC/CASTAFRICA/3, October 21, 1973, p. 1. Hereafter, doc. SC/CASTAFRICA/3.

16. The exercise went through five iterations. The first two began with a list of 132 technologies which might be applicable or useful to Africa before and after the year 2000 and a list of barriers to the introduction of the technologies. They also yielded a rating scale for determining the amount of effort needed to overcome the barriers. As a result, the number of feasible technologies was reduced to 44. In the next three iterations the effort was made to rank order the remaining technologies in terms of utility and feasibility, taking the agreed barriers to their implantation into account, and specifying the amount of special effort necessary to introduce them within the next five to ten years. The five most popular choices turned out to be helium-filled airships, all-terrain vehicles, pipelines, satellite communications, and small/self-contained power sources. Various agricultural technologies also proved popular, but less so. For a full description of the process and a carefully guarded interpretation of the results by the secretàriat, see UNESCO, *Results of a UNESCO Delphi Survey on Technological Feasible Futures for Africa,* doc. SC/CASTAFRICA/2, December 7, 1973. The number of participating experts hovered around sixty for each iteration, with the number of international experts always exceeding the African participants. However, the secretariat notes that "as a general rule, the African experts . . . showed themselves to be less ambitious than the international experts, and manifestly more realistic." Ibid., pp. 7 and 17.

17. For particulars on procedures and the construction of the indices, see UNESCO, "Results of a UNESCO/UNACAST Survey of Institutional Needs of African Countries in the Field of Science and Technology," doc. UNESCO/NS/ROU/296, January 4, 1974. Only twenty African countries furnished useable replies to the questionnaires. The assistance of UNESCO field offices was required to expedite the participation of national experts and officials. An effort was also made to specify whether national and regional research and training centers were adequate for overcoming dependence.

18. This and the following paragraph are based on doc. SC/CASTAFRICA/3.

19. For a discussion of these plans, see our subsequent treatment of ACAST.

20. Doc. SC/CASTAFRICA/3, pp. 96–7, 105ff. The priority area here turns out to be agriculture, even though the dependence index shows the engineering disciplines to be the salient ones. We cannot account for the difference in UNESCO's findings and arguments.

21. The summary which follows is based on the "Draft Programme of Studies on

Human Implications of Scientific Advance Including Misuse of Science," doc. 18/C/74, August 23, 1974, and on an internal draft produced by the official responsible for HISA, doc. SPI/1/3044, December 3–7, 1973.

22. Studies proposed include the following: case studies of the effects on society of specific technological innovations (for example, computers); technology assessment techniques and institutions; the impact of professions on society; impartiality, objectivity, and secrecy in research; involvement of youth in science; how to choose technologies in developing countries; case studies of innovation in developing countries.

23. Our UNESCO respondents broke down as follows in terms of their organizational ideologies: one rationalist, four skeptics, three eclectics, two not codeable (both delegates).

24. ECOSOC, *Official Records*, 41st sess. supp. 12 (E/4178), ACAST, Third Report, May 1966, p. 74. Hereafter referred to as E/4178.

25. See ACAST, *World Plan of Action for the Application of Science and Technology to Development* (E.71.II.A.18) (hereafter referred to as WPA), and *Science and Technology for Development: Proposals for the Second United Nations Development Decade* (E.70.I.23; hereafter referred to by its publication number).

26. For a recent self-diagnosis, see Committee on Science and Technology for Development, "Institutional Arrangements for Science and Technology in the United Nations System. Annex 1: Report of the *Ad Hoc* Group of the Advisory Committee on the Application of Science and Technology to Development" (E./C.8/29), September 23, 1975.

27. The membership breaks down according to profession and nationality as follows:

Geographical Distribution of ACAST *Membership, 1964–1977*
(percentages; N = 56)

North America, Western Europe, Australia, Japan	34
Eastern Europe	14
Latin America, Caribbean	14
South and Southeast Asia	13
Africa South of the Sahara	13
Middle East, North Africa	9
Israel	3

Professional Distribution of ACAST *Membership, 1964–1977*
(percentages; N = 56)

Biological scientists	36
Engineers	21
Physical scientists	18
Social scientists	16
Others and undetermined	9

The overwhelming majority of members concurrently occupy positions as administrators of scientific departments and agencies in national governments, or had occupied such positions prior to joining ACAST. In 1975 the developing countries mounted pressure to change the membership so as to increase the number of scientists from Third World countries, a demand resisted by France and the United States with the argument that no geographical quotas should be applied to a body of independent experts. Of nine individuals who have served as chairman, all but one came from developing countries. Of twenty-one sessions of ACAST, six each were chaired by Carlos Chagas (Brazil) and M. S. Thacker (India).

28. Our respondents included one rationalist, two pragmatists, and two skeptics. Two were members of ACAST and three were officials in the U.N. Office of Science and

Technology. Professionally, three were social scientists, one was an engineer, and one a physicist. The two ACAST members were, respectively, a physicist (who is a pragmatist) and a social scientist (who is a skeptic).

29. *WPA,* p. 70.

30. ACAST, Second Report, ECOSOC, *Official Records,* 39th sess., supp. 14 (E/4026), May 1965, p. 1. Hereafter referred to as E/4026.

31. *WPA,* p. 70.

32. ACAST, *The Application of Computer Technology for Development* (U.N. Publication sales no. E.71.II.A.1), pp. 54–5.

33. *WPA,* p. 3

34. E.70.I.23, p. 5.

35. *WPA,* p. 45.

36. E/4026, p. 7.

37. "Report of the First Session of the Advisory Committee on the Application of Science and Technology to Development to the Economic and Social Council" (E/3866), March 12, 1964, p. 29.

38. E/4026, p. 5.

39. *WPA,* p. *vi.*

40. E/4026, p. 47.

41. CSTD, "Eleventh Report of the Advisory Committee on the Application of Science and Technology to Development" (E/C.8/24), January 22, 1974, p. 6. Hereafter referred to as E/C.8/24.

42. E.70.I.23, pp. 12–15.

43. CSTD, "Science and Technology in the Second United Nations Development Decade. International Development Strategy: Note by the Secretary General" (E/C.8/10), January 31, 1973; "Quantification of Scientific and Technological Activities Related to Development" (E/C.8/18), December 26, 1973. The World Plan, like much of ACAST's work, is permeated by a predilection for the advanced and the expensive. It calls for collaboration among "ocean scientists of all nations" in the development of new marine technologies and prototype methods for deep-sea mining and processing. It alerts developing countries to the potentials of hovercraft, hydrofoil, and hydrojet services; of containers to replace break-bulk cargo transport; of the movement of gas, liquids, and solids in slurry form by pipeline; of short take-off and landing and vertical take-off and landing aircraft, which are examples of "developments on the technological horizon" to which the poor countries should be sensitive. It reminds them about recent progress in computers, "especially important for developing countries because so many of their applications have a direct bearing on some of the main facets of the development process." It cautions them about the opportunity costs, but nevertheless tries to "draw their attention to the benefits which they might obtain by an enlightened policy of selective investments and training" in nuclear technologies for agriculture, industry, medicine, and energy. It asks them not to overlook the promises of space technology in such areas as communications, education, resource surveys, and weather forecasting. (*WPA,* pp. 117, 196, 281, 265, 274.)

44. *WPA,* p. 73.

45. E/C.8/24, p. 17.

46. *WPA,* p. 152. The same objective is given for the development of water (p. 118) and energy resources (p. 123). The only disadvantage mentioned for the acquisition of nuclear power plants by LDCs is their high capital costs (p. 270).

47. ACAST, Tenth Report, ECOSOC, *Official Records*, 51st sess., supp. 6 (E/5288), April 1973, p. 4.

48. ACAST describes an appropriate technology in manufacturing as one "based on modern science which is in harmony with its environment" (E/4178, p. 61). It concedes that in LDCs with high unemployment the encouragement of labor-intensive technologies is "a sound policy . . . wherever this is possible" (*Appropriate Technology and Research for Industrial Development*, E.72.II.A.3, p. 5). However, the brunt of the argument is to show that LDCs should exercise much broader choices rather than those suggested by labor-intensive formulas.

49. ECOSOC Resolution 1621B (LI), July 30, 1971; "Terms of Reference of the Com-

mittee on Science and Technology, Report of the Secretary-General," ECOSOC, 52nd sess. (E/5116), March 31, 1972, p. 2. CSTD's mandate is spelled out in ECOSOC Resolution 1715 (LIII), July 28, 1972.

50. CSTD, "Report of the Intergovernmental Working Group of the Committee on Science and Technology for Development" (E/C.8/28), August 6, 1975, p. 10.

51. CSTD has recommended that the conference objectives should include adopting "concrete decisions on ways and means of applying science and technology in establishing a new international economic order, as a strategy aimed at economic and social development within a time frame." Ibid., p. 3.

52. CSTD, "Arrangements for Science and Technology in the United Nations System: Report of the Secretary General" (E/C.8/29), September 23, 1975, pp. 11–15. The issue is intertwined with planning the agenda for the upcoming U.N. Conference on Science and Technology. There is a good deal of pressure from member states on the U.N. Office of Science and Technology to select a few large priority items to serve as a focus for the entire U.N. effort. There is also uncertainty whether the interagency coordinating committee to plan the conference will in the future seek to implement these items or whether it will evolve into a separate specialized agency for science and technology. The role of ACAST in all this is certain to decline as pressure in CSTD mounts to arrive at programs featuring the immediate application of technology to development.

53. ECOSOC Resolution 1621B. The future status of both ACAST and CSTD—like that not only of other bodies involved in science and technology but of the entire U.N. institutional machinery as it bears on development questions—is uncertain. A study by a high-level expert group on structural reforms in the U.N. recommends that ECOSOC assume direct responsibility for the functions presently performed by its subsidiary bodies. Both ACAST and CSTD would be abolished, the former to be replaced by small ad hoc groups of scientists who would be selected, from an international roster representing a wide range of disciplines, to study specific problems. An eminent scientist would also be appointed as science adviser to the secretary-general, providing him with "timely advice . . . to help him anticipate the impact of advances in science and technology and identify the options that their application presents, especially for the benefit of the developing countries" (*A New United Nations Structure for Global Economic Co-operation*, E/AC.62/9, May 28, 1975, p. 19). CSTD in 1974 decided that ACAST would meet only every other year in the future, a decision which prompted the chairman of ACAST, Dr. Wilbert Chagula, to warn that many members would probably resign.

54. United Nations Industrial Development Organization, Industrial Development Board, *Annual Report of the Executive Director, 1974* (ID/B/150), March 5, 1975, p. 211. Hereafter, ID/B/150.

55. General Assembly, Resolution 2152 (XXI), November 17, 1966.

56. Slightly more than 10 percent of UNDP's indicative planning figure earmarked for country programs goes to UNIDO. UNIDO's operational program (as opposed to its "supporting" or "headquarters" work) cost about $20 million in 1973 and $24 million in 1974; the estimates for 1975 and 1976 are $26 million and $29 million. Of the other components of the budget for UNIDO field activities (which absorb slightly more than one-half of its total expenditures), a "trust fund" supported by voluntary contributions has elicited virtually no support from Western countries. U.S. contributions to the six pledging conferences held by the end of 1974 were nil. ID/B/150, appendix; Industrial Development Board, 9th sess., *Medium-Term Plan for 1976–1979* (ID/B/153), March 24, 1975 (hereafter, ID/B/153); Industrial Development Board, 9th sess., *Programme Budget for 1976–1977* (ID/B/154), March 24, 1975.

57. Resolution 2152.

58. *Annual Report of the Executive Director, 1973* (ID/B/140), February 13, 1974, pp. 6–7. Hereafter, ID/B/140.

59. Ibid.

60. Industrial Development Board, 5th sess., *Role of UNIDO in Co-Ordination of Activities in Industrial Development* (ID/B/83), April 27, 1971, p. 3.

61. Industrial Development Board, 7th sess., *Report of the Group of High-Level Experts on a Long-Range Strategy for UNIDO* (ID/B/133), February 23, 1973, p. 19. Hereafter, ID/B/133.

62. Our sample included six UNIDO officials and three delegates. In terms of professions, all the delegates were diplomats, five officials were engineers, and one a social scientist. Four of the respondents did not furnish answers which permitted their being coded in terms of organizational ideology.

63. ID/B/150, p. 20.

64. ID/B/150, pp. 81–2.

65. ID/B/153, p. 54.

66. *Industry and the Developing Countries* (P1/34/Rev. 1), 1973, p. 5. "Matchmaking" is also the method used for achieving increased capacity for industrial research. UNIDO "matches" experienced Western research centers with interested counterparts in developing countries.

67. Ibid.

68. However, a good deal of UNIDO's "supporting programs" also serve as a spur for investment promotion. One of the organization's main functions is that of a clearing-house for industrial information and know-how. The kind of information that has been communicated so far is preponderantly in the well-worn area of sources of technology available in the West. The main component of the clearing-house is an industrial inquiry service described as "a major line of communication and transfer between industries and industrial institutions in developing countries and the accumulated knowledge in industrialized countries" (Industrial Development Board, Permanent Committee, 5th sess., *A Clearing-House for Industrial Information* (ID/B/C.3/4), October 19, 1972, p. 8. The service dispenses, inter alia, names and addresses from continually updated rosters of industrial consultants and suppliers of equipment.

69. ID/B/150, p. 128.

70. Industrial Development Board, 9th sess., *Summary Records* (ID/B/SR. 168), June 16, 1975, p. 21.

71. ID/B/140, p. 12.

72. For descriptions of these and other projects undertaken by UNIDO in recent years, see ID/B/140 and ID/B/150.

73. ID/B/133, p. 7.

74. Ibid., pp. 8–10.

75. *Report of the Second General Conference of the United Nations Industrial Organization* (ID/CONF.3/31), May 9, 1975. This decision was opposed by the United States and greeted with profound reservations by other industrialized countries, Western and socialist. However, UNIDO's transformation into a specialized agency was made official at the Seventh Special Session of the U.N. General Assembly in 1975.

76. *Industrialization of the Developing Countries: Basic Problems and Issues of Action,* Second General Conference of UNIDO (ID/CONF.3/5), October 21, 1974, p. 11. Hereafter, ID/CONF.3/5.

77. *Industrialization, Employment and Social Objectives,* Second General Conference of UNIDO (ID/CONF.3/9), November 1, 1974, p. 6. It must be borne in mind that UNIDO's actual program does not even reflect the lopsided commitment to industrialization. The organization is caught between two fires: The developing members call for investment in heavy industry, and the industrialized members counter with suggestions for keeping UNIDO as an industrial referral service. The compromise has been a program of fostering the growth of "canneries and tanneries," satisfying neither group and violating the official program.

78. *Industrial Development Survey: Special Issue for the Second General Conference of UNIDO* (ID/CONF.3/2), pp. 112, 117.

79. ID/CONF.3/5, p. 20.

80. ID/B/133, p. 18.

81. The centrality of scientific research to food problems is symbolized by the creation in 1971 of the Consultative Group on International Agricultural Research, which advises FAO on research needs and provides funding for national and international research. It is unique in being composed of national governmental agencies, intergovernmental organizations, regional development banks, and private foundations. FAO hoped that the group would mobilize up to $35 million between 1971 and 1975 to finance the International Rice Research Institute (Philippines), International Center for

Maize and Wheat Improvement (Mexico), and the International Institutes for Tropical Agriculture (Nigeria and Colombia). The group is advised by a standing panel of scientists. Its secretariat is provided by FAO. See FAO, *The State of Food and Agriculture,* 1972, pp. 148–64.

82. The subsample is made up as follows: sixteen individuals associated with FAO, two with the World Bank's program on agricultural development, and one with a non-governmental group; twelve biological scientists, five social scientists, and two physical scientists; sixteen officials of intergovernmental organizations and three advisers. In terms of the total sample, this group is heavily skewed in the direction of IGO officials and biologists.

83. FAO, *The Director General's Programme of Work and Budget for 1976–1977,* Annexes, pp. 360–1, doc. C 75/3, July 1975. The conservative estimate includes activities in the agriculture, fisheries, and development departments relating to resource surveys, statistics, populations dynamics, pollutants, resource management, and diseases.

84. See *Report of the World Food Conference* (United Nations, 1975), doc. E/CONF.65/20; General Assembly, *Report of the World Food Council,* 1975, 30th sess., supp. 19, doc. A/10019.

85. The question is partly rhetorical. The excessively specialized character of FAO technical assistance operations and their lack of integration in national economic development plans were sharply criticized by the Jackson report. See United Nations, *A Study of the Capacity of the United Nations Development System* (Geneva, 1969), vol. 1, pp. 7–13, vol. 2, pp. 222–3. The reorganization of field operations and the increased authority of the UNDP-designated resident representative were designed to overcome these criticisms. In 1974/75 FAO received about $200,000,000 from UNDP, about 10 percent of which could be incorporated in the regular budget as reimbursable overhead. Other extrabudgetary revenue for 1976/77 was estimated at $436,500,000. UNDP's share of extrabudgetary contributions to FAO dropped from 73 percent in 1969 to 46 percent in 1975. FAO, *Review of Field Programmes, 1974–75,* doc. C 75/4, August 1975, pp. 2–3, App. A. Hereafter, doc. C 75/4.

86. One example must suffice. In 1968 FAO convened a conference of West African agricultural research administrators in order to persuade them to pool their efforts so as to address jointly a number of ecological issues common to the Sudanian zone. Very little happened as a result until the outbreak of the great Sahelian famine. "Report on the FAO Regional Conference for the Establishment of an Agricultural Research Programme on an Ecological Basis in Africa, Sudanian Zone" (Rome, 1969), doc. RU:AER/68/Report.

87. One recent example is progress made toward the control of pollution in the Mediterranean, covering both land- and ship-caused pollutants. The initiative came from FAO's department of fisheries which succeeded, after several years of studies and discussions with national officials, in getting eighteen states to negotiate a general convention on this subject, based on definitions and principles previously worked out by standing committees of experts convoked by the U.N. system. See doc. FID:PPM/73/6, October 1973, "Principles Suggested for Inclusion in a Draft Convention for the Protection of Living Resources and Fisheries from Pollution in the Mediterranean." The inter-governmental organ used for the purpose was the FAO-created General Fisheries Council for the Mediterranean.

88. Works recognizing such interdependencies include *The Assault on World Poverty* (Baltimore: John Hopkins University Press, 1975); Hollis Chenery *et al., Redistribution with Growth* (Oxford: Oxford University Press, 1974); Keith Griffin, *The Political Economy of Agrarian Change* (Cambridge, Mass.: Harvard University Press, 1974); Bruce F. Johnston and Peter Kilby, *Agriculture and Structural Transformation* (New York: Oxford University Press, 1975).

89. O. H. Frankel, *The Significance, Utilization and Conservation of Crop Genetic Resources,* FAO, doc. AGPE:Misc/71/1, 1971, p. 4. See also *Report of the FAO Technical Conference on Crop Genetic Resources, 1973,* doc. AGP:1973/M/4, May 1973. These activities resulted in the creation of the International Board for Plant Genetic Resources, composed of key agricultural research administrators, "to promote and support international, regional and national actions in the collection and conservation of the world's plant genetic resources." The board functions as an organ of the Consultative Group on International

Agricultural Research and thus participates in determining where research funds will be placed.

90. FAO, *Pollution: An International Problem for Fisheries*, World Food Problems, no. 14 (Rome, 1971), p. 82.

91. FAO, "Space Activities and Resources at FAO," doc. AGS:Misc/73/26, May 1973; "A Basis for Ecological Planning: Phyto-Geomorphic Classification," doc. AGS:Misc/73/ 76, May 1973.

92. William R. Furtick, "Pest Management: An Interdisciplinary Approach to Crop Protection," doc. AGPP:Misc.

93. FAO, *Provisional Indicative World Plan for Agricultural Development*, vol. 1, summary and main conclusions (Rome, 1970).

94. See "The Possibilities of International Assistance to Developing Countries in Research on Social and Economic Problems of Agricultural and Rural Development," doc. DDDR:IAR/74/14, January 1974, prepared by the technical advisory committee secretariat for discussion by the Consultative Group on International Agricultural Research.

95. Raymond J. Penn, "Environmental Aspects of Natural Resource Management: Agriculture and Soils," FAO, *Agricultural Services Bulletin*, no. 14, Rome, 1972; Milos Holy, "Water and the Environment," *Irrigation and Drainage Paper*, no. 8, Rome, 1971.

96. For an effort to achieve such a conceptual linkage, see Joint FAO/WHO Expert Committee on Nutrition, 9th Report, Rome, 1975.

97. Doc. C 73/21, September 1973. The proposal was worked out by the Interdepartmental Working Group on Natural Resources and the Human Environment, a group formed to refocus FAO programs in line with the thrust and opportunities provided by the U.N. Conference on the Human Environment. The working group, in fact, merely aggregated the separate programs of its constituent units and seeks UNEP support for collaborative programs with other specialized agencies; it does not integrate them.

98. A major effort made to operationalize the notion of ecological management is field operations designed to advise member states in the preparation of basic legislation on natural resources and environmental protection, as in the FAO program to so aid the government of Colombia.

99. Alan Berg, *The Nutrition Factor* (Washington, D.C.: Brookings Institution, 1973). Berg has since become the World Bank official charged with nutritional policy matters. See also Shlomo Reutlinger, "Nutrition Policy Research Priorities: A Perspective for the World Bank's Role" (internal paper, March 1976).

100. IBRD, Information and Public Affairs Department Paper, June 1976. The loan is designed to lay the institutional and research foundation for a $1.3 billion national program to combat malnutrition. The bulk of the funds is provided by Brazil. The program is the largest in the field of nutrition ever undertaken by a single country.

101. World Health Organization, Ninth Report of the Joint FAO/WHO Expert Committee on Nutrition (Technical Report Series no. 584, 1976), "Food and Nutrition Strategies in National Development," p. 13.

102. Doc. C 75/4, pp. 3–5 and App. A.

103. Ibid., p. 61.

104. *Agricultural Development: A Review of FAO's Field Activities*, FFHC Basic Studies no. 23, 1970; *Review of FAO Field Programmes, 1972–73*, doc. C 73/4, August 1973 (hereafter, doc. C 73/4); and doc. C 75/4.

105. Doc. C 75/4, p. 23.

106. Ibid., p. 18.

107. FAO, *Review of FAO's Field Activities* (FFHC Basic Studies no. 23), pp. 39–40.

108. Ibid.

109. The professed aim is to deal with "the implied interplay of the numerous interlocking and complex social economic, institutional and technological factors" of national development (doc. C 75/4, p. 109). Area development projects are defined as "projects concerned with the formulation and implementation of plans for the development of relatively large areas to which the multidisciplinary approach to agricultural development has been applied" (doc. C 73/4, p. 37).

110. Doc. C 75/4, pp. 133–5, and doc. C 73/4, pp. 37–47.

111. Doc. C 75/4, pp. 130–1, and p. 77.

112. On the implications for world order of satellite-mediated telecommunications, see Edward Miles, *International Administration of Space Exploration and Exploitation* (Denver: Monograph Series in World Affairs, 1971); Jonathan Galloway, *The Politics and Technology of Satellite Communications* (Lexington, Mass.: Lexington, 1972); and Steven A. Levy, "INTELSAT: Technology, Politics and Transformation of a Regime," *International Organization*, summer 1975. Spokesmen for underdeveloped countries frequently make the point that the technology is relevant to their economic and social development only insofar as it enables them to develop indigenous technical elites able to participate as equals in the management of international regimes, thus raising these countries from the status of "clients" of INTELSAT. See the comments on an ACAST study praising space technology as useful for education, meteorology, and resource mapping offered by Professor O. Awe of Nigeria, United Nations, Department of Economic and Social Affairs, *The Application of Space Technology to Development*, doc. ST/ECA/161, 1973, pp. 70–3.

113. The sample includes five United Nations respondents, five persons associated with COSPAR, and one each with the International Astronautical Federation and the International Radio-Science Union. Six are officials of nongovernmental organizations, three are United Nations officials, two are delegates to COPUOS, and one is an adviser. The nonphysicists include one engineer and two social scientists.

114. The International Astronautical Federation has a somewhat less prominent official role, though it is recognized as a consultative group by the COPUOS subcommittee on legal questions. The federation is perceived by COSPAR as a serious competitor for the attention of U.N. agencies and as a potential recipient of research funds. It appears to be more of an international lobby of industry-affiliated scientists and aerospace industries than an organization for scientific cooperation.

115. Miles, *Space Exploration*, p. 29; Eugene B. Skolnikoff, *Science, Technology and American Foreign Policy* (Cambridge, Mass.: MIT Press, 1967), pp. 86–8. Those who saw COSPAR as an international scientific panel that would weigh the permissibility of national experiments which might alter the environment were thus disappointed.

116. We encountered one interesting exception to this generalization. One respondent believes COSPAR's significance lies in sensitizing Soviet and American officials to the "new frontier for mankind" implications of outer space, in terms almost reminiscent of Arthur Clarke's. Space research because of its cognitive impact on man, and *not* because of its scientific qualities, has a profound role in reorienting consciousness and therefore has the unintended consequence of *denationalizing* policy approaches to space and its uses. Having to think about how one establishes new relationships to the planets is credited with a long-range significance far beyond the immediate application of space research to weather forecasting and remote sensing.

117. Miles, *Space Exploration*, pp. 2–3.

118. Ibid., p. 5. ITU regulation of the frequency spectrum for radio communication was not undertaken until forty-three space vehicles containing fifty-three transmitters had been launched. COPUOS, significantly, reports to the First (Political) Committee of the General Assembly and is staffed by the Secretariat Department for Political and Security Council Affairs. Delegates to COPUOS tend to come from ministries of foreign affairs and permanent delegations, not the technical ministries and services. Membership on COPUOS has always been arranged to overrepresent the Western and socialist blocs rather heavily. Among the ten member countries which are "underdeveloped" and "nonaligned," the following have active programs and maintain close ties to the United States: Argentina, Brazil, and Mexico.

119. For the unresolved issues, see UNGA, *Report of the Committee on the Peaceful Uses of Outer Space*, supp. 20 (A/10020), 1975, pp. 4–6.

120. See United Nations, *Practical Benefits of Space Exploration* (New York, 1969).

121. See the following notes by the Secretary-General to ACAST and ECOSOC: doc. E/AC.52/L.123, October 6, 1971; E/C.7/18/Add. 1, December 10, 1971; E/C.7/18, December 10, 1971.

122. "Report of the Scientific and Technical Subcommittees of the Work of Its Tenth Session," doc. A/AC.105/116, May 21, 1973.

123. UNESCO, *Communication in the Space Age: The Use of Satellites by the Mass Media* (Paris, 1968).

124. Committee on the Peaceful Uses of Outer Space, "Report of the United Nations

Panel Meeting in India on Satellite Instructional Television Systems," December 21, 1972, doc. A/AC.105/114, March 28, 1973. The UNDP participant defended the idea of using the system for teaching villagers participatory planning. The U.N. expert stressed national integration and the overcoming of cultural dependency. The UNESCO spokesman talked about systemwide planning of communications to "promote, reflect, and give new forms to change. It should also enable democratic participation in public affairs" (p. 34). While the bulk of the meetings was devoted to engineering design characteristics of the equipment, one cannot help wondering whose values were being propagated in the name of overcoming dependency and protecting traditional values.

125. A similar promotional effort in Africa resulted in a much less immediate and enthusiastic reception. The participants expressed a desire for more studies and evaluations and also considered the feasibility of having a regional satellite serve several countries in their instructional programs. "United Nations/UNESCO African Regional Seminar on Satellite Broadcasting Systems for Education and Development," October 22–31, 1973, doc. A/AC.105/120, November 29, 1973.

126. Statement by Academician Y. M. Kolossov, in *UNITAR News*, vol. 5, no. 2 (1973), p. 23.

127. Text of the UNESCO declaration on the use of satellite broadcasting, adopted on November 15, 1972 (ibid., p. 22). UNESCO's entry into this controversy was widely resented by members of COPUOS, who at their twenty-seventh session (1972) demanded to be consulted before any similar declaration of principles was adopted. Some delegations disputed UNESCO's right to be involved at all.

128. Miles, *Space Exploration*, pp. 32–3. The Soviet Union opposed the creation of a U.N. mandate in this field, though it subsequently fully participated in the working group.

129. Doc. E/C.7/18, December 10, 1971, p. 3.

130. "Background Paper by the Secretary-General Assessing United Nations Documents and Other Pertinent Data Related to the Subject of Remote Sensing of the Earth by Satellites," doc. A/AC.105/118, June 12, 1973, pp. 65–7.

131. Doc. A/AC.105/122, February 4, 1974.

132. UNGA, *Report of the Committee of the Peaceful Uses of Outer Space*, 30th sess., supp. 20 (A/10020), 1975, p. 8. The current consensus in COPUOS on this issue is summarized in ibid., pp. 5–8.

133. "Report of the Scientific and Technical Sub-Committee on the Work of Its Twelfth Session," doc. A/AC.105/150, May 7, 1975, pp. 8–12. Bilaterally operated receiving stations presently are maintained by NASA in Canada, Brazil, Italy, Iran, and Zaire. A consultant's report in 1973 suggested that only fourteen such centers are required for global coverage.

134. Philippe De Seynes, "U.N. and Technological Change," *UNITAR News*, vol. 6, no. 4 (1974), p. 4. De Seynes was U.N. Under-Secretary-General for Economic and Social Affairs from 1955 until 1974.

135. See the discussion among five participants in the March 1974 session of CSTD in ibid., pp. 6–8.

136. Marc E. Schieber, "Assessing Technology for Development," ibid., pp. 15–18. The author describes the role FAO well-digging projects played in contributing to the great Sahelian drought and the resulting famine.

137. Zdenek J. Slouka, "The Diplomat in a Technological World," ibid., p. 34; Alexandr Mironov, "Forecasting the Technological Future," ibid., p. 30.

138. These codes are discussed and some early drafts presented in ibid., pp. 26–9. The code on technology transfers was first prepared by a group of experts appointed by the 1973 Pugwash Conference. Their draft was inserted into international negotiations by the government of Algeria, in its role as the chairman of the Group of 77.

139. The speakers in the dialog and the opinions expressed are real. The general status of the discussion reflects the situation within the working group on remote sensing as of 1975. The technical information was taken from "Report of the Working Group on Remote Sensing of the Earth by Satellites on the Work of Its Third Session," doc. A/AC.105/125, March 13, 1974 (hereafter, doc. A/AC.105/125). The views of the governments on the issues are summarized in "Views and Comments of Member States on

Remote Sensing of the Earth by Satellites: Synopsis of Replies to the Secretary-General's Questionnaire dated 25 July 1973," doc. A/AC.105/C.1/WG.4/L.11, February 21, 1974.

140. Doc. A/AC.105/125, p. 6.
141. Ibid.
142. Ibid., p. 4.
143. Ibid.
144. Ibid.
145. The countries mentioned are the ones who indicated in their response to the secretary-general's questionnaire that such rules are needed. Several of them submitted draft conventions on the subject in 1974.

Chapter 10

Toward a Pragmatic World Order

Must we always settle for a few additional pieces of technical assistance as we harness science and technology to the creation of a better life on one planet? The answer determines whether unplanned and uncoordinated research tied to random application of the findings will continue to prevail, or whether the integration of knowledge will lead to the integration of its application to human needs.

In comparing the findings of Part 2 and Part 3 it becomes evident that our respondents see things somewhat differently from the authors. Among the respondents the skeptic reigns, and he is more likely to settle for random application of knowledge than the pragmatist and the rationalist. But our examination of the nine programs in terms of decision-making and institutionalization disclose a different pattern. There the trends are away from incremental tinkering and the random application of knowledge to social choice. Which perception should be featured when we seek to speculate about future world orders, about arrangements more coherent and consistent than the eclectic pattern of the present?

We begin with a systematic juxtaposition of the two sets of findings in summarizing the present status of the nine programs. We then develop two scenarios interpreting these findings. One is predicated on the assumption that scientists and politicians will continue to act out the attitudes and experiences we established as currently victorious. Change is envisaged as an outgrowth of presently discernible trends which do *not* imply that any significant actors will change their minds on the role of knowledge in the fashioning of international politics. The second scenario, however, changes this assumption. It is predicated on the possibility that actors displaying ambivalent views—many of the skeptics and eclectics—will reduce dissonance by accepting the primacy of their organizational programs. This projection leads to the conclusion that a pragmatic world order is within the realm of the possible.

ATTRIBUTES OF INTERNATIONAL SCIENTIFIC PROGRAMS AT PRESENT

We now go back to our international scientific programs and seek to place them in terms of their fit into one or the other of the models. The placement is made by judging the character of the programs as they were in 1975. The finality of this placement will be our ultimate concern.

The current situation suggests the popularity of the skeptic model, with the eclectic running a close second: The "old" order shades into the "new" (see Figure 6).

FIGURE 6
World Order Attributes of Nine Programs: 1976

Pragmatic	*Rational*
Public Health 73	
Science/Technology Agriculture 33	Science Policy 33
Science/Technology 44	
Developed Country 40	*Skeptic*
Eclectic	Oceanography/ Meteorology 64
European R & D 82	Water Resources 57
Outer Space 33	44
Global Environmental Protection (MAB) 32	32
Science/Technology-Industry 48	33

NOTE: Two coding rules were used in making the classification. If 50 percent or more of the sample professed a single organizational ideology, the program was placed in the appropriate world order cell. If no ideology scored 50 percent or more, the program was made to straddle the cells which account for the highest and the second highest ideological choices. The numbers in each cell identify the percentage of respondents in the category opting for that ideology. This classification is the result of the perceptions of the respondents we interviewed: They placed themselves in the cells by the responses they gave. They knew nothing about our interest in decision-making syndromes and institutional patterns. They are not to be blamed for the projections and interpretations of their perceptions which we have undertaken.

TABLE 16

Institutional Attributes of Nine Programs

Program	Purpose	Instrumentality	Division of labor	Ultimate authority
European R & D	maintain capability	common policy	sequential	diffuse
Developed Country Science policy	cope with consequences of capability	joint facility	pooled/ sequential	diffuse
Public Health	acquire capability	common framework	pooled	decentralized
Global Environmental Protection (MAB)	acquire capability to cope with consequences	common framework/ joint facility	pooled/tending toward sequential	decentralized/ tending toward diffuse
Oceanography/ Meteorology	acquire capability	common framework/ joint facility	pooled	decentralized
Science/Technology, Industrial Development	acquire capability	common framework/ joint facility	pooled/ sequential	decentralized
Science/Technology, Agricultural Development	acquire capability	common framework/ joint facility	pooled/ sequential	diffuse
Water Resources	acquire capability	common framework	pooled	decentralized
Outer Space	acquire capability	common framework/ tending toward joint facility	pooled/ some sequential	decentralized

We now classify the nine scientific programs in terms of the institutional and decision-making typologies developed in Chapter 6 (Tables 16, p. 318, and 17, p. 320). The mismatch between some of our judgments and certain perceptions of the respondents becomes obvious on Table 18 (p. 322).

The reader now has a choice: He may disregard the authors' judgments and make his own projections regarding the implications of these findings for a world order, or he may follow us in reinterpreting the findings in terms of the types of decision-making and institutions we elaborated. A straightforward projection will minimize any rapid evolution toward a more holistically structured relationship between knowledge and action. Issue-linkage, with the exception of the programs in public health, and perhaps in science policy among industrialized states, would not proceed beyond the incremental hit-and-miss expansion captured in the skeptic model. No major change in regional and world methods of collective choice is implied.

Before the choice is made we should explain our rationale for reinterpreting the findings.[1] The self-perceptions of the respondents result from their roles as officials, advisers, or delegates. They interpret *their* experiences in terms of the jobs *they* were asked to do, of *their* initiatives, *their* negotiations, *their* votes. The respondents were not asked to sum up their experiences by offering judgments of the collective and cumulative process of interaction. The authors, however, base their judgments on the interaction among advisers, delegates, and officials. We rated decisions and institutional behavior over a range of issues.[2] To put matters differently, if the respondents err on the side of missing the forest because they are understandably preoccupied with trees, the authors are more likely to be overimpressed with the forest at the expense of single trees.

For these reasons we may be forgiven for now speculating about the impact of scientific world order ideologies by subordinating the views of our respondents to our own.

In any event, respondents and authors agree on the classification of these four programs: oceanography and meteorology, science and technology for agriculture, water resources, and outer space. But we rate the public health program as meeting the requisites of the skeptic world order rather than the pragmatic. And the respondents credit these four programs with more disjointed incrementalism than we do: European research and development, developed country science policy, global environmental protection, and science and technology for industry. All but the last appear to us to meet the properties of the pragmatic model (see Table 18).

TABLE 17
Decision-Making Attributes of Nine Programs

Program	Knowledge	Learning	Relation to original objectives	Tactics	Bargaining
European R & D	deliberate search	partial scanning	sudden addition	resistance to reconsidering goals but forced reconsideration of means	variable-sum, side payments, complex package-dealing
Developed Country Science Policy	deliberate search	incremental	sudden addition	resistance to reconsidering goals	variable-sum, side payments by strongest actor
Public Health	search is sector specific	incremental	slow addition	resistance to reconsidering goals	none
Global Environmental Protection (MAB)	deliberate search	partial scanning/ rational analytic	sudden addition	periodic refocusing of goals	variable-sum, side payments, package deals

Oceanography/ Meteorology	search is sector specific	incremental	slow addition	periodic refocusing of goals	variable-sum, side payments by strongest actors
Science/Technology, Industrial Development	deliberate search	incremental/ some evidence toward scanning	slow addition	willingness to reconsider goals	zero-sum, unit veto, some package-dealing
Science/Technology Agricultural Development	deliberate search	partial scanning	slow addition	periodic refocusing of goals	zero-sum, unit veto some package-dealing
Water Resources	search is sector specific	incremental/ some evidence toward scanning	slow addition	periodic refocusing of goals	none
Outer Space	no search	partial scanning	sudden addition	resistance to reconsidering goals	zero-sum, side payments by strongest actor

Table 18
Nine Programs Classified: Self-Perception against Authors' Perception

	Institutional attributes of world order models		Decision-making attributes of world order models	
	Self-perception	*Authors*	*Self-perception*	*Authors*
European R & D	eclectic	pragmatic	eclectic	pragmatic
Developed Country Science Policy	eclectic/rational	pragmatic	eclectic/rational	eclectic
Public Health	pragmatic	skeptic	pragmatic	skeptic
Global Environmental Protection (MAB)	eclectic/skeptic	pragmatic	eclectic/skeptic	pragmatic
Oceanography/Meteorology	skeptic	skeptic	skeptic	skeptic
Science/Technology, Industrial Development	eclectic/skeptic	skeptic	eclectic/skeptic	skeptic
Science/Technology, Agricultural Development	eclectic/pragmatic	eclectic	eclectic/pragmatic	eclectic
Water Resources	skeptic	skeptic	skeptic	skeptic
Outer Space	skeptic/eclectic	skeptic	skeptic/eclectic	eclectic

What does this classification of current trends suggest for the future? How are science and technology and the social needs to which they are linked going to evolve? The rational scientist's way of viewing the future was our point of departure. We used his image as our focus for sketching possible paths of development, only to discover that his view is not shared by very many others. Nevertheless, his construct remains our frame of reference for evaluating what we found. All three world order models are conceived as dynamic frameworks for collective action. All three suggest that things will not remain as we found them to be. All three suggest *some* linkage between knowledge and action, expert and politician, though the linkages differ widely in detail and import.

How can this change be envisaged? The rationalist view suggests one answer, a dramatic conversion to a global vision of connectedness. Such a conversion could conceivably result from a nuclear war, a massive and sudden change in the climate, the mass poisoning of the water or air over a whole continent. An immediate and serious environmental crisis of unprecedented proportions could trigger such a conversion. So could a global famine, or a new wave of the Black Death. Less likely, but not to be excluded from consideration, is the possibility that the ideas of holistic ecodevelopment will acquire the force of a world religion, superseding the political ideologies familiar to us.

We do not take this scenario seriously, despite its popularity in the futurist literature which is predicated on the victory of new values and attitudes born from disenchantment with industrial society. We reject it because of our belief that a fully holistic notion of interdependence is logically untenable. Even if it were tenable, few decision-makers would accept the logic as binding on their options. The holistic view ignores what we know to be true of political choice and of the processes through which choice is brought to bear on the solution of problems.[3] We do not expect the sudden arrival of "a new ecological man." The rationalist model orients our thinking, but it does not dictate the details of international evolution we seek to capture.

This leaves us with two additional scenarios. We can imagine the impact on collective choice of the processes captured in the world order models as we found them. This would assume that whatever changes take place in and among programs will be captured accurately by the assumptions built into these models. Thus, perceptions will not change beyond the bounds of the models. Nor will experiences with these programs. No shift into another model is in the cards. But some evolution will take place just the same because some, however little, learning occurs. This scenario is our immediate concern.

The second scenario allows for the possibility that perceptions *will* change as a result of serious disappointment with current performance. Actors will then reconsider their assumptions and rearrange themselves in different mixtures for purposes of making decisions about the programs. If the first scenario involves development without transcendence, the second is predicated on the possibility of gradual transcendence. The consideration of this scenario will constitute our final effort to capture the way in which the present begets the future.

LEARNING AND SUBSTANTIVE CONNECTEDNESS

Both scenarios rely heavily on social learning. But what is learning in the context of the international politics of fashioning collaborative programs in science and technology? Surely the mere fact that since 1972 a number of major conferences have been convened on the role of science and technology in improving the global quality of life is not sufficient evidence of learning. The proof of the pudding is whether man goes about his business in any way different from the pattern which prevailed before UNCHE, the World Food Conference, the World Population Conference, HABITAT, the Seventh Special Session of the U.N. General Assembly, and UNCTAD IV.

We conceive of learning as the ability to redefine policy issues in such a way as to recognize the cause-and-effect connections among issues, to appreciate that increasing knowledge produces more complex cognitive images, and that these images may imply the need for more complex and comprehensive policies for improving the quality of life. Learning, for example, would be evident if there were collective recognition that it is no longer good enough to increase the volume of trade to increase income levels. An appreciation of complexity calls for the realization that changes in trade, income, nutritional levels, unemployment, and urban housing conditions are causally connected. An appreciation of the connection implies that government policy will *not* be directed only toward increasing the volume of trade; it will subordinate trade policy to the comprehensive consideration of the entire network of factors.

Each area of expertise in the programs we have examined incorporates a notion of certainty. Each is an island of certainty. The issue is are there consensual causeways connecting the islands? The more consensual the knowledge with respect to the clarity of the links among, say, trade, employment, nutrition, and urban housing, the larger the network of causeways becomes. But we know that each area of knowledge is highly particularistic. Experts on trade flows are confident of their expertise regarding trade; experts on housing feel they have "the truth" with respect to urban growth patterns. The more certain they are of their particularistic knowledge, the more hesitant they become to undermine that particularistic certainty by joining forces with other experts. In short, particularistic certainty is the enemy of generalized certainty: The desire to combine and integrate knowledge beyond the sector of specialization is restrained because the result may imply more contingency and less certainty. Scientists and engineers most confident of their knowledge make poor candidates for the kind of learning that seeks self-consciously to transcend the boundaries of particularistic certainty in the search for the more elusive general truth which, rationalists say, is there to be grasped.

The evolution of the nine programs suggests some commitment to grasp this general certainty. In OECD and the European Communities verbal homage is being paid to the proposition that it is no longer good enough to set permissible levels for pollution, plan for economic growth, look for alternative energy sources, and collaborate in industrial research *if these things are done separately*. In UNESCO, WHO, and FAO there is formal agreement that studies of environmental degradation and protection should be focused *on man as one agent of change and the main beneficiary of wiser management*. In the United Nations the new orthodoxy—at least at the rhetorical level—proclaims that technological innovation and diffusion *should be planned* so as to make the poor countries the chief recipients of the boon. Everywhere the emphasis is on joining islands of knowledge in the search for policies designed to realize a more ambitious set of linked social goals. Do these professions of faith constitute learning? Not if the *substance* of the programs contains few useable causeways.

One test of learning, therefore, is the existence or nonexistence of substantive progress toward the building of conceptual connections among islands of knowledge and more complexly linked collective social goals. Such progress can occur only if the actors involved in a program feel dissatisfied with the way in which they go about solving problems. There is little incentive to change one's ways of thinking if the familiar methods bring satisfactory results.

This formulation is dangerously close to the rationalist view which suggests that the dissatisfaction will soon arise and that all reasonable human beings will eventually slip into the rationalist's mode of learning. The logical and empirical links between unfolding knowledge and increasing social complexity, and the need to marry the two more firmly, leave no other option. Global government for the network of discovered causeways is the institutional implication. A technocracy of scientists becomes the decision-making elite.

Our definition of learning and our test for its existence in international politics do not call for this conclusion. Does *all* new knowledge suggest more integrated social action? Do *all* complexly linked social goals depend on better or more interdisciplinary knowledge for their attainment? We think not. The *substantive* characteristics of fields of knowledge and of social action do make a difference. If and when this is so, learning may well occur within a given world order model. Learning then need not approximate the rationalist extreme in order to merit the label.

Some illustrations are now in order. The combined knowledge of physics, astronomy, and biology may demonstrate that life exists, or has existed, on Mars. It is conceivable that we are on the threshold of a new basic concept of the position of man in the universe. Will this affect a single one of the international programs we examined? In short, however momentous the discovery may be on philosophical and theological grounds, however great a cognitive breakthrough it may represent, its impact on the achievement of collective social goals is unclear. In the short run, at least, it will have none. Take an area of knowledge closer to home. Imagine a development in the interaction among hydrology, agronomy, biochemistry, and agricultural economics which results in a comprehensive understanding of how to improve grain production in semi-arid areas in poor countries. Such expanding knowledge would surely bear on improved social planning for food, nutrition, and rural incomes. Would it seriously affect pollution, resource depletion elsewhere, trade in industrial goods, the stability of the pound? Not necessarily and not in equal measure everywhere.

Nor does the evolution of more complexly linked social goals depend always and everywhere on more integrated and expanding knowledge. The growing commitment to the global planning of food resources, because it links such goals as minimal nutritional standards, stable commodity prices, and adequate supplies of basic grains, does depend on the kind of confluence of knowledge just mentioned. But it also depends on the existence of adequate monetary resources, transport and storage facilities, and channels of distribution which have nothing to do with hydrology, biochemistry, or the knowledge of soils. Moreover, these are items of knowledge which are already available. In short, the mounting of an integrated world food policy may not require a daring marriage of discrete fields of knowledge.

Learning is the capacity to link islands of knowledge *to the extent that this is substantively necessary to attain sets of social goals* which are perceived as increasingly interactive. The extent to which they are interactive, however, is a function of the ways in which social actors perceive their interdependencies. For some purposes the pattern of pooled interdependence may suffice. For others the sequential pattern already institutionalized may do. As long as learning takes the form of redefining knowledge and social goals so as to remain within these strictures, no single new world order model can be envisaged. Moreover, the separate "world orders" implicit in each program would simply be reinforced without being transcended. Dissatisfaction would lead only to better performance within each model; it would not change the overall character of international cooperation in science and technology. Yet learning would have occurred because a better appreciation of substantive cause-and-effect links to specific social needs would have resulted in the particular adjustment in governance, albeit without triggering a new world order. Learning will take the form of recognizing that some needs can be met without a dramatic shift in consciousness. Our first scenario is designed to probe whether this has already happened or is now happening.

But learning may also mean something else. A shift in consciousness *is* involved when the better appreciation of substantive cause-and-effect links to new social needs results in demands and decisions for action which challenge the more diffuse and decentralized regimes created for making collective choices. Such a shift presupposes a perception of interdependence which borders on the reciprocal, which recognizes that the mere pooling of information or the sequencing of remedial actions is not good enough for doing justice to the knowledge and meeting the complex needs now articulated. However, the mere fact that the litany of ecosystemic interdependence is recited more and more often does not establish the arrival of such a consciousness. Our second scenario will inquire into the conditions of this form of learning.

HAS LEARNING CONFIRMED FRAGMENTED WORLD ORDERS?

We now seek to test whether the first pattern described here has actually occurred, or is occurring. If the answer is positive, the recent history of international scientific programs will suggest that the learning that has taken place implies no new comprehensive world order at all. Learning can be demonstrated if (*a*) the gap between official objectives and substantive programs narrows, (*b*) dissatisfied governments in certain programs press for more ambitious goals and ways to use knowledge. No learning has occurred if the gap between declaration and performance remains wide and if most governments are satisfied to operate at this level of diffuseness. Learning, then, is the equivalent of the kind of issue-linkage—among goals and appropriate bodies of knowledge—which respects the substantive limits of connectedness perceived as necessary to attain goals. The empirical limit on the amount of learning deemed necessary is given by the perceptions of the actors themselves. When they are satisfied that they have "learned enough" they will remain within the world order models in which they find themselves. We stipulate that some evolution in attitudes and expectations will occur; we do not stipulate that this evolution is defined by the canons of rational-analytic knowledge.

How Wide is the Gap?

The judgments as to the width of the gap between formal declarations and substantive programs are ours. They are based on the historical evolution of the programs as told in the previous chapters. We want to know whether the particularistic certainties embodied in single segments of single programs have been linked so as to result in an integrated program aimed at meeting social needs defined as a sum of quality-of-life considerations. We therefore have to ascertain to what extent a verbal commitment has been translated into programs linking fields of knowledge and to what extent the results of this knowledge have been applied to collective policy choices. The terminal point at which the judgment is made is the situation in 1975, as given in the "Authors" columns in Table 18. The point of departure is the situation in 1965. Was any cognitive distance traveled? To answer, we must know:

1. Which world order model describes the program in 1965?
2. Have discrete new sectors of activity been added, subtracted, has there been no change since 1965?
3. Have governments and international officials sought to define a concept of action designed to unify and order the sectors of activity to attain a *more* complex set of social goals? A *less* complex set of goals? No change?

4. Has the more unified concept succeeded in actually ordering the activities associated with the program? Not succeeded?
Or has there been insufficient time to determine?

5. Do the governments associated with the program evince
satisfaction with its status in 1975, dissatisfaction, or can we not
tell? We seek to answer this question by determining whether
governments feel that the purpose of acquiring a capability,
maintaining a capability, or coping with the consequences of a
capability is being met.

The answers are summarized on Table 19. In interpreting
this table we wish to pinpoint the programs which are likely to
undergo change so as to approximate a different world order
model in the future, even if knowledge does *not* become more
consensual and even if existing collective goals undergo *no*
change toward increasing complexity and interconnectedness.

We note first that five of the nine programs underwent a shift
since 1965. Developed country science policy and global environmental protection became more enmeshed with increasingly consensual knowledge, mixed scanning, and periodic refocusing of joint goals. Science and technology for industrial
development and outer space began to work out more complex
social goals in the absence of more consensual knowledge. Science and technology for agricultural development, however,
slipped from early dependence on consensual knowledge to the
incremental mode of learning and inchoate program expansion.
Only the pattern displayed by UNEP and OECD confirms the
optimism of the rationalist. UNESCO and FAO, however, suggest
that programs which were entirely in the hands of scientists
(both in nongovernmental and intergovernmental organizations) tend to lose cognitive cohesion as they attract the attention
of politicians and become subject to complex funding formulas.
The more evident the link between scientific knowledge and the
setting of social goals becomes, the more difficult it is to work out
a programmatic consensus. Perhaps too much knowledge is the
enemy of political agreement.

Is dissatisfaction a clue to suggesting a change in world order
arrangements? We stress again that our judgments are derived
from the *interaction* of experts and politicians, from observing
the political evolution of programs, *not* from the judgments of
the participating experts. Our entries in the column "Satisfaction with Purposes" is biased in the direction of the perceptions
of the participating governments. It is *governmental* dissatisfaction which serves as the predictive clue.

TABLE 19

Evolution of the Nine Programs, 1965–1975 (Authors' Judgments)

Program	World Order Model Attributes 1965		New sectors added	Unified action concept	Action concept implemented	Satisfaction with purpose	World order model 1975 institutions	Likely to remain as is
	Decision-making	Institutions						
European R & D	eclectic	pragmatic	yes	yes	somewhat	unclear	pragmatic	no[a]
Developed Country Science Policy	eclectic	skeptic	yes	no	—	yes	pragmatic	yes[b]
Public Health	eclectic	skeptic	yes	yes	no	yes	skeptic	yes[c]
Global Environmental Protection	eclectic and pragmatic	eclectic and pragmatic	yes	yes	somewhat	no	pragmatic	yes[d]
Oceanography/ Meteorology	eclectic	skeptic	yes	slight	somewhat	yes	skeptic	yes[e]
Science/Technology, Industry	eclectic	eclectic	yes	yes	no	no	skeptic	no[f]
Science/Technology, Agriculture	skeptic	skeptic	yes	slight	somewhat	no	eclectic	no[g]
Water Resources	skeptic	skeptic	yes	no	—	yes	skeptic	yes[h]
Outer Space	eclectic	eclectic	yes	yes	no	no	skeptic	yes[i]

[a]The pragmatic mode of action may be adequate to deal with the governments' dissatisfaction on industrial, environmental, and research questions, but it is doubtful that the resolution of inconsistencies among national policies can be dealt with separately from improving the coordination of economic and monetary policies. The periodic coupling of policy domains as knowledge changes may not be adequate for dealing with the entire nexus. Slipping back to the eclectic model is also possible.

[b] Since few governments expect any better performance and have no great commitment to a unified concept, there is no reason to expect any change.

[c] Since most governments never understood or sympathized with the attempt at a unified concept, the failure to integrate separate sectors causes no great dissatisfaction. The commitment to a global concept of well-being remains rhetorical, and there is no dissatisfaction connected with the gap between doctrine and concrete programs. However, this finding by no means implies that the WHO program will stagnate. Even assuming no conceptual or institutional changes of any magnitude, a computer model of the WHO budgeting process developed by Francis W. Hoole predicts increases in expenditures by 1980 within a range of 100 to 220 percent, calculated on the 1969 budget. Hoole, *Politics and Budgeting in the World Health Organization* (Bloomington, Ind.: Indiana University Press, 1976), pp. 112–29.

[d] Coding has to respect the fact that the MAB part of this program has been the province of nongovernmental organizations of scientists and continues to be heavily influenced by them even though UNESCO has ultimate responsibility. Global environmental protection policies under the direct purview of UNEP and some specialized agencies are more subject to governmental influence.

In 1965, MAB was subject to the pragmatic style of ICSU and the International Biological Programme. It featured and continues to feature sequentially arranged research missions, increasingly justified by an overarching concept. No follow-up in terms of national and international policies is as yet called for, and the financial burdens are minimal. Hence, there is no dissatisfaction. Once the work reaches the point where policy changes are implied, however, dissatisfaction is likely to increase. Change is then likely to take the form of deliberate refocusing of goals, confirming the pragmatic pattern.

With respect to intergovernmental programs of environmental protection, the developed countries are dissatisfied with the slow development of the "joint facility" and the developing countries complain that unless the facility meets their development needs they see little reason to support extensive coordinated monitoring. Probably the dissatisfaction can be worked out through a programmatic evolution quite consistent with the pragmatic model.

[e] In oceanography few governments expect any better performance and have no great commitment to a unified concept. In meteorology there is general satisfaction with the unified research and data-gathering approach. The material does not seem to call for any greater integration.

[f] The gulf between the developed and the developing countries is growing wider and the policy response of the developed countries is much slower than demanded by the developing. Any implementation of the plan for a New International Economic Order must feature more scanning, refocusing of goals, and non-zero-sum bargaining. Hence an evolution toward the pragmatic is implied by the tensions within the skeptic model.

[g] The eclectic mode prevails at the moment because commodity trade, price, and surplus questions have not yet been linked to policies of increasing the food supply through reliance on new scientific and technological methods. These two emphases coexist without being integrated. Food supply goals and the distributional solutions sought by the World Food Council can be worked out only if the interactions are resolved at least through the methods of the skeptic model.

[h] Since few governments expect any better performance and have no great commitment to a unified concept, there is no reason to expect any change.

[i] The clashing priorities and purposes of the various interested governments cannot possibly be made to coexist except in the skeptic model, and no emerging trend toward scanning, refocusing, and variable-sum bargaining is in sight. The more consensual the knowledge gets at the level of laboratory research, the more fragmented the goals of the actors seem to get. We have here a case of increasingly consensual knowledge triggering increasing political discord.

Dissatisfaction with Performance

On the hypothesis that dissatisfaction is likely to trigger programmatic evolution toward a different world order pattern, we
must conclude that the prime candidates are the programs in
science and technology for industry and agriculture, the outer
space program, European efforts to arrive at a common research
and development policy, and the program in global environmental protection. All but the last, of course, gain their special
salience from their position at the intersection of science and
economic development. There the stakes are high and immediate. And as we saw from our discussion on the disagreement in global environmental agenda-setting in Chapter 8, the
special salience of that program also owes something to its perceived relevance to economic betterment.

The question now is to what extent do the participating scientists and nonscientists share our judgments of disappointment?
Whose dissatisfaction is to be taken as the vital clue? Participating
scientists and political actors, of course, entertain widely differing expectations as to their potential success in engaging in collective international program-making. Those whose personal attitudes toward the utility of science in meeting social needs range
toward the skeptical and the eclectic do not put much stock in
expanding islands of knowledge, and these account for almost
half our total sample. But a more important consideration in
interpreting perceptions of satisfaction is the ambitiousness of
the social goals which the scientists associate with their work. To
be highly satisfied in a setting of modest ambition is one thing, to
be disappointed about being unable to attain a very ambitious
goal quite another. What is the criterion of ambition? Contributing to the rapid diffusion of scientific and technological
knowledge requires very little refocusing of thinking and planning because the continuation of the earliest policies is likely to
bring such a result. Working for the elimination of unwanted
physical side effects of these innovations requires very little more
ambition to envisage change since most developed countries
already follow such policies. But willingness to engage in systematic social forecasting and comprehensive planning so as to *subordinate* innovation, research, technical assistance, and future
policy *to* some overriding set of social goals (equality, a global
minimum living standard, resource conservation, or even peace)
is a much taller order. In short, our assessment of satisfaction
must respect the ambitiousness of the task.

We defined the dimensions of ambitiousness in the questions
designed to elicit the respondents' organizational experiences;

they rated themselves on that scale. Their perceptions of success, therefore, are their own judgments as to how well they did in terms of the goals of their programs. We now summarize our findings by ranking the three groups of programs along three dimensions: (1) the percentage of respondents who see themselves as determinist planners and social forecasters; (2) the percentage feeling they were successful in demonstrating the complexity of cause-and-effect links to governments; (3) the percentage feeling that their success is due to reliance on formal models and careful analysis rather than political bargaining. (See Table 20.) The fact that the rank orders are weakly correlated (Kendall's W = .168) confirms the great diversity of experiences included in these programs and emphasizes the impossibility of drawing a single strong conclusion. The uneven experiences of the participants simply confirm that there is no single built-in thrust toward a more holistic world order implicit in the work of international scientists and engineers.

In addition, however, the findings which emerge from Table 20 do *not* fully confirm our earlier judgments on disappointment and satisfaction. The greatest gap between ambitious goals and modest success is in oceanography and meteorology. A lesser gap is evident in the efforts to apply science to industrial development, confirming our first finding. On the other hand, there is no paradox in the modest ambitions of the participants in European R & D planning, outer space, and water resources and their optimistic perceptions of success. Given the low level of their objectives (on our scale), why should they not be successful in using formal models for their sectorally specific work and impress politicians that their fields of specialization are interconnected and complex? The level of interconnectedness is not very high to start with. The case of MAB confirms our suspicion that the spirit of comprehensiveness which gives cognitive unity to scientists is bound to suffer diffusion when it encounters the need to persuade politicians of possibly unpalatable measures to be taken. But the question remains: Why do self-perceptions of ambition and success fail to match the judgments of the authors?

The answer has to do with the fact that our samples did not include systematic representation of government delegates.[4] The self-perceptions recorded disproportionately capture those of scientists working as advisers, officials, and leaders of nongovernmental organizations. Some see themselves as very successful, but their success is a function of their present ambition. In certain programs we think it likely that their ambition *already reflects* the lessons learned in the past with respect to the difficulty

TABLE 20

Relative Rankings of Ambitiousness and Success of Nine Programs

Comprehensiveness	%	Complexity	%	Formal Models[b]	%
MAB[a]	81.9	Outer Space	66.7	Outer Space	100.0
Global Environmental Protection	62.2	Global Environmental Protection	66.7	Water Resources	71.4
Oceanography/Meteorology	54.5	Developed Country Science Policy	53.3	Oceanography/Meteorology	50.0
Science/Technology for Agriculture	47.4	Science/Technology for Agriculture	50.0	Science/Technology for Agriculture	41.6
Developed Country Science Policy	46.7	Water Resources	50.0	Global Environmental Protection	40.0
Water Resources	42.9	European R & D	38.5	Science/Technology for Industry	33.4
Science/Technology for Industry	34.8	Oceanography/Meteorology	33.3	MAB[a]	25.0
Public Health	25.0	MAB[a]	33.3	European R & D	25.0
Outer Space	18.2	Public Health	27.3		
European R & D	18.2	Science/Technology for Industry	25.0		

[a] We separated MAB from the program on global environmental protection for the purposes of this test in order to highlight the differences in perception between the two segments of this sample. MAB respondents were disproportionately biological scientists who served as their countries' delegates on MAB national committees, though functioning essentially as uninstructed individuals. Respondents associated with the global environmental protection program were all officials of U.N. specialized agencies and the United Nations, with various professional affiliations.

[b] Insufficient data to permit ranking for public health and developed country science policy programs.

of persuading governments of the imperatives implicit in consensual scientific knowledge, as in the cases of European R & D, and science and technology for industry.[5]

And so the reader once more has a choice. If he accepts the self-perceptions as persuasive, he will predict that programmatic evolution is suggested by what is already going on in MAB, oceanography/meteorology, and science/technology applied to industrial development. He will predict that MAB and industrial development will become consistently enmeshed in institutional practices of the skeptic variety, while oceanography and meteorology will slip into the pragmatic world order model. But if he accepts the judgments superimposed by the authors, he will decide that *all* the programs which seek to relate science and technology to human betterment, in industry, agriculture, outer space, R & D, and environmental protection, provide the substance for movement into a more pragmatic and a more skeptic mode.

The overall result of our test confirms two conclusions: No single world order model is going to dominate; change has taken place in fragments, by way of "fragmentary learning," without transcending the boundaries of the *general* pattern of world order. There is no reason to suppose that the main collaborative efforts in the field of environmental protection (water, MAB, public health, and oceanography/meteorology) will move away from the decentralized, hit-and-miss, unfocused institutional features which now dominate. But there is strong reason to think that, in the regional efforts among industrialized countries to build a different economic order, movement toward a more pragmatic set of institutions is likely. Orders, like social goals and bits of knowledge, will continue to coexist. If in the aggregate they do confirm something of the rationalist's view of the world, their variety in thought and their variable enmeshment with political objectives precludes any very uniform or markedly rapid enshrining of that view.

MORE LEARNING: TOWARD A HOLISTIC IDEOLOGY?

We now examine the scenario built on the assumption that disappointment will lead to a reconsideration of both knowledge and the appropriate linking of social goals. It presumes that actors enmeshed in a given model of world order *will* make a serious effort to transcend that model. We have no empirical evidence that speaks directly to this point, since we did not inquire of our respondents whether and how they changed their minds on these questions. We did not study specific decision-making sequences within our programs in sufficient detail to be able to tell who changed his mind as a result of what type of stimulus.

But we have an indirect way of approximating a test of holistic learning. What would the ideological picture be if a certain number of actors changed their views so as to increase the number of rationalists and pragmatists? What would the programmatic and institutional consequences of such a shift be? How can we imagine, given our data, a cognitive shift to a more holistic persuasion in the use of knowledge in policy-making?

We attempt such an approximation by relaxing the assumptions which informed the construction of our typology of organizational ideologies. The large number of eclectics in that typology is due, in large measure, to our unwillingness to apply rigorously the principle of dissonance reduction. Now, however, we will apply that principle. Originally, we declined to consider as pragmatists or rationalists those respondents who expressed some support for holistic organizational goals but whose personal attitudes failed to match the cognitive properties which holistic policies require. We refused to guess how such individuals would resolve their dissonant perceptions and took the conservative route of coding them as eclectics or skeptics. Our reclassification reduces their number by making the assumption that organizational experience, in the longer run, will prove more powerful to force the reduction of dissonance than will personal attitudes. We also reclassified those skeptics who do not believe in the special cognitive qualities of science but who nevertheless identify with ambitious organizational programs as determinist planners, social forecasters, and physical controllers. This reclassification gives us nineteen rationalists, fifty-nine pragmatists, twenty-two skeptics, and twenty-eight eclectics.[6] The results of the operation are presented on Table 21.

Using the same coding rules we employed in our first scenario, the shift means that the pragmatic world order model becomes the most popular (see Figure 7). We summarize the shift and contrast it to the transformations predicted by our judgments of the decision-making and institutional attributes of the various models in Table 22. In six cases out of nine, the evolutionary pattern we superimposed on the perceptions of our respondents corresponds to what they would do in accordance with their self-perception. If they were to learn that organizational commitments and experiences should make them overcome ambivalent

TABLE 21
Organizational Ideologies Compared: Programs

| Program | Organizational Ideology | | | | |
	Rationalists	Pragmatists	Skeptics	Eclectics	N
European R & D					
Original	0	18.2	0	81.8	11
Revised	0	18.2	0	81.8	11
Developed Country Science Policy					
Original	33.3	13.3	13.3	40.0	15
Revised	40.0	40.0	6.7	13.3	15
Public Health					
Original	9.1	72.7	18.2	0	11
Revised	8.3	75.0	8.3	8.3	12
Global Environ- mental Protection (MAB)					
Original	21.0	15.8	31.6	31.6	19
Revised	31.6	47.4	15.8	5.3	19
Science/Technology Agriculture					
Original	0	33.3	22.2	44.4	18
Revised	15.8	42.1	21.1	21.1	19
Oceanography/ Meteorology					
Original	0	27.3	63.6	9.1	11
Revised	0	81.8	9.1	9.1	11
Science/Technology Industry					
Original	9.5	9.5	33.3	47.6	21
Revised	8.7	34.8	21.7	34.8	23
Water Resources					
Original	0	14.3	57.1	28.6	7
Revised	14.3	57.1	14.3	14.3	7
Outer Space					
Original	0	22.2	44.4	33.3	9
Revised	0	36.4	54.5	9.1	11
N					
Original	12	29	36	45	122
Revised	19	59	22	28	128

NOTE: Percentaging horizontal.

FIGURE 7
Possible World Order Attributes of Nine Programs

Pragmatic Global Environmental Protection 47 Water Resources 57 Developed Country Science Policy 40 Oceanography/Meteorology 82 42 Public Health *Science/Technology* 75	*Rational* 32 40
Science/Technology for Industry 35 35 European R & D 82 	*for Agriculture* 21 Outer Space 55
Eclectic	*Skeptic*

personal attitudes, most of the programs would move in the predicted direction.

What about the exceptions? In the case of European research
and development our judgment of the decision-making and institutional character of the program differs appreciably from the
respondents' because we see a good deal of movement over time
which most of the officials and delegates fail to see because they
are immersed in day-to-day negotiations which proceed at a
snail's pace. On the other hand, we grant that the remaining con-
tradictions in the institutional and decision-making dynamics of
the European Communities are such that future movement may
be toward more skepticism *as well as* toward more rationalism,
thus reenshrining the eclectic pattern which the respondents see
as predominant in both typologies. In short, our prediction is not
absolutely at variance with self-perceptions.

In the case of water resources we suspect that the sharp increase in pragmatists will have little impact on the integration,
refocusing, and systematic negotiation of *global* water issues, and
hence we do not agree with our respondents. Most of them participated in national programs of the International Hydrological

TABLE 22
Self-Perceived and Predicted Shifts

Program	Self-perceived shift		Predicted by authors
European R & D	none	none	somewhat
Developed Country Science Policy	eclectic/ rational	pragmatic/ rational	yes
Public Health	none	none	yes
Global Environmental Protection (MAB)	eclectic/ skeptic	pragmatic/ rational	yes
Oceanography/ Meteorology	eclectic/ skeptic	pragmatic	no
Science/Technology for Industry	eclectic/ skeptic	eclectic/ pragmatic	yes
Science/Technology for Agriculture	eclectic/ pragmatic	pragmatic/ skeptic	yes
Water Resources	skeptic	pragmatic	no
Outer Space	skeptic/ eclectic	skeptic	yes

Decade, mostly in European regional programs, particularly in the Alpine region. An evolution toward integrated and refocused programs *in that region* is certainly implied by the learning pattern here assumed. But we do not see any reason why this should be reflected in the more global arrangements implied in our approach to world order. The pragmatic order our respondents see is a regional, not a global order.

Our disagreement with the oceanographers and meteorologists is due to a different factor. Here the introduction of the principle that organizational commitments and experiences will carry the day implies that the world order implications of systematic research on weather and climate will become dominant. The officials in our sample will then confidently expect the evolution of a single world weather forecasting system and an integrated monitoring network to facilitate environmental protection. The substantive work of such joint facilities and common policies, in our judgment, will still be confined to physical control and exclude social forecasting and planning. Major social goals will not be affected, a point to which WMO officials are rather indifferent. In short, the pragmatism implied in *their* self-perception falls short of what *we* would expect to happen in a pragmatic world order. As for the oceanographers, they are less affected by the shift in organizational ideologies than the meteorologists in this sample.

Who are the newly discovered rationalists and pragmatists? Are they evenly distributed among our professions and roles? Far from it:

TABLE 23
Organizational Ideologies Compared: Role

Organizational ideologies	Roles				
	Adviser	*IGO official*	*NGO official*	*Delegate*	*N*
Rationalist					
Original	17.9	8.1	8.3	9.8	12
Revised	26.7	10.9	14.3	10.0	19
Pragmatist					
Original	42.9	24.2	16.7	0	29
Revised	50.0	48.4	35.7	40.0	59
Skeptic					
Original	17.9	32.3	33.3	29.5	36
Revised	13.3	14.1	35.7	20.0	22
Eclectic					
Original	21.4	35.5	41.7	60.0	45
Revised	10.0	26.6	14.3	30.0	28
N					
Original	28	62	12	20	122
Revised	30	64	14	20	128

NOTE: Percentaging vertical.

Almost all the new rationalists are advisers and officials of nongovernmental organizations; two-thirds are biologists, and there are no diplomats among them. Over three-quarters of the new pragmatists, however, are delegates and officials of intergovernmental organizations. Half of all delegates are now rationalists and pragmatists; 60 percent of the IGO officials share these ideologies. The new pragmatists are disproportionately drawn from the engineering profession (about a third), while all the other professions share the increase in about equal measure. One implication would seem to be that among the rationalists a more consistent focus on ecosystemic constructs will prevail, while the systems engineering approach to problem-solving will be strengthened among the pragmatists, especially in the oceanography/meteorology and water resources programs in which most of our engineers are active.

Rationalism and pragmatism as bases for world order institutions share a dependence on increasingly consensual scientific knowledge. Does that mean that the scientists active in these programs can be assumed to agree on a greater proportion of

TABLE 24
Organizational Ideologies Compared: Profession

Organizational ideologies	Professions					
	Physical scientist	Biological scientist	Engineer	Social scientist	Diplomat	N
Rationalist						
Original	9.7	11.1	14.3	5.3	0	12
Revised	8.8	23.7	17.2	10.5	0	19
Pragmatist						
Original	22.6	36.1	17.9	21.1	0	29
Revised	41.2	50.0	51.7	42.1	37.5	59
Skeptic						
Original	35.5	25.0	39.3	15.8	25.0	36
Revised	38.2	13.2	6.9	10.5	0	22
Eclectic						
Original	32.3	27.8	28.6	57.9	75.0	45
Revised	11.8	13.2	24.1	36.8	62.5	28
N						
Original	31	36	28	19	8	122
Revised	34	38	29	19	8	128

NOTE: Percentaging vertical.

attitudes and experiences than was true under the assumption of fragmented learning? Obviously they cannot, since our reclassification only placed them in different cells without changing the data concerning their attitudes and experiences. The shift then means that, all other things remaining the same, there will be as much disagreement among actors in the pragmatically dominated world as in the skeptic model. Before exploring the implication of that dictum we illustrate the range of views.

In the pragmatic world order our respondents display a sharp increase in concern that science implies the substitution of knowledge of means, of technique, at the expense of values. They also worry more about the introduction of undigestible social change. But the number professing indifference to the unwanted side effects of scientific and technological innovation also rises sharply! Does this mixture of contradictory views imply more central control over the process of innovation, or less?

What are the views regarding representation and clients? Scientists claiming international organizations and the world interest as their reference group are more numerous now. But so are those who mention their home country as their client and scientists who identify primarily with their professional disciplines.

Does this suggest a greater conflict between parochial and universal interests than in the first scenario?

Much the same is true when we contrast the groups to be influenced by way of international action. National interest groups and international professional associations are no more popular as targets of action now than before. But international secretariats are. So are national governments and cabinet ministers, as well as specific *national* administrative agencies and *national* professional associations. A different pattern of international bargaining is suggested by this double impact, suggesting that both national and international decision-makers will be more important.

Is conflict over ends and means more likely to be resolved on the basis of scientific knowledge? Our scenario contains no clue that respondents are now *more* confident than before that their work has succeeded in demonstrating to national governments the complexity of cause-and-effect links; they divide in half on this question, as in the first scenario. More scientists now feel that careful analysis and good data are helpful in resolving conflict and that conflict has declined because of the acceptance of facts; but more also feel that building appropriate political coalitions is the best way to achieve agreement. Moreover, the number feeling that the issue never arises also goes up. And when asked whether it is easier now than earlier to achieve agreement among governments on the role of international scientific programs, the number answering yes declines to 58 percent, as opposed to 78 percent who answered positively when we used the original typology. Faith in the power of the scientific method as a technique for resolving conflict over goals does *not* consistently increase, even when the dominant model stipulates increasingly consensual knowledge.

Clearly, the pragmatic order is far from orderly, coherent, and cognitively unified. But it differs from the skeptic order because the integration of goals is no longer based on hit-or-miss lessons derived from incremental learning patterns, a spurious integration which can result in rapid disintegration with the next turn of the cognitive screw. In the pragmatic order the expansion of consensual knowledge provides the limits beyond which disintegration cannot occur. How, then, would the pragmatic order work in the setting of our programs?

CONTOURS OF THE PRAGMATIC WORLD ORDER

What are the consequences for a new world order if scientific knowledge applied to international programs becomes more consensual? Obviously the orderly march toward agreement on social goals "computed" from the consensus on means, which the rationalist expects, is not going to occur. But let us summarize the changes which *are* likely to occur:

1. Consensual knowledge implies the increasing importance of visible and invisible colleges of experts working together with political decision-makers. Joint decisions will be made on the basis of the cooperation of these types of actors in international organs of a consultative nature. These organs are likely to become more authoritative over time as increasing knowledge restricts the options, or at least orders them.

2. Joint decisions will become increasingly sequential, as a function of the ordering of knowledge, *if and when* the substantive character of the goals calls for a sequentially arranged international division of labor.

3. The integration of various social goals is a function of the actors' perception of substantive linkage. In the skeptic order, this linkage is not consistently informed by changing knowledge. In the pragmatic order, the extent of knowledge change predicts the linking of goals. But social goals remain substantively specific. Actors link them only when their own commitments permit them no other option. Increasingly consensual knowledge, therefore, predicts increasingly integrated and expansive social goals only when that knowledge unambiguously predicts improved welfare for most.

4. Centralization and decentralization of institutions does not follow a predictable course. The institutional pattern remains diffuse because goals will be linked and unlinked, aggregated and disaggregated, as a result of the learning that takes place. Since that learning is dependent on the extent to which knowledge and social goals cohere substantively, an indefinite pattern of institutional centralization followed by decentralization, to be followed by a different pattern of centralization, is to be expected.

5. Bargaining among actors will follow the rules of a cooperative, variable-sum game, using variable coalitions, and will feature package deals linking program demands which seem to be justifiable on the basis of changing knowledge. However, this pattern will not lead to uniform results since governments will not experience equal need and commitment to the bargains. Therefore, the degree of enmeshment of governments in the results of the bargains will differ by programs and regions. The political ideologies of governments, however, will become less important predictors of cooperation.

6. Changing knowledge does not imply a lessening of con-

troversy as a uniform and progressive trend. As knowledge is changing, the finality of the bargains is always in doubt. Controversy will wax and wane, depoliticizing and repoliticizing issues, to the extent that the consensus on knowledge does or does not preempt options on social goals. Hence there is no guarantee that a permanent cross-issue consensus will develop.

7. *But there is great likelihood that a much larger consensus on given issues, and issues closely related on substantive grounds, will emerge, thus permitting more knowledge-informed packages of policy on environmental, economic, and industrial issues.*

We now conclude our scenario by applying these maxims to our programs. We group them according to the pattern used in the substantive discussions: policy among industrialized countries, programs for global environmental protection, and programs seeking to apply science and technology to economic and social development.

Science and Technology for Highly Industrialized Societies

A commitment to pragmatism among the member countries of the European Communities and the OECD implies little basic institutional change: no federation or confederation of the classic type. The member governments are likely to continue the practice of deliberately seeking new knowledge designed to give them a cleaner environment, more wholesome cities, and a rate of economic growth and industrial modernization designed to assure, at least, the maintenance of standards of welfare now attained. They will use methods of mixed scanning indebted to systems analysis, without agreeing to a single comprehensive plan, but featuring the acceptance of explicit strategic targets which are to provide guidelines for appropriate national policies. The rate of technological innovation is not likely to slow down and therefore new, unforeseen issues will continue to arise and demand solutions as the older issues also remain on the agenda for joint action. Thus, there will be more demands for integrated regional policies of pollution control while demands for easing unemployment and inflation also continue. Trade is likely to be seen as a source of employment and monetary stability while also appearing as the devil causing urbanization, crowding, noise, alienation, and smog.

There is no guarantee that this syndrome of clashing perceptions will lead to the expansion of social goals jointly sought by the member governments on the basis of new cognitive linkages. The minimum common denominator among the purposes of the governments will be the maintenance of methods of action,

of capabilities to cope with the consequences of massive industrialization. But the achievement of this purpose is not likely to
elicit anything other than selective bargains, with the members
of the losing coalition not bound to participate in joint action.
The bargaining will be heavily informed by "joint facilities," international pools of research talent and data which, in demonstrating consensual knowledge, result in the coordination of national policies eventually adopted. In the area of pollution, at
least, the instrumentalities of action have already attained the
position of a "common policy," binding on all members but administered by each separately and superimposed on preexisting
national policies, without abolishing them. It is conceivable that
industrial R & D and energy policy will soon follow a similar
pattern, at least in the European Communities. The implementation of such policies calls for a sequential pattern of action, not
the simple pooling of information. It would call for a fully reciprocal pattern if systematic efforts were to be made to include this
package of objectives with the operation of an economic and
monetary union. But we cannot predict that this will happen. It
remains quite likely that the governments will succeed in decoupling certain of these issues to deal with them singly, as may be
the case with pollution once "the polluter pays" principle has
been routinized. While dependence on centrally marshaled and
legitimated information will surely increase, this implies no consistent and uniform centralization of institutional authority in a
single council or conference. Ultimate authority will remain diffused. The special role of governments enjoying an extraordinary capability for action (for example, the United States in
some, West Germany in other contexts) remains in the scenario
as a stick (through the exercise of vetoes) and as a carrot
(through the offer of side payments).

Science and Technology in Global Environmental Programs

The four separate programs grouped under this label all fall
squarely into the pragmatic model, with the global environmental protection program displaying strong affinities for the rational model. However, we also know that these programs differ
enormously among one another with respect to the substantive
issues of concern. While UNEP and IBRD, as well as personnel
committed to comprehensive ecological mapping, straddle
many issues, their concerns are not typical of the whole range of
activities. These programs and organizations *are* committed to
integrating consensual knowledge with more complexly linked
social goals; they seek to combine economic, social, and en-

vironmental desiderata. But these actors must coexist with oceanographers who are interested in much more modest objectives, such as making the oceans safe for scientific research. They share the spotlight with meteorologists preoccupied with one range of activity, understanding weather and perhaps making it amenable to deliberate control. Hydrologists are content to map water resources and to assume the social relevance of their work. Epidemiologists remain preoccupied with curbing specific diseases, and public health administrators worry about rural and urban population planning. What kind of minimum common denominator does a pragmatic model suggest?

The model suggests that _not all_ scientific disciplines and fields of knowledge will converge on a single set of priorities and options. The model also suggests that the mixture of universal and parochial clients and targets will make for more bargaining among actors and issues in the future. The uncertainties regarding the use of scientific methods in resolving conflict among actor objectives presage the same outcome. In other words, the confluence of objectives, issues, and new knowledge is most unlikely to result in a UNEP-dominated world order inspired by an ideology of ecological holism which also contains recipes for the solution of economic ills. The model suggests a long-range process of issue-linkage and -unlinkage, with many specific activities and programs going their own way.

There can be little doubt that scientific research on pollutants and natural environmental disturbances will lead to a consensus on thresholds, indicators, causative links, and remedial alternatives. When these are applied to policy-making, the result represents mixed scanning because the choice of strategic methods of observation then suggests ways of coping which are systematic. The fact that our four programs already represent efforts at a world division of the research effort simply establishes the deliberate international search for new knowledge. Each program is inspired by a desire to create a capability, to be able in the future to undertake measures of social control not now generally available outside the industrialized world. Once created, we can safely assume that governments will wish to maintain it, and eventually be able to use it for coping with the unwanted consequences of scientific and technological innovation, even in Brazil and India where an awareness of such consequences is rudimentary. The instrumentalities now in use are confined to pooling information and to providing guidelines to participating nations on how to collect and disseminate the information. But some joint facilities are emerging from the pooling process: the data collections of IBP and MAB, UNISIST, and the global data facilities being created by UNEP. These have the effect of not merely assembling information but of coordinating future research because they provide the cognitive limits and rules for the collection and utilization of data. The same can be said of SCOPE's environmental research center, the World Weather Watch, and of the results to be obtained from IOC's International Decade of Ocean Exploration, GEMS, and ICSU's Global Atmospheric Research Program. For the moment the instrumentalities of international action are those of the "common framework" for action. But the evolution of joint facilities implies that sequential patterns of remedial action will have to follow. The knowledge being accumulated, insofar as it bears simultaneously on several social goals, suggests that certain steps may have to be taken before other things can be done. Marine pollution, for instance, may need to be curbed *before* significant efforts to increase the nutritional significance of fish can be taken.

However, all this does not mean that integrated policies of global environmental protection must be fashioned. New knowledge does suggest that new social goals become recognized, but the older goals then *gain* in salience. If pollution threatens fish, the older goal of feeding one's population better by gaining a new source of protein becomes *more* significant. Policy-makers are forced to do justice to both sets of goals at the same time. But they are still attached to the principle of *national* development, and their experts remain concerned with the *national* clients and targets. The choice of means and tactics is likely to be instrumental: Couple issues when scientific and political consensus leaves you no alternative, but decouple them as soon as you have achieved the capability your purposes dictate. Thus, for example, one may well imagine that IDOE and GEMS will yield the kind of information which will enable underdeveloped coastal states to deal with environmental issues *while also* leaving them freer to assert more effectively an exclusive national jurisdiction over marine resources. Environmental and nutritional issues will then be effectively decoupled as an international issue area, though more effectively coupled nationally. Much the same can be said about most public health issues which do not raise controversies of world trade and industrial property (as in toxic chemicals and pharmaceuticals). There is no need to couple them tightly to *all* other environmental issues. If malaria is controllable by means of pesticides and if the pesticides are not generally harmful, why worry also about overall water or air quality?

The uneven dependence of these diverse scientific endeavors on one another with respect to satisfying old and new social goals then suggests that the bargaining process be dominated by variable coalitions playing a variable-sum game, with the losers under no immediate compulsion to join in the collective enterprise. If the North Atlantic countries decide to link environmental protection policies to fisheries conservation, the South Atlantic states may feel no need to join the effort. Hydrological mapping may disclose interdependence on sources of water in the Andes and the Alps, but not in North Africa or the Sahel. Integrated policies may be suggested in one context but technical aid to more sophisticated national measures may suffice in the other. Why then assume that governments will bargain with one another over programs in any way other than the diffuse pattern here suggested? Moreover, to the extent that knowledge remains issue and discipline specific, and as long as the implications of the knowledge do not carry a global significance, there is little incentive for especially capable actors to offer side payments in order to construct elaborate package deals. When, however, an interissue consensus does emerge, the incentive rises sharply. Perhaps UNEP suggests the growing momentum of such a process; UNESCO, IOC, WHO, and WMO do not.[7]

Pragmatism then means increasing dependence on joint facilities and sequential planning as the institutions appropriate for international programs of environmental protection. These may amount to a common policy eventually. But the emergence of a common policy remains subject to the built-in tendency to couple and decouple programs as rapidly changing knowledge and slowly changing social goals dictate.

Science and Technology for Economic Development

Much less can be claimed for the remaining programs. They continue to be much more infused with skeptic and eclectic attributes, even after our reclassification, than the programs devoted to global environmental protection. If we could be confident that the helter-skelter juxtaposition of linked but clashing social goals will not be ordered by the growth of new knowledge, we could dismiss these programs and not seek to link them to a pragmatic world order.

Such is the case in outer space. The greater the promise of new but unintegrated islands of knowledge becomes, the more political controversy seems to arise. The knowledge of outer space contains no single theme which can be made to support the achievement of single social objectives. Rather, it suggests many such themes: cheaper and more rapid telecommunications, more knowledge of weather systems, the ability to map resources with speed and accuracy, reaching isolated and illiterate populations with direct broadcast television. But these themes contain their own seeds of conflict over social goals. Who will control the telecommunications system, at whose expense? The knowledge of weather can be used as a means of economic and military warfare. The knowledge of resources can strengthen the power of multinational corporations and increase the dependency of developing countries. Direct broadcast television is perceived as a boon when it strengthens the capability of governments to send the messages which suit their purposes, but it becomes a worry when another government's broadcasts cannot be jammed. The diffusion of the knowledge, as long as it remains focused on hardware and technological capabilities, exacerbates conflict over social and political goals. And we see little reason to suppose that knowledge of outer space, as compared to ecological or economic knowledge, can be substantively integrated and unambiguously related to consensual social goals in the absence of a massive change in political values. Knowledge of outer space gives rise to fear because it may threaten the attainment of established objectives of national strength and development.

Still, activities seeking to relate science and technology to industrial and agricultural development do not exactly match this picture. The current world focus in industrial development is on the package of proposals known as the New International Economic Order officially proclaimed by the U.N. General Assembly in 1974. In agricultural development the world's attention is riveted on the group of measures associated with the World Food Council, which include special subsidies to the poorest countries to attain agricultural self-sufficiency, more systematic nutritional planning, and the creation of a decentralized world buffer stock system for key commodities. Commitment to such objectives suggests the emergence of a consensus on social goals, linked in addition to the parallel commitment to global ecological planning. Are these trends free from the fear of new knowledge? Are they more likely to be guided and informed by more consensual knowledge of economics, genetics, agronomy, and industrial engineering?

If the answer were simple and straightforward, these programs would occupy the pragmatic or rational world order cells, not straddle cells. In both programs the political stakes are very high. Politicians have pinned their future to the attainment of developmental and ecological goals, to the maintenance or con-

trol of growth rates, to the conquest of unemployment and un-
deremployment. Obviously, experts are less powerful in making
policy on these questions than politicians, in contrast to some of
the programs in environment mapping and research. Moreover,
the experts most involved in economic policy-making are social
scientists who tend to be more reserved in their embrace of scientific methods and assumptions than biologists and engineers.

The stakes are politically high also because these issues provide the substance for the split between the world's north and
south, with the socialist east occupying the sidelines. Unlike some
of the environmental programs we studied, these economic issues are defined in some measure by *permanent* coalitions of
states, engaged in seemingly *permanent* confrontation and
negotiation. While the majority coalition has the advantage of
numbers, the industrial minority has the benefit of the power to
withhold rewards, the power to veto change. The bargaining
process, therefore, is closer to a zero-sum game with permanent
coalitions and few side payments than to a variable- and
cooperative-sum game. Only the emergence of the OPEC bloc
softens the sharp contours of this picture somewhat.

Finally, we should recall that, in contrast to the views of scientists associated with global environmental programs, the clashing perceptions of scientists associated with economic programs
are likely to be important sources of internal conflict in the
industrial and agricultural development programs. Simultaneously held strong beliefs in *both* causal modeling and political
bargaining are not likely to aid in resolving conflict. Simultaneous appeals to *both* national planning bodies and international
secretariats are unlikely to guarantee the victory of the international network of experts. Simultaneous concern over the consequences of rapid social change *and* indifference to the impact of
technology do not suggest a formula for consensual decision-
making based on the expansion of knowledge. In what sense
does this picture add up to a gradual strengthening of the pragmatic attributes of world order?

We believe that the world is experiencing such a thrust because
international decision-making is clearly in the throes of simultaneously accommodating unchanging and established social
goals while also seeking to cope with new issues. The linking of
ecological goals with economic betterment through redistribution is evidence of the impact of new concerns. So is the linking of
industrial development with the global stabilization of commodity export prices. And so is the world's emerging acceptance of
nonmarket mechanisms for coping with food and nutrition. This

syndrome is certainly far from being internally coherent; but it exists, and it conforms to the travail of goal definition associated with a pragmatic world order. But the existence of the syndrome hardly justifies a prediction that goals *will* be meshed more coherently in the future.

Such a prediction would have to be based on a finding that knowledge is being sought deliberately and is becoming more consensual. Learning would have to be systematically informed by that knowledge. Tactics would have to reflect the learning process, and bargaining would thus become more cooperative. Bits and pieces of these features can be discovered now, and they support the finding that movement is toward a pragmatic order.

Unlike the nexus of environmental programs, the search for integrated knowledge in economic development is not in the hands of public international monitoring and research agencies. While some such work is done in the United Nations system, in FAO and in the Center for Development Planning, Programming and Policies, most of the search is done under private auspices, as through the Club of Rome, by a network of experts who know one another through prior service in United Nations agencies. Certainly the learning process is still largely incremental. The kind of mixed scanning favored by massive projections of resource, development, and population trends remains at the margin of the international decision-making process; it is not yet accepted as a tool. Hence, the tactics used in the design of programs and priorities are less dependent on new knowledge than is the case in the environmental programs. But it would be wrong to claim that such knowledge is ignored altogether. It shows up, in bits and pieces, even at highly publicized international conferences whose discussions are punctuated with old-fashioned ideological slogans. The zero-sum features of the bargaining process are still with us. Yet no conference that fails to reach agreement is ever broken off for good; it is merely adjourned for another round of negotiations a year later. No issue is ever dropped from the agenda; if not resolved, it shows up on next year's agenda. The "adamant refusal" of the large industrial states to share technology, guarantee minimum commodity prices, expand international lending capacity, forgive foreign debts, or subject multinational corporations to firm rules of conduct always becomes less adamant the next time around. In short, bargaining *has* become more cooperative, and the opposing coalitions are no longer frozen in membership.

What are the institutional implications of this picture? The purposes of the main actors remain at variance with one another.

The north is interested in *maintaining* an existing capability to act and to be able to cope with the unwanted consequences of that capability—in the environmental and energy fields predominantly. It is interested in guiding the evolution of international technology toward these purposes. The south, however, is concerned with *acquiring* the capability, if necessary at the expense of the north. Hence the road to designing global instrumentalities is a hard one. The "plans" of ACAST, UNIDO, and UNESCO can hardly be considered more than common frameworks to induce cooperative action. As long as the U.N. strategy for the Second Development Decade is not taken very literally by governments, it does not amount to a joint facility which actively coordinates national action by way of authoritative guidelines. The World Bank and the reorganized IMF, however, do constitute joint facilities and so does the world food machinery installed in 1976. And so the trend is toward the pragmatic model, particularly as the activities sponsored by these agencies must be planned sequentially in order to produce the results expected of them. Changing the methods of producing food, through integrated multilateral and national efforts, is more than pooling; it involves sequential financial decisions, choices on the procurement of fertilizers and pesticides, the selection of appropriate technologies, and consideration of earlier agricultural and genetic research, done for the most part by internationally financed private agencies.

But there is no sign of any centralized authority. Research, planning, and negotiations go on in widely scattered fora, coordinated by nobody. Issues are raised and adjourned as a result of separate conferences of the Group of 77, the OECD countries, meetings of experts called by the Club of Rome, by UNEP, by the World Bank. The orchestration of the total performance is influenced by strategic networks of experts, but there is no conductor. The totality does not approach the pattern of periodic centralization and decentralization of activity associated with the pragmatic model. Can it be expected to reach that point?

Probably. The substantive characteristics of the activities relating to environmental protection do not suggest an inevitable pattern of greater centralization of authority. Actors can be satisfied with results in many cases without being compelled to bring these activities under a single hat. We doubt that this is also true of the nexus of technological, ecological, and developmental issues. There *is* a substantive connection which cannot be ignored if the purposes and goals now prominent are considered important enough to serve as predictors of perceived interdependence. Economic issues are simply more salient to most people in most places than are ecological issues. If a hard choice has to be made between ecological and economic values, the recent history of the West suggests that it is the ecological values which people sacrifice more readily. We assume that the world's leaders and peoples will continue to consider economic welfare as the most important goal after the maintenance of political independence and military safety. Thus, any accepted demonstration of the interdependence between islands of knowledge in science and technology and increased human welfare is bound to be taken seriously. Any blockage of the benefits to be derived from that knowledge, which can be attributed to institutional scatteration and lack of focus, will then arouse the ire of politicians. Efforts at centralization will follow, as they did in the United Nations system after the publication of the Jackson report and the initiation of UNEP's program. That centralization will give way to decentralization, the coupling of issues to subsequent decoupling, as doubts about the new knowledge and its tie to social goals develop. But the trend will be away from the complete decentralization of authority which prevailed in global programs before 1970. The most significant trigger of evolution toward the pragmatic world order is the controversial set of economic issues. As knowledge here grows more consensual, the stated objectives of politicians leave them no alternative to using it, and to making the institutional adjustments necessitated by the need to use it.

CONCLUSION

We have now come full circle. We began this study by inquiring about the characteristics of science as a way of thinking about social and political objectives. We summarized these characteristics under the label of rationalism and wondered how scientists, acting as advisers to politicians rather than as philosopher-kings, could make their views prevail in international politics. We found that they cannot and do not make their views prevail consistently, in part because most scientists active in international programs fail to subscribe to these views. And yet we say that the world is evolving toward a model which gives increasing obeisance to the importance of scientific knowledge.

The cognitive threshold with respect to the interdependence

of scientific knowledge and political action was crossed in 1600, to pick a symbolic date which corresponds closely to the publication of Bacon's *The Advancement of Learning.* Science and technology, to be sure, existed before that date, in Greece, Rome, Egypt, India, and especially in China. Science and technology then remained part of the total texture of social values and institutions, and especially of religion. They seemed to carry no special, no supersocietal thrust which profoundly affected people's ways of thinking and acting collectively. Science and technology were part of society, the servants of its values rather than its mentors. All these civilizations used science and technology without drawing any single set of searing cognitive conclusions from the use.

In more modern days, science and technology have been used by Muslims, Christians, Buddhists, Hindus, Marxists, secular liberals, and agnostics. Each sought to subordinate the scientific way of thought to the value scheme embedded in its ideology and culture. Each was "right" in considering science and technology a servant of these values. Each was "right" in using science and technology as it saw fit, or not to use them at all. Where then was the universalizing thrust, the cognitive unification that is associated with science?

After 1600 there is powerful evidence that the subordination of science to cultural diversity is a thing of the past. There is compelling evidence that it is no longer possible to adopt a culturally relativistic attitude toward the impact of science. Scientists in China, India, Russia, Egypt, Brazil, and Indonesia seem to draw the same inferences as do their colleagues in Britain, Sweden, Canada, and the United States. Political ideology and cultural conviction seem not to block the making of discoveries and their application to social goals. With few exceptions, cultures and religious persuasions proved hospitable to the scientific way of thinking, to the acceptance that science is a special and universal way of "knowing." They all proved hospitable, at least in principle, to the application of technology in the political programs we call "modernization." It no longer seems to make much difference whether people are Hindus, Buddhists, Marxists, or liberal agnostics. They all want to modernize and use science and technology in the service of that goal. Few follow the model of Tokugawa Japan in the seventeenth century or of Nyerere's Tanzania in the twentieth.

Today, almost everyone accepts the proposition, derived from modern science, that man and society are part of nature and increasingly dependent on it for the fulfillment of political goals *even if that fulfillment calls for the manipulation and control of nature.* Modern man is "in science," not just a user of it, able to accept or reject it as his religious values dictate. To the extent that man and society have enmeshed themselves in these modes of thought—much to the chagrin of the counterculture—the scientific culture has become coterminous with political life. The claims to truth associated with science, if not objectively "true," have the function of being socially true and compelling because modern man has put himself in the position, by dint of his political values, of being unable to do otherwise, much as Bacon predicted. To take the argument a step further, if the view of evolution propounded by biologists is seen as compelling by politicians and articulate citizens, it will inform the political choices which will be made in the future. Biological laws will become social laws.

Notes

---

1. In our ratings we considered a program to be dominated by eclectic attributes if it differed from the requisites appropriate to a given world order model on more than one dimension. The mixed ratings which were the result of respondents' perceptions list first the model for which most respondents opted.
2. We illustrate our coding method.
    1. European R & D.

   Decision-Making Attributes (4 pragmatic, 1 skeptic)

   Knowledge: deliberate search; use of extended computer-assisted network of expert groups to arrive at a list of needs and priorities for new research to link goals in industrial development, environmental protection, education, economic growth.

   Learning: mixed scanning; effort to subordinate goals in specific sectors to certain strategic supergoals, without having a total plan for the entire nexus and without specifying all the causal links among goals.

   Original objectives: sudden addition; new objectives in environmental protection, energy, appropriate new industrial products and processes, and education added simultaneously to a preexisting and continuing commitment to maintain an economic union.

   Tactics: resistance to refocusing all goals; the governments proved unwilling to subordinate or reorder their old goals to the new concerns and simply added, in a rather inchoate way, the new to the old without respecting the scanning exercise of the experts.

   Bargaining: variable-sum game, with side payments and complex package deals; proposals from the Commission on each program are examined from viewpoint of each government and redesigned so as to meet the national goals of most governments; governments who opt for the program strongly will offer special inducements to the less interested and sometimes combine these with compromises in other domains; expectations of deferred benefits.

   Institutional Attributes (4 pragmatic)

Purpose: maintain a capability; the underlying purpose is to maintain the capability to grow economically and provide a better quality of life while taking into account the special problems of the "post-industrial" order which has emerged since 1968.

Instrumentality: common policy; the governments and the Commission must devise policies which result in parallel and mutually consistent *national* measures to protect the environment, conserve energy, steer investments into new industries, and arrange for the appropriate industrial R & D *while also* preserving the common market and advancing toward monetary union.

Division of labor: sequential; this can be done only if there is an agreement on which activities must be undertaken first, second, etc., and a specification of which sector (or country) must act first.

Ultimate authority: diffuse; power to decide is coordinated in Brussels, but implementation remains in the hands of nine governments.

2. Public Health

Decision-Making Attributes (5 skeptic)

Knowledge: sector specific; there is little effort to do research which links the increasing knowledge of specific hazards or diseases to a global concept of welfare. Increasing knowledge confined to radiation, toxicity, nutritional value, and so forth.

Learning: incremental; scientists are basically confident of their methods and uncomfortable with untried interdisciplinary approaches involving social sciences.

Original objectives: slow expansion; the initial objectives of improving health by attacking specific causes of ill-health remain intact; efforts at subordinating these to a comprehensive "plan" have failed, but the commitment remains.

Tactics: resistance to reconsidering goals; governments as well as experts are reluctant to sacrifice the "tried" objectives in favor of new and more comprehensive approaches. New programs are added ad hoc, for example, population planning, nutritional analysis and planning, radiation safety.

Bargaining: almost none; the addition of new programs is rarely a matter for political decision requiring bargaining among governments. Programs are implemented *(a)* through interagency agreements and *(b)* through agreement between an agency and individual governments. When bargaining does occur, as over agency budgets and divisions of labor among agencies, the coalitions are variable and the package deals limited to a few items.

Institutional Attributes (3 skeptic, 1 pragmatic)

Purpose: acquire a capability to improve health; for most developing countries public health programs are useful for creating an institutional infrastructure at the national level; for the developed countries (where the infrastructure exists) the purpose is to expand it to include new sectors of concern such as toxic chemicals, radiation.

Instrumentality: common framework; agencies do not "make policy." They do background research to enable others to make policy, and they set guidelines for appropriate national action on the basis of such research. When uniform standards are agreed to they do coordinate national policies so as to attain these standards, thus approaching a "joint facility."

Division of Labor: pooled; since there are no intersectoral priorities, the work is done by collecting and disseminating information pertaining to single sectors.

Ultimate authority: decentralized; there is no center since work is shared by WHO, FAO, IAEA, and UNEP, and none of these can "decide" so as to compel governments. Engage in functionally specific problem recognition and, if invited, implementation.

3. For detailed arguments on both grounds, see Robert O. Keohane and Joseph S. Nye, *Power and Interdependence* (Boston: Little, Brown, 1977), and Ernst B. Haas, "Is There a Hole in the Whole?" *International Organization,* summer 1975.

4. The rank-ordered presence of delegates among our samples is as follows:

Program	Delegates as Percentage of Sample
MAB	54
Water Resources	40
European R & D	31
Science/Technology for Industry	23
Developed Country Science Policy	19
Outer Space	17
All Others	0

5. That paradox is particularly striking in the case of European R & D. Personnel working in the E.C. Commission have earned a reputation for great political sophistication. They are correctly credited with the ability to link program proposals to social needs and emergent economic problems not yet uniformly experienced by the national societies united in the Communities, but to camouflage their true political and economic objectives under a façade of legalisms and earlier national commitments. However, their frequent failure to make such proposals prevail in the Communities' Council of Ministers may have taught them to scale down their expectations without sacrificing the underlying manipulative instinct. See David Coombes, *Politics and Bureaucracy in the European Community: A Portrait of the Commission of the E.E.C.* (Beverly Hills: Sage Publications, 1970); Glenda Goldstone Rosenthal, *The Men behind the Decisions* (Lexington: Heath, 1975).

6. See the breakdown on Table 10, Chapter 5, for the way our sample divided according to the original assumptions. Total N under the new assumptions was 128, since the full adoption of the principle of dissonance reduction permitted the inclusion of six respondents who were not classifiable at all originally. One respondent who appeared on the original typology could not be classified under the new rules. The two typologies compare as follows:

Original (N = 122)		Gain/loss of respondents		Revised (N = 128)
		recoded	reclassified	
Rationalists	12 +	8	−1	= 19
Pragmatists	29 +	26	+4	= 59
Skeptics	36 −	20 + 4	+2	= 22
Eclectics	45 −	18	+1	= 28

7. The reflections of an American scientist who participated in the U.N. Conference on the Human Environment support this conclusion. He found that scientists *are* extremely influential in preparing the materials documenting environmental degradation and demonstrating intersectoral cause-and-effect links. This influence is exercised in nongovernmental fora and through transnational networks. It effectively defines the agenda for the political negotiators. But he also concluded that the influence of scientists in the actual negotiations is much more restricted as the issue of trade-offs among rival goals rises to the surface. Scientists who prefer to retain their position as independent experts are not very successful; their colleagues who agree to join national delegations, and thus assume a role of influencing their fellow nationals while remaining within their instructions from home, are much more effective. We see no reason to doubt the continuity of this pattern, which suggests that the future role of independent experts will be strong in *preparing* and *monitoring* international decisions, but less pronounced in *making* the actual decisions. See Henry J. Kellerman, "The Stockholm Conference and the Role of Science," mimeo., U.S. National Academy of Sciences/National Academy of Engineering, n.d.

Glossary of Acronyms

AAAS American Association for the Advancement of Science

ACAST Advisory Committee on Science and Technology (U.N.)

CASTAFRICA Conference on the Application of Science and Technology: Africa (UNESCO)

CASTASIA Conference on the Application of Science and Technology: Asia (UNESCO)

CERN European Center for Nuclear Research

CGIAR Consultative Group on International Agricultural Research

CIDST Committee for Scientific and Technological Information (E.C.)

COPUOS Committee on the Peaceful Uses of Outer Space (U.N.)

COSPAR Committee for Space Research (ICSU)

COST Committee on Science and Technology (E.C.)

COSTED Committee on Science and Technology in Developing Countries (ICSU)

COWAR Committee on Water Resources (ICSU)

CREST Committee on European Research for Science and Technology (E.C.)

CSTD Committee on Science and Technology for Development (ECOSOC)

EC European Communities

ECOSOC Economic and Social Council (U.N.)

EURATOM European Atomic Energy Community

FAO Food and Agriculture Organization of the United Nations

GARP Global Atmospheric Research Program (WMO and ICSU)

GATE GARP Atlantic Tropical Experiment (WMO and ICSU)

GEMS Global Environmental Monitoring System (UNEP)

GESAMP Group of Experts on Special Aspects of Marine Pollution (IOC)

GIPME Global Investigations of Pollution in the Marine Environment (IOC and IMCO)

HISA Human Implications of Scientific Advancement (UNESCO)

IAEA International Atomic Energy Agency

IBP International Biological Program (ICSU)

IBRD International Bank for Reconstruction and Development

ICAO International Civil Aviation Organization

ICSU International Council of Scientific Unions

IDF Industrial Development Fund (UNIDO)

IDOE International Decade of Ocean Exploration (IOC)

IEA International Energy Agency (OECD)

IGOSS Integrated Global Ocean Stations System (IOC)

IGY International Geophysical Year

IHD International Hydrological Decade (UNESCO)

IHP International Hydrological Program (UNESCO)

IMCO Intergovernmental Maritime Consultative Organization

IMF International Monetary Fund

IMO International Meteorological Organization

INTELSAT International Telecommunications Satellite Organization

INTERSPUTNIK Soviet Telecommunications Satellite Organization

IOC Intergovernmental Oceanographic Commission

ITU International Telecommunications Union

IUCN International Union for the Conservation of Nature

JET Joint European Torus (E.C.)

LEPOR Long-Term and Expanded Program of Oceanic Exploration and Research (IOC)

MAB Man and the Biosphere (UNESCO)

NASA National Aeronautics and Space Administration (U.S.)

NATO North Atlantic Treaty Organization

NDF New Development Fund (WMO)

OECD Organization for Economic Cooperation and Development

OPEC Organization of Petroleum-Exporting Countries

OST Office of Science and Technology (U.N.)

PAHO Pan-American Health Organization (WHO)

PPBS Planning, Programming, Budgeting and Systems

PREST European Program on Research in Science and Technology (E.C.)

SCIBP Special Committee of the International Biological Program (ICSU)

SCOPE Special Committee on Problems of the Environment (ICSU)

SCOR Special Committee on Oceanographic Research (ICSU)

TEMA Training, Education and Mutual Assistance (IOC)

UN United Nations

UNCAST United Nations Conference on the Application of Science and Technology for the Benefit of the Less Developed Areas

UNCHE United Nations Conference on the Human Environment

UNCTAD United Nations Conference on Trade and Development

UNDP United Nations Development Program

UNEP United Nations Environment Program

UNESA United Nations Department of Economic and Social Affairs

UNESCO United Nations Educational, Scientific, and Cultural Organization

UNIDO United Nations Industrial Development Organization

UNISIST United Nations World Science Information System

WHO World Health Organization

WMO World Meteorological Organization

WWF World Wildlife Fund

WWW World Weather Watch (WMO)

Index

United Nations Educational, Scientific, and Cultural Organization. *See* UNESCO
United Nations Environment Program. *See* UNEP
United Nations Industrial Development Organization. *See* UNIDO
United Nations World Science Information System, 240–241, 262
United States National Academy of Science, 39

Water resources, 210–216, 223–227 passim; organizational ideology, 214–215; personal attitudes of sample, 215–216; world orders, 318, 329–331, 333, 335, 338, 345–348 passim. *See also* COWAR; IHD; IHP
Weather forecasting, 282, 284, 285. *See also* Outer space program; WMO; WWW
Whitehead, Alfred North, 5
WHO, 181, 186, 216–220, 325; with WMO, 201; with IOC, 204; with IHP, 213; with COWAR, 213; country health programing and intersectoral modeling, 219–220; with FAO, 273; nutrition and health, 275; world orders, 345–348 passim
WMO, 111, 181, 186, 199, 200–203; with IOC, 204; organizational ideology, 207–208; world orders, 207–208, 345–348 passim; with IHP, 212–213; with COWAR, 213; with FAO, 273; with COSPAR, 283, 285; with COPUOS, 286; with outer space program, 294. *See also* GARP; IMCO; IMO; Meteorology; WWW
WMO Voluntary Assistance Program, 202
World Food Conference (1974), 202, 266, 274
World Food Council, 267, 349
World Food Program, 266–267
World government, 48, 127

World Health Organization. *See* WHO
World Meteorological Organization. *See* WMO
World orders: responsibilities of scientists in, 3–11 passim, 15, 18–19, 27; defined, 16n2, 52–55, 57n16, 107n1, 111–113; rational world order, 31–33; and organizational ideologies, 46, 93–95; knowledge/action alternatives, 48–49, 80; and learning, 51–52, 324–329, 332–336; decision-making characteristics, 113–123; institutional characteristics, 124–129; in E.C., 134–135, 143–146; in developed country science policy, 155; in oceanography and meteorology, 207–208; in global environmental programs, 222–225, 227; in industrial development, 236–237, 261–264; in agriculture and fisheries, 278–279; in outer space, 285, 295; in economic development, 296–297; future rationalist scenarios, 323–324; future skeptic scenarios, 324–335, 342; future pragmatist scenarios, 335–344; science and technology for industrialized societies, 344–345; science and technology for global environmental programs, 345–348; science and technology for economic development, 348–353. *See also* Decision-making characteristics of world orders; Institutional characteristics of world orders
World Plan of Action, 248–251 passim, 254, 262, 263, 308n43. *See also* ACAST
World Weather Watch. *See* WWW
World Wildlife Fund, 180
WWF, 180
WWW, 201, 202, 207. *See also* Monitoring; WMO

Zuckerman, Sir Solly, 44